D1593109

Schooling in the contemporary world has a multiple agenda: the promotion of economic progress, the transmission of culture from generation to generation, and the cultivation of children's intellectual and moral development. This book explores the difficulties of achieving a synthesis of these objectives, in a case study of a rural African community. The analysis contrasts the indigenous perspective on child development with the formal educational model of cognitive growth. Teachers in the local primary school are shown to face the challenge of bicultural mediation, and the significance of schooling is discussed for each of the diverse individuals of the study in terms of his or her own reflections and interpretations. Two different attempts to activate a local dialogue about the school as a community resource are described, and the implications for approaches to educational planning are explored.

The significance of schooling

The significance of schooling

Life-journeys in an African society

ROBERT SERPELL

Professor of Psychology, University of Zambia

*Director of Applied Developmental Psychology,
University of Maryland Baltimore County*

CAMBRIDGE
UNIVERSITY PRESS

Published by the Press Syndicate of the University of Cambridge
The Pitt Building, Trumpington Street, Cambridge CB2 1RP
20 West 20th Street, New York, NY 10011–4211, USA
10 Stamford Road, Oakleigh, Victoria 3166, Australia

First published 1993

Printed in Great Britain at the University Press, Cambridge

A catalogue record for this book is available from the British Library

Library of Congress cataloguing in publication data
Serpell, Robert.
The significance of schooling: life-journeys
in an African society/ Robert Serpell.
p.   cm.
Includes index.
ISBN 0 521 39478 3
1. Education – Social aspects – Zambia – Case studies.
2. Developmental psychology – cultural – Zambia.
3. Communication in education – Zambia – Case studies.
10 24–92.   I. Title.
LC191.8.Z33S47   1993
370.19'096894 – dc20   92–8751 CIP

ISBN 0 521 39478 3 hardback

Contents

Illustrations

Tables

Preface

This book is about a large topic and a small community. If that disparity of scale seems to reflect a strategic weakness – an insufficient database to allow of generalisation – my defence is that I believe the disparity to be intrinsic to a central problem of education in the modern world. My broadest purpose here is to explore the nature of formal education and the reasons for under-realisation of its potential in societies of the Third World. The major stimulus for this ambitious venture has come from my intermittent acquaintance over a period of fourteen years with a cohort of young people born into a small-scale agricultural community on the periphery of Zambia, a newly independent African nation.

Contrasts of scale lie at the root of my analysis. Education is fundamentally about individual experience. But when its aggregate social significance is interpreted, a quantum leap is often made to the level of a province, state or region. As a psychologist I am interested in the significance of schooling for individual life-journeys, and as a social scientist my preoccupation is with those dimensions of community which are accessible to individuals in more than a token sense. As a citizen of the world, I have become increasingly sceptical of the rarefied, idealistic abstractions which proliferate in United Nations declarations concerning the universal brotherhood of mankind. Likewise on a national plane, although I have been an enthusiastic advocate of decolonisation, I find that the rhetoric of national development tends often to mystify rather than to empower the actors it recruits. A genuine sense of community can only grow from long-term personal acquaintance and trust.

In 1976 I concluded my book *Culture's influence on behaviour*, which reviewed the burgeoning literature on culture and psychological development, with two challenges: generation of radical theoretical alternatives, springing from an analysis by psychologists from non-Western cultural backgrounds of features of behaviour which are distinctive to their culture; and adaptation of those borrowed Western institutions, the factory and the school, to conform better with the aspirations and skills of other cultural groups. As an immigrant to Africa whose primary socialisation was in the West, it has seemed more appropriate for me to focus on the second of these tasks. But, as I hope this book makes clear, I do not believe it can be successfully addressed in isolation from the former. An indigenous theoretical conceptualisation of human development and socialisation is an essential adjunct to the adaptation of exogenous institutions for endogenous progress in the field of education.

The book has several themes which interpenetrate one another. Before making a case for their interconnectedness, each must be presented in its own right. The integrative principle, however, can be simply stated as follows. Human understanding not only is expressed in, but also arises from, the process of communication. In order to communicate successfully, an author (speaker, artist or theorist) must share certain presuppositions with her audience. We can describe this body of essential shared presuppositions in many different ways, some complementary, some mutually incompatible, none of them entirely satisfactory: we may say the author and audience must share a common language, a common culture, an agreed definition of the purpose of their interaction, an awareness of an implicit range of alternatives. When communication is proposed between two people about the behaviour or the experience of one or more others, this logical requirement is partially extended to the third party. There needs to be a connection between the presuppositions shared by the author and audience and those of the human subject about whom they are communicating.

In the chapters which follow, I argue that this requirement is seldom if ever met, and that the resulting imperfections of communication can be traced to the different perspectives afforded to each member of the triad by her position or point of view. I also argue that an awareness of the problem is the first step towards overcoming it. Perspectives are not hermetically sealed off from one another: we can, albeit often with great difficulty, understand a bit of what reality looks like from another person's point of view. The attempt to do so is an enduring, optimistic project of humanity, which deserves reaffirmation in the face of a growing bureaucratisation and commoditisation of knowledge in the modern world.

My indebtedness to others for inspiration and understanding is greater in the case of this book than anything else I have written. It extends along three dimensions. 1. I have discussed the topic and tried out drafts of my ideas about it with a wide range of people over a period of several years. 2. The data collection has brought me into contact with people at an unusual level of intimacy, so that I feel that the members of the study cohort and their relatives, neighbours and teachers have shared more of their time and experience with me than I have generally come to expect of the people whose lives I sample in the course of research. 3. The nature of the issues to which the study is addressed is so general that I find myself drawing many connections with my everyday life as a parent and teacher, and in earlier days as a child and a pupil.

My intellectual debts to individual writers and commentators are acknowledged in the notes appended to the text. The conception and writing of the book has been a preoccupation since 1982. Many colleagues and students at the University of Zambia have put up with my meandering thoughts on the subject since then, and have collectively sharpened my appreciation of the enduring significance of indigenous concepts and values in the process of education in Africa. Long-term participation in the affairs of the University has afforded me the privilege of feeling a member of Zambian society, a feeling which is too complex to articulate in this preface. I hope this distillation of ideas about our educational system will be received in the spirit of a contribution to our society's ongoing collaborative task of self-determination. Fieldwork, travel and data analysis were financed by the University of Zambia under a series of research grants for the study of intelligence, adaptation and education (1973–1987).

The Psychology Department at the University of Hull provided a hospitable haven for reflection and data analysis during my sabbatical leave in 1983–4. The Rockefeller Foundation provided both financial support at a critical period in 1987–8 and a uniquely congenial group of African peers with whom to exchange ideas in Dakar, Harare and Bellagio. And the Laboratory of Comparative Human Cognition at the University of California, San Diego, provided me with the encouragement I needed to persevere with trying to present a set of African issues to a Western audience. Most recently the Psychology Department of the University of Maryland, Baltimore County, has provided resources to enable me to complete the last phases of data analysis, writing and editing which have often seemed almost insurmountable hurdles.

Earlier drafts of several parts of the book were presented at two meetings sponsored by the Rockefeller Foundation under their Reflections on Development programme: one in Harare, Zimbabwe, in January 1988, the other in Bellagio, Italy, in July 1988. I received very frank and valuable comments on both occasions from several conference participants both on the argument advanced in chapter 1 and on its elaboration in other chapters. Without wishing to embarrass them with any suggestion that they would agree with all or part of what appears in these pages, I take this opportunity to express my gratitude to all of the following people whose comments significantly influenced my thinking about the study: Claude Ake, Ledvina Carino,

Michael Chege, David Court, Ariel Heryanto, Thandika Mkandawire, Penina Mlama, Resil Mojares, Joyce Moock, Micere Mugo, Alistair Mundy-Castle, John Ohiorhenuan, Ralph Scott and Crawford Young.

The community referred to as Kondwelani in the text is a real place with an actual school. I have tried to protect the privacy of individuals and villages by according them pseudonyms, except in those cases where the individual has explicitly granted permission for me to do otherwise. It is a striking reflection of the graciousness of Chewa social etiquette that I cannot recall a rude or unkind word from any of the people with whom I have spoken in this community over the years since 1973. Over and above that polite tolerance, I have been most kindly and hospitably received into their homes by the families of Chikomeni Banda, the late Godfrey Banda, Panganani Banda, Mr Chisi, Mr Chuni, Mr Masiye and Peter Phiri. To all these families and to the people whose lives and dilemmas I have tried to interpret in this book I am deeply grateful.

Both of my parents were scholars and teachers. The efforts they made to ensure that my education would be supportive of my personal development and understanding of the world have doubtless shaped my perspective on the topic more deeply than I can explain. In addition to their delight in the art of discussion which suffused my childhood, they provided what stand out for me as three crucially valuable opportunities: enrolling me in the Lycée Français de Londres for my primary schooling, tolerating an impetuous interruption of my formal schooling at the age of 16, and facilitating my informal admission to the multicultural University of Singapore for a year before I went to study at Oxford. In more recent years, my late father, Michael Serpell, introduced me to the work of Philippe Ariès, and my mother, Estelle Serpell, has discussed with me in depth drafts of several parts of this book. It is characteristic of her lifelong commitment to the tolerance of diversity that she wishes it well despite our many disagreements!

The other nuclear family of which I am a part has been established with my wife, Namposya Serpell, to whom I am indebted in multifarious ways. We have shared more than three-quarters of my lifetime in Zambia, savouring together the subtleties of communication across the interfaces among cultures, languages and generations which contribute so much to the quality of everyone's life in that society. We have had the joint privilege of parenting five children, Derek, Mwila, Zewe, Chisha and Carla, who have taught me more about developmental psychology than my professional work and yet have had to put up with a father for ever immersed in reading and writing. Apart from their all-important contribution to my sense of personal identity, each of the individual members of this family has shaped my perspective on schooling in significant ways by illustrating the diversity of educational experience and helping me to empathise with several varieties. I do not expect them to agree with this book nor indeed necessarily to read it, but I am grateful to them for being with me while I was writing it. Special thanks to Derek for drawing Figures 1.1, 1.3 and 6.2.

1

The multiple agenda of schooling

1   Three different agendas

Three ambitious programmes of social action have invested heavily in the concept of schooling. The process of education, institutionalised in schools of various sorts around the world, has come to be regarded as essential for each of the following areas of human endeavour: [the promotion of economic progress, the transmission of culture from one generation to the next, and the cultivation of children's intellectual and moral development] I shall refer to these three visionary rationales as the economic, cultural and pedagogic 'agendas' of schooling.[1] In theory, education might aspire to address all three agendas together in a harmoniously coordinated manner. Children would be assisted to grow intellectually and morally by expanding their knowledge and understanding of their cultural heritage. And this personal growth through expansion would empower the younger generation to build upon that heritage, discovering improved ways of managing the environment and generating greater wealth for society. In practice, however, educational programmes have consistently fallen short of such an ideal synthesis. In contemporary African societies – as in many other parts of the Third World, and also in disadvantaged minority communities within the rich, industrialised countries – the economic and cultural agendas of schooling often come into conflict.

The pedagogic agenda of schooling, cultivation of children's intellectual and moral development, presupposes a certain degree of social consensus on what constitute appropriate ways of preparing children for the responsibilities of later life. During the early years of childhood the human individual receives his or her[2] initial orientation to the nature of communication, social organisation and technology from a set of primary caregivers. Responsibility for the care and upbringing of the child is generally first entrusted to her mother and then gradually extended to a widening circle of people who make up the family and the community. These caregivers share both a physical environment and a cultural system of meanings, practices and institutions. The child's development is thus embedded in an eco-cultural niche[3] which sets the standards by which her adaptation will be judged. When institutionalised schooling is added as a component of this niche, the relationship between its cultural characteristics and those of other socialisation practices in the children's family and community environment becomes an issue of considerable complexity.

One model of this relationship which appeals to many contemporary educators is that a population of primary caregivers should agree on the need to organise some parts of their children's socialisation on a collective basis, building on and extending developmental processes initiated at home. Historically, however, this kind of cultural attunement, which allows for continuity in the child's socialisation, seems to have been a rather late and incidental arrival among the various defining characteristics of formal education. Schools as institutions arose initially as mechanisms for transmitting specialised bodies of knowledge to learners of various ages.

Culture, whether we understand it as a pattern of behaviour or as a system of meanings, is the product of a historically defined social group. When a school curriculum is designed in a manner which is alien to the cultural assumptions informing other socialisation practices to which its students have been exposed, discrepancies are liable to arise between the goals of that curriculum and the cultural goals of the social group. Religion and language are perhaps the most conspicuous domains in which such estrangement can arise. But many other dimensions of socialisation can pose analogous problems, which have been explored in fictional literature. How, for instance, can the social and emotional orientation of an individual as a woman in her earlier socialisation be harmonised with the developmental trajectory envisaged by a programme of schooling designed exclusively by and for men?[4] Or how can the indigenous citizen of a colonial dependency reconcile the values cultivated by his schooling in the metropolitan state with the demands of allegiance to a traditional home culture which that state has sought to suppress (cf. Achebe 1960)? In general, the greater the degree of alienation between the culture of a child's socialisation at home and the culture of schooling, the greater the resulting discrepancy between their goals.

But discrepancy is only part of the story: economic power attracts social prestige, with the result that the cultural practices of economically powerful groups often become a target of emulation by less powerful groups. In situations where economic power is controlled by a social group which differs systematically in culture from the group of which a child is raised as a member, the project of acquiring economically empowering cultural understanding at school easily becomes associated in the minds and practices of both teacher and student with devaluing the alternative culture of the child's family and home community (Roberts and Akinsaya 1976; Ogbu 1978; Howard and Scott 1981).

Just why this kind of conflict is so widespread has been interpreted in two broadly divergent ways. On the one hand, the resistance of some sections of the world's population to the package of Western schooling has been construed as a reflection of ignorance and/or narrow-minded conservatism. Originally pioneered by advocates of a unilinear, progressivist ideology of modernisation (McClelland 1961; Inkeles and Smith 1974), this point of view continues to be expressed in attenuated form by writers with a less global, but no less profound, commitment to the universality of certain values and practices intrinsic, albeit not exclusively, to Western civilisation (Goody 1977; Olson 1977). On this supposition, the traditional cultures of disempowered social groups may be held partially responsible for their disempowerment. For instance, the home culture may be held to give too much credit for compliance and not enough for autonomy, high levels of aspiration, analytical thinking, etc., to allow its bearers to compete effectively in the modern marketplace.[5] Even if this strategy of 'blaming the victim' is eschewed, proponents of this perspective generally hold that the traditional cultures are incapable of providing the ingredients required for economic progress in the modern world.

On the other hand, the same package of Western schooling has sometimes been construed as a vehicle for repressive political domination of marginalised communities. This view has been articulated mainly by proponents of radical political change in the macrosocietal arena, and is often phrased as part of an ideological critique of capitalism and imperialism (Freire 1972; Bowles and Gintis 1976; Carby 1982). From this perspective the promise of technical power is construed as a fiction, deliberately designed to mystify, domesticate and coopt the recipients of schooling as participants in a culture which legitimates the continued dominance of the group or class in power.

Each of these contrasting theoretical interpretations has been the target of persuasive criticism by advocates of the other. Analyses in terms of imperialism appear to suffer from a somewhat paranoid tendency to impute a 'conspiratorial' coherence to the mutually parasitic interdependence of capitalist imperialism with Christian evangelism and other branches of Western civilisation (e.g. Rodney 1972). Moreover, their exclusive focus on relations of social power fails to acknowledge the technological impact on quality of life which has been exercised by some applied branches of Western science such as agronomy, engineering and medicine (Habermas 1984). On the other hand, the widening gap in standards of living between the centre and the periphery, both within Third World countries and on the global stage, does seem to be causally linked to a continuing cultural and economic domination by the former metropolitan powers over their nominally liberated colonies.[6] Not only has the expansion of formal educational provision failed to deliver the promised fruits of economic growth and autonomy for African nations, but it seems in some respects to have facilitated their economic decline and increased dependency, by promoting the emergence of a national elite class whose externally orientated style of consumption drains the national economy of much of its productive energy.

Thus it seems important to acknowledge on the one hand that the Western package of schooling is more than a mere instrument of political repression, and on the other hand to allow the possibility that resistance to it by disempowered communities has a deeper rationale than ignorant conservatism. I believe that a valid resolution of this controversy requires a more direct focus on the pedagogic agenda of schooling: the cultivation of children's intellectual and moral development. If schooling is to be a source of empowering enlightenment rather than an instrument of domesticating indoctrination, its intellectual content must recruit the creative imagination of the growing child. And if the consequences for the local community are to be cultural enrichment and socio-economic progress rather than debilitating social conflict, cultural demoralisation and economic stagnation, an active dialogue is required among the varied perspectives of its multiple interest groups.

2   A case study in rural Zambia

In the chapters that follow, I shall develop this argument through several stages. My analysis will be centred around a case study conducted in a rural area of Zambia over the period 1974–88. The focus of the study has been on the anticipated and actual outcomes of various amounts of schooling (ranging from none to a full secondary and tertiary programme) among a cohort of some fifty boys and girls born into a Chewa community whose economy has traditionally depended primarily on subsistence agriculture and animal husbandry. The location of this cluster of villages, known as Kondwelani, is shown in Fig. 1.1. At the beginning of the project, members of the study cohort were aged between 6 and 14 years, and were assessed by adult residents of the same villages in terms of endogenously valued dimensions of intellectual and social ability and disposition. In addition their performance was measured on a set of locally developed tests of verbal and non-verbal intellectual skills, designed to tap dimensions of ability which receive support within this particular eco-cultural niche for development.

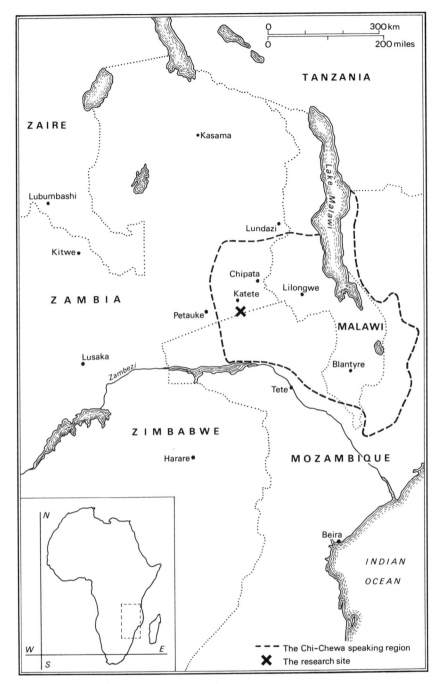

Fig. 1.1 This map shows the distribution of Chi-Chewa-speaking peoples and
the location of the Katete District community in which the author's
community study originated. The border of the Chi-Chewa-speaking region
is somewhat speculatively reconstructed from a number of different sources:
Mitchell, Fortune and Buchanan 1964; Ntara 1973; NELIMO 1988).

5

Over the ensuing years, records of school attainment were collected for those who entered school, and family discussions were held around broad questions of how parents construed the respective socialisation responsibilities of school and home, as well as specific considerations impinging on the decision whether a given child should be enrolled in school and if so how long she or he should continue to attend before withdrawing from the programme. At a later stage, members of the cohort were interviewed in person about their recollections of how these enrolment and withdrawal decisions were reached, about their present evaluation of those decisions, and in the case of those who went to school about what they believe they derived from that experience. Their current level of functional literacy and numeracy was informally assessed, and they were also asked about their life-goals and careers and about their views on schooling for their own children in the next generation.

3   The modern state of Zambia

Before I embark on the details of the enquiry, the socio-political context of my focus requires a few words of explanation. Zambia is a complex society caught up in a process of dramatic historical change, and its distinctive characteristics include an exceptionally high level of urbanisation relative to other nations in *Afrique noire*.[7] As a nation-state it is also distinctive on the continent in having experienced no military coups. At a certain level of abstraction, Zambia is often therefore plausibly characterised as a relatively modern, industrialised and stable nation-state. Conspicuous symbols of this modernity include:

> high-rise office blocks in the centre of Lusaka, the capital city
> high-technology copper-mining on a scale such as to make Zambia one of the world's three largest producers of copper, alongside the USA and Chile
> a state-of-the-art mass media complex which beams satellite news pictures from Beijing, Delhi, Berlin, London, Moscow, Paris, Washington, etc., to thousands of homes in Lusaka and the Copperbelt cities, as well as to several provincial towns as far as 500 miles away from the capital, reporting on the same day's current events around the world
> indigenous airline pilots trained in Zambia, who fly the national airline's Boeing 747 and other jet aircraft around the world.

Some other, less conspicuous, but to some Western audiences more significant, symbolic indicators of Zambia's modernity are the following:

> the University of Zambia, founded in 1965, which now boasts eight different Schools including Engineering, Law and Medicine, an

annual output of about 500 graduates and a body of more than
400 academic staff which includes many indigenous scholars in
the humanities, social and natural sciences[8]
the University Teaching Hospital where high-technology diagnostic
and therapeutic techniques are in place for a number of conditions, largely operated by indigenous personnel
the National Archives where government documents dating back
sixty or more years are accessible for study
the National Council for Scientific Research which sponsors applied
research in such fields as ecology and food processing technology
the Central Statistical Office which analyses by computer monthly
economic returns from government ministries and private
industries, a periodic national census of population, and various
other more frequent surveys of prices, employment, etc.

On the other hand, it remains true to say that more than 50 per cent
of the population live in rural areas without electricity or piped water,
that preventable and/or treatable diseases such as diarrhoea, measles
and malaria combine to claim hundreds of children's lives every year,
and that newspapers, books and radios are increasingly rare commodities in those rural areas. Moreover, the formal-sector labour force
which has never exceeded 25 per cent of the adult working population
has been shrinking steadily in both relative and absolute numbers
since 1971. The government's development planning rhetoric has shifted in the twenty-five years since independence (following fifty years
of colonial occupation by Britain), from an emphasis on the expansion
of free public education, health services and infrastructural resources
such as tarred, all-weather roads, towards a much more modest set of
basic needs and community self-reliance goals. 'Back to the land' is a
common slogan in this era. And this means a return to rural areas such
as the one on which this study is focussed.

In regions such as the Kondwelani area of Katete District, the people
live in small villages composed mainly of clusters of extended families.
They feed themselves from the crops they plant and the livestock they
rear. And they speak the dialect of their tribe. Much of the technology
on which their subsistence economy is based has changed only in
modest ways since the eighteenth century (cf. Fig. 1.2). Yet it is quite
adequate under normal circumstances to the demands of the pros-
perous survival of a human population within this ecosystem. Max
Marwick, who conducted anthropological fieldwork in an adjacent
area of Katete District between 1946 and 1953, observed that:

In general, the A-Chewa have a remarkably full knowledge of their bountiful
environment and a technology that is adequate for tapping its resources.[9]
Though occasional droughts threaten their subsistence, their main source of
insecurity lies in the fact that, in common with other non-Western peoples

Fig. 1.2 This photograph depicts pounding maize, a key stage in the traditional process for making the staple food of the A-Chewa, *unga*. As in many other rural African communities, this activity is reserved exclusively for women and is often accompanied by song. (Photo by the author)

living in the tropics, they do not have the technological resources for countering the diseases that are rife in their country.[10]

Western, or what is more properly now called cosmopolitan, medicine has made great strides in reducing the vulnerability of the A-Chewa to disease over the forty years since Marwick's research was conducted. Poliomyelitis, for instance, has been nearly eradicated through mass immunisation. Malaria and measles, however, continue to take a heavy toll, especially among young children.

The juxtaposition of technological inventions of the late twentieth century alongside ancient, labour-intensive economic practices is a recurrent feature of Third World societies which tends to startle visitors from the industrialised Western world. Yet in human terms, the capacity of individuals to adapt in a coherent fashion to the demands of both environments should not surprise us any more than the capacity of a New York banker to go tracking in the mountains for a holiday. Indeed, many citizens of countries where the affluence generated by industrialisation has become commonplace have begun to cast an envious eye on life-styles which are more directly attuned to the natural environment.

Parts of my analysis are designed to demonstrate the intelligibility and adaptive value of traditional indigenous ideas and practices among the A-Chewa. But my purpose in doing so is neither sentimentally nostalgic, nor romantically idealistic. Social change will undoubtedly result in the next generation of Chewa children being raised differently. But it is far from clear that those Zambians who have adopted a city life have a viable formula worked out for the future of Chewa society, or indeed of Zambian society as a whole.

When modern African politicians and planners are asked to explain the changes in their societies, a key ingredient of their answers tends to be education: a term which they use almost interchangeably with what is learned in school. My argument in this book will be that the connections among schooling, education and social change are complex and negotiable. As an illustration of their complexity I shall begin with an account of a widespread paradox.

4   An extractive definition of success

Since political independence from Britain was declared in 1964, Zambia has experienced a momentous expansion of formal educational provision, including the near attainment of universal primary education, an increase in the number of secondary schools from less than a dozen to more than 200, and the establishment of a university as well as various other institutions of tertiary education. These facts are often displayed with pride as some of the young nation's finest achievements, and as sure signs of national development. Not only politicians and public relations officers have adopted this stance: it is part of a widely endorsed ideological view of what the society has been trying to achieve in the brief period of history since independence, and is proclaimed as such by many citizens of Zambia when they are travelling abroad.[11]

Zambia is not unique in this respect. The project of 'universal primary education' has captured the imagination of politicians and social planners as a major contribution to national development in many if not all the nations of the Third World in the twentieth century. Yet the project is confronted with a moral trap which lies at the heart of the present study. The trap is experienced at the level of a single school with a catchment area in which most children are born into low-income families engaged in subsistence farming. Such schools are responsible for delivering the bulk of the primary educational provision administered by governments in sub-Saharan Africa: they are the prototype on which the project of universal primary education in Africa is based – the elementary cogs on whose operation the nation-wide machinery depends. Stated in its simplest form, the trap is for the school to find itself in the business of producing failures.

When we examine the profile of children going through a rural primary school over a period of years, what we see is that the vast majority of those who set foot in that institution leave school feeling that they are failures. Many of them believe that what went wrong is their own fault:

Nzelu ndalibe . . . linanikanga sukulu.

'I didn't have the brains[12] . . . school was too tough for me.'[13]

Ndinalephela kuphasa mayetso ya Grade 4 kuti ndipite mu Grade 5. Ndayetsa kucita lipiti koma ndalephela ndithu. Lomba ndangoti ndingoleka sukulu pakuti palibe cimene ndalikutengako. Uwelenganso sindinalikudziwa bwino.
Cifukwa ciani?
Nzelu zanga.

'I failed to pass the exam in Grade 4 to go into Grade 5. I tried repeating but I still failed. That's when I decided I might as well leave school since there was nothing I was getting out of it. I didn't even know how to read properly.'
'What was the reason?'
'My brains.'[14]

Not all school leavers choose to take all of the blame, but the vast majority of children who go into a rural primary school emerge with a feeling that something went fundamentally wrong with their education. Very few of them receive the crucial certificate which testifies that they passed Grade 7, and gained entry into secondary school. Technically these two achievements are independently certified in Zambia: a much larger proportion of the candidates qualify for the primary school-leaving certificate than the 15–25 per cent who qualify each year for a place in a government secondary school. This fine distinction is, however, disregarded by the general public, and in the absence of admission to secondary school, the school-leaving certificate (if and when it arrives, some six to twelve months later) is regarded as a certificate of failure. Admission to a secondary school – for the vast majority of parents, of teachers and of pupils – is the criterion of success. It is what they use to evaluate whether an individual's schooling was worthwhile.

And yet, given the scale of educational resources provided by the state, this particular achievement is automatically denied every year to the majority of aspirants. Figure 1.3 presents the so-called educational pyramid for Zambia. The tapering profile of the numbers of students enrolled at various levels represents with dispassionate quantification the morally outrageous definition as 'failures' imposed on the majority of primary school leavers. Sheer availability of space dictates that they cannot be squeezed into that narrow upper section of the pyramid which stipulates the number of places available for students in the secondary schools. Public discussion of this issue in Zambia has given rise to the neologism 'squeeze-outs' as a more appropriate catch-phrase than 'drop-outs' for referring to those students who do not complete the full twelve-year curriculum.

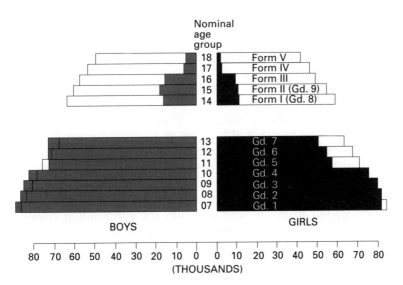

Fig. 1.3 Zambia's educational pyramid (1977). Number of enrolled students (shaded area) and corresponding age-groups of national population.

My reason for referring to this situation as a moral trap is as follows. If entry into secondary school is taken seriously as a criterion of success in schooling, then society is faced with the appalling conclusion that between 80 and 95 per cent of the children entering rural primary schools emerge as failures. This surely cannot be the purpose of the systems of public schooling in which many Third World nations have invested so much funding,[15] so much manpower and so much national pride. What is there to be proud of, if the result of all this expansion is that 95 per cent of our children in the rural areas go to a certain building, sit in front of a teacher for seven years, and at the end conclude that they are 'failures'? The search for an understanding of this paradox has provided a major impetus for the study reported in this book.

Some of the consequences of the dilemma are quite widely recognised. The national news on Television Zambia one evening in December 1987 quoted the District Governor of Luwingu (a rural district in Zambia's Northern Province) as being 'very disappointed' by what he saw at a certain local primary school. He said that he had found less than fifteen children enrolled in all the grades except one and that was Grade 1 where there were twenty children enrolled.

What a contrast with the complaints heard about enrolment figures in the big cities! In Lusaka, the capital, Education Officers are forever struggling to bring down the size of the classes to more manageable numbers. Until recently, when a system of written applications was introduced, every year in September long queues would form along the pavements outside each of the city's schools, where parents and young children would wait (sometimes all through the night) for a chance to enrol for a place in Grade 1 the following January. Although an official limit of forty was set for the maximum class size, enrolments often rose well above this target, resulting in predictable problems of instructional management. The phenomenal shortfall of school provision relative to public demand in urban areas is intensively publicised in the mass media, and features as a central theme in the analyses published by educational planners and deployed by politicians to back their demands for increased allocations to the educational budget.

In many rural areas, however, the 'market' situation is reversed: teachers go out from the school to tour the surrounding villages in search of children to fill the desks. This is not a universal pattern, but it is quite common at schools like the one visited by the District Governor of Luwingu. At the central school of our study in Katete District, this recruitment drive for pupils has been an annual event since 1974. Moreover, at almost all the primary schools around it, the headmasters have confirmed to me that they too go around looking for pupils to make sure that enough pupils will be enrolled in Grade 1 the following year.

The District Governor's comment was that parents in that area were 'sabotaging their children's future' – 'sabotaging' it, as he put it, by sending them to fishing camps and *chitemene* activities (slash-and-burn agriculture) at the expense of their schooling. Most literate parents will feel a certain degree of sympathy with the District Governor. We feel that every child has a right to an education, and that for a child of school-going age to be in a fishing camp where there is no school, or to be busy in the fields so much of the year that they cannot go to school, is a bit unfair. My contention, however, is that parents who assign such responsibilities to their children are not delinquent or abusive parents who do not care about their children: they are reacting to the situation which I have tried to characterise above – where they see the local school as being in the business of producing failures. They ask themselves, 'What is the benefit to my child of going to school?'[16] and some of them ask themselves the (perhaps higher-order) question, 'What is the benefit to the nation of my child going to school?'

Here is the formulation put to us during a family interview in 1980 by the father of two children, both of whom left school without completing Grade 7 in Katete District. He also had a third child who had not been enrolled in school. So we were asking him to explain how he reached the decision not to enrol the last child. The elder girl became pregnant while enrolled in school. She was the first one to stop, then the boy.

Lomba uja wamung'ono, Bauleni, nayenso ndidandaula. Bauleni wacita malipiti maulendo atatu, ndipo aka ndika 4. Lomba ndiye kuti mwana wanga uyu ndi wam'kulu. Lomba ndiko kuti adzalitukula liti dziko la Zambia? Cifukwa mwana wophunzila atukula dziko: lomba ine tate wake ndikhala wodandaula kweni kweni.[17]

'Now with this younger one, Bauleni, I'm beginning to wonder about him too. Bauleni has repeated three times, and this is his fourth try. Now the thing is this child of mine is getting big. So the thing is, when is he going to be uplifting the Zambian nation? Because a child with education uplifts the nation. But, as his father, I'm beginning to wonder about that really.'

What is it that has really gone wrong? How should we answer the challenge posed by this disappointed and confused parent? I shall argue in chapter 7 that the trap arises from the adoption by central planners of too static a 'bird's-eye' perspective on the patterning of enrolment and progression in the schools. Part of the explanation for this perspective is a set of assumptions about certainty of pedagogical method and the appropriateness of linking instruction in a graded sequence to the age of the student. The historical origins of these assumptions will be discussed in chapter 3.

5   Explanations for the prevalence of school failure

Some of the explanations most frequently offered focus on problems of implementation at a local level: 'lazy' or 'incompetent' teachers; 'ill-equipped' schools; 'ignorant' or 'delinquent' parents. It is often difficult to refute such arguments in specific cases, but the phenomenon of massive failure rates in rural primary schools is so widespread in Zambia that part of the problem must be of a more general nature. Moreover, Kondwelani School was in fact achieving a higher-than-average progression rate of its Grade 7 pupils into secondary school throughout a large part of the period of this study.

Three main lines of more general explanation were advanced in the course of our interviews in Kondwelani. The first is an extension of the self-blame cited above to cover a whole section of the student population. Thus one young woman interviewed[18] in Lusaka about her reasons for leaving school without completing the full primary course stated:

Uphunzila kufunika inu anzathu azimuna. Ife akazi sitikutha kwathu kuno.

'Schooling is useful for you menfolk from back home. We womenfolk from home aren't up to it.'[19]

Some readers may be inclined to attach little weight to such remarks, dismissing them as personal, idiosyncratic or parochial interpretations. But other, more pretentious explanations laying claim to the status of public policy, political ideology or scientific theory often advance a meritocratic rationale for educational selection: those who are given a place at the next level up the staircase of formal education are said to qualify for this exceptional opportunity for self-improvement by virtue of their demonstrated scholastic aptitude or general intelligence, which marks them out as 'suitable material for' higher education, as those most 'capable of benefiting from' it, or as 'potential' or even 'future' leaders of society.

In opposition to this argument, I will analyse in chapter 2 some of the characteristics of children's behaviour which are highly valued in rural Chewa society, and I will suggest that the quality of *nzelu*, which two of the early school leavers cited above felt they lacked, is a much broader concept than the English notion of scholastic ability. Moreover, in chapter 5 I will present evidence that various indices of intellectual functioning in early childhood, including ratings of *nzelu* by adults who knew them well, were poorly correlated with success in school in this population.

A quite different line of general reasoning is to condemn the current pattern of schooling as irrelevant to economic success. In another retrospective interview with a young man, who left school after Grade 6, the interviewer begins:

Kodi munacita bwino kusiya sukulu?
Koma, ee, nacita bwino.
Cifukwa ciani?
Cifukwa olo amene analikutsiliza Grade 7 ndipo uphasa sapeza ncito.
Mukamba zoona?
Eee. Kweni kweni olekeza Form III sapeza ncito. Ndipo tili nayo mumidzi m'muno kulima sunflower ndi ladyo.[20]

'Did you do a good thing to leave school?'
'Yes, I think so: I did a good thing.'
'Why?'
'Because even those who finished Grade 7 and passed – they didn't find jobs.'
'Are you telling the truth?'
'Yes, in fact, even those who leave school in Form III haven't found jobs. And now we're together here in the fields growing sunflower and garlic together.'

There are indeed cases of people who make quite a good living in this way. Much of the garlic sold in Lusaka and on the Copperbelt, Zambia's main urban centres, is grown in Eastern Province. It has become quite an important cash crop in recent years, and people who have never set foot in school earn substantial sums by growing and selling it.[21] Implicit in this young man's answer to our questions was a challenge to a widespread theory of how schooling 'brings up' the nation: schooling gets people into jobs, and in a job they produce, and so the nation's economy grows.

As this young man was aware, the facts do not really fit the theory. The facts are that nowadays to complete Grade 7 (that great criterion of formal educational success we noted above) does not guarantee formal-sector employment. Even finishing Form III (Grade 10) is no longer a secure passport to finding a job (Todd and Shaw 1980). So if the educational process that takes place in primary schools is to be justified as some kind of vocational preparation, it will have to be shown to be a relevant and useful preparation for what school leavers are actually doing.

Two major social scientific justifications have been advanced for the export of the Western package of schooling to countries like Zambia: modernisation theory (McClelland 1961; Inkeles and Smith 1974) and human capital theory.[22] According to modernisation theory, the moving force of economic development is a certain kind of individual, equipped with a coherent package of skills, values, motives and attitudes uniquely well adapted to the tasks of building, expanding and maintaining a modern industrialised society. Moreover, the argument goes, the recipe for moulding individuals into exemplars of this proto-type is known, and it has been incorporated (with varying degrees of accuracy) in the design of various types of school curriculum.

According to human capital theory, development programmes should therefore invest public resources in the creation of a stock of such individuals, by exposing the younger generation to appropriate school curricula. An elitist perspective on education, which is often expressed among those who have reached the top of the educational staircase in Africa, adds to these premises a couple of 'common-sense', good husbandry assumptions: that given limited resources for school-ing it is wiser to do the job properly for a small section of the popula-tion than to do it poorly for everyone; and that it is wiser to select for the 'full treatment' those individuals who show promise of internalis-ing its message efficiently.

The fact that tests of intelligence and scholastic aptitude are 'validated' in terms of their power to predict performance in settings of higher education or formal-sector employment tends to result in a closed circle of self-confirmation, whereby the most intelligent are seen to be those who are selected for opportunities for which their superior intelligence 'qualifies' them. By focussing attention on the 'match' between school attainment and performance at higher levels of the school system or in formal-sector employment, this kind of analysis tends to obscure from view more fundamental questions regarding the legitimacy of designing an educational system or a labour economy in such a way that only a minority of the population can have access to it.

There also exists a less elitist version of the modernisation theory of schooling which asserts that, even in small doses, 'schooling has a variety of beneficial socio-economic consequences' which are somewhat independent of access to employment in the formal sector of the economy. These include 'improved agricultural productivity, better health, nutrition and fertility regulation' (Court 1985, p. 1; cf. Court and Kinyanjui 1985). The data from our case study, which will be presented in chapter 5, do not consistently conform with this pic-ture. Moreover, a perplexing feature of the supporting statistical evidence cited by its proponents is that these alleged beneficial conse-quences of schooling appear to occur independently of either the cur-riculum focus or the quality of the schooling: 'the primary school has a powerful influence upon "development behavior", especially of young women, but specific curriculum content seems paradoxically unim-portant' (King 1988, p. 6). I shall argue in chapter 7 that much of the correlational evidence is open to alternative interpretations and that the underlying conception of education as an economic investment is flawed by pseudo-quantification and commoditisation.

The cohort whose lives we followed in our study was by 1987 composed of young people in their mid-20s. Their adult occupations included predominantly rural, quasi-subsistence economic activities: farming, wholesale and retail marketing of home-grown agricultural produce, livestock husbandry, food processing and storage, house-building and maintenance, child-rearing; while those who had migrated into the urban regions of the country were engaged in economically fragile and socially peripheral activities, such as domestic service, manual labour in a factory, delivering and selling retail goods. The only exceptions were two young men who were still full-time students in the secondary or tertiary levels of the educational system.

The relevance of the primary school curriculum to these various current occupations and also to these young people's aspirations for the future is debatable. Their own diverse views on this subject, expressed in 1987, will be discussed in chapter 5, in the context of an analysis of the significance of schooling for the pattern of the various individuals' life-journeys. It is noteworthy, however, that even if schooling does eventually contribute in a positive way to the efficacy of some of these young people in the kinds of occupation I have listed, such an outcome was regarded as nothing more than a 'fringe benefit' by their parents and other family sponsors in deciding whether to enrol their young in school and how long to keep them there. The objectives expressed by those adults in the course of family discussions during 1980 were exclusively premised on a conception of primary schooling as the first steps on a staircase which leads up through secondary school to an effective credential for entry into well-paid, formal-sector employment. Success in schooling was therefore conceived by implication as a process by which young people are extracted from the local community into a superior and external realm.

6 Cultural ambivalence and social change

It is almost inevitable that parents who have received little or no schooling themselves should experience a deep ambivalence about committing their children to a system whose objectives they understand in this way. Collectively the elders of any community are conscious of a responsibility to pass on the accumulated wisdom of their culture to the next generation. The Chi-Chewa word for this traditional wisdom is *mwambo*. But, in a community which is conspicuously involved in a process of rapid social change, those who endorse attempts by the political leadership to give direction and coherence to that process of change, under the banner of 'progress', national development, etc., must also acknowledge alternatives to tradition as a frame of reference for the definition of wisdom. A variety of formulations are available such as 'modernity', 'science and technology', the national political ideology – be it 'scientific socialism', *Ujamaa* (Nyerere 1968) or Zambian Humanism (Kaunda 1974), etc. The school, as the public institution *par excellence* charged with preparation of the younger generation for their participation in the life of this changing society, is readily construed as a repository of this alternative wisdom. Thus a Katete District Regional Secretary for UNIP (the national political party) intervened in one of our local family discussions to explain:

Muno m'mudzi tili nawo mwambo, ndipo mwambo wamuno m'mudzi . . . ku sukulu kuli mwambo wina . . . mwambo wa dziko.[23]

'Here in the village we have our traditional wisdom, and it's the wisdom of village life. In school there is another kind of wisdom . . . the wisdom of the nation.'

This speaker's political commitment leads him to construe the school as representing what, at a national level, UNIP and the national government are trying to do in terms of transforming the nation.

As I shall illustrate with further citations in chapter 4, this view of schooling is tied to other aspects of the curriculum which mark it as not only technologically powerful but also culturally alien. If we take at face value the speaker's affirmation of the validity of each of the two kinds of wisdom in its own particular context, we are confronted here with a position of extreme relativism. Alternatively, if the nation is construed as superior in power and importance over the local community, the two kinds of wisdom may be regarded as stratified, with that of the school held to be more general and more modern, while that of the village is more locally restricted and less relevant to the demands of the modern world. I shall argue in chapter 4 and the Appendix that this is an unsatisfactory resolution of the problem of relativity, and that different world views are neither necessarily superior one to the other, nor impenetrably insulated from one another in watertight compartments.

One of the most destructive consequences of the extractive definition of success is the 'brain drain' which it imposes on the community. In a questionnaire[24] addressed to primary school teachers at various rural schools in Eastern Province in 1983, I asked respondents to compare the migration pattern of their local primary school 'squeeze-outs' with that of those who qualify for a place in secondary school. Table 1.1 shows the pattern of responses to this question. Clearly, the more of the process[25] known as 'schooling' one receives, the less likely one is to remain a member of the community. That the teachers know this themselves, of course, has an influence on their thinking about how to talk to the parents. They cannot hide this information. The parents

Table 1.1 *Teachers' expectations regarding their former Grade 7 pupils: frequency of various categories of response among a sample of 52 teachers currently serving in rural primary schools in Zambia's Eastern Province*

Among the few who go on to secondary school from your Grade 7, how many do you expect will come back to live in the area close to your school within the next 10 years?

almost none	less than one third	about half	more than two thirds	almost all
8	21	12	8	3

Among those who do not go on to secondary school, how many do you expect to remain living in the area close to your school after they reach the age of 20?

almost none	less than one third	about half	more than two thirds	almost all
1	8	11	12	20

know it, and they know it. So it constitutes an area of overlap between their perspectives on the level of shared information. But their evaluation of that shared information may be quite different.

To the extent that teachers subscribe to the theory that schooling helps to 'build the nation'[26] by giving young people a way to climb up and out of their natal community (to rise above it, some would say), to that extent they will construe this demographic pattern as evidence of the success of the enterprise in which they are engaged. More school leavers entering secondary school and moving into occupations which keep them in town means that the public schooling system is doing its job well, performing its assigned role in society, in nation-building. Conversely, to the extent that parents subscribe to the theory that schooling is an alienating process, estranging young people from their cultural roots and from the community of kith and kin into which they were born, to that extent we would expect them to construe the same demographic data as evidence of the power of schooling to undermine the welfare of the local community by extracting some of the finest of its human resources. More secondary school entrants means that the community will have fewer of its able and enterprising youth available to participate in the production of food, in the organisation of local development projects and, of course, in the reproduction of the traditional way of life.

Yet, paradoxically, most parents appear to feel most of the time that they agree with this educational process. It is seen as a necessary kind of sacrifice – 'we lose him, yet it is for the better'. This is the message conveyed by most of our adult respondents in this rural community. The ultimate absurdity of their position is revealed by a phenomenon which will be further discussed in chapter 7 on educational planning. Every year we read in the Zambian press about cases where the parents in a certain community refuse to let any of their children come back to school. They declare: 'We want a change of staff because these teachers are useless – they didn't get anybody into secondary school.' This is perhaps the most paradoxical index of the extractive definition of success. The community condemns the school for not extracting any of its youth into the outside world. They have become prisoners of a self-defeating formulation: that what education is about is schooling, and what schooling is about is getting into the next level.

7   An overview of the book

Two complementary branches of theory sustain this peculiarly self-defeating definition of formal education. One branch concerns the nature of social and economic opportunity; the other concerns the nature of pedagogy and instruction. The first of these theoretical branches construes educational qualifications as rigid credentialist requirements for entry into specific occupational slots, and hence portrays the future prospects of pupils and school leavers as a closed, narrow staircase, rather than an open-ended adventure. Complementary assumptions within the second branch of theory represent the primary goal of education as conditioning, moulding and transforming the mind of the learner, rather than cultivating, nurturing and feeding it, and the guilding principle of teaching as professional expertise rather than public accountability. Each of these theoretical notions will be considered in a later chapter of the book, and I will try to show where it comes from, why it is so seductive, why it is mistaken, and how it can profitably be replaced with an alternative formulation.

In chapter 2, I shall explore a number of lines of evidence concerning how developmental change and individual differences in intellectual functioning are conceptualised and assessed by indigenous members of this particular rural community in Zambia's Eastern Province. The extent to which this analysis can be generalised to other rural communities in Africa and elsewhere in the Third World will also be discussed. I shall argue that the humane and rational principles informing the pedagogic practices of this indigenous African cultural perspective have important implications for the design of an educational psychology which is comprehensible, illuminating and empowering for parents and young people living in this community.

In chapter 3, I shall describe some of the theoretical ideas informing the curriculum of Zambia's primary schools, tracing their cultural and scientific origins, as well as exploring its ideological status in contemporary Zambian society. Significant differences will be highlighted between the culture of the school curriculum and that of the local community.

Teachers posted to a rural primary school are confronted with a set of social realities which are at variance in significant respects with the model of educational provision held up to them during their professional training. The latter included an orientation towards the values and conceptual structures of the school curriculum. On the other hand, their earlier socialisation was in many cases informed by a culture similar to that of their pupils' home community. Moreover, as residents in the community these primary school teachers necessarily interact on a daily basis with parents and other adult members of the local community. Chapter 4 will consider some of the ways in which teachers interpret and coordinate the different moral and intellectual concepts and values embedded in the contrasting cultural perspectives at whose interface they live and work. My analysis will pay special attention to issues of language and how they affect people's conceptualisation of the educational process.

In chapter 5 a set of individual life-journeys will be presented, illustrating the varied ways in which the experience of schooling can be of psychological significance. Some of the people in our cohort never set foot in school; a few completed the whole curriculum; and the majority sampled its wares for between two and five years. The reasons why individuals did or did not enter school and why they left will be analysed in the light of interviews with their parents and their peers, of records of their academic performance, and of their own retrospective interpretations in young adulthood.

An attempt has been made at various stages of the project to promote a dialogue between teachers and their pupils' families concerning the goals of education and problems impeding their attainment. Chapter 6 will describe these encounters and the mutual perceptions they revealed, as well as trying to explain why they generally fell short of genuine dialogue. In the second half of chapter 6 an alternative approach using popular theatre will be described. In collaboration with a team of theatre specialists, we mounted within the local community a participatory drama to highlight for reflective consideration some of the paradoxes and conflicts which emerged from earlier phases of the research.

Yet another perspective, somewhat independent of those favoured by most parents, teachers or pupils, is that of the educational planners who are responsible for national policy on the content and structure of the school curriculum, on the allocation of funds for the supply of teaching materials and for the provision and maintenance of school buildings and equipment, on the regulations concerning enrolment of pupils and their progression to higher grades, on the training, posting and remuneration of teachers, etc. The managerial and economic aspects of this task tend to dominate both planning and decision-making in the field of educational policy. I shall argue in chapter 7 that attempts to define a point of articulation between these concerns and those of students, their parents and their teachers have generally been hampered by two kinds of problem. The first is a tendency for planners to confine their attention to the highest and most abstract levels of aggregation. The second is a reliance on quantitative indicators which often bear only a very tenuous relationship with the concepts which scientists claim that they 'measure'.

After arguing that current planning models overlook many of the complexities of schooling described in earlier chapters, I will go on to discuss briefly a number of steps which could be taken within the framework of existing rural primary schools to increase their responsiveness and accountability to the local communities they are supposed to serve, and at the same time to enhance the value of the education they offer to the hopeful young people who continue to turn up at their door.

In the Appendix I propose a broad theoretical account of the relations between alternative cultural traditions of thought, and illustrate its application to the topics of human development and education. The philosophical position of perspectivism which undergirds this account serves as a loosely integrative theme for the topics of the other chapters: qualitative variations in the conceptualisation of psychological functioning, child development and socialisation (chapter 2); historical construction of institutionalised interpretations of pedagogy (chapter 3); cross-cultural mediation and translation in the practice of school-teaching (chapter 4); individualised, phenomenological patterning over time of the significance of what school offers (chapter 5); public communication strategies and their cognitive consequences (chapter 6); problems of conceptualisation underlying the use of quantitative indicators of psychological and social processes, and problems of articulation between smaller- and larger-scale perspectives (chapter 7). Some readers may therefore prefer to read the Appendix first, others to turn to it at the end of chapters 1 to 4 or after reading the whole book.

As the argument of the book unfolds, I will suggest the following way forward out of the trap described in this introduction. In order to grasp the larger problem of which it is a part, we need to 'unpackage' the concepts of schooling, education and children's development, and to recognise the historical contexts from which the present pattern of institutionalisation of schooling in Zambia has evolved. We need to acknowledge, on the one hand, the intrinsic coherence of the evaluative principles guiding the socialisation practices of families in rural Chewa society. On the other hand, we need to understand the logic of the pedagogical principles informing the school curriculum, and to acknowledge certain distortions and inconsistencies in the way those principles are currently instantiated.

As well as confronting these two perspectives on how children should be raised, we need to acknowledge their potential for harmonious coexistence even within the mind of a single individual. Such harmony is unlikely to be achieved by a group of experts sitting down to design an ideal school curriculum, which is handed down for implementation by another cadre of expert teachers. It must be worked out by each individual in the course of her personal development, and negotiated by each neighbourhood school through active dialogue with parents in the community from which its students are drawn.

The legitimacy of the national project of universal primary schooling can only be sustained if it is grounded in a psychological understanding of human development and pedagogy which acknowledges the primacy of moral accountability. The mandate of rural primary schools needs to be redefined in a more flexible and multidimensional way so that education can play a more constructive role at the interface between local cultural tradition and social innovation.

2

Wanzelu ndani? A Chewa perspective on child development and intelligence

1   Reasons for investigating this perspective

The interface between culture and psychological development is open to various lines of interpretation. According to one research tradition of cross-cultural psychology (Segall, Campbell and Herskovits 1966; Serpell 1976; Jahoda 1980), culture is construed as a source of structure in the environment within which children develop. More recently, as the complex interrelationships among psychology, anthropology (LCHC 1978, 1979, 1983; Jahoda 1982) and history (Hareven 1986) have been explored, a peculiarly human feature of the niche for human development has begun to emerge. The ecosystem within which humans develop (Bronfenbrenner 1979) is jointly structured by the physical environment and a cultural community with a socio-political and economic history. The forces which impinge on the behaviour of the developing child are mediated by mental processes generated through conscious interaction among the persons who constitute a social group. And this interaction is in turn mediated by their accumulated cultural stock of cognitive resources, language, theories and technology.

Thus an account of the eco-cultural niche of child development requires the scientist to specify not only the 'physical and social settings' (Super and Harkness 1986, p. 552) which provide opportunities for practice and elaboration of skills and dispositions, and the 'culturally regulated customs of child care and child rearing' (p. 552) (including social structures and institutions), but also the implicit psychology of the caregivers:[1] the cultural models (D'Andrade 1984; Quinn and Holland 1987) or 'ethnotheories' with which adults responsible for management of the child's everyday experience conceptualise psychological resources, processes and outcomes.

An examination of the psychology endogenous to a non-Western culture can be justified scientifically on several grounds. The behaviour of human caregivers such as parents is informed and thus indirectly structured by their conceptions, however vaguely formulated, of why children behave as they do and of how their own caregiving behaviour influences the child's immediate behaviour and/or the child's development. These conceptions incorporate a number of theoretical ideas, some of which may suggest hypotheses for scientific research. More immediately, when scientists or professional practitioners of the human sciences put forward new explanations of human behaviour or experience, they would do well to take cognizance of their audience's pre-existing theoretical ideas if they aspire for their new explanations to be intelligible, acceptable and empowering to ordinary people.[2]

In this chapter, I will describe four complementary lines of enquiry[3] which have informed my approach to the task of specifying an appropriate perspective for the interpretation of children's development in rural Zambian communities:

> the terminology available for evaluative discussion of children's behaviour and dispositions
> conversational usage of that terminology
> cultural practices and opportunities for development
> traditions and theories as cultural capital.

The initial impetus for my research in the Kondwelani community was an attempt, starting from the bottom and working my way up, to generate an account of intelligence which would make sense in the context of children's development in a rural African community. The decision to return to this fundamental task of conceptualisation arose from my dissatisfaction with the ways in which existing measures of intellectual performance were being used in Zambia's school system. It seemed to me that we had no firm basis for asserting that any of the psychological tests in use measured an aspect of Zambian children's minds which could properly be termed intelligence. Such tests consistently elicited less successful performance from rural children than they did from urban children in Zambia, while the latter in turn performed less well than children growing up in Western cultural contexts – a finding which was essentially concordant with those of other researchers elsewhere on the continent.

Much of the early cross-cultural research on cognitive development in Africa centred around trying to explain how such differences came about. My own preferred interpretation was that the tests sampled a highly specific set of perceptual, linguistic and other cognitive skills which depend for their development on certain environmental conditions which are more closely approximated by urban settings in Africa than by rural settings (Serpell 1969, 1971, 1979). Stated in this way, this was not a very controversial interpretation. But some authors believed that a further conclusion could be derived from these findings, namely that schooling and other social services should be

designed to 'compensate' for 'deficiencies' of African home environments. Only if such 'enrichment' were programmed into the environment could African (especially rural African) children be expected to
develop intellectually on a par with their privileged peers in Western,
industrialised societies (Witkin 1967; Okonji 1969; Vernon 1969).

In contrast with those authors, I have favoured the view that the
generally poor performance of African children on Western psychological tests reflects not a deficient but a qualitatively different cultural
environment (Wober 1969; Cole and Bruner 1971; Serpell 1976). As I
see it, the construal by certain researchers of rural African children as
intellectually 'deprived' rests on the ethnocentric premise that there
exists just one supremely desirable and adaptive pattern of intellectual
development: namely that which is measured by Western psychological tests, and which is optimally promoted by Western forms of
socialisation and education.

That Eurocentric assumption, of course, fits very well with the kind
of unilinear, progressivist conception of cultural, social and economic
development discussed and rejected in chapter 1 under the heading of
modernisation theory. As Philip Vernon put it,

the developing countries of Africa, the West Indies and elsewhere, together
with the incompletely acculturated minorities such as Indians and Eskimos,
are aiming at economic-viability and self-sufficiency. In other words, they wish
to achieve civilisations comparable to those of the Western technological
nations, but are severely handicapped at present by lack of intelligent, well-
educated manpower to provide the necessary professionals, teachers, administrators and technicians. Under these circumstances, it becomes reasonable to
study their performance on Western-type tests, which are known to be
relevant to educational and vocational success, in an attempt to determine
their present strengths and weaknesses and to point to the environmental
handicaps which must be remedied if they are to make more rapid progress.
(Vernon 1967, p. 335)

I contend, on the contrary, that when their leaders are thinking most
clearly, the so-called 'under-developed' nations of Africa, as elsewhere
in the Third World,

tend to be eclectic about Western values; they aim for computers and motor-
cars but not for Old People's Homes. To what extent do we defeat this aim by
insisting that they must develop their minds along Western lines? (Serpell
1974, p. 594)

Vernon's claim that Western-type tests are relevant to educational
and vocational success in Third World countries has been widely endorsed by practitioners of applied psychology in Africa (e.g. Durojaiye
1984). But, as I have argued in detail elsewhere (Serpell 1977a,
1984a), the supporting evidence is essentially circular. The managers

of higher education and of industry set the standards to which primary school instruction is geared, and it follows easily that what becomes defined as 'intelligent' behaviour in the context of such schooling will reflect the values of those external goals. Yet, if we pause to consider a different context in which psychologists are sometimes asked to assess intelligence, these prospects of future attainment in an external, prestigious world lack even superficial plausibility as criteria for the validation of intelligence tests. Consider the case of an adult who never attended school, who has been living all of her life in a subsistence agricultural economy, and who because of some socially unacceptable behaviour is referred to a psychiatric clinic. Part of the standard procedure for investigating such a case will be a psychological assessment of the patient's intelligence.

A psychologist would ... deserve ridicule if he were to assess such a patient as being of 'low intelligence' on the basis of a test which shows ... that she would certainly not qualify for a place in secondary school. What is needed in such a case is an objective method of assessing the patient's adaptability within the constraints of ... her normal environment. (Serpell 1977a, p. 184)

Arising from these considerations, the goal of our initial study in Kondwelani was to arrive at an understanding of what is meant by intelligence in a rural Zambian community. We approached the question in a somewhat indirect manner for methodological reasons which I have analysed elsewhere (Serpell 1977b). Adults who were familiar with a group of children of the same gender and age-range living in a single small village were asked to select one among them for each of a series of imaginary tasks – tasks which could be regarded as high in 'ecological validity' (Brunswik 1956) but which contained a sufficient element of novelty to demand more from the child than mere repetition of a well-established routine. The tasks as they were presented to our informants are listed in Table 2.1.[4] After the respondent had selected a child, she or he was asked to justify the choice and a record was made of the precise terminology used in these replies. Note that none of these tasks had any connection with the activities of schooling.

The reader may find it useful, as a preliminary to interpreting the results of this study, to try the thought experiment of answering the questions in Table 2.1 with respect to a group of children of the same age and gender with whom she or he is familiar. This will not be equally easy for all readers. The authors of a somewhat similar enquiry in Guatemala reported that their 'efforts to duplicate the study in two [urban] U.S. communities proved to have serious difficulties...'. Not only were many families unwilling to cooperate, but 'most critical, unlike Guatemalan communities, nonrelatives rarely could identify a

Table 2.1 *Situations in which elders of A-Chewa villages were asked to choose one child out of a group of age-mates*

1 (a) If a house catches fire and there are only these children present which child would you send to call others for help? Why would you choose this child?*

(b) Which child would you want to stay with you to help you?

2 Suppose you go to a house early in the morning where you are not expected and you find all the adults are absent having gone to work. Then these children come to you shouting 'thief', 'knife', 'he has run away'. The things the children are saying are not clear at all. Which child would you ask to explain clearly what happened?

3 (Girls)
Suppose you are washing your clothes and you see that the place where you usually spread them out (to dry) is muddy (dirty); which of these girls would you send to search for another good place to spread your clothes?

(Boys)
Suppose you are doing some work on a house, such as repairing the thatch where the roof is damaged or replacing an old door, and you see that a tool such as a hammer is needed. However, you do not have a hammer. Which of these boys would you send to make a substitute tool which you could easily use to finish the job quickly?

4 If you are sitting together in the evening and you tell a riddle, which one of these children would you expect to answer well?

5 Suppose when you have left your friend's home you remember that you forgot to tell him/her something. You think it would be good to send a child to tell him/her what you forgot to tell before. Which one of these children would you send with the message?

Supplementary situations:

6 (Girls) lighting the fire for cooking
(Boys) going in search of lost cattle in the evening

7 (Girls) looking after a pot of food on the fire
(Boys) soaking strips of bark to prepare them for use as twine

*This rider was also repeated every time a child's name had been given in response to any of the remaining questions.

sufficient number of the photographs by name of the child to be included in the study (Klein *et al.* 1976).

In our Katete study, we also excluded close relatives of any child in the group to be assessed, since our experience in a pilot study had been that parents tended to choose their own child with a high degree of consistency if one was present in the group. A few of our informants in Katete offered as an explanation for their choice that this child was their relative — 'after all, why send someone else's child if mine is there?' The interviewers explicitly discouraged this kind of reply, since what we were after was an account of children's personal qualities rather than 'ascribed' traits. We would ask what was the nature of the relationship cited and stress that all the children under consideration could be regarded as the informant's children in the extended family sense which pervaded the population of these A-Chewa villages. By and large the elders accepted this suggestion and, as can be seen in Table 2.4, explanations in terms of kinship ceased to be offered by the time we reached Question 4 of the interview.

Of the forty-six children for whom data were complete in respect of all the variables of our research design, twenty-seven were boys and nineteen girls. They ranged in age from 6 to 14 years with a median of 8 to 9. Only fourteen of them were enrolled in school: five in Grade 1, seven in Grade 3 and two in Grade 4. The sixty-one adults whose evaluative judgements about the children's behaviour, abilities and dispositions were analysed were long-term residents of six neighbouring villages who had received little or no schooling themselves. Most of them were over the age of 40 and had raised two or more children of their own. In order to eliminate one obvious source of bias from their choices none of the respondents in this part of the study were parents of the children under discussion. Several aspects of the lives of these children will be explored in this book. In the present chapter my main concern is to articulate the cultural framework within which their behaviour and personalities were interpreted by the community into which they were born.

2   The Chewa language and culture

Chi-Chewa is spoken as their principal medium of communication by about 10 million people living in a region of Africa which straddles the borders of three modern nations: Malawi, Zambia and Mozambique (see Fig. 1.1).

In Malawi it is the national language and is spoken as a first language (or mother tongue) by the great majority of the population (6 million in 1980).

In Zambia it is spoken as a first language by the A-Chewa and the A-Ngoni peoples of Eastern Province, and taught under the name of Chi-Nyanja (literally 'the language of the lake' – a reference to Lake Malawi) in all the primary schools of Eastern Province. Because of the predominance of Chi-Chewa speakers among early migrants to Zambia's capital city of Lusaka, a variant known as 'Town Nyanja' became the principal lingua franca of the city and Chi-Nyanja is the preferred official language for most functions in Lusaka alongside English, and is supposed to be taught in all its primary schools. Chi-Nyanja is one of the seven indigenous languages which have an official status in Zambia, and one of the two languages other than English which are accorded the most air-time on radio. According to a mass media audience survey conducted in 1971–2 it was spoken and understood by 42 per cent of the nation's adult population, less than half of whom had learned it as a mother tongue (Mytton 1974, 1978). According to the latest national census, about one million people (18.2 per cent of the total 1980 population of 5.7 million: Central Statistical Office 1985) speak one of the Nyanja group of languages as their mother tongue.

In Mozambique the latest estimate states that 385,000 people spoke Nyanja in 1980 (NELIMO 1988), and if related languages are included the figure rises to about 1.2 million (10 per cent of the total national population of 12 million) (Katupha 1984).

Nyanja is also spoken quite widely in Zimbabwe where large numbers of A-Chewa men migrated for work during the period of British colonial administration in the first half of this century, culminating in the Central African Federation, which linked the three territories now known as Zambia, Zimbabwe and Malawi.

Allowing for the natural increase of the population (over 3 per cent per annum in all countries of the region) we can thus estimate that the Chi-Chewa or Chi-Nyanja language is used as their main language in 1990 by about 10 million people in Central Africa.

Because of its different socio-linguistic context in each of these bordering nations, this is a difficult language to document in a standardised fashion. As Guthrie, one of the founding fathers of Bantu linguistics, recognised (Guthrie 1948), the distinction between what constitutes a language, a dialect or a more transient variety depends as much on socio-political factors as on linguistic characteristics. Depending on the context in which the question is phrased, a Zambian respondent interviewed about her linguistic competence will, at one extreme, sometimes describe herself as a speaker of Nyanja, a relatively inclusive term which incorporates, along with the dialect of the Chewa people of Katete District, variants characteristic of several neighbouring tribes of Zambia's Eastern Province, including the A-Ngoni of Chipata District, the A-Kunda, and even the A-Nsenga and the A-Tumbuka, as well as the urban dialect of Town Nyanja shared by much of the multilingual speech community of Lusaka. At other times, for a variety of reasons associated with ethnic identity, social status or 'impression management',[5] the same individual may describe herself as a speaker of Chi-Chewa, contrasting the variety she speaks with all of the non-Katete variants of Nyanja listed above, but perhaps equating it implicitly with the Chi-Chewa spoken in Lilongwe and elsewhere in Malawi. The linguistic characteristics in respect of which these dialects differ include phonological and lexical forms. But the basic grammar and a substantial core of vocabulary are shared, and mutual intelligibility under favourable communication conditions is generally high.[6]

Given its predominantly oral character, it is hazardous to rely on dictionaries as a source of authoritative information about the Chi-Chewa language. The written literature is confined to a few short novels and social studies (probably less than 200 in all), the Bible and a couple of newspapers. Probably of greater significance than many of the novels as a corpus of creative composition in Chi-Chewa is a series of radio dramas by Julius Chongo under the title *Fumbi Khoboo!*[7] But above all else Chi-Chewa is a language of daily conversation about current affairs, both public and more especially domestic, a medium for informal discourse concerning the intimate dimensions of social life in communities such as the Katete District neighbourhood on which the present study was centred.

The analysis of Chi-Chewa terminology which follows is based in an eclectically integrated fashion on all of these types of source, and I rely for its validation on a series of conversations spread over several years with a variety of insiders to Chewa culture, people who grew up with Chi-Chewa or a cognate dialect as their first language in the home, and who still use it fluently for various types of discourse. Some of these informants also have a strong command of English, having used it for study and other communication functions over a period of ten or more years. Others, especially long-term residents of the rural community on which our study is centred, have shared their intuitions about the subtleties of Chi-Chewa terminology with me in a more indirect manner by deploying it in evaluative discussions of the behaviour and character of actual persons, or in reflections on the respective responsibilities of home and school in fostering the development of their community's children. Overall there have been few dissonant voices regarding the connotations of the terms which I have chosen to foreground below, and these will be discussed at later stages of the book in relation to the particular contexts in which they occurred and the background of the speakers in question.[8]

3 Terminology in Chi-Chewa and some other African languages

3.1 Nzelu, -chenjela, -tumikila: *the Chi-Chewa terminology of assessment*

A succinct distillation of our initial findings on this subject was formulated as follows in Chi-Chewa by my colleague Chikomeni Banda, who had worked for some time with me on the project and who grew up in the Kondwelani area:

What leads us to call a person *wanzelu*? Among the A-Chewa a child with *nzelu* is a child who is clever (*-chenjela*), trustworthy (*-khulupilika*), who listens, understands and obeys (*-mvela*), who is prompt (*-changu*), and who cooperates with others (*-mvana ndi anzake*).[9]

The concept of *nzelu* has a good deal in common with the English concept 'intelligence'. But the temptation to treat these concepts as equivalent needs to be resisted. At least in the formal psychological literature, the English term has a primarily, if not exclusively cognitive thrust. *Nzelu*, on the other hand, appears to have three dimensions, corresponding roughly with the domains covered in English by 'wisdom', 'cleverness' and 'responsibility', or in French by 'sagesse', 'débrouillardise' and 'serviabilité' (Serpell 1989b). Both literary and conversational usage draw on the contrast between the two dimensions *-chenjela* and *-tumikila*, and yet the full meaning of *nzelu* seems to embrace both of them. The central thrust of Chewa culture's definition of *nzelu* is thus a conflation of cognitive alacrity with social responsibility.

Table 2.2 presents a rough taxonomy of the words and expressions used by the Katete elders we interviewed in 1973–4 to express the attributes which led them to choose a given child for one of our imaginary situations listed in Table 2.1. According to this taxonomy the superordinate concept is *nzelu*, which has three dimensions: 1. *nzelu* (wisdom); 2. *-chenjela* (aptitude); 3. *-tumikila* (responsibility). The second dimension is subdivided into (2a) *-chenjela* (cleverness); (2b) (particular aptitudes); (2c) (ability to perform particular activities). And the third dimension is subdivided into (3a) *-mva/-mvela* (attentiveness, obedience); (3b) *-khulupilika/-mvana* (trustworthiness, cooperativeness).

Ku-chenjela was the commonest term used by these informants. The classical dictionary compiled between 1892 and 1929 by the Scottish missionaries, Scott and Hetherwick (1929), with acknowledged contributions by Che Ndombo, J. Bruwer and E. W. Chafulumira, defines its meaning as: 'to be clever, cunning, quick; in speaking, buying, etc.'. These days, a child who is doing well in school is conventionally described as *wo-chenjela*. But a child can be *wo-chenjela* and still be without *nzelu* (*alibe nzelu*). The distinction is illustrated in a fable told by E. W. Chafulumira in a popular school reader entitled *Mfumu watsopano*, 'The modern chief':

The animals' first choice of a chief to look after (*-sunga*) and instruct (*-weluza*) them was Lion, mainly because they feared his fierceness. At the feast which they prepared to mark his installation, the animal womenfolk sang a song, with words of traditional wisdom (*mwambo*) designed to advise their chief to be well-behaved (*ndi ma-khalidwe a-bwino*) and wise (*ndi nzelu*). In the song they proclaimed that a wise chief (*mfumu wa-nzelu*) rules his people without jealousy. Lion did not heed this advice but continued his habit of killing and eating other animals. As a result when he died there was no sorrow in the animals' hearts at his funeral, and they decided to choose a different animal for their next chief. They argued that lions only like meat for their food. But the other lions thought the chieftainship should pass to them and went around boasting that it would always remain with the lions because there was no other animal as clever (*-chenjela*) and fierce as Lion. (Chafulumira 1957, pp. 1–4)

In some contexts the term *-chenjela* carries a more explicitly derogatory nuance. A striking example occurred in the course of a recent interview with a member of our cohort who is now living in Lusaka. He had lost touch with most of his childhood contemporaries – the group whose behaviour we had discussed when they were growing up together in Kondwelani in 1973–4. At that time we had asked adults about them: 'Which one is the most intelligent, who has the most *nzelu* among them?' Now, fourteen years later, we were asking the same questions of the young people themselves. They were in their twenties now, and we asked them to talk to us about their peers. At the beginning of the interview, when we listed the names of his contemporaries, this young man remarked: 'This one I haven't seen for a long time; and this one is a thief now; and yeah, this one I see regularly...', and so on. So, we said: 'You know them all somewhat: let's compare them. Which one is the most *wa-nzelu*? Which one is the most *wo-tumikila*?' And so on. In these trace interviews we asked each of our respondents to rank these childhood acquaintances of theirs in respect of a series of attributes. Now when it came to *ku-chenjela*, he replied with a laugh: 'Of course this one is the most *wo-chenjela*: because he knows how to steal!' (*Poti iye adziwa kuba*)[10] What struck him as relevant in that context was the cunning side of the word's meaning. Yet he had rated the same individual as the lowest of the group in respect of *nzelu*, and confirmed this contrast when we questioned him.

It is when this derogatory meaning of *-chenjela* as a sly, devious kind of cleverness comes into play that *nzelu* can be seen to involve something more than *ku-chenjela*. Since the English term clever can also be used with negative connotations of 'craftiness', should we conclude that it likewise stands in contrast with true 'intelligence'? There seem to be different perspectives on this question even within contemporary, urban American society. Robert Sternberg and his colleagues[11] asked two different groups of US respondents to rate each of 170 'behaviours' (a) for 'how important [it] was in defining their conception of an ideally ... intelligent person', or (b) for 'how characteristic [it] was of their ideal concept of intelligence'. Generally these two

Table 2.2 *Words and expressions used by elders to express the attributes which led them to choose a given child in response to researcher's questions*

	1. or 2. *ndi wanzelu* *ali ndi nzelu*		
1. no examples.	2. (a) *achenjela*	2. (b) i. *akamba zolongosoka* *akamba zomveka*	2. (c) *achenjela ku ....* *adziwa ku ....* *akhoza ku ....* *anga-*
		(a/b) *achenjela ku kamba zomveka* *achenjela pa kamwa*	... *fotokoza* ... *thandiza* ... *yanika bwino* ... *masulila* *mwambi* *ayankha bwino*
		ii. *akumbukila* *(bwino) sangaiwale*	(2.b.iv/3.a) *angacite zintbu mofulumila* *akhoza mwamsanga* *omvela msangu mau*
		iii. *adziwa kusamala* *poika zinthu*	(2.c/3.b) *akhoza kuthandiza*

3.
atumikila
ndi wotumikila
(ndi wabwino)
(makhalidwe ake)

(a)
i. *akumva*
amvela
ndi womvela
ndi wamatu
akumva zocitika

ii. *alola*

iii. *changu*
ndi wam 'changu

(b)
i. *ndi wokhulupilika*
akamba zoona

ii. *alibe mwano*
ndi wopanda mwano
sakana
sangakane

iii. *athandiza nchito*

iv. *timvana*

34

English translations for terms not underlined (underlined terms are explained in the text)

2. (b)(i) talks sense, sensibly, in an orderly way speaks clearly, intelligibly

(2.b.iv/3.a) can do things in a hurry
is able to (act) fast
mvela words fast

3. is good
his/her behaviour/manners

3. (a)(i) 'has got ears'
mva what is to be done

(a/b) ... at speaking intelligibly ... 'on the mouth'

(2.c/3.b) is able to help

(a)(ii) obeys, is obedient

(b)(ii) remembers (well) doesn't, can't, wouldn't forget

(b)(iii) knows how to put (place) things carefully

3. (b)(i) tells the truth
(b)(ii) is not insolent, doesn't complain, doesn't, wouldn't, couldn't refuse

(b)(iii) helps with work

2. (c) knows how to ...
is able to ...
can ...
... inform
... help
... lay out clothes well
... explain riddles
answers well

35

kinds of rating were very highly correlated; however, the sets of behaviours rated high by their two groups of respondents were rather different.

One group consisted of 140 psychologists with doctoral degrees doing research on intelligence, while the other group comprised members of the general public recruited through advertisements in local newspapers in New Haven, Connecticut. A factor analysis of the ratings revealed two consistent major factors across various sets of ratings by these 'laypersons' – which the researchers termed, respectively, 'problem-solving ability' and 'social competence'. But the second of these factors was conspicuously absent from the ratings by the 'expert' respondents. The behaviours most highly correlated with this factor were as follows:

> accepts others for what they are
> admits mistakes
> displays interest in the world at large
> is on time for appointments
> has a social conscience
> thinks before speaking.

The personal qualities underlying such behaviours as these are more or less antithetical to the devious, crafty aspect of cleverness. What these ordinary people of the USA seem to be looking for in an intelligent person, and which theoretical psychologists seem to have defined as out of bounds, is a reflective kind of social responsibility.[12]

A key concept for describing the socially responsible dimension of intelligence in Chi-Chewa is *-tumikila*. The nearest English equivalent is the archaic word 'biddable' (cf. Kingsley 1977), but in order to grasp its significance it is essential to recognise the pervasive nature of 'sending' (*ku-tuma*) people on errands in Chewa society. This practice is very widespread in Zambian and other African cultures, beginning with asking toddlers to bring you something which you cannot reach without standing up, and extending to commissioning friends and acquaintances to make small purchases for you when travelling abroad. To be 'sent' on such an errand is a sign of recognition both as a responsible person and as a comrade. The dictionary explains *ku-tumika* as 'to be able to be sent, to be one who is sent ... one who is willing to go' (Scott and Hetherwick 1929, p. 567).

A child who is *wo-tumikila* is reliable (*-khulupilika*) both because she can understand the demands of the task and because she has a cooperative attitude. These two notions fall within the range of meaning of the root form *-mva* and its various derivatives: '*mva, ku*: to hear, feel; *ku mve-la*, to listen, obey; ... *wo-sa-mve-la*, disobedient; also *wo-sa-mva*, as *wo-mve-la*, obedient; *ku-mva-na*, to listen to one another as in an orderly *mlandu* [hearing of a legal case]' (p. 350). Hence Chikomeni

Banda's summary expression cited above: *o-mva-na ndi a-nzake*, 'one who gets on with others, listens to their point of view and reaches agreement'.

To recapitulate, among the set of words describing children's and adults' intellectual dispositions which together form the family of *nzelu* characteristics, we can discern three main groups of terms, one of which can be subdivided into two subgroups. The dimensions of meaning which this lexicon articulates can be characterised as follows: 1. *nzelu*, in addition to its function as an overarching term, specifies a dimension of wisdom whose primary thrust is the notion of the complete person, who has all that it takes to be truly *wa-nzelu*; 2. the *-chenjela* dimension which corresponds quite closely to the English notion of cleverness, intellectual alacrity – this is a component part of *nzelu* so that the term *nzelu* is sometimes used to connote just this subdimension, whereas the term *-chenjela* is more precisely attuned to this dimension; 3. the *-tumikila* dimension, which is perhaps best expressed in English by responsibility and includes two subdimensions: 3a. the *-mvela* subdimension, which comprises the domains of listening, hearing, understanding and obeying; and 3b. the *-khulupilika* subdimension, which comprises the notion of trustworthiness. For the kind of responsibility connoted by *-tumikila*, both of these complementary characteristics are required: a cooperative responsiveness to others, and a commitment to honesty and truthfulness. These together make up a person who is known as *-tumikila*, a person who can be sent, who can be entrusted with responsibility.

The tension I have described between the *-chenjela* and *-tumikila* dimensions arises from the possibility that the intellectual alacrity of the *-chenjela* dimension is potentially either creative or destructive. It is capable of being deployed in a socially productive way in which case it is indeed part of what is required of a true *nzelu*. On the other hand, it can also be deployed in a selfish, self-advancing manner which is socially counterproductive and results in the individual being perceived as lacking in true *nzelu*. One well-known illustration of this tension is the character from African folklore known as Kalulu in Chi-Chewa (and indeed in several other Zambian languages), who is a hare. This character is known to the English-speaking culture of the United States, through an oral tradition imported from Africa, and eventually welcomed into the annals of English literature under the name of Brer Rabbit.[13] The character of Kalulu is primarily endowed with the *chenjela* dimension of *nzelu*. He is a clever fellow whose mischievous, manipulating attitude is by and large socially counterproductive. Both the humour and the moral implications of his various pranks hinge on a recognition by the audience of the essentially self-interested nature of his brand of intelligence.

Table 2.3 *Ranges or clusters of personal qualities covered by the meanings of words in different languages*

	1	2	3	3a	3b
Chi-Chewa	nzelu	nzelu -chenjela	nzelu -tumikila	-tumikila -mva/-mvela changu	-tumikila -mvana ndi anzake khulupilika
Ichi-Bemba (Zambia)[a]	mano	-chenjela (-chenjeshi)	mano	mfwila	
Lu-Ganda (Uganda)[b]	-gezi	-gezi -kalabakalaba -kujukuju			
Kipsigis (Kenya)[c]		ngom kwelat	ngom	kaseit	iyanat
Baoulé (Ivory Coast)[d]	n'glouèlê angundan	n'glouèlê i gni ti . . . . . . klè klè	n'glouèlê o ti kpa		
Tale (Ghana)[e]	yam	u mar . . . . . . nini pam	yam		
Djerma-Songhai (Niger)[f]	lakkal	ciermey	lakkal		
English	wisdom prudence intelligence	intelligence cleverness smartness skill	sense responsibility intelligence	attentiveness obedience	cooperativeness trustworthiness
French	sagesse diplomatie intelligence	intelligence débrouillardise habileté	serviabilité	obéissance	honnêteté
Spanish[g]		listura			

[a] discussed by Kingsley (1977)
[b] discussed by Wober (1974)
[c] discussed by Super (1983)
[d] discussed by Dasen *et al.* (1985)
[e] discussed by Fortes (1938)
[f] discussed by Bissiliat *et al.* (1967)
[g] discussed by Klein, Freeman and Millet (1973)

3.2.   *Other African languages*

Echoes of this taxonomy can be found in the vocabulary of evaluative discourse about intellectual functioning and development in several other African cultures. Table 2.3 lists some of the key terms identified in studies independently conducted among the Ba-Bemba in northern Zambia, the Ba-Ganda in Uganda, the Tale in Ghana, the Djerma-Songhai in Niger, the Kipsigis in Kenya and the Baoulé in Ivory Coast. Only the last two of these studies were conducted with any knowledge of our findings among the A-Chewa. Yet many of them underline the importance of the social responsibility dimension represented by column 3 of the table.

The recurrence of this pattern of meanings across various African languages cannot plausibly be explained in terms of etymology. The various cultures of Africa share a number of historical experiences, each of which has left its marks. But although some of the broad lines of linguistic evolution can be reconstructed (albeit with a fair amount of controversy) we cannot expect to be able to trace for non-literate cultures how the subtler meanings of words have emerged or shifted over the centuries.

Admittedly the first three languages in Table 2.3 are all members of the Bantu group and this group of languages may in turn share some common origins with West African languages such as Baoulé, Tale and Djerma-Songhai. But the linguistic roots of the words *nzelu*, *mano* and *-gezi* are quite distinct within common or proto-Bantu.

Some of the cultures in the southern Saharan belt of Africa have adopted and incorporated into their languages the Arabic word *al'aql*, meaning 'the intellectual turn or capacity in man either for understanding, by way of thinking ... or for receiving this understanding from above (Wober 1974, p. 273). Thus in Djerma-Songhai we find the form *lakkal* whose meaning and usage are discussed in depth by Bissiliat and his colleagues (1967), in Hausa *hankali* (intelligence) and even in Ki-Swahili *akili* (intelligence). Wober describes this process as one in which, under 'the influence of Islam ... the concept of *al'aql* has been worked into African cultures', while in some cases 'the word itself has taken root and ... its meaning has developed' (p. 274).

In the case of Bantu root-forms, like *-mva/-mfwa*, we are dealing with much earlier processes of diffusion dating back thousands of years, which are only accessible by very indirect means of historical reconstruction, such that the details remain the subject of controversy. Alexis Kagame considered that the basic vocabulary shared by the Bantu languages was evidence of a fundamental cultural unity, expressed as the 'incarnation' of certain philosophical elements which he enumerated as follows: 'the mental structuring of the sign of ideas, the categorisation of beings and objects, the conception of the world and of the supernatural' (Kagame 1976, p. 55).

Kagame's approach is attractive for two reasons. By considering the Bantu languages as a whole, it seems to offer a sub-continental perspective which escapes us when we look at the different cultural groups within it. And by considering linguistic root-forms it seems to tap into a system of expression for human conceptualisation which has far greater historical depth than any other type of record available.

However, the focus of Kagame's analysis on phonological forms seems to have limited potential for mapping commonalities of conceptualisation in the domain of intellectual functioning and development among different cultural-linguistic groups within the African region. Etymological linkages often fail to generate exact equivalence among the most closely cognate forms in contemporary languages. Shifts of nuance within the range of the subtle differences between the columns of Table 2.3 seem quite likely as we move across the continent. Variants on the root-form *-chenjela* may be traceable throughout the Bantu language region, but there is no good reason to expect its subtler connotations to remain constant. Indeed, it would not be particularly remarkable if in a given language the root-form *-chenjela* came to carry the connotations which *-tumikila* carries in Chi-Chewa and vice versa. Each of the studies cited in Table 2.3 will therefore be discussed separately.

Phillip Kingsley analysed the responses of elders in a Bemba village community of Zambia's Northern Province to questions about generally 'desirable behaviours and qualities in children'.[14] The open-ended request to 'explain how a good child is, his character or quality, what can/does he do?' most often received the reply 'uku-mfwila' or 'icu-mfwilo'. These two cognate words contain the same Bantu root-form (*-mfwa/-mva*) as the Chewa word *ku-mvela* which defines the focus of column 3a in Table 2.3. Kingsley comments: 'the term *icu-mfwilo*, which we have translated as "obedience", probably does in fact have a rather prominent cognitive dimension or connotation. In many contexts it is most appropriately translated into English as "harken", "hear", or "understand"; "to understand" in particular is a very frequent meaning of the verb *uku-mfwa* and this verb thus has a very clear, cognitive reference' (Kingsley 1985, p. 286).

The word *ubu-chenjeshi* has the same root as the Chi-Chewa *ku-chenjela*, which defines the focus of our column 2. Elders were asked to compare this quality to *-mfwila* in two ways:

(Q.2) Is there a difference amongst these: a child who is clever/intelligent [*-chenjela*], a child who is obedient [*-mfwila*] and one who is respectful [*-muchinshi*]? Amongst these three types, which is best? Why? . . .

(Q.9) One child is more obedient [*-mfwila*], another is more respectful [*-muchinshi*], the third is cleverer [*-chenjela*] than his friends; amongst these three children, which one has the best character? Which one would have a good place in the future?

In both cases a clear preference was shown for the other two qualities over *-chenjela*. 'A number of the respondents commented in relation to "uwa-chenjela" that a child with this quality may only be "clever at talking"' (Kingsley 1977, p. 19).

Kingsley concludes that '(despite the advice of qualified speakers of Bemba and English) *ubu-chenjeshi* may not be the best translation of "intelligent". *Ubu-chenjeshi* appears to have at least a slight negative connotation of slyness and perhaps superficiality ("clever at talking only"), making it understandably a less than highly desirable trait. Replies to some of the other questions in the interview schedule suggest that a term like *mano* (sense, wisdom, intelligence) has a more positive connotation and would probably have elicited more choices as a desirable quality (although it may possibly be somewhat less applicable to young children than to adults)' (Kingsley 1985, pp. 286–7).

Thus *mano* seems to have a range of meaning similar to the primary meaning of *nzelu* in column 1 of Table 2.3, but also perhaps some of the connotation of 'sense', or 'good sense' covered by column 3. The latter range of meaning becomes more apparent in Audrey Richard's account of *mano* as 'that important social attribute of every Bemba – *mano*, or social sense' (Richards 1956, pp. 75–6).

Another language in the Bantu group was the subject of one of the first systematic investigations to be published in this field. Mallory Wober set out to 'study the goals of mental development set within [Kiganda] culture and see how these may or may not resemble Western specifications of intelligence' (Wober 1974, p. 262). In the Luganda language three different terms are cited for this domain. *Amagezi* (or in a more abstract form *obugezi*) is 'related to the verb *okugera*, meaning "to measure, evaluate", and the root *-ger* is that which appears as *-gez* in *amagezi*. A related word is *kutegeera*, "to understand"' (p. 264). Wober analysed the account of traditional means and goals of education given by a Mu-Ganda writer, Paul Kibuuka (1966). Then he proceeded to ask a number of different samples of Ba-Ganda people to rate the word *obu-gezi* on scales in a questionnaire. He concluded from Kibuuka's account, from the responses given to his questionnaire by ten male and fourteen female adult Ba-Ganda villagers: 'as well as from the dictionary and most informants, it is clear that the word *obu-gezi* has a meaning that includes the English referents of wisdom, as well as of intelligence; and where there are any differences between the two English concepts, for example concerning speed, or social conformity, *obu-gezi* is more like wisdom than intelligence' (Wober 1974, p. 277). In this respect, then, *-gezi* seems, like *nzelu*, to have as its primary meaning the focus of column 1 in Table 2.3.

On the other hand, there exists at least an extended form of *-gezi* with some of the connotations of column 2, which Wober illustrates with a Luganda proverb:

Omu-gezi-gezi, akuguza ekibira ('a clever fellow sells you a forest' – since a forest is a nuisance to basically agricultural people who have to cut it down to use the land, this is like 'selling refrigerators to Eskimos').

Interpretation of the situation here hinges on whether the proverb refers to a *mu-gezi* (one who is imbued with *obu-gezi*) ... it appears that the form *mu-gezi-gezi* represents a mutation in meaning from *ama-gezi*, and it means 'tricky' or 'cunning' rather than 'intelligent'. In this case the proverb refers to a concept of narrower relevance, the cunning man ... (p. 279).

This evokes the same range of meaning covered by *-chenjela* in Chi-Chewa and in Ichi-Bemba. In Luganda too it seems that this dimension is coded separately in the lexicon: 'Luganda also has the words *obu-kalaba-kalaba* and *obu-kuju-kuju*, but these apparently refer more to "cunning" or "cleverness", of less scope than *ama-gezi*' (p. 264).

Not far from the Ba-Ganda, in western Kenya, live the Kipsigis people of Kokwet, members of the Kalenjin grouping of Highland Nilotic peoples whose languages are quite different from the Bantu group. Charles Super describes the source of his information about their vocabulary as follows:

Exploration of local concepts about the differences among children was begun in a discussion and advisory group organized with six women of Kokwet. Meeting sporadically over the course of my three years' residence, the group served as counselor and guide for the design of research and for understanding local customs, values and beliefs concerning child rearing and child development. One topic presented to the group and discussed over several occasions was what words and ideas they used to note differences among children between 3 and 10 years old. Further clarification of the meaning of the 20 or so words and phrases identified was obtained through detailed inquiry with 11 particularly helpful informants, including three men. (Super 1983, p. 201)

Super's qualitative account derived from this 'ethnographic enquiry' suggests that the Kipsigis word *ngom* may cover the meanings of columns 2 and 3 in our Table 2.3:

Although *ngom* is universally translated as 'intelligent', elaboration of its use reveals a strong component of 'responsibility' as well ... A few informants distinguished a separate meaning of *gnom ngom* for the child who gets good marks in school. This could be specified as *ngom en sukul* rather than *ngom en ga* ('intelligent at home'). The informants stressed, however, that the two meanings (domestic and academic) were not necessarily related, and that a child may do well in school while often forgetting to do chores at home.

Ngom is not normally used to refer to adults. Rather a native speaker is more likely to use *utat*, which has a stronger connotation of inventive and clever, or sometimes wise and unselfish. *Kwelat* may also be used, meaning 'smart' or 'sharp'. A man who is *kwelat* dresses smart and is clever in dealing with his family, though not necessarily educated or even potentially successful in school. (p. 202)

Super identifies two other important 'conceptual clusters' used by the people of Kokwet to describe differences among children. First is 'a large group of concepts referring to a child's helpfulness and

obedience', including 'kaseit, derived from the word gase, to understand, meaning a child who understands quickly what is to be done
and does it, hence translated by native speakers as "obedient"' (p.
201). The parallel with -mvela in Chewa and -mfwila in Bemba is very
striking, and this word seems to belong in column 3a of Table 2.3. Less
clearly, perhaps, we may detect a relation between column 3b and
Super's third cluster, 'centered on the term iyanat, meaning "trustworthy" or perhaps "honest", and related words' (p. 202).

This preliminary ethnographic enquiry was supplemented by more
formally presenting sets of three words at a time to a sample of
ten female and thirteen male adult residents of Kokwet. They 'were
asked to indicate for each triad which of the two words were most
similar in meaning' (p. 202). The pairings of words generated by this
procedure were then pooled across all the respondents, and the aggregated data were subjected to a mathematical procedure which
represented their pattern in terms of spatial arrangements on three
dimensions.

The results of this multidimensional scaling analysis are difficult to
interpret. As with Wober's semantic differential technique (1974), it
seems unlikely that many respondents would have the confidence to
reject outright the possibility of giving a meaningful response.
Moreover, the dimensions which emerged presumably reflect in large
part the particular subset of words selected for comparison. For
instance, since four of the twelve words used in this part of the study
were chosen from the cluster 'referring to a child's helpfulness and
obedience', it is hardly surprising that one major dimension to emerge
was a contrast between social submissiveness (with all four of these
words ranged at that end) and individual expression. It is, however,
interesting to note that ngom features near the middle of this dimension, about half-way between kaseit and nyigan (brave).

An earlier study in yet another African language group was reported
by a multidisciplinary team comprising an ethnographer, a sociologist,
a psychologist and a psychiatrist (Bissiliat et al. 1967). The language
whose usage they describe is Djerma-Songhai, which is spoken in
Niger. This report provides only very sparse details of the data collection procedures followed by any of the four researchers. But it is rich in
illustrative quotations. The word lakkal, which is derived from the
Arabic 'aqal, clearly has both an overarching meaning in Djerma-
Songhai and a bias towards the meanings represented by columns 1
and 3 of Table 2.3, in contrast with the word ciermey, which focusses on
the chenjela dimension of column 2.

The most recent study to be published in this field is from West
Africa and discusses in French the nature of Baoulé evaluations of
children's intellectual development (Dasen et al. 1985). The authors
are Pierre Dasen, who spent three years in Ivory Coast directing a study

of early child development and nutrition (Dasen *et al.* 1978), and six Ivorians (two Baoulé and four Agni, 'culturally and linguistically very close to the Baoulé' (Dasen *et al.* 1985, p. 300), Démbelé Barthélémy, Ettien Kan, Kabran Kouamé, Kamagaté Daouda, Koffi Kouakou Adjéi and N'guessan Assandé. Their first approach was to ask adults to define what is meant by the statement that a child of about 8 or 9 years will have *n'glouèlê* (will be intelligent). This question was posed in the setting of a family discussion and responses were provided by a total of sixty-one women and eleven men, all adult members of a single Baoulé village (cf. Dasen, 1984).

Eight 'components' of *n'glouèlê* emerged from this procedure. The expression most commonly used spontaneously by elders was *o ti kpa*, literally 'he [or she] is good'. The authors translate this with the French word *serviabilité*, a concept which seems easier to capture with a single word in Chi-Chewa (*ku-tumikila*) than in English. A person who is *serviable* is one who is always ready to be of service, perhaps 'obliging'. The research team expand on this interpretation of *o ti kpa* as follows:

serviabilité, or the performance of tasks which contribute to the family's welfare ... with the connotation of responsibility and a touch of initiative as well as know-how ... What is important is that the child should help out, pull his weight in domestic and agricultural work. But it is not just a matter of performing these tasks: the child is more *o ti kpa* the more he performs them well, spontaneously and responsibly. Honesty is also mentioned in this context... (pp. 303–4; all translations by the author)

Almost as frequently mentioned was *agnyhie* (respect, obedience and politeness), a concept which seems close to *-muchinshi* in Ichi-Bemba (discussed above) and *-ulemu* in Chi-Chewa. The authors link *agnyhie* to *o ti kpa* as representing together 'the most important dimension of the concept of intelligence among the Baoulé: a profoundly social dimension' (p. 304). But it is clear from a later part of the same report that they are seen as independent attributes of children by Baoulé parents. *O ti kpa* seems rather a vague designation for a focus of meaning if we rely on the literal translation 'he is good'. But if we accept the authors' interpretation of *serviabilité* as representing the conventional connotation of the phrase *o ti kpa*, then it seems to correspond very closely to the Chi-Chewa concept of *-tumikila* which defines the focus of column 3 in Table 2.3.

A quite different expression used by Baoulé elders to define *n'glouèlê* was *i gni ti kle kle*, literally 'he has eyes which follow everything'.

Thus this applies to an attentive, observant child, but also to a child who learns quickly and retains what he sees. The expression also covers memory and manual dexterity, and can be applied to educational achievement, characteristics which are also designated by more specific terms ... But the child whose eyes are too observant can become curious, sly, wily, even a thief and then one can no longer speak of intelligence ... it is necessary to consider *i gni ti kle kle* in its context to know whether it designates a virtue or a fault; in the latter case it is often accompanied by the term *ngboko*, which means 'too' or 'excessively'. (pp 306–7)

This ambivalence of *i gni ti kle kle* is reminiscent of *-chenjela* in Chi-Chewa and Ichi-Bemba, and the authors draw attention to the similar contrast drawn by Wober between *obugezi* and *obukujukuju* in Luganda. They also point out that a similar account was given by the research team in Mali for the Djerma-Songhai term *ciermey* by contrast with *lakkal* (Bissiliat *et al.* 1967). The French translation of *ciermey* is *débrouil-lard*, another word for which an exact equivalent in English is hard to find. *Se débrouiller* is to cope or work things out on one's own, and a person who is *débrouillard* is good at fending for himself. Harrap's French–English dictionary suggests 'resourceful, canny, especially at getting out of difficulties'. This aspect of the meaning of *i gni ti kle kle* suggests that it has more the focus of column 2 in Table 2.3 than that of column 3a, where attentiveness shades into obedience.

Another 'component' of *n'glouèlê* seems to have been intuited by the research team rather than suggested by elders. The term *angundan* (wisdom) was never mentioned spontaneously by elders in response to the request for a definition, but the great majority of them agreed, when they were asked, that it 'could be included in *n'glouèlê*'. The word is, however, regarded as

too strong in itself to be used routinely about a child ... Among the people interviewed, three consider that *angundan* cannot truly apply to a child:

> given his immaturity, a child cannot think (or reflect) very much;
> for a child that would be exaggerating.

It is quite clear that many adults would not be regarded as wise. It is necessary to be intelligent in order to be wise, but it is not sufficient. *Angundan o ti kpengben o tra n'glouèlê*, says a Baoulé proverb: Wisdom (or thought) is older than intelligence. (Dasen *et al.* 1985, p. 306)

This weighty quality of *angundan* is reminiscent of Kingsley's misgivings about the applicability of the Ichi-Bemba word *mano* to young children, and evokes the primary meaning of the Chi-Chewa *nzelu* represented by column 1 of Table 2.3.

The last account I wish to consider of an African community's vocabulary for discussing children's intellectual development was published by Meyer Fortes in 1938. His account draws on a period of immersion for two years as 'participant observer' in a rural community of the Tallensi in Northern Ghana – without enumerating his informants. At an early stage in his account of the social psychological character of traditional education in Taleland he emphasised:

the concept of *yam*. Tallensi often use the concept of *yam* when discussing social behavior. It corresponds to our [i.e. the English] notion of 'sense' when we refer to a 'sensible man', or sound 'common sense'. As the Tallensi use their term it suggests the quality of 'insight'. Its range of usage is wide. If it is said of some one *u mar yam pam*, 'he has a great deal of sense', the implication is that he is a man of wisdom, or is intelligent, or experienced in affairs, or resourceful. If some one commits a *faux pas*, or shows lack of understanding, or misbehaves morally, the comment is *u ku yam*, 'he has no sense'. The concept is used to refer both to qualities of personality and to attributes of behavior. It is applied also in a genetic sense to describe the social development of the child. (Fortes 1938, pp. 14–15)

This account clearly indicates that *yam* in the Tale language has both the ranges of meaning identified in columns 1 and 3 of Table 2.3. Whether the terms 'intelligent' and 'resourceful' in Fortes' explanation are sufficient to conclude that it also covers the range of column 2 is somewhat less clear. But another Tale expression is cited by Fortes for this aspect of intelligence, which bears a striking similarity to the Baoulé notion of *i gni ti kle kle* discussed above:

Rapid learning or the acquisition of a new skill is explained by *u mar nini pam*, 'he has eyes remarkably', that is, he is very sharp ... This conception of cleverness is intelligible in a society where learning by looking and copying is the commonest manner of achieving dexterity both in crafts and in the everyday manual activities. (p.13)

It is tempting to add to the display in Table 2.3 other terms cited in the literature. For instance, Sid Irvine, whom Berry credits with being the first to conduct 'an empirical study in psychology of folk conceptions of intelligence' (Berry 1984, p. 345), mentions in a discussion of theories of intelligence that 'the Shona word for intelligence, for example, is *ngware*, meaning "to be cautious and prudent", particularly in social relationships' (Irvine 1969b, p. 98). It is not clear, however, from this brief allusion what kind of investigation it is based upon. Hannan's *Standard Shona Dictionary*, to which Irvine refers in his article, defines the root-form -*ngwara* as to 'be cautious, prudent, intelligent, wisdom (endowed or acquired)'.[15] It is difficult to guess from such succinct entries what significance the reader should attach to the absence of 'prudence' from the second definition. Probably such variations are indicative of an imperfect match between English and Shona vocabulary rather than of some sharply defined borders of meaning. Irvine himself phrases his point rather more cautiously in another paper: 'that the Shona word *ngware* which means caution, prudence and wisdom, should be translated as *intelligence* is not without significance' (Irvine 1970). *-Ngwara* may belong in column 1 of Table 2.3, and probably extends across the scope of column 2 also.

But for a full analysis we would need more examples of how this and other Shona words are used. Hannan's dictionary, for instance, also defines the word *uchenjeri* as 'practical wisdom, caution, prudence, cleverness'. This is derived from the verb *-chenjera*, the Shona equivalent of Chi-Chewa *-chenjela*, and listed as one of the core words of 'common Bantu'. *-Shona* and *-Chewa* are quite closely related languages within the Bantu family, and the dictionary also lists words of similar derivation and meaning to the Chewa *-tumikila* and *-mva*. The Shona form *nzero*, however, which is undoubtedly related to Chewa's *nzelu*, is defined by the dictionary as 'ability (mental): agility of mind'. If the word is really as restricted in usage as this implies, it is an example of a phenomenon widely recognised in urban Zambian society – that the 'same' root-form (of 'common Bantu') often acquires quite different shades of meaning in different Bantu languages.[16]

Another striking observation appears in the account by Michèle Fellous of child-rearing practices in a Bambara village in Mali:

Man, according to the Bambara, is destined to live communally. The 'complete' or 'educated' individual is one who has acquired *mogoya*: good manners or tact, sociability, self-awareness in relation to oneself, one's brother, one's family and the community, self-control and mastery of one's emotions, tenacity of character. (Fellous 1981, p. 201; my translation)

It is tempting to place *mogoya* in column 3 of our Table 2.3, but I hesitate to do so because Fellous' report does not include information about the Bambara vocabulary for designating other characteristics. It may be that *mogoya* is a rather broader, more general term than those featuring in Table 2.3, with something like the connotations of *umutima* in Ki-Rundi.

Among the Ba-Rundi of Burundi, we learn from Nicephore Ndimurukundo, citing an essay by Barbara Ndimurukundo, that 'a man of heart [*umutima*] is one who is wise or sensible [*sage* in French is given as a translation for *yitonda*]; who thinks or reflects [*qui réflêchit* is given as a translation for *mbazu-mutima*]; who respects others, *yababa*, etc' (Ndimurukundo 1981, p. 230). It seems as if *yitonda* belongs in columns 1 and 3 of our Table, but does it also cover column 2?

In the adjacent and culturally cognate society of Rwanda, an indigenous psychologist, Dorothée Mukamurama, undertook a systematic investigation of conceptions of intelligence in her culture, focussing her enquiry exclusively around a single indigenous term *ubwenge*. From her intuitive knowledge of everyday and literary usage, she concluded that this term is polysemic, including the meanings of intellectual maturity, adaptability, perspicacity, memory, comprehension, reasoning, skill, problem-solving resourcefulness, knowledge and canniness (Mukamurama 1985; all translations by the author).[17]

In the Rwandese proverbs and oral literature she reviewed, the dominant themes seem to be primarily focussed on the *chenjela* dimension of column 2 in our Table 2.3. But, as she points out, the admiration evoked for this quality of the hare (*Bakame* in the Ki-nya-rwanda language) seems paradoxical, 'given that the Rwandese conception of wisdom prohibits deception and malice'.[18] She defends the integrity of this heroic celebration of the *u-chenjela* of Kalulu (if I may be allowed the licence of translating her analysis into Chi-Chewa terminology) on the grounds that the hare represents the interests of the small and the weak, and that the brand of intelligence he champions is not that of 'a presumptuous person who thinks himself superior to all others and wants to ignore social norms' (p. 99).

Perhaps the most interesting of the many Rwandese proberbs analysed in this report is:

Ubwenge burarahurwa.

'Intelligence is obtained from one's neighbour like fire.'

Mukamurama interprets this, in the light of the customary willingness of neighbours in the village, if requested, to provide a light to start up one's fire, as follows: 'One must know how to come out and open oneself to another person to be able to collaborate with him in order to benefit from his knowledge' (p. 91).

Mukamurama also explored the understanding held by four different groups of contemporary Rwandese (youngsters and adults, with or without any school-based education, all of them with at least a home base in the rural area), starting with the question: 'For you, in our Rwandese culture, what are the characteristics of someone who has *ubwenge*?' More than half of the respondents in each of her four groups cited one or more characteristics pertaining to (1) good social relations, to (2) knowing how to derive advantage from anything, and (with the exception of her sample of university-educated adults) a majority in all groups cited one or more characteristics pertaining to (3) *débrouillardise*, which we noted as a feature of our -*chenjela* dimension, and to (4) a capacity for initiative. Perhaps even more interesting than these commonalities are the following contrasts. (5) Being polite, respectful and obedient was stressed by many young respondents, but never mentioned by the adults, whereas the opposite was the case for being (6) foresightful, (7) discreet and (8) frank. (9) Manual skill and (10) clairvoyance were cited almost exclusively by respondents who had no schooling.[19] Further probing with a request for respondents to rank order a list of twenty-two selected characteristics yielded no clear patterns of variation by age, formal schooling or gender, perhaps because such exercises are somewhat artificial and tend to focus the attention of respondents more on the meaning of words than on the substantive concepts they are used to describe (cf. Serpell 1977b).

Mukamurama developed a somewhat different taxonomy of dimensions of intelligence from that of our Table 2.3, and showed that, in each of the published accounts of 'indigenous terms designating intelligence' in five different African cultures (Bissiliat *et al.* 1967; Wober 1974; Serpell 1977b; Dasen *et al.* 1985; and her own study), references can be traced to 'social intelligence', 'practical intelligence' and 'cognitive intelligence' (Mukamurama 1985, Table V, p. 171). The limitations of this analysis can be illustrated with reference to the case of the Chewa culture in Zambia, where she chose to focus on the term *chenjela*. As I have argued above, this term, although the commonest among those cited by our adult informants in the first phase of my research among the A-Chewa, is conceptually subordinate to the term *nzelu*. Searching for equivalents to the English or French word intelligence is an inadequate basis for articulating the nature of another culture's conceptualisation of the domain of intelligence, and can easily lead one astray, especially when operating without a wide-ranging knowledge of the language. Nevertheless, Mukamurama's study confronted in the case of *ubwenge* many of the semantic issues I have discussed above, and makes it clear that this single term in Ki-nya-rwanda vocabulary is an overarching, polysemic term like *nzelu* in Che-Chewa, *n'glouèlê* in Baoulé and intelligence in both English and French: 'with all these diverse aspects of intelligence, we cannot say that there are several intelligences. We are dealing with a single concept with several components' (p. 102).

Another society closer to the A-Chewa, whose conceptualisations appear to be in tune with others we have considered, is that of the A-Ngoni. This offshoot of the Zulu people in South Africa moved north across the Zambezi river in the nineteenth century and fought battles of conquest against the A-Chewa and other peoples in what is now Zambia's Eastern Province. By and large, although retaining a distinctive social structure, the A-Ngoni have now adopted the language of the A-Chewa, often preferring the non-ethnic name for it, Chi-Nyanja, which derives from the word for lake that also gave the state of Malawi its colonial name of Nyasaland. Margaret Read's account of 'growing up among the Ngoni', which is cited later in this chapter in relation to the use of proverbs, includes a number of suggestive remarks about the -Ngoni concepts of intelligence and other personality traits, but provides only occasional items of the indigenous vocabulary. She does not, for instance, indicate whether it is *nzelu* that she has translated as 'wisdom, which was sharply contrasted with being clever, and which included knowledge, good judgement, ability to control people and keep the peace, and skill in using speech' (Read 1959, p. 48).

Likewise, something of the contrast between columns 2 and 3 of Table 2.3 seems to be implied by Robert and Barbara Levine's account of a Kenyan community who speak the Bantu language Gusii: 'Smartness or brightness by itself is not a highly valued characteristic, and the Nyansongo concept of intelligence includes respect for elders and filial piety as vital ingredients' (Levine and Levine 1963, p. 181). But without an account of the indigenous vocabulary it is not possible to assess how this pattern of values is represented in the lexicon.

4   Conversational usage

So far I have described (in section 3.1 of this chapter) a set of linguistic resources for the expression of a system of meanings. This 'meaning-system' constitutes one dimension of Chewa culture.[20] A certain amount of 'fuzziness' about the distinctions emerging from that analysis of terminology reflects the open-ended nature of the rules which constitute a cultural meaning-system. The competence of an insider who has mastered those rules is not restricted by a set of static, bounded categories. Her knowledge is revealed by the success with which she communicates to other insiders, who share the same cultural knowledge, particular ideas (some of which may be quite original) about particular persons (each of whom is unique) acting in concrete, observable ways in specific situations, some of which may be examples of familiar routines, while others are quite new to both the speaker and her audience. While creative innovation is one of the most exciting possibilities of such an open-ended system for the expression of meanings, in order to characterise the system we need to consider ways in which the topic of discourse places certain semiotic possibilities at risk relative to others.[21]

In this section I will discuss how some of the Chi-Chewa terms were used by Katete elders in conversation with members of our research team. Later (in section 6) I will consider some less direct evidence on ways in which particular verbal expressions such as proverbs are deployed for communicative purposes among the A-Chewa and in other African societies; as well as providing a brief account of stories, rituals and symbols, whose accessibility colours in more intangible

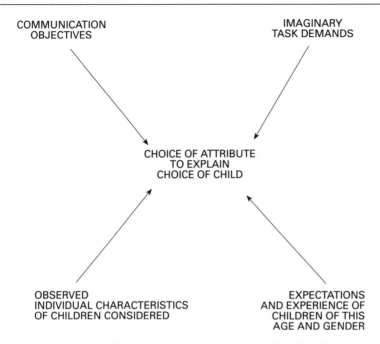

COMMUNICATION
OBJECTIVES

IMAGINARY
TASK DEMANDS

CHOICE OF ATTRIBUTE
TO EXPLAIN
CHOICE OF CHILD

OBSERVED
INDIVIDUAL CHARACTERISTICS
OF CHILDREN CONSIDERED

EXPECTATIONS
AND EXPERIENCE OF
CHILDREN OF THIS
AGE AND GENDER

Fig. 2.1 Factors influencing the choice of an attribute by elders in
conversation with researchers.

ways A-Chewa people's everyday interpretations of action and their
discourse involving such interpretations. And in chapter 6 the importance of these issues will be further explored in the context of a particular case of rhetorical theoretical discourse which drew on symbolism
indigenous to Chewa culture in an attempt to promote active reflection
within the community on contemporary issues of education.

Figure 2.1 illustrates the convergence of several types of factor on
the decision by an elder to cite one or another of the attributes in one
of the imaginary situations. (More general aspects of the interaction
between psychological explanations and the audience to whom they
are addressed are taken up in the Appendix.)

The conversations which gave rise to the sample of Chi-Chewa
vocabulary in Table 2.2 were conducted with reference to the vignettes
summarised in Table 2.1. Each of these qualities of mind or character
or behaviour was cited as a reason for selecting a child in response to
one of those questions.

First, there is a set of considerations arising from the respondent's
interpretation of the conversational activity of which their speech was
a part. What did they think the research team was after? What kind of
image did they wish to project to the team, of their culture, of their
community, of themselves, of their children?[22] We emphasised in our

Fig. 2.2 The scene depicted in this photograph illustrates something of the quality of our first round of interviews, although it was in fact taken by the author during one of the trace interviews with a young woman I had first encountered as a child some fourteen years earlier. The interviewer in this picture is Peter Phiri who was a near contemporary of the respondent, Mrs A., and who grew up in a near-by village, attending the same primary school.

preliminary explanation of the purpose of the interview that we hoped to learn from the elders about their knowledge of the children, since they knew them well as a result of living with them in the village. It is difficult to gauge how this was interpreted. Certainly the sight of two 'teacher'-like adults, one of them also foreign, sitting with pen and paper in hand, ready to record what they said, was unusual for all of our informants. And to some of them it may have appeared either suspicious or ominous (cf. Fig. 2.2).

On the other hand, certain explicit misconceptions had already been dispelled during a preliminary demographic survey (including initial surmises that we might be tax-collectors or water-surveyors!). Moreover, since all of our informants were parents and many of them grandparents, it did seem appropriate to many of them that their wisdom should be sought out by a group of people who were manifestly very interested in children's behaviour. And, although (as later chapters will illustrate) elders who had never attended school themselves[23] were often ambivalent about the local school, they were all well aware of its existence as an institution devoted to activities with children. So, the idea that teachers should be interested in children was presumably a plausible one.

Rereading the transcripts ten years after they were recorded I was impressed by the coherence and pertinence of almost all of the replies, and by the scarcity of signs of rigid perseverance with choices of the same child or of the same attribute across successive questions. Applying a fairly conservative criterion,[24] the overall proportion of responses which were 'perseverative' was 11 per cent in respect of names and 16 per cent in respect of attributes, and only four of our thirty-nine respondents persevered in naming the same child four or more times in succession, while only six (including one of the same respondents) did so in respect of attributes.

A different way of scrutinising the quality of an informant's responses is to consider whether their overall impressions of the group of children in respect of a preferred attribute is consistent with the frequency with which they cited the various children across the series of imaginary situations.[25] Again, using fairly conservative criteria fifteen of our twenty-four male informants and eight of our fifteen female informants were rated highly consistent, and of the remaining sixteen informants, fourteen met a slightly less stringent criterion of consistency.[26] If these two measures were indices of the quality of an informant's comprehension of the interview's concerns, we might expect them to correlate positively, with those informants who show signs of a perseverative 'response bias' tending to be less 'consistent'. In practice, however, the opposite was the case: seven of the nine most 'perseverative' informants were rated 'highly consistent'.

By and large these analyses of the superficial patterning of responses appear to confirm our intuitive, on-the-spot impressions that the elders understood the nature of the topic under discussion and gave it their concentrated attention. If their choice of attributes was biased by communication objectives hidden from us at the time of the interviews, those objectives have remained hidden.

Table 2.4 presents the results of a re-analysis[27] of the responses by our adult informants in response to the questions listed in Table 2.1. The frequency distribution pattern shows that, although there was a great deal of overlap, terms relating to the *-chenjela* dimension were significantly more often introduced to justify the choice of an individual for the imaginary tasks of giving a clear account of an event and answering riddles, whereas the *-tumikila* dimension predominated in the case of finding a makeshift tool or place, and carrying a message to the next village.[28]

Furthermore, a slight but statistically unreliable trend was found for girls to be more often chosen for being outstanding in respect of *ku-chenjela* and boys in respect of *ku-tumikila*, both tendencies being more

Table 2.4 Percentage of replies to each question which invoked each type of explanation

	Q.1: the fire a) send	b) keep	Q.2: confused account (new)*	Q.3: (Boys) makeshift tool (new)*	Q.3: (Girls) substitute drying place (new)*	Q.4: riddles (new)*	Q.5: messages (new)*	All questions (1–7)
nzelu	0	2	4 (6)	3 (3)	0 (0)	13 (13)	7 (0)	4
Col. 2. (*-chenjela*, etc.)†	30	25	61 (64)	15 (14)	50 (45)	62 (70)	47 (50)	40
Col. 3. (*-tumikila*, etc.)†	42	52	18 (13)	61 (60)	28 (36)	13 (9)	40 (48)	38
age or maturity	10	10	6 (3)	12 (13)	6 (0)	10 (7)	7 (3)	9
relationships or familiarity	9	8	0 (0)	9 (10)	0 (0)	0 (0)	0 (0)	6
other reasons	0	2	10 (13)	0 (0)	17 (18)	3 (0)	0 (0)	4
(N)	(50)	(48)	(49)	(33)	(18)	(39)	(45)	(304)

*New explanations were defined as those which used terminology that did not feature in this respondent's reply to the immediately preceding question.

†Terms appearing in Column 2 or Column 3 of Table 2.2.

Table 2.5 *Percentage of various types of attribute* cited by elders to explain their choices of younger and older boys and girls*

(Number of attributes cited)	nzelu	-chenjela and specific abilities	-tumikila -mva/mvela -changu -khulupilika and related disppositions
Younger girls (N=47)	6	70	23
Older girls (N=31)	0	55	45
Younger boys (N=26)	0	38	62
Older boys (N=142)	7	39	54

*Excluding all attributes except for those falling into one of these three categories.

pronounced in the case of younger children (cf. Table 2.5) (Serpell 1989b). One way of interpreting such a trend would be that the speakers' evaluative judgements of individual children derive part of their focussed significance from background assumptions of what is expected in Chewa society of girls in general or of boys in general.[29] The behaviour of different gender and age-groups of children poses different recurrent problems for the adults who interact with them. Girls, for instance, may tend in general to pose fewer disciplinary problems to their mothers, aunts and grandmothers than boys do to their adult male relatives. As a result, adult men of the village were more likely to be preoccupied with the dimension of -*tumikila* (pertaining to behaving responsibly) in their assessments of boys, whereas adult women, who assumed a generally high level of compliance and cooperativeness in girls, centred their assessments more on -*chenjela* (cleverness) or on specific skills and aptitudes. The tendency for greater compliance to be expected (and successfully enforced) from girls than from boys, in many rural communities of Africa and elsewhere, has been documented in an extensive literature (e.g. Erchak 1976).

The contrast between women's expectations of girls and men's expectations of boys is just one example of ways in which the relationships that prevail among different sets of people are liable to influence their assessment of one another's behaviour and personality, and still more so their criteria for deciding on a course of action towards one another in the context of a particular situation and a particular constellation of other people. Parents, as noted earlier, tend, other things being equal, to assign their own children responsibility in preference to others. Children probably have a similar tendency to 'send' on errands their younger siblings, their 'playchildren', or failing that other younger playmates. Grandparents in many African societies, including the A-Chewa, have privileged access to intimate, almost egalitarian relationships with their grandchildren. These relationships doubtless create quite different opportunities and incentives for interaction from those prevailing between adjacent generations.

Over and above the factors summarised in the first three quadrants of Fig. 2.1, our assumption in designing this particular format for the interviews was that the attributes chosen by our informants would reflect individual differences among the children which they had observed in the course of their everyday interactions with them. Certain researchers with prior experience of studying children's cognition in other African societies, however, have formulated a fundamental critique of the method we used in two slightly different ways. (1) Does not the whole study impose on this community an alien conceptualisation of ability or abilities whose origins can be traced to the organisation of industrialised societies – as a resource which is limited in quantity and unevenly distributed across individuals? (2) Is it not possible that age, kinship and discipline are sufficient criteria for the allocation of responsibility in these imaginary situations and that intelligence is actually irrelevant to them?

The answer to these intriguing challenges seems to be that they are not consistent with the actual responses of our informants. One of our supplementary questions concerning looking after a pot on the fire elicited a few times the reply 'any one of them could do that'; while at the other extreme, the tasks of lighting the fire or answering riddles occasionally elicited the response 'they are none of them old enough for that'. But these were exceptional responses. The more usual form of response to these and other questions was for the informant to cite one or more names quite readily. Moreover, the explanations they offered only infrequently alluded to age or maturity alone, and often invoked specific abilities (cf. Table 2.2).

Which is more important? Is it more important to be *wo-chenjela* or *wa-nzelu*? Some of the village elders to whom we put this question replied that it is important to have a combination of both qualities – a wise, but evasive answer. But when the young adults whose lives were traced in this study from their childhood were requested to rank them along with eight other qualities in order of desirability, the great majority rated *-nzelu* significantly higher than *-chenjela*.[30]

Because of the intimate linkage I have described between social cooperation and intelligence in Chewa culture, it may still be tempting for some readers to conclude that intellectual ability and maturity are not really valued traits among Chewa adults. For instance, Ammar's account (1954) of indigenous education in a village of southern Egypt

Table 2.6 *Aggregate rank order of desirability of various personal characteristics according to a sample of young Chewa adults* in 1987*

Chi-Chewa	Rough English equivalents	Mean rank
ulemu	respectfulness	2.8
chifundo	kindness, compassion	3.6
chikhulupililo	to be trustworthy	4.4
kudzichepetsa	humility	5.4
chilungamo	to be straight, or just	5.5
chigwilizano	to be cooperative	5.8
nzelu	intelligence, wisdom	5.8
zikambidwe	to be articulate, good with words	6.2
changu	to be prompt	7.0
uchenjela	intelligence, cleverness	8.6

*14 men (Kendall's coefficient of concordance, w=+.43, p<.001)
 14 women (Kendall's coefficient of concordance, w=+.24, p<.001)

described parental socialisation as focussed on imparting to children the quality of *adab*, defined as discipline, politeness and conformity with adult expectations. *Nzelu* is a much more explicitly intellectual quality than this, and other words exist in Chi-Chewa which are closer in meaning to *adab*: for instance, *ulemu* (respectfulness) and *manyazi* (shame, including the observance of taboo). When the members of our cohort were interviewed as young adults we requested them to place in rank order of desirability a set of ten characteristics, including several of the key terms in Table 2.2, as well as *ulemu* and some other, non-intellectual characteristics. The aggregate rank order which they generated is shown in Table 2.6. Clearly, for most of these young people respectfulness and compassion were considered even more important than trustworthiness, cooperativeness or intelligence. I will return to the significance of this point in chapter 5, when discussing the relevance of schooling to the course of their various individual life-journeys.

Two dimensions of variation are generally recognised in respect of characteristics such as *nzelu*: variation across the range of individuals of a given age, and variation in developmental status. The characteristic is thought of as emerging gradually as a child grows up and an informal consensus exists on what constitutes a normal rate for this development. In societies like our rural A-Chewa community, where chronological birthdates are accorded very little significance, the behaviour indicative of growing *nzelu* is an important index of general maturation. Indeed, it may carry more weight in arriving at the decision that an adolescent is 'ready' for formal initiation into adulthood than do the organic signs of reaching puberty.

Richards, for instance, describes *mano*, the Bemba term cited from Kingsley's study in column 1 of Table 2.3, as 'that important social attribute of every Bemba -*mano*, or social sense'. The context is a symbolic 'test' of maturity in the girls' initiation ceremony conducted at puberty, which was interpreted by one local participant as designed to 'find out if the girls have grown up' and by another to the effect that, if the girl fails, 'the women all know she has not yet acquired *mano*' (Richards 1956, p. 76). An explicit parallel occurs in the account by Robert and Barbara Levine (1963) of the criteria by which Gusii children are admitted to initiation in the rural Kenyan community of Nyansongo:

As the parents put it, they want to see evidence of -*okongainia*, a verb which is variously translated 'to be intelligent' and 'to have sense.' In the case of a girl, 'having sense' means primarily being willing and able to do the work of an adult woman around the house and, to a lesser extent, in the fields. She should be able to grind a fine flour with the grinding stones and should perform these duties without having to be ordered and reminded by the mother. There is an assumption on the part of Nyansongo parents that any girl who has enough 'sense' and seriousness of purpose to do these things well will be able to undergo the painful operation of clitoridectomy without screaming or running away. (pp. 185–6).

The boy who wants to be initiated through the ritual of circumcision 'proves that he "has sense"' not only by continuous sleeping in the children's house' (a sign of reduced dependency on his mother) 'but also by wearing shorts to show that he is developing a proper sense of modesty, and sometimes by doing agricultural work to indicate seriousness of purpose' (p. 197). This account of *okongainia* (reminiscent of the illustrations considered above of Kipsigis *ngom* and Baoulé *n'glouèlê*) clearly implies the prevalence in Gusii culture of a concept of developmental 'readiness'. The use of this concept in Western educational theory is discussed in chapter 3. Also implied by this developmental perspective are the notions of 'precocity' and 'retardation' representing, respectively, the emergence of mature behaviour patterns either earlier or later than usual. In a recent account of socialisation among the Aba-Luyia, another Kenyan group, Tom Weisner argues that 'mothers use evidence that a child has the ability to give and receive social support, and assist others, as markers of a child's more general developmental level, much as an American parent might use literacy skills such as knowing the alphabet, or verbal facility, to show how grown-up or precocious his or her child is' (Weisner 1989, p. 86). Such notions have featured prominently in Western theories of differential psychology and their application to educational policy.[31]

What role do adults assume in the mobilisation of these intellectual developments? At least three aspects of the answer to this question may be variable across cultures:

(1) the division of responsibilities among adult members of the community;

(2) the kind of interest in a child's behaviour taken by those adults who regard themselves as responsible in some way for the child's 'socialisation'; and

(3) the range of a child's daily behaviour falling under adult observation and control.

The particular situation in respect of these variables in our rural A-Chewa community will be described in the next section.

5   Cultural practices and opportunities[32] for development

In traditional Chewa society the distribution of responsibilities for a child's socialisation changes as the child grows up:

the parents are responsible for bringing forth children ... The mother feeds the baby till it is weaned. From then on the responsibility for further rearing and education lies with the grandparents. When the child leaves the ... [house] of his grandparents [at the approximate age of seven] he passes on to the sleeping quarters of the unmarried and his training becomes more of a community concern than of individual parents. (Bruwer 1949, p. 197)

Moreover, because of the matrilineal system of inheritance, a maternal uncle tends in Chewa society to have as great, or sometimes greater, authority over a young boy as his father. Although the specifics of age and relationships vary from one culture to another, the existence of important roles for grandparents and other adults in the day-to-day control of a child's behaviour is described in the ethnographic accounts of many African societies. Even in the earliest phase, before a child is weaned, multiple caretaking (or caregiving) is the norm rather than an exception in many parts of Africa. This means that a great deal of the psychology of child-rearing based on the nuclear family typical of middle-class Western societies needs to be reconsidered for its relevance to the context in which most African children grow up.

A second aspect of child-rearing which is relevant to the conceptualisation of intellectual development is the kind of interest in a child's behaviour taken by those adults who regard themselves as responsible in some way for her socialisation. Table 2.7 illustrates some of the ways in which such an interest may be expressed. The categories of intervention listed in the first column are not construed as an exhaustive list, and various combinations or subdivisions could be envisaged.

Table 2.7 *Practices relating to the development of* nzelu *in children*

Interventions	Processes (assumed to be stimulated by interventions)	immediate ✓	longer-term ↓	cumulative ↘
demonstration	observation			
guidance	attentiveness	mimicry	addition of techniques to repertoire	
task-sharing	guided learning	repetition		expertise
commanding	discovery	rehearsal	appropriate application of techniques	
sending	practice	refinement of skills	promptness (compliance and efficiency)	
delegating			cooperation with other members of the community	responsibility
supervision				
ignoring	play exploration	exercise maturation	know-how self-reliance	
rebuking	understanding of causal relations			
chastising	fear	inhibition	conformity with social norms	wisdom
story-telling	understanding of human behaviour/social institutions		moral rectitude	
inclusion in/exposure to adult activities	acquisition of factual knowledge and values		avoidance of socially disapproved behaviour	

Rebuking and chastising might, for instance, be combined under the heading of punishing; sending might be subsumed as a special case of commanding, which could also be expanded to include bribing and threatening; and so on. The particular items listed were chosen in accordance with two guiding principles. They are all forms of intervention which have been clearly described in several different ethnographic reports on child-rearing in different parts of Africa, and they all seem to me likely to be immediately intelligible concepts for any adult with experience of managing children's behaviour.

To put this in more ambitious terms, I would hypothesise that all these concepts would find a place in the vocabulary of any cultural group's naïve educational psychology. The categories of intervention listed range from zero (ignoring), through minimal (exposure, inclusion), to direct and highly purposive actions (commanding, punishing). The extent to which these active interventions are construed as having an instructional goal is also variable. Demonstration and punishing are perhaps the most unambiguously instructional activities in the list. Finally, the amount of explanatory structure contained in an active and explicitly instructional intervention ranges from nil in the case of some types of demonstration to a great deal in the case of moral tales. The last two columns of Table 2.7 are also construed as part of the explicit naïve theory guiding socialisation practices. They are examples of the sort of broad objectives on which most adults with responsibility for child-rearing in any culture will agree. But whereas the cumulative outcomes (expertise, responsibility and wisdom) will be expressible in everyday terms in every natural language, the more exact specification of what leads to them is phrased in more technically focussed terms. In order to communicate the nature of the longer-term objectives listed in Table 2.7 to a non-technical audience it would often be necessary to express them in more concrete and culturally specific terms. The addition of techniques to a child's repertoire, for instance, could be rephrased for rural Chewa society as learning such techniques as how to prepare flour from cobs of maize or how to thatch a roof, whereas in the Zinacanteco society of Mexico a more appropriate example might be weaving cloth on a loom (Childs and Greenfield 1980). Conformity with social norms would likewise be differently specified in different cultures.

The processes and immediate outcomes listed in Table 2.7 are technical in a more psychological sense. The justification for including them in the same table alongside the everyday concepts of the earlier and later columns requires a more elaborate kind of argument. Carla Childs and Patricia Greenfield have analysed video-tapes of the naturally occurring sessions in which Zinacanteco novices began learning to weave, in order to highlight the systematic nature of the teaching and the immediate behaviour which it elicited. Meyer Fortes has described in much more general terms what he regarded as the 'fundamental learning processes' which were operative in rural Tale education in northern Ghana in the 1930s: mimesis, identification, cooperation and play (Fortes 1938).

He also draws a number of contrasts between the contexts and methods characteristic of Tale education and those of Western school-

ing. Western instructional practices, Fortes notes, often involve participation in 'factitious activities' that demand 'atomic modes of response'.
(The historical origins of these will be discussed in chapter 3.) In the
case of Tale education most learning takes place in 'real situations'
which require 'organic modes of response' (p. 28). As a result, a child's
education proceeds not so much by an accumulation of discrete elements, but rather through a process which Fortes likens to embryonic
evolution. The desired behavioural outcomes 'are present as *schemas*
from the beginning ... the child acquires a well-defined interest associated with a postural diagram of the total pattern ... as it were a contour
map, extremely simplified and crude but comprehending the essential
elements and relations of the full pattern ... which evolves from the
embryonic form' (pp. 42–3).

Little research has been done until recently on how the 'instructor'
intervenes to promote this kind of learning. Patricia Greenfield and
Jean Lave offered some preliminary insights from a comparison
between the case of Zinacanteco weaving and the training of appren-
tice tailors in urban Liberia. They concluded:

that there exists a great variety of instructional techniques in informal learning
situations ... such as trial and error, verbalization, and cooperative participation ... Often techniques are combined to yield scaffolded learning, which is an
active, organized enterprise. Teachers present verbal instructions coordinated
with demonstration and actual performance, and fit these to the needs of
learners. (Greenfield and Lave 1982, p. 206)

The concept of 'scaffolded learning', introduced by David Wood and
his colleagues (Wood and Middleton 1975; Wood, Bruner and Ross
1976; Wood 1989), is a good example of the kind of interpretive
metaphor which psychologists can sometimes add to the explicit
theoretical ideas of a community, in order to clarify for them what
previously they were doing on the basis of unarticulated intuitions.[33]
The scaffolding used by builders to hold up parts of a building
temporarily while the permanent structure is still too weak to stand on
its own is presented as a metaphor for the control exercised by the
instructor over those parts of the task which a learner has not yet
mastered. This support by the instructor enables the learner to concentrate upon those parts of the task which are within her range of
competence to learn. An effective instructor starts by controlling the
most difficult parts of the task while the learner tackles the easier parts,
and, as the learner's skill improves, the instructor gradually removes
the scaffolding to allow the learner to take on responsibility for more
and more of the difficult parts of the task. Childs and Greenfield
observed this structured sequence in the behaviour of Zinacanteco
mothers when they were teaching their daughters to weave, but those

effective instructors had apparently not articulated what they were doing as an explicit theory.

Recently Jean Lave (1988) and Barbara Rogoff (1990) have begun to explore the implications of this model, now known as the 'apprenticeship' model, for various aspects of cognitive socialisation. Rather than focussing only on the particular cognitive strategies, schemas, etc., which the individual internalises in the course of training, they have drawn attention to the ways in which 'guided participation' by immature and/or inexperienced individuals in activities structured by the culture provide an account which retains the context of the activity as an intrinsic element of what the novice is learning. Analysis of the processes through which such guidance is provided to apprentices has often drawn on the concept of the 'zone of proximal development' introduced by Vygotsky (1978) to account for the dramatic improvements in performance which can often be achieved when a novice has access to support from an expert. As Michael Cole has pointed out, this concept of a developmental zone within which instructional support can extend the learner's competence provides an illuminating meeting point between the microgenetic processes of cognitive development and the macrosocietal processes of social organisation and change: indeed, it may be seen as a point of articulation between the individual and societal levels of analysis, 'where culture and cognition create each other' (Cole 1985, p. 146).

Many of the interventions listed in Table 2.7 are ambiguous in purpose. Sharing a task, commanding an act, sending a child on an errand may seem at first glance to be acts designed to achieve a reduction in work-load of the agent. Consider, for instance, the following account of child-rearing in rural Kenya:

Parents begin obedience and responsibility training very early, often as soon as a sibling is born. The child begins by carrying dishes of food from one house to another within the homestead. As time goes on, more and more errands of this kind are demanded of him. When the father wants to smoke a cigarette or the mother her pipe while sitting in the yard, any nearby child will be sent for a coal from the fireplace to ignite the tobacco. When visitors come, a small child is sent into the house for a stool. When a beer party is planned, children are sent to notify neighbours, and once it is underway they may be sent to other houses to borrow pots, kettles and cups. An adult will never get something for himself if he can order a child to do it, even if the child is farther from the object than he himself is. (Levine and Levine 1963, p. 181)

This account describes a pattern of recurrent practices which is closely akin to what I have observed among the A-Chewa and in other Zambian village communities. But in a society where obedience (*ku-mvela*) is regarded as a sign of responsibility (*ku-tumikila*) rather than of weakness or lack of imagination, errands are more of an opportunity for displaying competence than an infringement of freedom. If adults are asked to interpret their own or other people's behaviour in this domain, they may well tend to emphasise the concrete purpose of the errand, followed by the goal of instilling discipline. But it is probably incorrect to describe the less obvious purpose – that of affording the child an opportunity to learn through practice – as incidental. Adults presumably keep some kind of mental tally of the proportion of errands that a given child performs adequately, and this serves as an index of how *-tumikila* the child is. In the short term this attribute is used to choose which child to send on another such errand; in the longer term it feeds into an assessment of that child's expertise and responsibility.

5.1   *Individual differences in parenting*

In addition to these broad characteristics of prevailing cultural practices it is important to acknowledge the existence of individual differences in styles and methods of parenting, child-rearing and instruction within a single community. Many of the ethnographic reports of child-rearing practices in rural Africa have been written by authors (like myself) who did not grow up as a child in such a context and who have little or no experience of bringing up a child of their own in a village. As a result, many of the judgements they contain are contrastive with a different set of cultural reference points. In the case of reports published in the early part of this century such comparisons are often explicit and sometimes quite ethnocentric in tone, with expressions like 'we', 'us' and 'our society' standing for some idealised concept of 'mainstream' Western, European or North American culture. Reports by indigenous African writers and by some exogenous researchers in more recent years have tried in various ways to distance themselves from this tradition. But one consequence of the comparative perspective has been remarkably persistent: the tendency to portray the practices of parents in rural African communities as homogeneous with little differentiation between families, between different children of the same gender in a given family, or across different situations.

Yet such variations are surely commonplace within everybody's circle of personal acquaintances. Phillip Kingsley (1977, pp. 23–4; cf. Kingsley 1985) designed a set of sharply focussed questions about one's preferred methods of training and disciplining children, which were put to a sample of fourteen men and seven women, most of them middle-aged or elderly, in a Bemba-speaking village in which one of the interviewers (Sophie Kasonde Ng'andu) had grown up as a child:

Techniques recommended for instructing children ... varied with the content of the lesson; abstract knowledge such as customs and kinship are best conveyed by verbal explanation according to a majority of respondents (some said kinship should be taught in concrete situations ... i.e. when kin are present relationships should be explained with reference to them). Practical skills (e.g., cooking), on the other hand, were thought by more than half of the respondents to be best taught by demonstration. A couple of respondents said that trial and feedback (correction) is a good way of teaching practical skills, and a large number took this position in relation to the development of speaking ability. (Kingsley 1977, p. 21)

Opinions were clearly divided on the question of corporal punishment:

a minority of respondents expressed unqualified approval of beating as a technique of discipline but many apparently felt that it should not be used or should only be used very selectively. Various other forms of punishment were mentioned, prominent among them being scolding and withholding food. A number of respondents felt that nothing should be done to a child who grumbles about work, and a few even said this in relation to a child who refuses work. (p. 23)

A similar degree of variability probably prevails in rural Chewa communities. The views of some A-Chewa parents on this subject will be considered in relation to the practices of the local primary school in chapter 4.

5.2   *Children's games*

A third aspect of child-rearing which may vary significantly across cultures is the range of a child's daily behaviour falling under adult observation and control. In many rural African societies children are expected, from the age of about 3 or 4 years until adolescence, to spend a large part of the day in the company of elder siblings and age-mates from neighbouring families. Much of this time, as in other societies, is devoted to playing – an activity regarded by most adults as essentially childish, and therefore unworthy of adult attention.[34]

Unsupervised play activities thus constitute a major component of children's experience, defining the goals to which they aspire and the contingencies affecting their learning of skills. Some of these activities are quite effectively hidden from adult eyes, either because adults are not interested in them or because children do not wish them to be observed. Yet within this partly hidden realm, there exists a semi-autonomous subculture of childhood activities encoded in the rules of games, in a slang lexicon and in a pecking order or dominance hierarchy. Our informal interviews and observations and the more recent research of Mapopa M'tonga (1985)[35] revealed a rich child folklore of Chewa games, riddles and songs. Parents seem to acknowledge the educational value of these activities through passive tolerance.

In the first phase of our research in Katete District in 1974 groups of children were interviewed about the games they play, mainly by Shadreck Sipu whose experience of growing up in the neighbouring rural District of Petauke inspired him to pose a number of leading questions. The initial question to a group of children about what games they play together usually elicited reference to games of the rough-and-tumble variety, like 'hide-and-seek' (*kalondo-londo*, or *ku-bisalana*), or *nkuku (yoyela) yakuda*, a game similar to the English game 'fox and geese'. The progress of the interview beyond this point depended critically on the intuitions and experience of the interviewer. Through a process of probing it emerged that a variety of more intellectually demanding recreational activities were common in most of the villages.

Children of both sexes played a game called *nyepe*, which consists of one person guessing in which hand another person has hidden a stone. In one case this was demonstrated by a group of girls, the pair-formation moving around the circle and each individual recording her score by the progress of a stone around a stylised maze drawn in the sand. *Sine-sine*, also played by both sexes, starts with piling up a long mound of sand; then the actor slides a stone into one end of the mound under his finger, runs the finger right through the mound emerging at the other end without the stone, and then divides the mound into several separate smaller mounds. The other participant in the game now has to guess, aided by observation, in which mound of sand the stone is concealed. This game, like the next, was demonstrated with great manual dexterity. *Mtengo wampando* is played with one hand and consists of drawing regular geometrical patterns in the sand by alternating the number of fingers and the direction of movement. The object is to make the patterns as regular as possible and to perform the whole exercise in a smoothly coordinated series of swift movements.

All the groups make models out of clay, often congregating close to a good supply, such as an ant-hill. On a more recent visit to another part of Katete District, I spent a morning with a group of herdsboys, and with the assistance of George Phiri, who grew up there, quizzed them about their favourite games. Some of the boys made models of cattle and later used them in imaginative games representing various aspects of the local economy, such as ploughing. Girls, on the other hand, more often make *ti-ma-doli*, little model people, and play imaginative family games with them. The skills involved in making a clay model of a person have been explored over the past few years in Zambia, giving rise to a semi-standardised test known as the Panga Munthu Test (Make-a-Person Test), whose use is discussed in chapters 5 and 7. Children of both genders also sing songs, dance and play drums.

A game confined to girls is *chiato*. This is played sitting in a circle

Fig. 2.3 *Nsolo* game-board, discussed on p. 67. (Photo by the author)

around a small hole in the ground. A number of small stones are placed in the hole and the player's task is to scoop out specific numbers of these during the time between throwing up another stone and catching it in the same hand. Other skilful recreational activities confined to girls were threading beads and plaiting hair. Girls aged 5 to 8 years old were said to be too young for plaiting. Older girls sometimes practise the complex designs used in hair-plaiting by plaiting blades of grass. Boys also plait blades of long grass but this is for use as cattle-whips.

The well-known pan-African game *nsolo* is only played by boys. It calls for two or four parallel lines of holes along which stones are moved in accordance with elaborate rules which call for considerable planning as well as numerical calculation. Under a tree close to one of the villages in our study there stood for many years a wooden '*nsolo*-board' carved out of a tree trunk, with no less than twenty-seven holes in each of the four rows (see Figs. 2.3 and 2.4). More commonly the game is played with holes in the ground, and one of our groups of boys demonstrated their ability to play with a small array of four holes to a line. Generally, however, boys only start playing this game seriously in early adolescence. The gradual emergence, with increasing maturity and playing experience, of strategic forms of play in this complex and intellectually challenging game has been documented in detail by Retschitzki, Assandé and Loesch-Berger (1986; see also Retschitzki 1990)

67

Fig. 2.4 Game of *nsolo* in progress, discussed on p. 67. (Photo by the author)

with a painstaking analysis of video-taped games among expert players of various ages in Côte d'Ivoire.

All our groups of boys were keen on trapping birds, most of them relying on the sap of a tree to get the bird's feet stuck, but in one case using a more elaborate noose technique (cf. Kidd 1906). A few boys expressed an interest in fishing, but the techniques were not discussed. A number of boys had constructed model cars out of wire, and one or two had carved them out of wood. All the models we saw had operational wheels and steering and were apparently of similar quality to those seen in Zambian towns (Fig. 2.5) (Serpell 1979). The herdsboys, in addition to their specialised whips, had perfected whistling as part of their stock in trade. Their technique involved using cupped hands as a resonator and moving their fingers to vary the pitch.

6   Traditions and theories as cultural capital

One of the distinctive characteristics of the biological human organism seems to be our tendency to treat our young as individual persons from the outset. We talk to them and try to meet their gaze in the same way that we interact with adult humans (cf. Trevarthen 1980); we name them and impute moods and feelings and a personality to them from a

Fig. 2.5 Model car constructed from scraps of wire by an 11-year-old boy in Lusaka, discussed on p. 68. (Photo by the author)

very early age. The beliefs which seem to underlie these transculturally universal phenomena include the following:

Children are voluntary agents, capable of reflection on their own actions (cf. Shields 1978), capable of learning, accessible to intersubjective mutual awareness with others. They are also immature, which implies that they have limited competence, are ineligible for full moral responsibility, and yet are destined for full adult competence and eligibility for responsibility at some future time.

Parents are mature, have generally greater competence than children, especially in the domains in which they interact with them, and have special rights and obligations with respect to certain children arising from, and sustained through, an enduring personal relationship with them. These include: protection, nurturance, guidance and socialisation.

Can we infer from this analysis that humans speculate in every culture about how their children grow up, that they care about the kind of person their child is becoming, and that they see themselves as to some extent responsible for that developmental process and for its outcome? Such attitudes may be held with varying degrees of self-consciousness in different cultural groups, and opinions may differ both across and within groups as to the domains in which parental influence is greatest, and as to the mechanisms by which that influence has its impact. But there seems little reason to doubt that every human group accepts some degree of responsibility for shaping the development of its young. In the case of Chewa society such a collective sense of responsibility is encoded and stored for reference in appropriate contexts in some of the proverbs presented and explained in Box 2.1 (e.g. *tsamba likagwa manyazi agwira m'tengo; mbeu poyamba*).

A key concern of developmental psychology has been to provide a coherent account of the transition from the condition of early childhood to that of adulthood. The difficulty experienced in arriving at a consensus on what this account should be like suggests to me that there probably exists no clear transculturally uniform, intuitive interpretation of the transition: rather it is a source of perplexity to most human beings which underlies many crises of interpersonal relations, which invites investigation for the sake of curiosity and which holds promising opportunities for effective practical application of specialised knowledge for the amelioration of the human condition.

All societies seem to have a somewhat ambivalent attitude towards children. They are accorded the status of humans as far as our basic orientation is concerned. We do not treat them like animals: we talk to them, greet them, expect them to eat, to toilet and to dress like humans; but we do not expect them to take responsibility for their actions or their words. They are thus incomplete humans, in a state of transition, creatures about to be persons. Their actions are promissory, provisional, subject to correction and to being forgotten. It is this ambivalence which motivates the activities we call rearing, socialisation or education – through which we attempt to prepare children for adult personhood. The proverbs cited in Box 2.1 include theoretical analogies which serve to legitimate and guide such purposeful activity (e.g. *madzi saiwala khwawa; kuongola m'tengo ndi poyamba*).

On the question of how best to organise education, an ongoing debate in cross-cultural psychology is addressed to the question how much explicit awareness characterises the guidance afforded by non-specialised adults to their young charges and apprentices (Greenfield and Lave 1982; Strauss 1984; Segall *et al.* 1990). Some Chewa proverbs seem to represent the beginnings of a theoretical account of instruction, though none of them is explicitly linked to childhood or parenthood (see Box 2.1: *pfupa loumiliza linaswa m'phika; ziliko nkulinga utatosa; saweluzika anamanga nyumba pa mchenga*).

The succinct distillation of cultural wisdom contained in proverbs has drawn them to the attention of many anthropologists. Typically the focus of a proverb is both interpretive and prescriptive. Since they

Box 2.1 Proverbial Wisdom

The following Chewa proverbs show that three themes, which will be developed in the course of this book, are not completely unfamiliar to Chewa society.

Theme 1: elders have a responsibility for the upbringing of children.

Tsamba likagwa manyazi agwira m'tengo.
'When a leaf falls down the shame will be on the tree.'
Whenever a child does something wrong very often it is the parents who bear the shame. They have not brought up their child well apparently.

Mbeu poyamba
'The harvest depends on the beginning.'
Well begun is half-done. Success depends on the way a thing is started. Note that the word *mbeu* means both 'harvest' and 'seed'.

Theme 2: early experience has a profound influence on later behaviour; hence the effectiveness of educational intervention early in life.

Madzi saiwala khwawa
'The water does not forget its bed.'
Things learnt when young are not forgotten easily. The conditions of life may change but a man rarely forgets his native customs, language, etc., just as water will always trace back its own brook as soon as the rain falls, even if during the dry season the brook has dried up.

Kuongola m'tengo mpoyamba
'A tree is straightened when it is young'.
The older one becomes, the harder it is to change. So if corrections are to be made, they must be done when one is young and supple.

Theme 3: instruction is essential for success in life, and it requires an awareness of how learning takes place.

Saweluzika anamanga nyumba pa mchenga
'The man who did not accept advice built his house on sand.'
The man who does not heed advice of others can meet misfortunes.

Pfupa loumiliza linaswa m'phika
'A bone forced in broke the pot.'
A person should never be forced to do something against his will. Not only may he do a poor job, but he can also do more harm than good.

Ziliko nkulinga utatosa
'You can say "the mice are there" only after you have checked by poking a stick into the hole.'
'The proof of the pudding is in the eating.'
One gets to know something when one has some close contact with it. The image of this proverb is taken from the sport of hunting field-mice, especially popular among the A-Chewa's neighbours the A-Ngoni.

Note: all of these proverbs and their translations/interpretations appear in Milimo 1972, pp. 16, 111, 108, 15, 6, 111, 96 respectively.

are anonymous there is a temptation to treat them as collective representations of opinions commanding a high degree of consensus in the society. Paradoxically, however, different proverbs within a single culture not infrequently contradict one another. In English culture, for instance, we find both: 'Many hands make light work' and 'Too many cooks spoil the broth'. Read's account of the ways in which proverbs are deployed in conversation in A-Ngoni rural society illustrates how this diversity is used in debate (Read 1959). Proverbs differ from theories as we know them in contemporary social science by being much less explicit, but the discourse practices which Read describes for their use (in a community closely akin to that of the A-Chewa) are far from the image of effortless consensus implied by statements of the form 'this proverb shows that among the *** intelligence is defined as...' or '...regarded as...' (e.g. Irvine 1970). Like many theoretical hypotheses in scientific psychology, well-known proverbs may be regarded as summary statements of a line of reasoning about a recurrent phenomenon in human experience which has been generated through shared observation and interpretation and stored in capsule form for transmission across generations as part of society's cultural capital.

Other instances of such cultural capital are the games, songs and riddles described above, which are often regarded by adults as ethically trivial, and yet which have a remarkable continuity across many generations (Opie and Opie 1959). A number of African studies (e.g. Kaboré 1981; M'tonga 1985) have suggested that the content of children's songs and even the rhythmic patterns of their music and dancing provide a symbolic representation of behavioural norms which sustains and reinforces many of the principles of social organisation enshrined in other institutions which only proclaim their messages intermittently. Certainly this body of child folklore provides a bridge for communication among children and its broad outline is known to their parents, which may be a source of reassurance that part of the private world of child play is intelligible to them (or would be if they cared to inspect it) as people who have been children in their own time.

The most prestigious forms of cultural capital tend to be religious, political, legal or technological. During the twentieth century the A-Chewa, like the other ethnic groups of Zambia and most other countries in the region, have surrendered a great deal of their traditional religious and political autonomy to ideas imported from Western culture. The central government of the modern Zambian state affords nominal recognition to the institution of chieftainship, but most legal and political issues affecting the community as a whole are determined by laws made and enforced by the central government. Domestic disputes, however, over marriage or children (including, until recently, issues of inheritance) are often settled under local traditional laws interpreted and enforced by the Chief or his representative (cf. Marwick 1965; Mvunga 1979). The rites of passage into life, adulthood, marriage and death are generally celebrated in ways which incorporate elements both of indigenous spiritual tradition and of Christianity.

Many of the concepts and values I have described can also be traced within the ritual forms of the boys' secret *Nyau* society and the songs and proverbs pronounced on the occasion of *Chi-namwali*, the traditional puberty rite for girls. The ideation of *Nyau* will be discussed in chapter 6 where I describe an exploratory dramatic representation for and by the local community of the themes analysed in this research project. But it is clear from our discussions with contemporary residents that only limited sections of the community participate in those rituals which are, moreover, confined to specific occasions. I have preferred therefore in this introductory chapter to concentrate on the texture of ordinary conversation and daily life in search of characteristics of 'everyday cognition' (cf. Rogoff and Lave 1984; Dasen 1987; Segall *et al.* 1990) which embody this implicit educational philosophy.

Conclusion

My purpose in this chapter has been to evoke the principal characteristics of the indigenous Chewa point of view for conceptualising children's intellectual development. This point of view, as we have seen, is articulated in the cultural practices of everyday relations between adults and children in Kondwelani, outside the framework of schooling. Its main dimensions are:

1. *nzelu*, an overarching, superordinate concept which encompasses both the notion of cognitive alacrity (*-chenjela*) and the notion of social responsibility and cooperativeness (*-tumikila*, which requires both *-khulupilika* and *-mvela*);
2. an awareness that *-chenjela* in the absence of *-tumikila* is a negative social force which would certainly not be part of the objectives of the indigenous educational philosophy;
3. shared responsibility among adult members of the community for the socialisation of children;
4. a set of assumptions, largely implicit, about the psychological processes in children's minds stimulated or enabled by various types of adult intervention and their likely, desirable outcomes over various periods of time (cf. Table 2.7), which collectively constitute a way of building an educational function into the everyday interactions of adults with children;

5. a range of elaborately structured, unsupervised play activities through which various cognitive skills and social dispositions are practised and elaborated by children, over and above those acquired in the context of their various domestic and economic chores.

Despite the rarity with which its dimensions are explicitly articulated or affirmed in public discourse, and despite its low prestige in the arena of national and international debate about education, this system of constructs and practices encoded in Chewa culture constitutes a coherent alternative to those represented by the system of formal schooling, whose nature and origins will be described in chapter 3. Moreover, the point of view represented by this indigenous system derives great strength from the facts of its familiarity and its continuity with many other aspects of contemporary life in the community.[36] These subjectively experienced features of its social reality, perhaps more than any explicit commitment to a historical tradition, underlie its informal legitimacy and its capacity to pose a real challenge on the local stage to the might of the establishment view represented by the primary school.

3

The formal educational model of cognitive growth

1   Introduction

The philosophy underpinning Zambia's system of schooling differs from the indigenous Chewa perspective on children's intellectual and moral development with respect to each of the characteristics highlighted in chapter 2. Its theories of pedagogy and instruction are much more explicit; cognitive functions are conceptually segregated much more sharply from the conative and emotional aspects of human thought; technological mastery over the environment is construed as an intrinsically desirable feature of mental function and perhaps the pre-eminent goal of human development. Moreover, the responsibility for children's socialisation is highly differentiated, with a clear division of tasks between the home and the school (as well as more individualised control over decision-making by the nuclear family relative to the wider community), and a consequent professionalisation of pedagogy complete with a mystique of what constitutes education.[1]

My purpose in this chapter is to trace the historical origins of the developmental psychology (both implicit and explicit) which informs the practices of Zambian schools, to show how and why it differs so markedly from the psychology reconstructed in chapter 2 for the eco-cultural niche of rural Chewa society, and thus to lay one of the foundations for an understanding of the paradox presented in chapter 1. I shall argue that the kind of education offered in a rural Zambian primary school contains an ambitious set of promises, which in general have not been fulfilled.

The account of cultural resources presented in chapter 2 stressed their empowering function, as amplifying tools[2] of thought. In this chapter I shall argue that a complementary facet of such cognitive empowerment is a canalisation which tends to restrict the scope of thought, obscuring the value of alternative ways of interpreting experience, either by hiding them from view or else by misrepresenting them. A common metaphor for the former effect is that of the protective eye-shades, known as blinkers, fitted to the harness of horses used for drawing carriages through the busy streets of Western cities in the nineteenth century, in order to prevent them from being distracted and frightened by the near-by movement of other vehicles or pedestrians. A number of authors have likened the latter effect to that of a distorting lens.[3]

In chapter 1, I characterised Zambia's system of schooling as outward-looking and extractive. Part of the key to understanding this apparently self-defeating orientation lies in the historical fact that the seeds of the present were more or less consciously exported to Zambia, as well as to many other parts of the world, by British educators during the first half of the twentieth century. Much has been written by political analysts about the motives of those pioneering teachers and their sponsors in the missionary and colonial administration, concerning whether their goals were emancipatory or oppressive, humanitarian or exploitative (see Snelson 1974; Serpell and Mwanalushi 1976; Ball 1983).

Yet, in a longer-term perspective, it may be less important to interpret the intentions of those actors than the nature of the ideas they left behind. For, since the independence movement gained momentum in countries like Zambia, these ideas have been appropriated by an indigenous leadership, and they have continued to evolve while the provision of formal education has expanded far beyond the scope of what was established, or indeed probably ever envisaged, by its missionary and colonial pioneers.

During the modern era – which some would trace back to the end of the nineteenth century, others to the beginning of Europe's industrial revolution in the eighteenth century, or even earlier to the Renaissance – extraordinary increases in human power over the environment have been achieved through the systematic elaboration in Western civilisation of the cognitive amplifying tools of literacy, mathematics and science. This human empowerment has been intimately linked to the particular institutional structures within which that elaboration was conducted, structures whose form was often dictated more by considerations of communication and social control than by intrinsic properties of the cognitive technology itself. As a result a great deal of *packaging* has taken place, such that other societies wishing to benefit from the incorporation of Western technological inventions have been encouraged to believe that this is only possible if they import (a common metaphor is to buy, or buy into) Western institutions and their embedded practices.[4] A major theme running through the chapters that follow will be that this wholesale importation of institutionalised packages has led to anomalous and dysfunctional applications of what were potentially valuable principles and techniques for the amplification of cognitive power. In particular my

argument centres around the practices of schooling as a mode of transmission of cognitive tools.

Several principles and processes can be distinguished in the historical
genesis of the conceptual model of cognitive growth which lies behind
the practices of formal education in contemporary Zambia. Many of
them are shared with the philosophy of education endorsed by educational professionals and planners in other parts of the world. I shall
discuss them under the following headings: (1) the gradation of school
instruction; (2) projection of school grading onto child development;
(3) stigmatisation of unschooled persons as incomplete; (4) infusion of
the teacher–learner relationship with condescension; (5) the
emergence of a formal concept of didactic process; (6) a growing faith
in the certainty of method, culminating eventually in (7) the concept
of educational expertise.

The modern elementary or primary school (of which the Kondwelani community's local school is an example) is a remarkable
cultural invention, designed as an instrumental approach to ecological
adaptation, through a specialised method of child-rearing. Its origins
are complex and readers may need to hold their breath occasionally as
I attempt to trace within a few pages the story of its evolution over a
period of several thousand years! After examining the historical and
philosophical pedigree of the ambitious promises embedded in the
programme of contemporary schooling, I will turn in chapter 4 to the
particular challenges confronting those entrusted with the task of articulating those promises in the context of a contemporary, rural African
community, taking account of its cultural and economic expectations. I
will draw attention to the institutional constraints within which these
brave teachers are required to operate, the compromises which those
constraints have precipitated and the public confusion which has been
generated. Later, in chapters 5 and 6, I will describe some of the
strategies evolved by citizens for surviving the assaults on their
energies and on their self-respect by this social crisis.

The historical processes which I wish to review extend over an
immense span of time and space, and are interwoven in complex ways.
At the risk of simplification, I shall identify (for the sake of clarity in
presentation) the following successively emergent phases:

A. urbanisation and craft specialisation beginning in the Mesopotamian
   civilisation about 5000 years ago;
B. the invention of writing and the gradual refinement and standardisa-
   tion of scripts, beginning about 3000 years ago (Diringer 1948;
   Havelock 1976; Cole 1990);
C. the evolution of Western archival scholarship from the first great
   libraries of Alexandria and Pergamon, through the Byzantine and
   Islamic libraries and the early Christian monasteries to the establish-

ment of university libraries in medieval Europe and the invention of
the printing press;

D. the transformation of formal educational institutions in Europe from
the medieval monasteries through the universities of the Renaissance
to the public schools of the eighteenth century;

E. the deployment of teaching as a vehicle for religious proselytisation,
democratisation of knowledge and cultural imperialism;

F. the philosophical articulation of education as a means of enlightenment, closely tied to the emergence of the ideology of Western
science in the seventeenth and eighteenth centuries;

G. the politics of culture contact and social change in Africa during the
nineteenth and twentieth centuries;

H. the ideology of decolonisation and centralised manpower planning
for the establishment of autonomous nation-states in the second half
of the twentieth century.

The most obvious contrast between the implicit educational philosophy described in chapter 2 and that which informs the formal education system arises directly from those two qualifying attributes: implicit
and formal. Unlike the traditional Chewa perspective which is
pervasive throughout everyday life, taken for granted and implicit, the
educational philosophy underlying formal schooling is formalised as a
deliberate undertaking, with an explicit purpose and design. The
school's very *raison d'être* is to change the children who enter it: some
educators would say to enlighten them, others to transform them,
others to prepare them, others to assist them. The differences among
these various conceptions of what it is the school is trying to do to its
pupils, important though they are, are secondary to the premise shared
by all philosophies of formal schooling: that they are going to add
something, that without schooling life would be different.

It is difficult to make such a claim in the case of an implicit philosophy embedded in the practices of everyday child-rearing such as the
one described in chapter 2. In that context adult interventions in the
lives of children (cf. Table 2.7), although they have educational functions of the kind I have suggested (ranging from the immediate promotion of certain psychological processes to a more indirect contribution
to certain cumulative long-term psychological outcomes), also have
other, more immediately pragmatic functions in the flow of daily life. If
there were no child around to be educated, many if not all of these
activities would still take place in the interactions between adults,
albeit perhaps in a slightly different form. Individually and collectively,
adult members of the community are aware that in the process of these
activities they influence children's development, that the adult who
performs these interventions is assuming some kind of responsibility
for a change in the child's outlook. But in many cases the activity did

not come into existence solely for that purpose. Even story-telling, which might appear to be a deliberately pedagogical activity, has a self-justifying celebratory quality which enables the story-teller to derive a reflexive satisfaction from its performance. It is thus less factitious[5] than the educational activities of formal schooling, which are designed explicitly for the purpose of instruction.

2   Western cultural premises

The conceptual underpinnings of contemporary practices in Western-style formal education include psychological premises regarding the nature of cognition and human development which found their way into the design of curriculum and the training of teachers long before the formal articulation of the various, seemingly diverse yet philosophically cognate, theories of cognitive development and in-struction which dominate the scientific and professional journals of Western academia. Education in Western culture, whatever its socio-economic functions, has from its earliest philosophical origins expres-sed a preoccupation with promoting cognitive growth, the expansion of knowledge and understanding.[6] Cognition, in post-Renaissance Western thought,[7] has been persistently conceived as private, tran-scendental, absolute and independent of will. That which I think (*cogito*) is inalienably my own. My consciousness exists in a dimension which is not physically defined,[8] so that it may persist after the death and decay of my body (including the brain) and is capable of appre-hending an infinitude of new ideas. The character of that apprehension depends on nothing and no one else: it is immediately given and personal to the holder. And finally, what I think bears an asymmetrical relation to what I want. I may and, if rationally inclined, generally should take account of what I think I know in formulating my inten-tions. But for my motives to influence what I think I know is unsound and to be avoided.

Humans are conceived as developing not only physically, but also spiritually. Children are not merely weak, but incomplete as human beings. The work of Philippe Ariès (1962) has been widely cited as demonstrating that this idea is the product of a series of gradual changes in Western thought between the fourteenth and sixteenth centuries. But there is a danger in inferring from this historical analysis that what preceded it was a vacuum – that, as Ariès puts it dramati-cally, European society 'discovered' childhood. This view seems to rest on a version of the 'deficit' theory discussed in chapter 2 with reference to cross-cultural comparisons.

Ariès contends that prior to the sixteenth century the child was considered 'an unimportant little thing' whose death was so much to be expected that it was treated with an 'indifference' suggestive of 'callousness' (1962, p. 39). And Barbara Tuchman's study of 'the calamitous fourteenth century' provides a similar, more superficial sketch of a view of childhood bereft of compassionate fostering of development:

> On the whole babies appear to have been left to survive or die without great concern in the first five or six years ... Possibly the relative emotional blankness of a medieval infancy may account for the casual attitude toward life and suffering of the medieval man. (Tuchman 1978, p. 52)

Like Ariès, Tuchman seems to mistake the relative paucity of visual (and literary) representation of children engaged in childlike pursuits as evidence of a lack of sensitivity to the unique characteristics of children.

Authors writing in this vein seem to have embedded their interpretation of emotional experience so deeply in the culturally specific practices of their contemporary, local subculture that they misconstrue any radical departure from those practices as evidence of a condition in which the emotions they know and value are inconceivable. Inspired by something akin to a strong version of Maslow's (1954) hierarchy of needs, both Ariès and Tuchman argue that only when societies have managed to protect mothers and infants from the hazards of disease, heavy economic labour and the like can mother–infant interaction acquire the depth and intensity of emotion which is now heralded by Western psychologists as a foundation of healthy social and emotional development.

The notion of childhood familiar to pre-fourteenth-century Europeans and indeed in many contemporary non-European cultures is assuredly a different one from that which has been legitimated through the world-wide promotion of a certain model of schooling, but this should not be confused with the highly improbable notion that these other cultures have or had *no* concept of childhood. In my view, this interpretation of history has reversed the sequence of causation. When particular economic conditions allowed certain societies to plan the division of labour in such a way as to institutionalise mothering as a full-time occupation, the pre-existing salience of the special emotional quality which normally characterises mother–infant relationships was a prime candidate for articulation as an explicit cultural theme in literary and visual artistic representations.

Tuchman in fact cites a number of counterexamples to her own thesis. How, for instance, could a thirteenth-century English encyclopaedist advocate breast-feeding 'for its emotional value', or an Italian physician of the same period advise 'ample playtime and unforced teaching at school' in a cultural atmosphere where, as Tuchman puts it, 'the investment of love in a young child' was 'so unrewarding that ... it was suppressed'? Likewise Ariès, even more forcefully, concedes that 'countless mothers and nannies had already felt the same way' (1962, p. 49), but focusses on the fact that among all those mothers 'not a single one had admitted that these feelings were worthy of being expressed in such an ambitious form' as became conventional in European writing in the seventeenth and eighteenth centuries (p. 49).

The most conspicuous examples of non-modern representation of childhood in Ariès' book are in fact pictorial rather than verbal. And here his reasoning is flawed by insufficient attention to the contextual framework which informs an artist's communicative goals and thus constrains the directive schema (Freeman 1972) from which his or her product emerges. Ariès acknowledges the significance of the gradual detachment from religious iconography of a quite different genre of painting, but fails to consider what communicative inhibitions medieval artists may have felt against portraying the infant Jesus or indeed the children of powerful gentry in an immature, playful or vulnerable light. Artistic representation is an attempt to communicate with a given audience in relation to a background of shared presuppositions, which include what types of activity it is appropriate to represent in a given medium. Once this is recognised, it ceases to be surprising that putti were represented in all sorts of playful poses throughout the sixteenth century while the tradition of portraiture continued to portray children like miniature adults (Ariès 1962, p. 44). Once it is acknowledged that purposive communicative strategies inform and constrain the form of representations produced by artists of all ages (Gombrich 1960; Goodnow 1977), there is less temptation to infer that the medieval artists who painted children devoid of immature characteristics had no conception of childhood as a state of immaturity.[9]

The largest and, in my view, most informative part of Ariès' book is concerned with the practices of schooling. When the full range of his arguments and detailed supporting evidence is considered below, a somewhat different formulation will be suggested of his central insight. Rather than construing the historical change in Europe from the fifteenth through to the nineteenth century as a process of *discovering* childhood, I suggest that it was a process of *redefining* the nature of childhood, indeed almost *inventing* a particular version of childhood. Just as it has been said that man created God in his own image, so it would seem that during this period European professional pedagogy created a version of child development to fit its own agenda.

This agenda was designed in response to a variety of pressures and demands, some indeed arising from the observable nature of children, others from effective principles of instruction, and yet others from a particular set of social norms, some of which reflect quite incidental issues of economic convenience, such as the number of children who can be successfully managed at one time by a single teacher and the number of points of view a single teacher can hold in mind when talking to a group. The homogenisation of stages in children's development is a convenient fiction for the teacher who would like to present a packaged instructional message to a group of children simultaneously. Based on the fiction of a specifiable stage of cognitive readiness, the curriculum can be divided into a logical sequence of modules. On the one hand, this modularisation may be held to systematise the task of learners. Yet, on the other hand, it tends to create an artificial demand for an audience attuned to each particular module.

3   The rationale for formalising education

Given that education can and does take place informally in the context of everyday life, why was it felt at a certain point in history that a more explicit, deliberately instructive set of activities should be introduced in the form of schooling? A need for focus seems to be one of the earliest rationales. Philosophy as taught in the early schools of ancient Greece was seen as requiring analytic thought, of a kind which does not take place without concentration and effort. The purpose of this kind of schooling was to enable the minds of young Athenian citizens to ·truggle with something difficult. This theme still persists in the contemporary prospectus of formal schooling: schooling is about difficult things. Indeed, so strong is this theme that parents sometimes reject the idea of including certain topics within the school curriculum on the grounds that they are too easy or obvious. More than one of the non-literate parents we interviewed about the benefits their children might have derived from a terminal primary schooling rejected as ridiculous the suggestion that it might be justified as an opportunity to acquire some of the skills required for routine agriculture. They recognised the value of knowing how to grow food, but seemed to regard the skills involved as too straightforward and accessible to warrant any kind of formal instruction.

A second major reason for the formalisation of instruction is the desire to transmit an accumulation of knowledge. Michael Cole posits this as one of the crucial historical factors responsible in ancient Babylonian civilisation for the establishment of one of the earliest recorded prototypes of schooling. The newly expanded, city-based economies needed an improved form of record-keeping, which gave rise to the elaboration of the cuneiform writing system. This

could not be mastered in a day. It required long, and systematic study. Nevertheless, so important was the power associated with this new system of written communication that societies began to support young men who otherwise might be engaged directly in a trade or farming with the explicit purpose of making them 'scribes', people who could write. The places where young men were brought together for this purpose were the earliest schools. (Cole 1990, p. 95)

At a much later juncture in history, the Renaissance in Europe took as one of its guiding themes the rediscovery, reactivation and application to the solution of contemporary problems of the accumulated knowledge and wisdom of classical Graeco-Roman civilisation.[10] Education was, of course, an important vehicle for the implementation of that agenda. Although the democratisation of access to cultural knowledge was to be a later development, an important early precursor was the project of imparting to the next generation of elites this 'rescued treasure', and the principal way of doing so was systematically to introduce the young to the languages of those cultures and to imbue them with its mythology, its history and its ideas.

The assumption that the wisdom of a past civilisation can be acquired by the study of its books is akin to another major ingredient of the European educational tradition, the study of the Bible, or 'the Scriptures'. The very concreteness of text has served in all the great world religions as a reassuring constant in the hazardous process of transmitting ideas, be it in proselytising or in passing on cultural tradition (see Goody 1986). And the requirement of literacy as a precondition for extracting information from text has become a recurrent subtopic within the school curriculum. It is noteworthy, however, that the philosophical justification for this emphasis on the particular factitious activity of reading resides not in any intrinsic characteristic of print or books, but in the access which is thus afforded to accumulated cultural knowledge. Indeed, in the modern era, when a myriad of applications have been devised for printing, the educational establishment regards many printed documents as not only extrinsic to their agenda, but even antithetical to it. It is thus not unknown for educators to strive at times to prevent children from reading certain material, on the grounds that its content is potentially corrupting. The project of imparting literacy is in principle conceived as subsidiary to the acquisition of a selected body of knowledge through the medium to which literacy gives the child access.

As in the implicit educational philosophy of the A-Chewa, the transmission of traditional wisdom is a dominant theme of the rationale for schooling. In both cases the transmission of culture from one generation to the next is a primary justification for the endeavour. The selective aspect of this transmission (choosing the best, highlighting the important points) is reflected, in the case of oral traditions, in proverbs and symbols which succinctly and pungently epitomise a key idea in a form which will stay in the mind. The design of a school curriculum is likewise very selective and the selection is guided by explicit organisational purposes. This purposeful selection is itself an area of vulnerability to cultural bias. Once the need to select is recognised, criteria have to be applied and much of the debate about the ideological intrusiveness of Western education in Africa emerges from this necessity to spell out what shall be transmitted.

4   Gradation of the curriculum

Two kinds of selection can be distinguished in the design of a school curriculum. The first, which informed the original formalisation of education as schooling, is dictated by the range of ways in which the content can be used (for the salvation or perdition of one's soul; for greater or lesser economic production; for loyalty or disloyalty to the state, etc.), and by the internal structure of the accumulated wisdom of a culture (for example, which are the most important and powerful ideas for integrating that body of knowledge?). A second kind of selection, which has found its way into curriculum design more recently, is motivated by more narrowly pedagogical considerations. What information is a child of a certain age able to absorb? Given that a child will be under the tutelage of the school for a period of several years, what is the most appropriate order in which to introduce various parts of the corpus of cultural knowledge selected by the first set of criteria?

Once a decision has been taken to enrol pre-adolescent children in the school, it becomes self-evident that certain aspects of what an adult member of society should know will not be comprehensible to the pupils at the beginning of their studies. Moreover, given that a programme of instruction will be spread over a period of years it is natural to reflect on the question of how to segment and order the curriculum. A recurrent principle of curriculum design is that of preparation of the learner for what is coming next: each stage of the curriculum is designed to build on the previous one and to lay foundations for the next. This criterion tends to supplant those arising from the content of the subject. What is most basic to the body of knowledge gives way to what is easiest to grasp.

In modern schooling at least (available accounts of earlier forms of schooling tend to be silent on this issue) the assumption is regarded as axiomatic that before a child can address the deeper aspects of the curriculum, she must acquire a number of preliminary, enabling skills. The child must first be prepared as a learner to receive certain types of information. The most obvious case of this is the preparation for reading. Before the student is exposed to Cicero, to Shakespeare or to Dewey, she must be taught the basic skills of extracting meaning from print. This technical pedagogical requirement gives rise to a peculiar separation in elementary schooling between the focus of the learner's attention and the broader, higher-order goals of the curriculum. This is sometimes formulated as a separation between knowledge and skills. The skills are conceptually subsidiary to the knowledge, but for instructional purposes they are accorded temporal priority. The skills are imparted as tools for enabling the student subsequently to handle tasks which would be intellectually unmanageable without such tools. Arithmetic is likewise taught first as a cognitive tool for coping with more complex mathematical topics to be introduced later in the curriculum. Even the recent innovation of starting with the elements of set theory can be understood as facilitatory rather than substantive in purpose.

Two historical factors appear to have been critical in generating this focus on gradation of the curriculum, which has now become a crucial tenet of modern educational orthodoxy: the formalisation of didactic process and faith in the certainty of method.

Ariès has documented the gradual, and somewhat uneven, emergence between the sixteenth and nineteenth centuries in European schools of the modern concept of the school class or grade:

the constituent cell of the school structure ... [which] corresponds to a stage in the progressive acquisition of knowledge (to a curriculum), to an average age from which every attempt is made not to depart, to a physical, spatial unit, for each age group and subject group has its special premises (and the very word 'class' denotes both the container and the contents), and to a period of time, an annual period at the end of which the class's complement changes. (1962, pp. 176–7)

It is quite clear from his account that (a) schooling was institutionalised long before the gradation of students into a succession of classes was attempted, and (b) that the original function of this gradation was

to separate students according to their capacities and the difficulty of the subject-matter, not to separate students according to their ages. The new penchant for analysis and division – which characterised the birth of modern consciousness in its most intellectual zone, namely pedagogics – inspired in its turn further distinctions and divisions. The desire to separate the ages was only gradually recognised, and separation asserted as a principle, when separation had already been established in practice after lengthy empirical experiments. (p. 188)

5   The concept of didactic process and faith in the certainty of method

The Great Didactic of Comenius was published in 1657 and drew on a number of contemporary European educational practices and treatises.

Although some of his immediate successors in European educational circles appear to have regarded his formulation as excessively radical, it was a supremely explicit version of the pedagogical principles which began to accumulate in the context of formal schooling during that period, which survived in multiple editions of his textbooks throughout the eighteenth century, and was aknowledged in the nineteenth century as an authoritative statement of the paradigm:

> The function of pedagogy, as Comenius sees it ... is a mechanical operation. Comenius freely admits this and, in fact, boasts of it – 'Hitherto the method of instruction has been so uncertain that scarcely anyone would dare to say: "In so many years I will bring this youth to such and such a point; I will educate him in such and such a way ... we must see if it be possible to place the art of instruction on such a firm basis that sure and certain progress can be made"' ... 'a suitable environment must be provided and materials prepared, impediments must be removed, difficulties avoided and assistance given where required. Then the timing must be right and the programme must advance through the simplest steps possible, with everything necessary for success and nothing irrelevant.' (Sadler 1966, p. 202)[11]

Sadler's account of Comenius' systematic approach shows that it foreshadowed not only many of the principles of programmed machine instruction but also some of the ideas which are often associated in the twentieth century with Piaget and Froebel. But most important was his commitment to the formalisation of a set of methods which could be reproduced on a massive scale, through concretely specified instructional procedures, teaching aids and above all textbooks:

> 'It is evident', he writes, 'that the success of my scheme depends entirely upon a suitable supply of encyclopedic text-books', and since 'this task transcends the strength of one man or one life-time' it should be entrusted to a body of learned men. His hope was that eventually a series of books would be produced covering the whole range of education from birth to maturity which would standardise the process of instruction and make it possible for children to work under the direction of subordinates or even on their own. (p. 107)

The attraction of Comenius' project was greatly enhanced by the *Zeitgeist* of European culture in the eighteenth century: the so-called philosophy of the Enlightenment. Isaiah Berlin has observed that:

> the 18th century is perhaps the last period in the history of Western Europe when human omniscience was thought to be an attainable goal ... The application of mathematical techniques – and language – to the measurable properties of what the senses revealed, became the sole true method of discovery and of exposition ... A science of nature had been created; a science of mind had yet to be made. The goal in both cases must remain the same: the formulation of general laws on the basis of observation ('inner' and 'outer'), and, when

necessary, experiment; and the deduction from such laws, when established, of specific conclusions. To every genuine question there were many false answers, and only one true one; once discovered it was final – it remained for ever true; all that was needed was a reliable method of discovery. (Berlin 1956, pp. 14–16)

It was essential to guarantee the efficacy of the instruments of investigation before its results could be trusted. This epistemological bias characterized European philosophy from Descartes's formulation of his method of doubt until well into the nineteenth century, and is still a strong tendency in it. (p. 16)

What science had achieved in the sphere of the material world, it could surely achieve also in the sphere of the mind; and further in the sphere of social and political relations ... Men were objects in nature no less than trees and stones; their interaction could be studied as that of atoms and plants. Once the laws governing human behaviour were discovered and incorporated in a science of rational sociology, analogous to physics or zoology, men's real wishes could be investigated and brought to light, and satisfied by the most efficient means compatible with the nature of the physical and mental facts. Nature was a cosmos: in it there could be no disharmonies; and since such questions as what to do, how to live, what would make men just or rational or happy, were all factual questions, the true answers to any one of them could not be incompatible with true answers to any of the others. The ideal of creating a wholly just, wholly virtuous, wholly satisfied society, was therefore no longer utopian.

Nor is this view confined to the natural scientists and their allies and spokesmen. It was held no less confidently by the rationalist followers of Leibniz and his disciple Wolff. (pp. 27–8)

The 'noble faith' in the possibility of a 'final true philosophy which could solve all the theoretical and practical problems for all men everywhere for all time' ... was 'common ground' among 'theists and atheists, believers in automatic progress and skeptical pessimists, hard-boiled French materialists and sentimental German poets and thinkers'. All 'seemed united in the conviction that all problems were soluble by the discovery of objective answers which, once found – and why should they not be? – would be clear for all to see and valid eternally' (p. 28). It was within this *Zeitgeist* that the foundations were laid of the educational model exported to Africa by missionaries in the nineteenth and twentieth centuries.

6   Schooling as an age-graded instructional process

Philippe Ariès in his widely cited work, *Centuries of childhood*, argued that whereas 'the age groups of Neolithic times, [and] the Hellenistic *paedeia* presupposed a difference and a transition between the world of children and that of adults, a transition made by means of an initiation or an education, Medieval [European] civilization failed to perceive this difference and therefore lacked this concept of transition' (1962, pp. 411–12). As I have explained above, this seems to me an unlikely interpretation. His detailed analysis, however, clearly shows how the institutional forms of European schooling evolved along a tortuous path. The early medieval schools were strictly vocational training establishments designed to recruit a few boys to the priesthood. Their curriculum was not dissimilar in form from that of contemporary Quranic schools, consisting principally of chanting in unison the Psalms and Canonic hours, in Latin – what in modern, Western educational parlance would be called recitation aimed at rote memory. To this core curriculum were gradually added some of the Latin *artes liberales*, mainly grammar, plus a little rhetoric and logic, arithmetic and music, residual elements of ancient Greek and Roman scholarship, along with Christian theology and common law. It was the gradual emergence of masters specialised in these subjects, who resented the domination of the Church authorities, that gave birth to the first medieval universities.

The students of those early universities ranged very widely in age and it was the residential arrangements of the colleges – originally conceived as boarding houses – rather than any pedagogical principles of curriculum design that provided the initial impetus for the definition of age-grades which has come to dominate educational theory and practice in modern times. It took about five centuries for a gradual consensus to emerge among the professional educators and the upper and middle classes of European society that children's minds develop along a course from vulnerable innocence to maturity which can be charted in a stepwise fashion corresponding to grades of instruction.

Whereas parents and teachers in the twelfth to fifteenth centuries apparently saw nothing wrong with mixed grouping of students ranging in age from 10 to 20 years, thereafter, especially during the seventeenth century, a doctrine arose that childish innocence requires 'safeguarding against pollution by life' (p. 119) This was held by those responsible for pedagogy to entail the need for adults to display 'modesty' in the presence of children, avoiding the use of any behaviour (including speech) with sexual connotations, segregating boys from girls, and as far as possible separating pre-adolescent students from adolescents. Yet it was not until the early nineteenth century that:

the regularization of the annual cycle of promotions, the habit of making all the pupils go through the complete series of classes instead of only a few, and the requirements of a new system of teaching adapted to smaller, more homogeneous classes, resulted ... in an increasingly close correspondence between age and class. (pp. 239–40)

This projection of the curricular gradation onto teachers' and parents' expectations of children at different ages has since become a Western cultural theme of such importance that twentieth-century Western visitors to Third World primary schools are frequently astonished and dismayed to find a spread of eight or more years among the ages of pupils enrolled in a single class. Yet the data presented by Ariès show that this was commonplace in French schools in the seventeenth century and that even at the beginning of the nineteenth century the modal age-range for a given class had only dropped to six years (pp. 219–30).

Both the conception of education and that of child development were profoundly influenced in Western society by this matching process. On the one hand, it legitimated the organisation of knowledge into a hierarchy of elements best taught and learned sequentially, working up from the basics to higher and advanced stages. And, on the other hand, it came to inform the notion that a child's maturation is incomplete in the absence of specifiable learning experiences which follow a natural progression in the school curriculum.

The theme of stepwise regular progression through a graduated curriculum provides the rationale for the popular metaphor of schooling as a staircase or ladder – somewhat analogous to the 'steps of the ages of life' which Ariès notes originated in an iconography of fourteenth-century European art and became the schema for a type of print of a 'popular, commonplace type, which lasted with very few changes from the 16th century to the beginning of the 19th century' (p. 24). The logic of such progression fits well with the theme of a certainty of method. It is regarded as so essential to have completed one step of the curriculum before proceeding up to the next that each stage is treated as subsuming those which preceded it. Thus, even in contemporary Western society, when assessing the qualifications of a student for admission to a select course of higher education or of a university graduate for a professional post it is conventional to pay little or no attention to earlier stages of the individual's *curriculum vitae*, and to focus only on her final level of accomplishment.

Another consequence of the projection of gradation onto the implicit theory of child development occurs in comparisons across cultures, across nations and across historical eras. The latter is a popular exercise among literate parents when setting their internal standards for their childrens' academic progress: 'when I was your age...'. All such comparisons are typically made on the basis of the metaphor of the ladder. Each step on the ladder is treated as a static category in which a certain age-group should be enrolled, learning a certain prescribed (developmentally appropriate) step of the curriculum.

If enrolment ratios have changed dramatically over time, as they did in Zambia between the early 1950s and the 1970s, and in Japan between 1947 and 1971 (see Inagaki 1986), such comparisons are as sytematically distorted as comparisons by matching grade-levels across nations, e.g. Zambia vs. UK, US vs. Japan. The meaning of success in a competitive entry examination (to secondary school in Zambia, to University in Japan) changes as a function of the ratio between the base and the target. Thus selection for one of the 20,000 places in the first grade of secondary school in Zambia in 1975, although draconian, was nevertheless far less competitive at a ratio of about 1:6 than selection for admission to the same level of schooling in the early 1950s when less than 200 places were available (see Coombe 1967). But the uninformed (or unreflective) observer sees only the upper level as a determinant, and is encouraged by the age-gradation principle to think in absolutes. A less stiff competition is thus misinterpreted as evidence of lesser ability in the pupils and/or of falling standards of teaching.

To recapitulate, the regularisation of the ages at which children were enrolled in successive grades of the school curriculum took place very gradually in European history. The endurance of this age-by-grade matching as an integral feature of public education around the world reflects a commitment to the principle of certainty in pedagogical method, and underpins the metaphor of educational progress as climbing a staircase: a unilinear sequence of somewhat arduous movements along a predetermined path with a known set of discrete intervals and a specific, exalted destination.

The prototype of a public primary school which has emerged in Zambia and in many other countries around the world symbolises in several ways this conception of education: in the design of its physical premises, its time-schedule of instruction, its record of students' attendance and its periodic assessment of what students have learned. Hence the following characteristics of Kondwelani School, all of which are standard across all Zambian government primary schools whether in an urban or a rural area. The premises consist of rectangular blocks, each divided into several rectangular classrooms, each a discrete compartment separated from its neighbours by opaque walls. In each classroom a rectangular chalk-board is mounted in one wall facing the students' desks which are aligned in three or more parallel columns, and are separated from the chalk-board by a larger teacher's desk.

On the wall of the Head's office a rectangular timetable likewise compartmentalises each of the week's five school-days into 'periods' of time. The beginning of each scheduled period is proclaimed to the school community by the chiming of a 'bell'. (At Kondwelani School, as at many other rural schools, the chimes were produced by a designated pupil striking a stick against an old car-wheel with the tyre removed, suspended from the branch of a tree.) The duration of these study periods is prescribed by the headquarters of the national Ministry of Education, as is the proportion of the week's teaching time allocated to each subject.

Another document in the Head's office classifies and orders the social roles of the teachers in accordance with which grade they are teaching for the year:

> Grade 1 Mrs Banda
> Grade 2 Mr Phiri
> Grade 3 Miss Mbewe, etc.

Each teacher maintains a class 'register' in which the names of enrolled pupils are neatly laid out in a list[12] (often subdivided into a section for each gender) followed by a row of narrow columns in which daily attendance is recorded with a series of ticks.

At the end of every term (a period of thirteen or fourteen weeks stipulated each year by the Ministry), tests are administered in each class and the results are tabulated with a numerical grade next to each pupil's name, and usually a rank position in the class derived from the distribution of grades on the test. Depending on their performance on these tests, a decision is taken after every three-term year as to whether each student is ready for 'promotion' to the next step in the hierarchy.

Thus are the spatial, temporal and social coordinates of the school classified into a compartmentalised, taxonomically ordered set of elements, susceptible to efficient management, and conceptualised as reflecting a rational analysis of the school's pedagogical agenda of promoting the intellectual development of the students it 'processes'.

7   The exaggeration of pupils' puerility

Several peculiar consequences have flowed historically from this, at first sight rather harmless-looking, conceptualisation.

First, 'adult education, widespread in the 15th and 16th centuries disappeared in the 17th century and its place was taken by an education confined to children' (Ariès 1962, pp. 300–1). Concomitantly, the role of 'learner' became institutionalised as intrinsically suited to an immature mind. As a result, since adult education was reinvented in the nineteenth century it has had to struggle to throw off an image of education as a condescending process in which the teacher has an obligation to control and direct the student along a predetermined path. The implications of this theme of condescension include an asymmetry in the flow of information between teacher and student, that the timing of class activities will be strictly controlled by the teacher and that any deviation by a student from prescribed forms of behaviour is subject to authoritarian correction by the teacher.

Second, this asymmetry has become available as a legitimating ideology for the stigmatisation of whole sections of adult society, such as women, the poor and foreigners, who for social and political reasons have not had access to the socialisation institutionalised in our kind of school. Rather than seeing these out-groups as different but equal, the equation of schooling with normal child socialisation has encouraged the 'products' of Western schooling to look down on them as incomplete human beings, either to be pitied for their deprivation or else to be despised as not deserving this essential ingredient of becoming fully human. Cook-Gumperz points out that this tendency has been accentuated during the twentieth century by the accumulation of more and more ideological baggage around the concept of literacy:

As literacy becomes ever more precisely yet expansively defined, the notion of illiteracy takes on a new specificity as the absence of all such 'functional' skills and so makes the negative association with limited ability even more likely. (Cook-Gumperz 1986, p. 20)

This stigmatisation of the unschooled as incomplete also found fertile ground in the missionaries' project of evangelisation. The recipients of schooling in Africa were not only perceived by these exogenous teachers as needing 'civilisation', but as lost souls in danger of perdition:

Although separated by considerable distances, and with little or no contact between them, there was close agreement among the early missionaries in their assessment ... They regarded the people as immoral, lazy, and drunken, steeped in superstitions and witchcraft, and doomed to spiritual damnation. There could be no question of grafting the Christian message on to the traditional culture. That whole culture was rotten, in their view, and had to be replaced, root and branch. (Snelson 1974, p. 11)

Schooling was conceived as an effective instrument for deliberately inducing a process of cultural change. It is interesting to note the recurrent use of the term 'intelligence' in the formulations by early missionaries of this role for schooling in their project of evangelisation. The Foreign Secretary of the London Missionary Society in 1908 wrote:

It is easy to see that if the converts from heathenism are to have any real intelligence or stability they must be in a position to read for themselves the Word of God. (T. R. Wardlaw, cited in Snelson 1974, p. 11)

92

And a Church of Scotland missionary in the Northern Province wrote in 1918:

The aim in view is to enable the people to read the Scriptures for themselves in an intelligent manner ... The village school, by enabling the people to read the Scriptures for themselves and intelligently decide on the question of Christianity, has been one of the most powerful agencies at the command of the Missions. Any other instruction imparted, such as writing and counting, is given largely with a view to quickening the intelligence and increasing the ability to understand the Scriptures. (R. D. McMinn, cited in Snelson 1974, p. 12)

The missionaries were not only uncompromisingly committed to a particular religious interpretation of social and moral behaviour, but were also deeply and for the most part unquestioningly attached to the principles of contemporary Western civil life, including commerce and administration. As a result they generally saw little or no conflict between their evangelising objectives and the imperialistic expansion of their governments' spheres of influence. In Central Africa they were thus, at best unwittingly, often instrumental in paving the way for colonial occupation.[13] Yet their vision was a different one from that of most colonialists in that they believed in the capacity of education to transform Africans into fully fledged persons. Here lay the seed of future conflict with European politicians who tried to use the ideology of cultural superiority to rationalise the continuation of colonial oppression, even when a body of African spokesmen had emerged claiming the right to self-government in precisely the language of the Western culture which missionary schools had so successfully implanted.

When missionaries exported the Western model of schooling to Africa, it seems that the other corollary of nineteenth-century schooling ideology, the packaging of stepwise gradation of the curriculum from elementary to advanced material with the assumption that the beginning student is immature, was effortlessly compounded with an ethnocentric assumption of cultural superiority to justify a condescending style of pedagogy. This condescending, indeed often authoritarian, style has remained such a salient feature of schooling, even in those institutions which are now run by indigenous lay teachers employed by the government, that we may almost call it a local or regional educational tradition.

Not only is there a preponderance of trivial content in primary readers and arithmetic texts, but the style of classroom management favoured in most African schools still resembles the 'chalk and talk' model of early twentieth-century Western schools.[14] Largely content-free drills are used pervasively to impart much of the curriculum, with an apparent rationale of memorisation. Progress is assessed by the criterion of accurate recitation of the alphabet, the times-table and 'factual' lesson-notes copied from the black-board into exercise-books. Moreover, most teachers administer their classes in a highly directive ('didactic') manner, demanding deferential silence from their students except when called upon to answer specific questions, and enforcing the adherence to rigid procedural routines with authoritarian discipline. It is somewhat ironic that in the last twenty years following a shift of emphasis in Western pedagogy in the direction of self-regulated discovery-learning under the influence of Montessori and Piaget, many Western observers of the actual schooling practices in contemporary African classrooms have been moved to ask whether the prevailing pedagogical methods are adequate to capture or canalise the pupils' intrinsic motivation to explore and learn by discovery (e.g. Gay and Cole 1967).

In our rural Zambian community many of the individuals whose lives we traced started their schooling around the age of 12. At this age much of the content of the syllabus in the lower grades must have appeared strangely puerile. These young people, by the criteria of their home culture, were already on the verge of being treated as responsible adults. They were about to enter the age-grades of young man or young woman, where although they would not be assigned leadership responsibilities they were expected to take charge of their own lives in important ways. By about the age of 14, for instance, a young man is expected to build himself a house, while a young woman is expected to start conceiving children and very soon to give birth and start nurturing a baby. In the ceremonially institutionalised instruction offered to young women of this age in the traditional culture, the focus would be on the responsibilities of a marital relationship. Yet because of a theoretical rationale developed for much younger learners, the instruction offered to them in school was composed of largely content-free drills in reading, writing and number work. There is simply no provision in the official primary school curriculum for adjusting the content to the age of the learners.[15]

This is probably true of 90 per cent or more of the formal educational provision on the African continent, at least if provision is quantified in units of student-hours engaged in formal learning. The predominant form of the learning activities constituted by that provision is designed in accordance with a model developed as a content-free preparation of immature children for subsequent cognitive activity which will have more content.

At the period of history when missionaries from Europe first introduced schooling to local residents in Central Africa, educational thought was in the throes of highly controversial transformation in

Europe. How much of this controversy was familiar or significant for the missionaries is a subject deserving of thorough investigation. Richard Tignor (1976) points out that there was a good deal of diversity in the amount and type of formal education Western missionaries had received before coming to Africa. In Kenya at the beginning of the century, whereas many of the missionaries working under the auspices of the Church Missionary Society (CMS) and the Church of Scotland Mission (CSM) 'had graduated from leading British universities (Tignor 1976, p. 122), most of those working under the auspices of the African Inland Mission (AIM) had received their only post-secondary schooling from American Bible institutes which offered 'a narrow religious training, usually of two years, with a strong evangelical emphasis' (p. 120). Evangelical education was linked both conceptually and institutionally (e.g. through the Society for the Propagation of Christian Knowledge) with the goal of democratising access to enlightenment. But the inequalities of political power between the bearers of European and indigenous African cultures seem to have ensured from the outset that the meeting of minds was always phrased in a very asymmetrical way. Rather than sharing or exchanging ideas, the participants construed the process as one of unidirectional transfer of information, skills, understanding and civilisation.

It is not necessary to take a position on how oppressive was the tenor of early missionary education in order to recognise that under its auspices there occurred a misapplication of an originally well-intentioned scheme carefully designed in the light of sound theoretical principles of pedagogy. The rationale of that scheme, whose origins can be traced back to early European educational theorists in the tradition of the Englightenment such as Comenius, is that the learner will in due course reach the real heart of the curriculum where the substantive issues will be addressed, concerning the accumulated cultural knowledge for the transmission of which a system of public schooling has been established. It makes sense under those circumstances to start by teaching some basic skills in a format which will be intelligible to young children.[16]

8   The use of a foreign language as medium of instruction

The most problematic of these deferral strategies in the education offered by contemporary Zambian schools involves the teaching of a foreign language which is to serve as the medium for all transmission of the substance of the curriculum.[17] Not only is the language in question unknown to the vast majority of school entrants before they start schooling, but it is mandated to be taught on an 'immersion' basis as the sole medium of instruction from the very beginning of the curriculum.

Jack Goody has pointed out that the situation has in fact arisen at several different points in world history:

> where the language of 'scholarship' (i.e. the school) is totally distinct from the vernacular language spoken by the teachers or the pupils, that is, from the vernacular. Such a situation already existed in Mesopotamia; Assyrian scribes had to learn Sumerian before they could learn to read. A similar course of events took place in Phoenicia (Ugarit) with Assyrian itself and it happened with Aramaic, Hebrew, Greek, Latin (throughout Western Europe), with Sanskrit and Pali in Asia, while written Chinese has been described as a totally different language from any of the spoken versions. (Goody 1977, p. 125)

Goody argues that these occurrences are 'virtually (but not entirely) pure artefact of writing', and that they 'did not simply entail a mechanical job of learning another language. The categories of the understanding were also influenced by the preservation of the unspoken language . . .', e.g. in the imposition on English grammar of forms better suited to Latin (p. 125).

During the first two centuries of post-Renaissance education, schooling in England was exclusively couched in Latin. There were even statutes in the sixteenth and seventeenth centuries where 'the speaking of English in school is dealt with as a heinous offence, on the same level as slipping into "barbarous" Latin' (Kandel and Tate 1966). Similarly, many Africans who attended secondary schools in the 1950s in Zambia, Kenya and other British colonies have recounted the dire penalties imposed on any student caught using a vernacular language in the school grounds. The seventeenth-century English poet, John Milton, and his contemporary, the philosopher John Locke, both complained of the excessive emphasis on learning of a new language or languages in the school curriculum of their times. Yet despite the gradual emancipation of English and Scottish schooling from this oppressive influence of Latin during the eighteenth and nineteenth centuries, the English language now occupies a position in the public school systems of many African countries quite similar to that of Latin in seventeenth-century Britain.

The first step towards the institutionalisation of English as the language of education in Zambia was taken when the colonial administration imposed English legal and administrative documentation on the affairs of the colony. The *de facto* dominance of English in all official spheres of public life by the time political independence was won in 1964 posed a massive dilemma for the new indigenous government. Economic opportunities contingent on the completion of schooling had hitherto been closely dependent on competence in the language of the alien people whose political oppression was now being formally terminated. In the short term at least, competence in English was likely to continue to be a credential of overwhelming importance in determining the material benefits to be derived from education.

Yet an opportunity existed at such a historical turning-point to institutionalise through public policy the political pre-eminence of one or more of the local indigenous languages, which, as I have discussed for the case of Chi-Chewa (Nyanja) in chapter 2, are intimately bound up with many of the society's traditional practices and which enshrine in multiplex and subtle ways the epistemological foundations of indigenous moral values. Given the dramatic expansion of local employment opportunities in the Civil Service which accompanied independence in Zambia and elsewhere on the continent, systematic indigenisation of the language of legislation and administration would undoubtedly have generated concrete rewards for corresponding changes in the school curriculum such as a greater emphasis on acquiring literate competence in an indigenous language.

In practice, however, most African governments stopped far short of this, confining their affirmation of the national authenticity of the indigenous languages to a rhetorical, almost ritualistic, level. Without any legal, administrative or economic backing this rhetoric has been powerless in Zambia to counterbalance the economic and neo-colonial political weight of English.[18] Ironically, a radicalisation of the control of English over the school curriculum was introduced in Zambia in 1965, just one year after independence, in the wake of a series of British Council and UNESCO conferences and technical advisory missions in various parts of Africa (Higgs 1980; Shana 1980), where the previously established conventional wisdom of the educational establishment was called into question. The earlier consensus view that children should be first introduced to the foundation skills of reading, writing and arithmetic in the medium of their home language was challenged on three grounds. (a) *Practicality*. The use of any single indigenous language was held not to be practically feasible in multilingual communities, especially in the large cities. (b) *Malleability*. 'Immersion' programmes in Canada (Lambert and Tucker 1972) were cited as evidence that young children can learn equally well in a second language. (c) *Preparation*. It was argued that students who acquire proficiency in the medium of secondary education earlier in life would have a 'head start' in mastering that more advanced part of the school curriculum, and Zambia like many other former British colonies expected to continue, for largely economic reasons, to rely on English as the medium of secondary and tertiary formal education. In the light of this set of purportedly technical arguments, as well as pressing political considerations (Mwanakatwe 1976), the nation's first indigenous Minister of Education persuaded the Cabinet to establish English as the exclusive medium of instruction in all Zambian schools with effect from the First Grade.

Prior to the introduction of this policy, the medium of instruction for the first four grades had been determined on the basis of zones, such that in linguistically homogeneous rural communities like Kondwelani all children learned to read and write in Chi-Chewa before they started to study English. The controversy surrounding how and why the policy was changed just after the exodus of the colonial regime has been analysed elsewhere (Serpell 1978b; Sekeleti 1985). Whatever merits may be claimed for the new scheme on a national level, it should be noted that the pressing political considerations stressed by the Minister pertained to the racial desegregation of privileged urban schools, to which the residents of rural communities distant from the urban centres have never had any access. Moreover, the practicality argument has no relevance for a community like Kondwelani, where all families raise their children in a single local language. The preparation argument has relevance only for the tiny minority of pupils who qualify for progression to the secondary level, and therefore feeds on and reciprocally reinforces the extractive definition of school success discussed in chapter 1.

The malleability argument strikes at the heart of the pedagogical agenda of basic schooling. But increasing numbers of critics have argued that the special socio-cultural conditions under which the initial immersion experiments were conducted were almost certainly responsible in large part for their success (Riegel and Freedle 1976; Serpell 1981). In Zambia, one consequence of requiring children to become literate in English as a precondition for understanding the rest of the curriculum has been effectively to deprive a large number of pupils of the opportunity even to sample the accumulated knowledge on offer, let alone experience cognitive enrichment from it. The dilemma which this aspect of the curriculum presents for rural primary school teachers will be analysed in chapter 4, and some of its consequences for individuals passing through the system from rural communities will be illustrated in chapter 5.

9   The ideology of literacy

What of those who, despite the odds against them, do succeed in mastering the basic curriculum of the primary school? A recurrent theme in the autobiographical and semi-autobiographical writings of African intellectuals about their childhood is an exhilarating sense of liberation through the acquisition of literacy.[19] Even in the chains of South Africa's white supremacist regime, despite the tutelage of a hostile racist professor, Sibiya, the central character of Lewis Nkosi's tragic novel *Mating birds* reflects:

I went to school, then to university, and I know what my father did not suspect: the white world that he hated and feared so much is built on shifting sands. It will not last. It will be swept away. That is what history teaches us. It is the history Professor Van Niekerk should have taught me, because it was getting to know that history, independently by private study and diligent reading, that saved me ... from a self-destructive rage. I became strong and defiant without real hatred in me. (Nkosi 1986, p. 101)

This is the 'true' value of education which Sibiya has found, in contrast with the 'illusory' expectations of the non-literate members of the society in which he was raised, which ranged from a belief that schooling would impart to the learner some 'awesome powers of the occult' (p. 85) to the conviction that it would breed contempt for their indigenous culture, treachery towards their own people, or sheer insanity (pp. 86–7).

Nkosi's vision reflects a faith in the transcendental power of literate education. Habermas has proposed the most ambitious philosophical statement of this position in his critical theory:

A structure of prejudices that has been rendered transparent can no longer function as a prejudice ... Authority and knowledge do not converge. To be sure, knowledge is rooted in actual tradition; it remains bound to contingent conditions. But ... we can turn back on internalized norms ... Reflection recalls that path of authority along which the grammars of language games were dogmatically inculcated as rules for interpreting the world and for action. In this process the element of authority that was simply domination can be stripped away and dissolved in the less violent force of insight and rational decision. (Habermas, *Logik der Sozialwissenschaften*, 1967, cited in McCarthy 1978, p. 182)

One of the axiomatic underpinnings of the political programme of educational expansion in Africa seems to be the notion that becoming literate does much more to the individual than granting him or her access to printed information: that it transforms the student's intellect. Jack Goody in a series of influential publications (Goody and Watt 1963; Goody 1977, 1986) has argued with extensive documentation the case that:

writing establishes a different kind of relation between the word and its referent, a relationship that is more general and more abstract, and less closely connected with the particularities of person, place and time than obtains in oral communication. (Goody 1968, p. 44)

From this he believes a crucial link can be traced to the cultural awareness of the possibilities of logic, history and science. Several elements of the argument have been challenged. Some critics have seen its tendency to dichotomise the world's cultures artificially into literate and non-literate as rendering it susceptible to manipulation for mischievous ideological purposes. For instance, Goody's intended 'irony' in entitling one of his seminal works 'the domestication of the savage mind' (1977) has apparently not always been 'appreciated' (1986, p. xiv). Although the final chapter of that work repays careful study as a critique of 'the great divide' theory of literate vs. non-literate thinking, the ideological baggage which literacy has accumulated is such that his arguments can sometimes be read as endorsing rather than challenging that notion. Others have focussed attention on the implicit determinism of Goody's analysis and, perhaps most significantly, the 'autonomy' which it imputes to literacy as a factor in socio-cultural and psychological change (Street 1984).

The historical processes through which the Western literate tradition has been transmitted include a number of paradoxes which defy any inference of simple causal connections between the culture and its unique literate forms: the essentially oral nature of Christ's message which became fossilised after his death in Scriptures; the preservation of much of classical Graeco-Roman written culture in Islamic libraries during a period when the societies which generated it were in a period of cultural recession (the so-called 'Dark Ages'); and the preservation in Christian monasteries of the Greek invention of alphabetic script in a form very different from that which gave it the unique power attributed to it by Havelock (1976), as he indeed acknowledges in later chapters of his book.

The precise nature of the cognitive changes which arise from the individual's acquisition of literacy has received attention in a number of comparative psychological studies of the cognitive consequences of various different types of schooling. Sylvia Scribner and Michael Cole (1981), for instance, studied three different forms of literacy (in the Arabic, Roman and Vai scripts) among the Vai people of Liberia. They concluded that the effects of learning to read and write are rather specific and that the uses to which these skills are put depend on the wider social context in which they are acquired. Patricia Greenfield and Jean Lave (1982) reached similar conclusions about the extent to which other cognitive skills learned in the curriculum of a school or a craft apprenticeship are generalised by learners beyond the range of applications which they were explicitly taught.

Barbara Rogoff (1981) has provided a critically analytical review of studies on the cognitive correlates of schooling, showing that many variables may be involved, including a selective bias affecting which children are sent to school in societies where it is not universal. Nevertheless, a strong hypothesis emerges from these studies which is worthy of consideration: that schooling may promote a pattern of competencies which are especially wide in their scope of generalisability, by focussing the pupils' attention on formal, abstract principles outside the context of concrete activities, and by encouraging them to search for general rules to order the large body of information they are required to assimilate. Don Sharp, Michael Cole and Charles Lave (1979) suggested that children with experience of schooling in Liberia and in Mexico may differ from their unschooled peers in the competence and disposition to provide their own structure for organising the information contained in new and unfamiliar tasks.

If this were true it would indeed be a powerful vindication of the hopes widely expressed in developing countries that formal education will dramatically enhance the quality of their human capital. On the other hand, serious doubts have been expressed about this hypothesis by Cole (Sharp *et al.* 1979) himself and by others such as Greenfield and Lave (1982). Ginsburg provides the following critique. First, he restates the conclusion of Sharp and his colleagues as follows:

if a task 'tells' the subject what to do, the poorly educated person generally has the competence to do what is required. But if the task is relatively open-ended, the uneducated person may not be able to determine which of his available competencies to use ... 'It seems' [he writes] 'self-evident that the hypothesis cannot be true for intellectual performance in general. For example it must be the case that uneducated subjects familiar with, say, navigation or car repairs or hunting would require less task structure to perform the appropriate cognitive operations than would educated subjects unfamiliar with these areas. (Ginsburg in Sharp *et al.* 1979. p. 94)

Thus we return once again to a more specific question: what is it that the child learns in school? Evidently many things, but all of them, perhaps, specific in their range of generalisability. Ginsburg suggests that much of what is learned consists of 'non-cognitive skills ... such as attentiveness, obedience and persistence' (p. 100).

Another major hypothesis is that mastery of the cognitive forms and procedures distinctive to a written culture is intrinsically empowering and by the same token also domesticating, committing the graduate to conformity with a powerful but none the less limited mode of thought (Goody 1977). David Olson argues that: 'Literacy in general and schooling in particular are instrumental in the construction of a *particular* form of knowledge that is relevant to a *particular* set of socially valued activities...' (Olson 1977, p. 67). He further contends that:

because prose is such a valuable intellectual tool we have underestimated the bias it puts upon knowledge. It is *not* the most appropriate tool for the establishment and maintenance of social and authority relations. It is *inappropriate* to practical actions in immediate social and physical contexts ... the means has become the end. The acquisition of knowledge has become nothing other than the construction of a particular view of reality appropriate to the requirements of explicit logical text ... The exclusive reliance upon text may lead to the undervaluation of practical knowledge and the 'mother tongue'. (p. 86, my emphasis)

The work of Scribner and Cole on literacy among the Vai, however, suggests that the impact of schooling in the Western mode is quite distinct from the impact of literacy *per se*. Literacy in Arabic served to amplify skills of memorisation, reflecting the context in which it was taught, whereas literacy in the syllabic Vai script enhanced skills of syllabic segmentation. The particular cognitive accretions acquired by becoming literate in a Zambian primary school likewise reflect the overall orientation of the curriculum.

Rather than tracing key aspects of the cognitive consequences of modern education to the early invention of script (Havelock 1976; Goody 1977, 1986), I would argue that we need to see texts as elements of the complex cultural system whose evolution Ariès and others have described, deployed in particular ways for particular purposes (Clanchy 1979; Scribner and Cole 1981; Heath 1983; Street 1984). As Jenny Cook-Gumperz has noted, 'the making of literacy into a school-based skill changed for ever the relationship of the majority of the population to their own talents for learning and for literacy ... Schooling and a pedagogy that was based on schooled literacy assured that knowledge became stratified in its transmission' (Cook-Gumperz 1986, pp. 27, 31). But each society's 'historical heritage in this regard is particular rather than general' (p. 22). For instance, two distinctive themes of the contemporary Zambian school curriculum, reverence for text and mastery of true facts, have quite different origins in Western culture (religion and science, respectively). Their convergence in modern education is neither a necessary consequence of literacy nor an intrinsically empowering, autonomous mode of cognition. It constitutes a culturally situated syndrome incorporating strategic approaches to the retrieval and utilisation of information as well as tactical skills in understanding and/or generating it.

Resnick and Resnick (1977), like several other commentators, have construed the persistence of a powerful link between schooling and religion throughout most of the nineteenth century in Europe, and on into the twentieth century in Africa, as a source of conservatism, which they hold responsible in large measure for the dominance of a domesticating orientation towards the acquisition of literacy over a liberating or empowering one. They contrast the capacity to (1) read aloud familiar religious texts on demand with an ideal of being able to (2) derive new information inferentially from unfamiliar text, and/or (3) interpret a complex text with literary allusions and metaphoric expression and relate it sensibly to other texts. The nature of this contrast is exclusively cognitive. The historical progress of educational development is thus construed in terms of technical improvement in ways of elaborating a set of cognitive skills. As a result these authors appear to celebrate the removal of moral content from the curriculum as a necessary expedient for the enhancement of the efficiency of the cognitive skills training programme.

This line of reasoning appears to me to give too little weight to the ultimately moral purpose of education – whether we call it liberation or empowerment. Dogmatic religious teaching is offensive to that moral purpose for more than technical reasons. It suggests a closed approach to understanding which undermines the creative and innovatory potential of human thinking on which society must depend for its continuous readaptation to a changing world, and for the time-honoured challenge of working out ways of reconciling the desires of individuals with the collective welfare of the group. But to suggest that the problem of dogmatism can be solved by banning all moral content from the curriculum would be at best naïve.

The forum of analytic reflection on the accumulated knowledge of prior generations is an ideal one in which to equip the growing person with strategies for self-expression. To rely on the family and outside society to do this work is an abnegation of pedagogical responsibility. The preoccupation with certainty of method and educational expertise which I have traced in this chapter has generated a spurious dilemma for the professional educator: either teach only that which is devoid of moral content or else risk being seen as unprofessional when tackling with your students the deeper issues of life.

Nevertheless, lest I seem to be devaluing the cultural invention of literacy, I should emphasise that I do recognise an extraordinarily intimate reciprocal dependency between social and psychological aspects of literacy, and I am inclined to agree with Goody's view that this is more than accidental: it has a peculiar appropriateness which, if it falls short of logical implication, is nevertheless intrinsically harmonious. It seems to me that what Goody has termed 'restricted literacy' has a similar status to Habermas' construct of 'symstematically distorted communication' (McCarthy 1978; Habermas 1984, 1987). There is a sense in which the cognitive potential of literacy to perform nobler, more liberating, more empowering functions is an implicit premise of the activity itself which is at least accessible with a little guidance to all who participate in even its most restricted form, and whose absence they can recognise as disappointing if this is pointed out.

Brian Street has cited as a counter-argument to this view the deep suspicion of the literate world engendered in medieval England by the phenomenon of forgery (Clanchy 1979; Street 1984). I believe the significance of this phenomenon should not be overstated. The very idea of forgery presupposes an appreciation of the value of genuine documents. It is no more legitimate to argue from the possibility of forgery that documentation is an intrinsically unreliable source of information than it is to argue as did Hume, adapting Descartes' argument, from the possibility of sensory illusion that we therefore live in a solipsistic world unable to rely on any evidence from our senses. For reasons which have been fully articulated by Wittgenstein (1958) and Austin (1962), such exceptions are really more informative about the general reliability of experience than grounds for an all-embracing scepticism. In contemporary Zambian society, certain types of document are treated with widespread scepticism. For instance, in an attempt to regulate the competition for access to limited places in the overcrowded urban schools described in chapter 1, the government requires parents to produce evidence that the children they are seeking to enrol are of an appropriate age. Since birth certificates have been difficult to procure because of a variety of bureaucratic problems, provision was made for an alternative, in the form of a legal affidavit, declared before a magistrate at a minimal fee, attesting to the place and date of birth of the child. School age in Zambia, however, continues to be a distinct concept for many young people whose function is to gain enrolment and has no particular relationship to one's biological age (see Serpell 1983a).

It seems evident that the invention of writing was a necessary precursor to certain other cultural inventions, such as the accumulation of information in libraries and experimental science based on detailed records and mathematical computation, without which modern education could not have taken on its present form. But this is not to say that the cognitive strategies required for scholarship and science are directly imparted to the individual by the acquisition of literacy. The structuring of cognition by culture takes place through a series of stages, some of them displaying regularities at the level of social macrosystems or microsystems embedded within them (to use the terminology of Urie Bronfenbrenner's 'ecology of human development' (1979)), others arising through the mediation of unique practices.

At the macrosystematic level, in John Ogbu's formulation (1978), valued social roles and a social mobility system 'generate cognitive problems to be solved by individuals', while microsystems such as family socialisation and schooling 'seek to equip children with competencies to solve those problems'. In a modern, industrialised society whose political, legal and economic institutions are all organised around written documents, the performance of almost every valued social role hinges on a sufficient command of the particular cognitive skills demanded by the cultural practices surrounding the generation and utilisation of those documents. A cultural practice, as formulated by Syliva Scribner and Michael Cole, be it weaving, law, literacy or schooling, constitutes 'a recurrent sequence of activities, using a particular technology and particular systems of knowledge directed to socially recognised goals ... [And] a skill is a coordinated set of actions involved in applying this knowledge in particular settings' (1981, p. 236).

The interconnectedness in Zambian society between the cultural practices of schooling and literacy tends to be regarded as axiomatic. Yet as we shall see in chapter 5, the everyday opportunities for the deployment of literate skills by most rural adults are only tenuously connected to the school curriculum.

10   The educational impact of Western schools in post-colonial Africa: a crisis of credibility

At the peak of nationalist confrontation with colonialism every institution and every cultural practice associated with the European presence in Africa came under intense and polemical scrutiny. The rationale of each was questioned with a profound scepticism fired by an angry indignation at the hypocrisy which was so widespread among colonial administrators, settlers and missionaries. These self-appointed trustees of civilisation were (in my view, rightly) seen as narrow minded, bigoted and often self-interested to a degree which they themselves barely understood.

Schooling in the context of this confrontation was often construed somewhat analogously to a piece of technological hardware in the hands of a malicious enemy. Just as the independence project involved taking over guns and cars and typewriters and turning them to the purposes of national development, so factories and schools could also be reoriented. But what was not always clearly understood was that in the case of schools and factories, far more than in the case of guns and cars and typewriters, the software is deeply 'buried in' (or cleverly built into) 'the hardware' (Cherns 1984). In order to understand how this came about we need to become more conscious of the long historical process through which it was achieved. It is not enough to recognise that the 'educators' in Africa in the nineteenth and early twentieth centuries lacked a profound educational philosophy and any genuine commitment to the autonomous development of the individuals and communities they were claiming to serve (or to 'save'). We need also to understand the structure of the systems they exported, its pedagogical focus, the latent premises about children, learning and human development on which it was based. For in many cases these premises gave to the structure a transforming potential which extended well beyond the conscious awareness or control of the teachers and administration who were nominally 'in charge' of the schooling process.

The historical perspective of many social scientists, including many of my African friends and colleagues, on Africa's experience of Western education has focussed on the distortions introduced by colonial and missionary practitioners when transferring European education to Africa. But very little attention has been paid to the sociocultural context of the agenda set by early nineteenth-century educators in Europe. What Ariès' analysis helps to reveal is that European educators were not addressing objectively pre-existing needs of children but a set of needs implicit in a particular culture's conception of childhood – a conception which was in fact largely formed in its turn by a set of socio-historically specific institutional practices.

It seems that no one asked when exporting European education to Africa: how do African societies conceptualise children and their needs for socialisation? Instead, a set of interdependent equations, which had become established within orthodox Western thought and which are deeply ingrained in the institutionalised practices of formal education, were exported wholesale to the peoples of the Third World under the label of opportunities for enlightenment, liberation and enrichment, and which in practice often serve the very opposite purposes of mystification, oppression and impoverishment:

> civilisation=urban life-style
> education=schooling
> intelligence=aptitude for school subjects.

Modern education promises to deliver at the end of its process: a mind better equipped to confront the challenges of adult life, to surmount practical difficulties, to act responsibly, and to reflect wisely on the implications of experience for future action. How can it justify its claim to be in a position to deliver this extraordinarily appealing package of benefits? One of school's most tangible outputs is literacy. Most apologists for education would have us believe that it transforms the mind, imparting greater freedom from the demands of the immediate environment in the form of a pervasive attitude of detachment, objectivity and rationality. My own view is that these possibilities are indeed inherent in the project of acquiring literacy but that they do not flow automatically from it.

On a social plane, literacy brings with it new possibilities for the accumulation and sharing of knowledge, empowering successive generations to build upon their predecessors' culture. Not only can a literate culture bring together more readily the insights of its various participants across time and space, it also becomes more readily accessible to outsiders who may borrow from it elements for incorporation into their own culture. Such contact between cultures, however, is notoriously asymmetrical, particularly when one of the two is literate and the other is not (Goody 1986). Thus the enrichment implied by access to Western culture's literate accumulation of science and technology has often been accompanied in Africa by a loss of continuity in the non-literate indigenous cultural traditions, sometimes approaching total disintegration.

The psychological consequences of literacy cannot be understood in isolation from their socio-cultural context. Not only does the individual who becomes literate in Africa need a coherent sense of how his or her knowledge relates to that of other members of her society. More fundamentally, she needs a cultural framework within which to explore and realise the potential of the amplifying tool she is acquiring. But as I shall seek to illustrate in chapter 4, little or no attempt has been made to establish such a framework at the local or community level in Zambia. Rather, those who aspire to use their literacy are steered towards a career in the upper echelons of the modern state, which centre around the activities of a distant urban bureaucracy and only impinge on the life of rural communities in tangential ways.

This extractive definition of success within the school curriculum is fundamentally alienating. Instead of empowering a community to take charge of its own destiny, to secure greater control over its physical resources, to channel them into a more productive and harmonious 'way of life', schooling has served to fragment and stratify society, and to devalue indigenous cultural forms: language, music, socialisation practices, even the basic concept of *nzelu*. The principal pedagogical goal of Zambia's primary school curriculum is conceived as cognitive growth, defined in terms of the acquisition of skills and knowledge. Moral development is only marginally if at all on the agenda. Even centrally issued directives to incorporate political conscientisation within the curriculum have encountered deep resistance from teachers. Our interviews with parents described in later chapters showed that the school's clientele share the view that 'political education' does not belong in the primary school. Thus in terms of the vocabulary of Chi-Chewa discourse about intelligence discussed in chapter 2, the curriculum is construed as a way of promoting the growth of the -*chenjela* dimension. The complementary requirement for complete *nzelu*, a sense of social responsibility, is expected to be cultivated in other ways.

By way of alternatives, what the school has offered is a strictly credentialist entry route to various occupations defined in bureaucratic terms by the modern state. The route is uncompromisingly narrow and most of the aspirants are doomed in advance to failure by the rules of the game, which revolve around the fundamental axiom that only a few deserve advancement, while the majority belong down there, out in the cold.

Paradoxically the universalisation of access to primary schooling, widely heralded as a democratisation of education, has tended to aggravate the crisis of credibility for schooling in Zambia. For the more people are herded into primary schools, the smaller the percentage who can go on to make something out of it in the present set-up. Unless and until success is redefined in a less extractive, narrow staircase mode, the crisis is likely to continue to grow more severe. Schooling can only vindicate its deeper educational objectives by articulating a concrete relevance to the socio-cultural and politico-economic opportunities existing within the communities it aspires to serve. And in Africa these continue to be predominantly small-scale, rural communities.

4

Bicultural mediation: local challenges for teachers

1   Introduction

Two different formulations of intellectual development and its relation to moral development and socialisation have been articulated in chapters 2 and 3, one of which is embedded within the indigenous cultural tradition of a rural community, while the other informs the curriculum of the local primary school. Primary school teachers in Zambia and in other independent African countries occupy a strategically important but also culturally ambiguous position in this scenario. On the one hand, their professional training commits them to the rationale and practices of the school curriculum; on the other hand, their personal identities are often rooted in indigenous norms of socialisation.

Their training prepares them to adopt explicit instructional methods and condescending attitudes as the best way of instilling cognitive skills for technological mastery over the environment. It also provides an elaborate rationale for the belief that stepwise progression through the prescribed curriculum imparts a special quality of mind ideally suited to responsibility and leadership. And it certifies their membership of an intellectual elite whose knowledge, skills and attitudes set them apart from (and, in some respects, above) the rest of society.

On the other hand, their early child socialisation was in most cases couched in the medium of a culture very similar to, if not directly continuous with, that in which their pupils are now growing up. Their own relationships with their parents and other elders were negotiated within the terms of reference explored in chapter 2, including the notion that cognitive alacrity (*-chenjela*) requires interpersonal, social responsibility (*-tumikila*) as a necessary complement for the development of a wise intelligence (*nzelu*). They acquired many of their practical and verbal skills through the medium of peer-group play and informal apprenticeships to adults. And the resulting network of personal relationships with the kin and peers of their childhood neighbourhoods accords them enduring membership of a community in which all adults share responsibility for the socialisation of children.

This chapter seeks to analyse the ways in which teachers mediate the interface between these different cultural systems of meanings and values. The stimulus for this mediation comes from several directions. Their professional role mandates intensive interaction with other people's children (see Delpit 1988), and most of the parents whose children they are expected to educate have little or no experience of schooling themselves. They need therefore to have 'a position' on the differences and commonalities among the two cultural perspectives when interacting with parents. Moreover, as parents themselves they are subject to the pressures of social comparison, and often have to decide between culturally contrastive alternatives on their childrens' behalf. Often the existence of points of conflict are communicated to teachers indirectly by the behaviour of their students as they commute between the worlds of home and school. The teachers are then called on to take a position on the conflict when interacting with their pupils. Finally, it is arguable that within their own personal identities, teachers have to find ways of integrating the different themes of the two cultures which have contributed to their own development.

2   The cultural background and professional training of rural Zambian primary school teachers

The individual life-journeys analysed in chapter 5, as well as the attempts described in chapter 6 to promote a dialogue between teachers and parents about the nature of education, were all centred around the experience of a single, particular school, its teachers and its client community. In order to generalise from the findings obtained in that context, it seemed important to broaden the focus of our enquiry to include the relations between other rural Zambian primary schools and the communities they serve. A questionnaire was therefore administered in November 1983 to several teachers at the school in whose catchment area the local study is focussed, as well as a sample of fifty other teachers currently posted at ten different primary schools in Zambia's Eastern Province.[1]

A total of fifty-five teachers at ten different primary schools[2] in Zambia's Eastern Province completed the qestionnaire:

     31 teachers at 6 schools in Katete District,
     11 teachers at 2 schools in Chipata District, and
     13 teachers at 2 schools in Petauke District.

Thirty-six of the teachers were men and nineteen were women, six were Head Teachers and four were Deputy Heads. The extent of their teaching experience was distributed as follows:

14 had between 1 and 5 years,
9 had between 6 and 9 years,
11 (including 2 Deputy Heads) had 10–14 years,
11 (including 2 Heads and 2 Deputies) had 15–19 years,
8 (4 Heads and 4 Deputies) had more than 20 years.

All but one of our thirty-nine respondents with five or more years of teaching experience had children of their own, thirty-two of them including one or more children currently enrolled in primary school, generally at the same school at which the parent was teaching. Eight of these teachers had one or more children who completed primary school but had not proceeded to secondary school, while fourteen had one or more children currently enrolled in secondary school. Nearly three-quarters of our respondents received most of their own primary education in Eastern Province, while about half of them received most of their secondary schooling and/or teacher training there. All but one claimed a knowledge of Chi-Chewa, and 60 per cent of them stated that this was their most fluently spoken language other than English.

It is clear, then, that their experience, knowledge and skills in respect of residence, language and parenthood were adequate to impart a sensitive awareness of the alternative classifications, values and norms which inform the expectations held by their pupils' families with respect to their child's intellectual and moral development. Indeed, I have met many teachers who manifest such sensitivity in the context of discussing the challenges of teaching at a rural primary school. Because many of them grew up themselves in communities like this, they are aware of many of the points of conflict I have described in chapter 1. Moreover, they have children of their own enrolled in school who face some of the same kinds of problems, although teachers' children always tend to do systematically better than other children in a village school.

On the other hand, the ideology internalised by teachers in the course of their formal training and their socialisation into the profession has several sources. Some parts of it are interpretive products of personal experience, others are directly derived from an explicit theoretical idea or professional principle, and yet others serve to rationalise and legitimate the group's self-image or to advance an agenda of 'impression management'.[3]

From personal experience in their chosen professional occupation, primary school teachers can point to many particular work activities for which their formal education provided a uniquely appropriate preparation, as well as concrete benefits which have accrued to them from their acceptance of the school's formulation of individual progress and from their persistence in addressing the challenges of that curriculum. These may be extrinsic benefits such as a regular income, decent housing and long holidays, or more intrinsic ones such as the pleasures of reading, or of following through the mass media the public debate of national and international issues. Although theory is probably not a common focus of explicit discussion among such teachers, many of the concepts and maxims which feature in their everyday discourse originate from Western educational theories and principles.

I have argued in chapter 3 that the conception of schooling as an age-graded instructional process is in part responsible for the attitude of condescension which has become a widespread feature of the self-image of the teaching profession. Any claim on the part of a student to know better than – or even as well as – the teacher tends to be construed in this context as threatening to undermine the legitimacy of the teacher's claim to a specialised role.[4] Not only, therefore, do primary school teachers seldom entertain critical questions from their pupils, but they can generally rely on consistent support from all of their colleagues, including the school Head, for almost any disciplinary step they may take to suppress unacceptable behaviour by pupils.[5]

As Erving Goffman has shown in many insightful analyses of face-to-face interaction (1967, 1974), any social encounter tends to draw on an elaborate set of shared presuppositions concerning what is appropriate to the relative social status of the individuals who are interacting. Each participant in the encounter deploys his or her knowledge of this background information to lay claim to a certain role in the current interaction. Through a process of mutual ratification they acknowledge or challenge the legitimacy of each other's claims and thus construct an agreed interpretation of the activity in which they are engaged. To an outsider, or indeed even to an enlightened insider, much of this aspect of social interaction takes on an appearance of a ritual or dramatic performance of a predetermined script.

Over and above their various reasons for 'believing in' their professional activity, much of the daily decision-making by teachers is tightly constrained, if not fully determined, by considerations of administrative convenience. And the demands of administration arise not only from the interaction between teachers and their clientele, the pupils and their families, but also from a highly structured set of institutional practices which constitute the school's routine.

Adherence to routine is an important index of appropriateness for all participants in the subculture of schooling. Teachers are judged by the Head of the school to be 'on task' if their voices can be heard during class periods, if the pupils can be seen through the window, seated at their desks, reading or writing. If an approved activity involves departures from this paradigm, its temporal and spatial borders are sharply defined: calisthenic exercises in the school courtyard at a prescribed time of day, in another slot of the timetable gardening in the school production unit, etc. The appropriateness of a pupil's behaviour is likewise monitored by the teacher in terms of being in the right place at the right time.

This conspicuous orchestration of group activities serves two complementary functions: one instructional, the other dramaturgical. On the one hand, it orientates participants towards the requirements of learning, by foregrounding what the curriculum defines as essential texts and scripts, and filtering out or controlling extraneous 'noise'. Theoretical accounts of skilled performance in the information processing tradition (e.g. Sternberg 1984) construe routine as a strategy for reducing the demands on central processing mechanisms, in order to make available the maximum amount of processing capacity for a particular task (often the most difficult component of a complex of several tasks). On the other hand, public adherence to a routine also constitutes a dramatic script for managing the impresssion of schooling conveyed both to the immediate participants (teachers and pupils) and to an external audience constituted by the local community. The parents in this audience expect their children to be engaged in joint activity with their teachers as an opportunity for the latter to apply their specialised expertise to the guidance, preparation or moulding of young people for the technical requirements of work in the bureaucratic world.

Teachers, like any cadre of professionals, are generally acutely aware of their special status as performers of a particular social role. In a rural school in Zambia (and this is probably true for most other parts of sub-Saharan Africa), several factors conspire to define the role of teacher as requiring a kind of thinking which is distanced from the wider community: the extractive social goals of schooling linked to the national political agenda of modernisation; the teleological, progressive structure of the school curriculum; and the special status of the English language in which the curriculum is couched. Teachers therefore do not expect their pupils' families to show more than a superficial understanding of the pedagogical process in which the school is engaged, and they rely heavily on their professional training for planning the way in which they perform their societal role. Many of the parents we interviewed seemed to share the view that they were ill qualified to comment on or contribute to the processes of curriculum development and instruction impinging on their children's school education.

3   Two areas of potential conflict: agricultural work and starting a family

So long as all parties are in agreement that a young person should be in class, this insulation between the worlds of home and school might

Table 4.1 *Views of primary school teachers in Zambia's Eastern Province on school children helping in their parents' fields during the rains*

Favourable (45); detached or ambivalent (6); unfavourable (2)

Reasons in favour of the practice

7	to gain knowledge and/or experience of agriculture
3	to learn self-reliance
3	to learn responsibility
1	to learn hard work
1	it keeps the physique in good shape
5	to show parents the good methods pupils have learned in production units
9	it will help parents to buy the pupils' school requisites
5	they live on the food grown in their parents' fields
1	their parents are too old and need help
3+	it is a duty

Reasons against the practice

1	they lose interest in schooling
1	children must be given time for schoolwork
1	they would not have enough time to tend their own production unit where crops are grown
1	after harvest they aren't cared for – so the balance isn't fair enough

seem to reflect nothing more than a rational division of labour: a mutually agreeable division of responsibilities between parents and teachers. But sometimes the dictates of the school timetable enter into direct competition with the demands of socialisation in the traditional framework. The cycle of agricultural work, for instance, follows the weather, which in Zambia generally means that weeding is a major concern for subsistence farmers throughout the months of January and February. Agriculture is the mainstay of most families in Katete District, and the principal methods in use are highly labour intensive. Traditionally, adult men are responsible for clearing the land and fertile women for planting the seeds. But once the rains have set in during the months from December to February, every able-bodied member of the family is expected to participate in the work of weeding, including children over the age of about 5 or 6 years.

The school year, however, begins in mid-January and many teachers at rural primary schools report that class attendance is typically very low until after the weeding season has ended, several weeks into the first term of the school year. One item in our questionnaire asked, without any lead-in explanation: 'What are your views on school children helping in their parents' fields during the rains?' The great majority of respondents (forty-five out of fifty-three) expressed favourable attitudes. Table 4.1 presents a summary of the reasons cited in favour of or against the practice.

Only a small number of our respondents construed this widespread practice as an unacceptable collision between the values of the school curriculum and those of the indigenous socio-cultural system. These negative responses, listed at the bottom of the table, reflect the official policy position that children of school-going age are entitled to exemption from such chores and should concentrate all of their energies on their studies. Most teachers appear to favour some kind of compromise, perhaps to suspend the school timetable informally in deference to the demands of the local economy. Nearly half of the explicit reasons they advanced for approving of school children participating in this work focus on intrinsic developmental benefits to the child: in respect of knowledge, skills, social attitudes or physical health. These respondents were thus able to incorporate an out-of-school activity which lies beyond their control as teachers within their vision of the child's overall socialisation. A somewhat larger number of reasons for approval (eighteen) focus on extrinsic social obligations: duty, helping infirm parents, earning their keep, helping to defray some of the costs of their schooling. Finally, a small group of five responses ingeniously construe work in the fields as an opportunity to demonstrate to rural families the practical benefits of schooling. The validity of this optimistic view was explored in some of our efforts to promote a dialogue between teachers and parents, discussed in chapter 6.

Another topic with potential for more subtle and perhaps less easily resolved conflict between the cultures of home and school is the period of adolescence. Since many children are first enrolled in rural Zambian primary schools after the age of 9, and substantial numbers repeat one or more grades, it is normal for the Seventh Grade of such schools to include students over the age of 15 and not uncommon for them to include some over 18, the age at which, under the law, they are entitled to vote, to purchase and consume alcohol in public bars or to get married without parental consent. Our questionnaire asked: 'What are your views on Grade 7 pupils who are over the age of 18?' The following responses were given to the three riders:

			Yes	No
(a)	'Should they be encouraged to register as voters?'		49	2
(b)	'Should they be allowed to drink alcohol in public?'		3	48
(c)	'Should they be punished for entering into sexual relations?'			
		male teachers	21	13
		female teachers	15	2
		total	36	15

As young adults, most female students over the age of 15 in rural areas would be expected by their families to be contemplating marriage. Among our cohort, for instance, several of the women bore their first child before they reached the age of 17. Patrick Ohadike reports for a sample survey of 400 rural families in Zambia's Central Province, conducted in 1968–9, that the mean age of the women at marriage was 16.4 years, and that 30 per cent were married before the age of 15 (Ohadike 1981, p. 116). In the rural areas of Lusaka District national census data for 1969 gave an estimated average age at marriage of 18.0 years for women and 24.5 years for men (p. 100).

Teachers, however, especially female teachers, clearly regard enrolment in school as precluding the appropriateness of marriage, sexual intercourse and child-bearing. They themselves, we may infer from the general pattern of educational administration in Zambia, had almost without exception postponed marriage until after completing their secondary schooling (around the age of 19–21). And they clearly regarded this as an appropriate strategy in relation to the agenda of their own education. As we shall see in chapters 5 and 6, the conflict between this perspective on marriage and reproduction and that endorsed by the local community was almost certainly a major consideration leading to the low level of school participation by the women in our trace study cohort after reaching the age of adolescence.

The majority view that students over the age of 18 should be punished for entering into sexual relations is consistent with the view, also endorsed by most of our respondents, that they should not be allowed to drink alcohol in public places. In conformity with the theme of condescension discussed in chapter 3, Zambian teachers tend to exaggerate the puerility of their students. Pupils are construed as immature and subordinate persons who should not aspire to adult roles until after leaving school. Thus among the comments written by teachers on this part of the questionnaire were the following:

A child is a child and a pupil is always a pupil regardless of its age.

A child cannot drink alcohol in public places with his parents, because the child cannot give respect to the parents.

If it's not controlled, schools will become marriage centres.

Married life will confuse them.

Children over 18 should not be enrolled in primary schools.

An exception was made, however, in respect of registering as voters. Since they were responding to a written questionnaire, teachers may have felt it unwise to acknowledge any reservations they felt about this issue, which has been a sensitive one in Zambian politics. On the other hand, it is possible that in the current political climate, registering as a voter was construed by rural teachers as a passive duty, calling for compliance rather than for a mature sense of civic responsibility.

4 Cognitive strategies for the integration of a bicultural repertoire

I have argued up to this point that the perspective on children's development informing the practices of schooling in Zambia differs significantly from the perspective of indigenous Chewa culture, and that the teachers based in Katete primary schools have access from two different dimensions of their socialisation to each of these perspectives. In principle, at least, they appear to have inherited a dual cultural repertoire. How does an individual deal with such a dual heritage? Must she decide between the two, or can they be combined?

4.1 Contrasting views of the potential for productive synthesis

When two or more varieties of language (or other cultural meaning systems) come into contact, two opposing tendencies come into play: boundary maintenance and diffusion. Early theoretical accounts of the interface between such different, juxtaposed varieties tended to interpret the potential for conflict as arising from fundamental incompatibilities, and to view participation by a single individual in more than one cultural system as a source of stress. Kavadias, for instance, suggests that in many parts of the Third World people 'are torn by conflicting emotions aroused by their awareness of the fact that they ought to adopt the innovation but cannot adapt it to their situation' (Kavadias 1966). Turnbull's melodramatic account of *The lonely African* (1962) builds on this idea to argue that urbanised Africans are alienated and disorientated by being cut off from their roots (*déracinés*, as the French put it). When confronted with signs of cultural assimilation in the behaviour of modern citizens in African and other Third World societies, the proponents of this position generally focus on minor variations imposed on Western cultural practices by these 'newcomers' as evidence of a superficial and irresponsible eclecticism. In the domain of language, for instance, derogatory terms such as 'degraded' or 'corrupted' are often used in popular parlance to characterise the grammatical and phonological features of the ethnic dialects of English or French used in former colonial dependencies of Britain and France, and in various groups of established immigrants within the populations of those former metropolitan powers.

This pessimistic picture contrasts with an equally popular but much more optimistic historical interpretation of the broader trend over time of intercultural interaction and synthesis. The progress of so-called Western civilisation over the centuries seems to have been characterised by enthusiastic adoption and adaptation of inventions and ideas from many other cultural traditions.

On the pessimistic view, cultural artifacts, practices and principles are construed as the property of a group or population, who, as 'culture-bearers', are uniquely attuned to the demands of an integrated system which cannot be adaptively altered or eclectically sampled without loss of coherence, intelligibility and authenticity. On the optimistic view, the best thing that can happen to a cultural invention is that it inspires further developments beyond the context in which and for which it was originally created. Thus, far from being corrupted or degraded, Egyptian hieroglyphs were fortunately caught up in a process of progressive adaptation when they were simplified in hieratic script, varied in Aramaic and Phoenician and eventually radically transformed from a logographic to an alphabetic system in Greek (Diringer 1948; Havelock 1976).

Yet the notion that the English language is evolving in new and progressive ways as it meets, mingles and merges with the phonologies and lexicons of other languages in India, Africa and elsewhere (Pride 1982) has proven highly contentious. Instead of welcoming these signs of adaptive incorporation and development, many teachers of English have tended to treat it as a degrading process which needs to be checked by a heavy emphasis on conservative adherence to a set of standards which are perceived by many users as foreign or archaic or both.

Differences in political ideology have doubtless played an important part in the debate concerning what degree of tolerance should be displayed towards new and transitional linguistic forms. But it seems likely that one reason for the conservatism traditionally favoured by the teaching profession is the difficulty of conceptualising education as an open-ended process of cultivating development, rather than as training towards a predefined end-state. So pervasive is the tendency for school pedagogy to insist on standardisation that in societies where an exogenous language is adopted as the medium of elementary school instruction, teachers often drill their pupils towards mastery of 'fossilised', locally standardised forms which deviate in significant ways from the national or international standard (Selinker 1972).

4.2   The challenge of bilingualism

One reason for suspecting that the hypothesis of fundamental incompatibility is inadequate to account for the full range of interactions between adjacent cultures and languages is the existence in the linguistic domain of the phenomenon of fluent bilingualism. An individual who is bilingual integrates in some way within her cognitive repertoire the two different systems for expression of meaning. Studies of the ways in which this is achieved have generated a set of theoretical constructs tied to concrete examples which provide a preliminary basis for analysing more generally the psychological processes involved in functioning at the interface between two cultural systems.

One construct is the social stratification of speech varieties. Beginning with the classic work of Ferguson on diglossia (1959) and Fishman's (1967) application of that construct to formerly colonised nations, socio-linguistics has now established as a general principle that in speech communities where most members claim fluency in more than one distinct speech variety (be they termed styles or forms or dialects or languages), typically one variety is systematically regarded as more appropriate for use in some social situations than in others. Considerations of social power and prestige almost always enter into the definition of this type of situational appropriateness.

Linguistic competence in such a speech community includes not only mastery of the lexicon, grammar and phonology of both (or all) the speech varieties in question, but also a knowledge of the conventions governing such appropriateness. This socio-linguistic dimension of communicative competence (Fishman 1972; Hymes 1972) turns out to reflect a complex body of cultural knowledge which varies in the details of its patterning from one society to another. Theoretical accounts of the cultural and cognitive processes at work have been developed to explain the observed patterns of alternation among speech varieties or 'codes' in recorded samples of naturally occurring speech.

The simplest case is known as situational code-switching:

Distinct varieties are employed in certain settings (such as home, school, work) that are associated with separate, bounded kinds of activities (public speaking, formal negotiations, special ceremonials, verbal games, etc.) or spoken with different categories of speakers (friends, family members, strangers, social inferiors, government officials, etc.). (Gumperz 1982, p. 60)

This kind of situationally appropriate behaviour is mediated by a semiconscious attempt to match one's behaviour to the normative expectations of one's interlocutors and/or those of bystanders.

The empirical data, however, demand additional constructs to account for the full range of switching. As a first step, Gumperz proposed the notion of metaphorical code-switching, suggesting that when a code is 'imported' into an unusual speech situation it carries with it some of the connotations arising from its more usual context. In speech communities marked by stratified usage (often known as diglossic following Ferguson's usage (1959)) such that one variety is associated with situations of higher prestige than others, the use of the high-prestige variety in an informal discourse context will thus evoke an impression of incongruous formality which demands an interpretation, be it that the speaker has decided to display his or her superior sophistication or that the idea being expressed is quoted or borrowed, or that the speaker is making a joke of some sort.

Eventually, however, it has become clear that code-selection is better understood in a more integrated way as a pragmatic aspect of linguistic communication. A fluent bilingual conversing with other bilinguals deploys the codes at their joint disposal in much the same way as monolinguals make use of register:

> The ultimate semantic effect of the message ... derives from a complex interpretive process in which the code juxtaposition is in turn evaluated in relation to the propositional content of component sentences and to speakers' background knowledge, social presuppositions and contextual constraints. (Gumperz 1982, p. 84)

The particular meanings evoked by a given code are never fixed, even within the framework of a speech community, let alone carried forward from one community to another. Thus Gumperz describes how in a rural European community close to the borders between Austria, Italy and Yugoslavia,

> two forms of German have assumed special meanings of their own within the village context. They have become incorporated into network specific pragmatic conventions, where conversational inference is signalled by a juxtaposition of codes within what are semantically single messages rather than by choice of one code over another. We use the term conventions to highlight the fact that what is involved are not rules which must apply throughout but context dependent interpretive preferences affecting the quality of interaction. (p. 49)

4.3   Frames for the cross-cultural importation of new forms

At any given point in time two broad types of alternative strategy are open to the bicultural or multicultural individual: coordination and fusion. As Rogelio Reyes (1976) has noted, a multiple linguistic repertoire places the speaker in a position to produce three different types of mixed utterance: code-switching, incorporated borrowing and spontaneous borrowing. Incorporated loan-words in the usage of a Chicano community of the south-western USA studied by Reyes, typically showed extensive phonological adaptation and conformed, with their inflections, to the grammar of the host language system. Spontaneously borrowed words, on the other hand, retained more of their original phonological form, and were introduced in the context of special syntactic frames that protect them from the need for inflection in accordance with the rules of the host system.

One of Reyes' examples of such a syntactic frame in Chicano is the Spanish verb *hacer* (roughly meaning 'to do'), which is used to introduce English verbs in cases of spontaneous borrowing. A close parallel occurs in the urban dialect of Chi-Nyanja where *ku-chita* is used to the same effect. In the other main urban dialect of Zambia, Town-Bemba, a different syntactic frame is used to achieve this effect: *uku-* [borrowed verb]-*ing-a*. Thus in Town-Nyanja we find: *a-chita report kuti a-mai a-dwala* (he is reporting that his mother is sick), whereas a corresponding sentence in Town-Bemba would be: *ba-li-reporting-a kuti ba-mayo ba-le-lwala* (same meaning as above).

In both cases the syntactic frame serves a dual function: on the one hand, it alerts the audience that an exogenous vocabulary item is being introduced into the flow of indigenous-language speech (thus warning against trying to retrieve its meaning by looking it up in the indigenous lexicon), and, on the other, it specifies within the host system a recognisable grammatical role for the word within the sentence into which it has been inserted (thus providing a limited kind of legitimacy for the word within that linguistic context).

Extension of this concept of frames to a deeper level of conceptualisation provides a way of interpreting the process of tentative, innovatory deployment of exogenous cultural resources. A graduate of the formal schooling system may wish to incorporate some element of the culture she encountered in that context into her daily life in the largely non-literate community in which she resides. In order for that element to be intelligible in the unschooled community it must be encapsulated in the first instance in an introductory, presentational envelope which enables her fellow participants in the 'mainstream' of the local, 'host' culture to recognise that the behaviour in question is exogenous and to locate it within the grammar of the host culture.

The frame used by teachers for introducing exogenous forms of practice with children is constituted by an agreed definition of their role in contemporary Katete society. Just as the syntactic frame *ku-chita* serves as a mechanism for spontaneous borrowing of English words into Chi-Chewa speech, so the role of Teacher defines a cultural frame within which an exogenous, cross-culturally borrowed practice can be acknowledged as intelligible. Thus a teacher may engage in the following patterns of behaviour towards children which would be regarded as anomalous if they were displayed by other adults towards children known to them in other contexts of everyday living in this community: known-answer questioning; eye-contact interaction with children of the opposite sex; verbal praise for appropriate performance of simple, assigned tasks. Like verbal utterances in a foreign language, each of these culturally exogenous behavioural practices requires a foreign 'grammar' for its interpretation.

Cross-linguistic homonyms are probably quite rare in the linguistic case; but in the case of behavioural practices, introduction of an exogenous practice without the frame could easily lead to misinterpretation. An adult male teacher striving to maintain eye contact with an adolescent female student, for instance, might be taken to be making a sexual advance; known-answer questions would probably be regarded as insulting; and praise for the performance of simple assignments would be interpreted as condescending or even ironic.

Another example of framed innovatory deployment of exogenous cultural resources is described by Wim Hoppers (1981). Many young men and women who had completed primary school in Zambia's North-Western Province in the early 1970s had decorated the walls of their homes with cuttings from magazines, and written their names on the door. These are clearly practices which had no counterpart in the indigenous tradition of housing, and the fact that they were confined to the young person's private domain illustrates the tendency to circumscribe such cultural imports in such a way as to minimise the chances of their being misinterpreted. One of the Grade 7 school leavers in our Kondwelani cohort had adorned an interior wall of his house in the same manner, and entertained me to a meal, seated facing the display of magazine cuttings. As far as I was able to discern there was no explicit personal theme connecting his life to the colourful cuttings he had selected, which showed various European and African men and women, all smartly dressed in urban Western attire.

Gumperz in a wide-ranging overview of socio-linguistic patterns around the world (1968) describes a continuum of multilingual speech communities ranging from compartmentalised at one extreme to fluid at the other. In the former, the various elements of the speech repertoire are sealed off from one another by watertight barriers, such that one speech variety is reserved exclusively for use in one set of domains and another for use in a different set of domains. When a bilingual person follows social convention in this regard, she or he can be said to switch codes according to the demands of the situation. Other cultural resources seem to be deployed in a similar situationally sensitive manner in a multicultural society. People, for instance, often change their clothes to 'suit' the occasion. And, in Zambia at least, many musicians adjust their performance style to the apparent taste of their audience (Serpell 1978a).

Such situational switching is a strategy for the coordination of alternative cultural forms in a socially acceptable fashion while maintaining their distinctness. A more radical type of integration involves the fusion of elements from two different cultural systems in such a way that they no longer 'belong' exclusively to either system. In the case of incorporated loan-words, such as *sitima* in Town-Nyanja, or *menu* in contemporary English, the genetic origins of the 'borrowed' terms are generally unknown to the population using the form, and they acquire the character of endogenous cultural resources. The English form *steamer* gave rise through a fusion with Nyanja phonology to the Nyanja word *sitima* meaning a railway train, which has persisted long after the disappearance of steam-engines from Zambia Railways, which now uses German and Chinese diesel engines. The French term *menu*, abbreviated from *menu détail* – minute detail – was borrowed into English in the context of the British fascination with French cuisine, and has long since lost any connotations of minuteness, or indeed of French cuisine. In this case also the host language has shifted the phonological realisation of the underlying form so that the English term *menu*, with a stress on the first syllable and a diphthong [yu] in the second syllable, is almost unrecognisable to a monolingual speaker of French.

The tendency of incorporated borrowing to disguise the resulting word's etymological derivation is of lesser theoretical interest than its successful fusion of two disparate cultural forms. In the domain of Zambian schooling, the challenge confronting an educator who wishes to promote indigenous ideals of socialisation within the existing institutional structure is whether it would be acceptable to teachers, pupils and parents to introduce indigenous cultural forms within the framework of the curriculum. The fused outcomes might be rejected as deviant anomalies or welcomed as imaginative syntheses.

One such attempt was the development by the Ministry of Education of a curriculum module of basic reading in seven of the Zambian languages. Peter Higgs (1978) conducted a detailed content analysis of these reading primers and concluded that they missed a significant opportunity to inject indigenous cultural themes into the curriculum by confining the indigenous elements introduced to superficial aspects of form. Although the primers are expressed in grammatical versions of the indigenous languages and their illustrations represent indigenous children in local scenarios, the themes of the stories and their implicit values were found to be indistinguishable from those of the English-medium materials they were designed to replace, and to lack the deeper, distinctive characteristics of traditional African folktales. Cultural authenticity is an elusive notion, and it is only through a process of trial and error that acceptable, creative integration will be achieved of the various strands of Zambia's multiple cultural heritage.

4.4   The status of English in Zambian education

The English and Chi-Chewa languages interact at several types of interface in contemporary Zambian society. At the level of collective representation their interaction is situated in a complex historical drama which includes the intertwined themes of political domination/liberation and of traditionalism/modernisation. The wider socio-political ramifications of this interface between English and all the indigenous languages of Zambia have been eloquently articulated over the years by Mubanga Kashoki.[6] At the level of interpersonal communication their interaction reflects, negotiates and deploys those broad societal themes while building on the cognitive resources of the interlocutors. Education constitutes a unique blend of these two types of interface. On the one hand, schooling is construed as a process through which children are introduced to and encouraged to appropriate collective representations as part of their cultural heritage. And, on the other hand, the student is construed as undergoing a guided process of personal development in which she acquires certain cognitive tools and learns how to deploy them.

Unlike a society in which the medium of school instruction is the children's 'mother tongue', in Katete District (and all over Zambia's rural areas) pupils are introduced to the peculiar cognitive challenges of reading, writing and arithmetic in the medium of a language they have scarcely ever used before they enter school and which is not in current usage in their everyday lives at home, in the fields or in any other part of the ecosystem they inhabit. The physical locale of the school, its personnel and the curriculum are thus all symbolically tied to the connotations of the collective representation of the English language. Going to school is frequently equated with learning to speak English, which in turn is construed by many families as becoming a different kind of person, internalising a set of cultural values, skills and knowledge which entitle the bearer to certain privileged social roles in the national arena.

Because of the low frequency with which it is used in everyday life, and its connotation as the language of a bureaucracy based in the distant capital city, English is perceived not only as powerful (both as a cognitive amplifying tool, and as a credential for gaining access to a more affluent life-style) but also as somewhat alien. The flavour of English in Zambia is not foreign in the sense of total unfamiliarity, since it has been a part of the local cultural panorama for more than fifty years; nor is it perceived as inaccessibly sealed off within a closed social system like the Indian languages which traders are heard speaking with one another and with members of their families. Indeed, the ethnic load of English is probably lower than that of any other language with Zambian currency. Rather, its distinctive character is deeply tinged with connotations of power, which influence both the range of ideas and the range of interpersonal relationships it is used to express.

In Halliday's theory, the ideational component of language is reflected in the *field* of an utterance, the interpersonal component in its *tenor* and the textual component in its *mode* (cf. Gregory 1967). English in Zambia may be said to represent a distinctive register or group of registers applicable both to certain specialised fields such as bureaucratic affairs, science and technology, and above all 'educated folks' topics', and to either a formal personal tenor or a didactic functional tenor. These several aspects of diatypic variation are fairly autonomous in the speech of urban Zambian adults, but in the experience of children of primary school-going age, especially those residing in a rural area like Katete, most of whose families use English very rarely, the three features hang together in a coherent package. The topics of bureaucracy and science are presented to them almost exclusively in English by a teacher in an interpersonally formal, functionally didactic tenor.

This strictly bounded domain of usage is not characteristic of how the English language is used by teachers in their daily lives. Many of them conduct a good deal of social conversation with their colleagues (in many cases including their spouses) in English, particularly when the topic is public affairs. They listen to radio broadcasts in English, read English newspapers when they can get them and in some cases deliberately speak to their own children in English. Code-switching between English and Chi-Chewa is deployed within this social group as a means of conveying subtle connotations, as it is in urban Zambia. Paradoxically, however, the orthodoxy of educational practice discourages teachers from drawing this communicative resource to the attention of their students, since code-switching tends to be construed as deviant, non-standard, incorrect usage (cf. Serpell 1978a, 1980a).

5   The perceived benefits of schooling

In addition to providing a profile of these teachers' cultural and linguistic background and of their status as parents of pupils and school leavers, our survey collected a body of opinions on the following subjects: the goals of education, contact with pupils' parents and other family members, teaching as a profession and children with special needs.

Regarding the goals and the consequences of primary schooling, the teachers were in some respects more detached and willing to criticise the enterprise of which they are a part than I had expected. The views

Table 4.2 *Benefits of primary schooling for young men and women living in rural areas of Zambia's Eastern Province as perceived by serving primary school teachers (N=53)*

SECTION A	Young men	Young women
(Intrinsic good)	0	1
Adaptability/intelligence	10	7
General knowledge	10	5
Articulacy	10	4
Literacy	109	82
Further education prospects	7	3
Employment prospects	7	6
Initiative	16	10
Skills for local economy	66	24
Domestic skills and knowledge	4	123
Personal hygiene and health	23	12
Social status	7	13
(Religious outlook)	1	0
(Marriage prospects)	0	3
(Cross-gender association skills)	0	4
Recreational skills	7	8
Cooperative social attitudes	45	28

A high score indicates that many respondents to the questionnaire stressed this type of benefit, while a low score indicates that few did so. Specifically, one point was entered for each of the benefits cited by a respondent up to the limit of 3 benefits stipulated in the format of the question. (No benefits were cited by 3 respondents.) Thus the highest possible score would be 150 (=50×3).

Section B of the table provides a breakdown of selected categories.

SECTION B: *Breakdown of larger categories in Section A*

	Young men	Young women
Literacy	109	82
(a) Literate: literacy, can read and write; reading and writing	62	54
(b) as for (a) but specifying 'in English'	13	5
(c) as for (a) but specifying 'in mother tongue'	18	11
(d) Read and write letters; can help parents read and write letters from/for relatives in town; read and write letters for unschooled; communicate in writing with others away from them; read books or letters	8	13

SECTION B: *Breakdown of larger categories in Section A (cont.)*

	Young men	Young women
Literacy	109	82
(e) Read and understand things; reading	6	0
(f) communicate with written work	3	0
Skills for the local economy	66	24
(a) Agricultural knowledge; farming; production unit experience	32	21
(b) Modern agricultural skills; fertiliser applications; *lima* gardens	11	0
(c) Vegetable gardens	8	0
(d) Hoeing	3	2
(e) New methods of looking after livestock	3	0
(f) Woodwork (carpentry) – all entries from one school	10	0
(g) How to make and sell articles using local materials (cf. (a) sewing and (b) knitting in next section)	0	1
Domestic skills and knowledge	4	123
(a) Sewing	0	25
(b) Knitting	0	13
(c) Cooking/cookery	0	21
(d) Budgeting/cost of living; wise spending of money	4	5
(e) Home economics; homecraft	0	27
(f) Home care; look after family; house care; sweeping	0	28
(g) Child care; good mother; family planning; what to do when they get married	0	6
Personal hygiene and health	23	12
(a) Cleanliness	19	6
(b) Health care; primary health care	3	2
(c) Sanitation	1	0
(d) Diet	1	1
(e) Help mother keep family healthy	0	3
Social status	7	13
Tidy; neat; smart; well-dressed; more conscious of their personal appearance	7	4
Look civilised; customs of behaviour; education	0	8
Setting an example for others to send children to school	0	1

expressed were certainly not suggestive of stereotyped idealism. The questionnaire opened with a presentation of statistics for the nation as a whole and for Eastern Province, showing that 'most pupils in Grade 7 do not get a place in Form I the next year'[7] (cf. Fig. 1.3). 'When you meet one of the pupils from your school who did not get a place at secondary school after completing Grade 7, do you regard that boy or girl as...' The alternatives provided were chosen with the following frequencies:

		never	seldom	sometimes	often	always	no response
(a)	a failure?	3	0	6	0	0	45
(b)	unlucky?	1	2	25	7	1	18
(c)	normal?	0	1	3	1	3	46

Most respondents only chose a response for one of the three alternatives (a), (b) and (c), making analysis slightly difficult. But it is apparent that these teachers strongly reject the notion that Grade 7 pupils who are not selected for a place at secondary school should be regarded as 'failures'. Although their pedagogical efforts are explicitly and unashamedly geared to preparing pupils for the selection exam as the pre-eminent criterion of success, they recognise that there is a sense in which this is unfair, and that there is more to evaluate in a school leaver than his or her success in the exam.

As we noted in chapter 1, teachers in Katete District recognise that most of their school leavers will not proceed to secondary school and will remain living in the area close to the school after they reach the age of 20. It is in this context that their views regarding the value of school education were sought in the remainder of the questionnaire.

5.1   *Gender role stereotypes*

'What are the three most important benefits these young people have derived from their primary education?' The responses to this question concerning pupils who complete more than half of the primary school curriculum (Grades 4 to 7) are presented in Table 4.2. These data show that teachers' perceptions of such benefits were quite different for the two genders. Literacy was far and away the most important benefit that boys are expected to derive from the curriculum, whereas for girls this comes only in second place, below domestic skills and knowledge. Economically productive skills, in the conventional sense of those which can be applied in work outside the home, rank even lower among the benefits expected for girl pupils. Thus, although there is no official differentiation along these lines in the national educational policy, these rural primary school teachers (both male and female) evidently regard their educational objectives as systematically different for the boys and girls enrolled in their classes. Presumably, these differentiated objectives are pursued through selective focussing of attention and differential rewarding of achievement in particular fields of study. For there is only minimal opportunity for teachers to separate their pupils by gender, with perhaps one or two periods per week for subjects like domestic science, in which only girls are normally enrolled.

Like many of the parents we have interviewed, most teachers defined the goals of education differently for boys and girls. Not only were boys expected to derive more benefit than girls from schooling in the fields of personal hygiene and social cooperation, but literacy and skills for the local economy were also regarded as more important for boys than girls. These judgements (by both men and women teachers) reflect similar attitudes to those documented in Zambian secondary schools (Shifferaw 1982; Maimbolwa-Sinyangwe 1987) and confirm the grave concerns expressed by university-educated women's groups in Zambia (Longwe and Shakakata 1985) about obstacles to real equality of educational opportunities for girls and boys.

5.2   *Entrepreneurship or alienation*

Table 4.3 presents the pattern of responses to a set of questions which required the teachers to compare their impressions of Grade 7 school leavers with their contemporaries without schooling. In the case of each attribute they were also asked to specify whether they regarded it as a mark of success or of failure for the school. Ignoring the small number of anomalous responses and the cases where respondents declined to comment, the results show a clear majority view with respect to just four attributes. Young people with a complete primary schooling were perceived as:

> more enterprising in their agricultural work;
> more likely to question their parents' ways of doing things;
> more likely to indulge in frequent heavy drinking;
> less honest.

The first two attributes support the theme of modernisation which, as I noted in chapter 1, has been emphasised by many of the more optimistic accounts of the significance of schooling for economic development. A proclivity for alcohol abuse, on the other hand, could be interpreted as a symptom of alienation, a theme which emerged in some of the discussions with families described in chapter 5. The last attribution was the most startling: that teachers should regard their former pupils as generally less honest than their contemporaries who

Table 4.3 *Differences between primary-schooled and unschooled young people perceived by teachers at rural primary schools in Zambia's Eastern Province*

Compared with those who have not been to school, young people who have completed primary school are generally found to be	For the school this is regarded as		
	a mark of success	*no comment*	*mark of failure*
(a) more enterprising in their agricultural work	28	0	2*
no difference	3	3	8
less so	1*	1	7
extremes of success index (e.s.i.) $\left(\frac{28-7}{35}\right) = +.60$			
(f) more intelligent	19	0	0*
no difference	1	5	6
less so	2*	3	16
e.s.i. $\left(\frac{19-16}{35}\right) = +.09$			
(g) wiser	14	0	3*
no difference	2	4	13
less so	3*	1	11
e.s.i. $\left(\frac{14-11}{25}\right) = +.12$			
(h) more responsible	16	3	0*
no difference	3	0	8
less so	1*	2	17
e.s.i. $\left(\frac{16-17}{33}\right) = -.03$			
(i) more honest	6	1	0*
no difference	7	3	11
less so	3*	2	17
e.s.i. $\left(\frac{6-17}{23}\right) = -.48$			
(e) more likely to question their parents' ways of doing things	19	1	3
no difference	3	5	6
less so	8	3	6
e.s.i. $\left(\frac{19-6}{25}\right) = +.52$			

Table 4.3 *(cont.)*

Compared with those who have not been to school, young people who have completed primary school are generally found to be	For the school this is regarded as		
	a mark of success	*no comment*	*mark of failure*
(b) more critical of the Party and its Government	14	1	7
no difference	1	4	5
less so	7	1	12
e.s.i. $\left(\frac{14-12}{26}\right) = +.08$			
(d) more religious in their outlook on life	12	1	1
no difference	6	4	11
less so	4	1	13
e.s.i. $\left(\frac{12-13}{25}\right) = -.04$			
(c) more likely to indulge in frequent heavy drinking	9*	4	13
no difference	6	0	9
less so	6	2	5*
e.s.i. $\left(\frac{6-13}{19}\right) = -.37$			

*Cells starred with asterisk were identified in advance of the analysis as counterintuitive, on the supposition that respondents making several such responses might be inferred to have misunderstood the question and/or the response format.

Fourteen respondents made only one such response, eight of them in response to item (c) (see discussion in text), while five respondents made two or more such responses. Thus, although this is a complex response format to handle, requiring the respondent to refer back to his or her reply to Question 6 in order to reply to Question 7, the majority of respondents dealt with it in a careful and coherent fashion.

have not been to school. None of the teachers to whom a preliminary report of these data was circulated responded to my written invitation to comment on them, but this particular paradox became a focus of discussion at two seminars among Zambian educators held in Lusaka during 1987.[8]

   The most plausible interpretation of this negative evaluation of the outcome of a terminal primary schooling which has been suggested to me is that it reflects the ambivalence of the indigenous culture noted in section 2 with respect to the *-chenjela* dimension of intelligence. There is a sense in which teachers may feel they can see the effects of school-learning in the behaviour of their former pupils as a manipulative kind of cleverness. Consistent with this interpretation is the finding that a large number of respondents felt that there was no difference between primary-schooled and unschooled young people in respect of wisdom and regarded this as a mark of failure by the school.

The teachers, as we have noted, partake simultaneously of the cultures of the school and the village. It is in the latter context that they interact with school leavers and it is by its standards that they must now evaluate these young people's behaviour. If our interpretation is correct, it represents a poignant dilemma for the teachers: on the one hand, their professional orientation demands that they conceive of schooling as intrinsically beneficial to the development of all those who experience it; yet, on the other hand, the standards of evaluation favoured by the cultural milieu in terms of which they interact with their neighbours on everyday, non-professional matters tell them that the impact of schooling is often morally sterile and even damaging.

6   The nature of teachers' sense of accountability

How is this potential conflict between the evaluative standards of the culture of schooling and the indigenous culture of the community dealt with in the interactions of teachers with their pupils' parents during the period of the child's actual schooling?

The principal cognitive strategy used by the teachers appears to be one of compartmentalisation, with certain subjects being construed as legitimate topics of conversation with parents, while others are reserved for a different kind of discourse protected by a professional mystique against intrusion by the uninitiated. I have argued elsewhere (Serpell 1978a) that Zambia's multicultural urban society displays a highly fluid linguistic repertoire in which children display from an early age much greater flexibility than is acknowledged by the current language policy in education. Adult migrants into these cities seem to slide effortlessly into their fluid multicultural repertoire. Why, then, do these teachers, most of whom received part of their training in such an environment, adopt a compartmentalised strategy with respect to coordinating the two cultures of Chewa homes and formal schooling?

The teachers in our survey, especially the men among them, reported quite a high level of social familiarity with the pupils' families. Three-quarters of our respondents claimed to know the families of half or more of the pupils in their current class 'well enough to greet them by name when ... meet[ing] them on the road', and about half had visited half or more of their pupils' families at their home. According to their reports, when they talk about school matters with the family of a pupil, the focus of most discussions was on the concerns of the school as an institution: family support for the pupil's schooling, followed by the pupil's moral, social and personality development, the pupil's abilities and performance in classwork and exams, and then other aspects of education. Especially frequent were references to issues of attendance, punctuality, absenteeism, discipline and good and bad behaviour.

Some teachers expressed the view that they are unwelcome in villages. Many, however, are actively involved in local politics (twenty-two out of fifty-three) and/or in the affairs of a local church (twenty-eight out of fifty-three), and hold positions of civic responsibility (judge, demonstrator, voter registration, census enumeration, official celebratiorís, health committee). Most respondents (forty-five out of fifty-three) were of the opinion that their responsibilities as a teacher extend to activities outside the school. A number of respondents cited an obligation to set an example (or serve as a model) of upright moral behaviour (nine), and a few to instil discipline (two) or regulate their pupils' out-of-school behaviour (two). Others felt they had a special role to play in visiting the sick or attending funerals (two). By and large the teachers seem to view themselves as a cut above the general population, with more to offer the local community than to gain from it.

The substance of the curriculum and pedagogical practice, on the other hand, appear to be virtually taboo as subjects of conversation between teachers and their pupils' parents. It is not just that these subjects 'never come up'. One question was phrased as follows:

Sometimes other people may have a different idea from you about how your job should be done. If they suggest a different approach in a polite and friendly way, do you think you should take account of their point of view and change your behaviour at work accordingly?

The responses are summarised in Table 4. Clearly, parents are not expected to have anything useful to contribute in this professional sphere, and teachers do not feel directly accountable to them in respect of their schooling activities.

Given the nature of the responsibility entrusted to teachers, this is a quite remarkable state of affairs. Yet it is certainly not unique to Zambian primary schools. Very similar attitudes have been described among secondary school teachers in Cambridgeshire, England (Elliott *et al.* 1981). In the introduction to that study, John Elliott distinguishes between two forms of accountability in the teaching profession. The first, which is much the more prevalent both in England and in Zambia, is a hierarchical, bureaucratic, contractual form of accountability to the Governors and Local Education Authority through the Head, in which accountability is interpreted as ' "fitting in" with role expec-

Table 4.4 *Perceived obligation to take account of other people's ideas about how one's job should be done among primary school teachers and heads in Zambia's Eastern Province*

	Mean likelihood that one should change one's behaviour at work accordingly: (ranging from never = −2 to always = +2)		
	Heads and Deputies	*Other Teachers*	*Total*
Source of idea	(N=10)	(N=43)	(N=53)
Circular from the Ministry	+1.00	+0.64	+0.71
Inspector of Schools	+0.10	+0.43	+0.37
Head of your own school	+0.20	+0.37	+0.34
Parent of one of your pupils	−0.60	−0.77	−0.73
One of your pupils	−0.70	−0.81	−0.79

tations pre-determined by others'. The second is a moral, informally negotiated answerability, in which accountability is interpreted as 'explaining and justifying to others the decisions and actions one has taken' (pp. 15, 19).

Dave Ebbutt (Elliott *et al.* 1981, chapter 2) argues plausibly that a neighbourhood school is more exposed than one with an extended catchment to immediate surface evaluation and to product evaluation by its clientele and should therefore experience greater pressure to identify psychologically with the locale. The central school of the present study, like almost all primary schools in Zambia's rural areas, is a neighbourhood school in this sense: all of its pupils walk to and from school every day.[9] The reluctance of Zambian teachers to extend the scope of their identification with the life of the community to include a moral, informally negotiated answerability to parents in respect of their pedagogical activities seems to me to arise from what Elliott terms a technological perspective on schools shared by teachers and parents, which stresses product criteria, i.e. examination results. But this criterion is precisely the mechanism through which schooling exercises its essentially extractive impact on the local community. A much more constructive perspective for evaluation of schooling would be the humanistic alternative advocated by Elliott (1981, chapter 3) in common with many contemporary educators in the West. Here the stress would be on process criteria relevant to the personal and social development of the child.

Most of the teachers at Kondwelani School have appeared to me in our discussions over the years to be equipped with the cultural knowledge and the humanitarian motives required for undertaking this kind of education. The impediments to their construing their responsibilities in these terms are institutional rather than personal. Like other Zambians who have completed a secondary education, most of them have developed a multiple cultural and linguistic repertoire which they deploy eclectically and flexibly in dealing with everyday social interaction.

But the public definition of their professional role is embedded in a highly stratified social system which, as we saw in chapter 1, functions as an allocation mechanism for scarce economic resources. Powerful political pressures therefore operate to maintain an image of technical infallibility for the examinations, the curriculum and the teaching profession. The certainty of pedagogical method, exogenous in origin and suspect though its intermediary bearers had become, was seized on by apologists of the post-colonial state as part of a legitimating ideology for centralised control of the curriculum and for an emphasis on quantitative expansion with only minimal attention to qualitative curriculum reform. Thus, paradoxically, an already dated Western educational orthodoxy was incorporated as a methodological package into the very heart of one of the most intimate strands of national policy.

In matters of teaching, clearly teachers regard themselves as primarily accountable to their professional and administrative constituency, not to the families of the children they teach. There is perhaps nothing surprising about this, given that they receive their salaries from a central Ministry. But what it underlines is the tremendous responsibility which lies with the planners, administrators and trainers to 'represent' the interests of those primary clients, to gear the incentive system, the reward system and the disciplinary system of schooling in such a way as to maximise the responsiveness of serving teachers (however indirectly or 'for the wrong reasons') to the needs of the children they teach, of their families and of their local community. In chapter 7 I will discuss some specific ways in which policy could, in principle, be geared to these ends.

7   Public expectations

Compartmentalisation is more than a cognitive strategy for an individual. It is sustained by a process of mutual distrust. Identifying a theoretical strategy for enhancing local accountability is not likely in itself to give rise to significant changes in educational practice in areas such as Zambia's Katete District. Any attempt to open up a dialogue with parents, let alone students themselves, concerning the fundamental validity or usefulness of any part of the established practice of schooling is potentially threatening to the politico-economic order, and is liable to encounter fierce resistance from powerfully entrenched interests in the wider society.[10]

It is not only teachers who rationalise the segregation of the content of the school curriculum from other more generally accessible discourse about intellectual and moral development. Many parents who had little or no schooling themselves evidence a deep ambivalence about committing their children to a system which they interpret in the extractively promotional terms described in chapter 3. On the one hand, they are conscious of a responsibility to pass on the accumulated wisdom of their culture to the next generation. The Chi-Chewa term for this traditional wisdom is *mwambo*. But, in a community which is conspicuously involved in a process of rapid social change, those who endorse attempts by the political leadership to give direction and coherence to that process of change, under the banner of 'progress', national development, etc., must also acknowledge alternatives to tradition as a frame of reference for the definition of wisdom. A variety of formulations are available such as modernity, science and technology, the national political ideology (known in Zambia as Humanism (Kaunda 1974)), etc. The School, as the public institution *par excellence* charged with preparation of the younger generation for their participation in the life of this changing society is readily construed as a repository of an alternative brand of wisdom.

Thus a Katete District Regional Secretary for UNIP (the national political party) intervened in one of our local family discussions to explain:

Muno m'mudzi tili nawo mwambo, ndipo mwambo wamuno m'mudzi . . . ku sukulu kuli mwambo wina . . . mwambo wa dziko.[11]

'Here in the village we have our traditional wisdom,[12] and it's the wisdom of life here in the village. In school there is another kind of wisdom, the wisdom of the nation' (*mwambo wa dziko*).

This speaker's political commitment led him to construe the school as representing what, at a national level, UNIP and the national government are trying to do in terms of transforming the nation.

Another reflection of the compartmentalisation subscribed to by the families is the differentiation of responsibility with respect to dealings with the school. In an unpublished study in Lusaka, Mrs Yaona Mwale in 1980 asked a sample of eighteen fathers and twenty-one mothers of children enrolled in early grades of primary schooling in Lusaka: *Ndani ayenera kuikako nzelu kumaphunzilo amwana pa banja?* ('Which member of the family should take responsibility for the child's education?') Thirteen out of eighteen fathers and fifteen out of twenty-one mothers answered that it was the father who is responsible. In our rural Katete sample the question of who had taken the original decision to enrol the child in school was put in the course of family discussions held during 1980 concerning sixteen of the children in our cohort who either were in school at that time or had been in school and had subsequently withdrawn. In about one-third of these interviews the answers given were somewhat ambiguous. The following breakdown is based on the most plausible interpretation of the tape-recorded protocols:

	Boys	Girls
Father	2	4
Other male relative (uncle or brother)	2	0
Father and mother	0	2
Mother	2	1
Self only	2	0
No clear answer	1	0

This preferential allocation of responsibility to the father is all the more striking in the light of the general tendency for the care of children of this age to be seen as primarily the mother's responsibility. The father acquires this ascribed role, not as a result of an intimate involvement with the child but because of his authority status *vis-à-vis* the state bureaucracy, mediated and rationalised through his greater competence in the English language, and his more advanced level of schooling. Each of these connections reinforces and underpins the other: men are seen as better able to negotiate access to schooling for their children because they understand its content better, and this will still be so in the next generation so that it makes more sense for young men to continue their schooling than for young women.

Another compartmentalised interpretation was formulated as follows by an unschooled elder of the village in the context of the same wide-ranging family discussion concerning the community's child-rearing philosophy, their hopes and aspirations for particular children and the value of schooling:

Ku sukulu kufunika maphunzilo olemba. Ife tikondwela ngako chifukwa ana akhala azungu.[13]

'At school what's called for is learning about writing' (i.e. literate education). 'And we're very pleased about this because our children *akhala a-zungu.*'

We could translate this last phrase as 'becoming Europeans', but it is more than that. The term *mu-zungu* is in fact quite widely used in Lusaka to designate one's boss or employer, even if he or she is an indigenous African. So it has acquired a wide range of connotations. In the context of this rural family's discussion of schooling, I interpret the speaker as claiming that for children to become literate makes them part of that culture that came from outside – a culture which is tied to the authority system, tied to the white-man's way of life.

In support of this interpretation, consider the following experience recounted by my colleague, Dr Mapopa M'tonga, who grew up in Zambia's Eastern Province. He described members of his extended family as saying of a child who had completed five years of formal education at secondary school: 'This one we have given to the *azungu*.' Then they went on to say of another, younger child in the same family, for whom a move to the city had been mooted, to stay with his educated relatives and go to school: 'Don't take this one away from us, we must at least keep one here.' This particular conversation is not an archaic anecdote: it took place in 1986. Even today[14] there are old people in the villages who regard sending a child to school as giving him or her away. Giving him away to the agenda of some external power: maybe it's for the *dziko* (for nation-building); maybe it's for something even a bit more alien than that – for the *azungu*. But it's for something which is not *mwambo wa muno m'mudzi* (the wisdom of life here in the village).

This kind of alienation between the process of schooling and the mainstream of the local culture is still very much a reality in many parts of rural Zambia. It provides one kind of legitimation for the extractive definition of success in our system of public education which stipulates that a successful person gets out of the community, climbs out of the village way of life, 'up' – and this directional metaphor of upward movement is a pervasive feature of public discourse about education – up into the city life of the *apamwamba* (the people on top, or the upper class). This image is very clearly expressed in the following passage of a letter written to me recently by the one member of our cohort who is now studying at university:

Later in life it's inevitable for one to go out of the village if he has to keep that burning desire to learn in himself/herself. One has to go to the right places and mix with the right people so that you don't plateau in one's quest for advancement.[15]

The myth of personal advancement, up and out of the indigenous culture of the village is highly seductive for those who succeed in mastering the curriculum of the nation's stratified public educational system, and it generates in some teachers a sense of superiority to the rural community whose children they are assigned to teach.

8   Perspectivism and social responsibility

Underlying each of these compartmentalised views (that schooling is a technical process only intelligible to those with the relevant specialised training, that it represents a radically different brand of wisdom from that of the village, uniquely well suited to the programme of national development, or belonging to an alien and powerful people) is an epistemological stance of 'perspectivism', where a perspective is defined as:

a more or less closely related set of beliefs, attitudes and assumptions that specify how reality is to be understood. They concern the appropriate field of observation, the proper domain of explanation (that is, where to seek it, and when to regard it as sufficient), the necessities and possibilities of social life and how the self and its relation to society is to be conceived and human interests identified. (Lukes 1982, p. 301)

The 'strong' version of perspectivism, which states 'that there can be no perspective-neutral interpretation and explanation' (p. 302) poses a number of difficulties for any kind of applied psychology, including education. A practising psychologist has a professional obligation to formulate prescriptive statements based on the best evidence available. If intersubjective meanings are construed as the primary defining criteria for social facts, what line of action should the practitioner prescribe in cases where her own interpretation of the relevant social facts differs significantly from that favoured by the subjects whose behaviour is involved?

How should an educational practitioner proceed when deciding what kind of education is best for the children of a rural African community? On the one hand, she may be convinced by arguments in favour of a number of crucial curriculum components and pedagogical principles developed in the context of a modern, industrialised society. Yet several of these ingredients of an ideal education may seem to be not only impracticable but also counterproductive as a preparation for life in the community into which these children were born. If she decides on relativistic grounds to eschew those ingredients as inappropriate, the objection can be raised that she is discounting the possibility of social change, and indeed neglecting her responsibiltiy as a broker of technical knowledge to contribute to the guidance of such change in a 'progressive' direction.

The phenomenon of individual biculturation seems to promise a solution to this dilemma by suggesting that it is in fact based on an epistemological misconception. Beliefs and practices which appear to 'belong' to two contrasting cultural systems often coexist within the cognitive and behavioural repertoire of a single, multicultural individual. While some writers have interpreted this as a condition fraught with internal conflict and frustration (e.g. Turnbull 1962; Kavadias 1966), I am more inclined to portray it as an adaptive kind of flexibility particularly well suited to the demands of life in a rapidly changing, Third World society (Jahoda 1970; Serpell 1977c). As we have seen in section 4, not only can different cultural perspectives coexist harmoniously within a multicultural community; they are also amenable to various forms of psychological integration within a single person.

Yet in some important respects the potential of this biculturation seems to be underrealised. The challenge for teachers as bicultural mediators is to identify (or build) bridges between the cultures of home and school. Such bridges can most readily be constructed through a process of dialogue and negotiation. But teachers tend to regard the school culture as privileged territory, on which parents should not be encouraged to trespass.

Teachers share with parents a repertoire of concepts for discussing home-based socialisation practices. They also share certain constructs pertaining to the domain of school. But the latter are strictly confined to an external, instrumental view of the activities of schooling. These constructs are encoded in incorporated loan-words: *ma-pensulo* (pencils); *ma-uniform* (uniforms); *ku-pasa* (to pass an exam); *ku-feluka* (to fail); etc. But there are no incorporated loan-words for curriculum; for revision; for practical subjects; for fieldwork projects.

Embedding the curriculum in the English language includes among its various dangerous consequences the temptation for teachers to think of parents as incompetent to enter the discourse of curriculum planning. Yet a parent might have very useful and relevant knowledge for discussion of how to teach agricultural science, which could contribute both theoretically and practically to the enhancement of the primary school curriculum. Or in the 'subject area' of civics, parental views of *mwambo* (traditional wisdom) could be integrated in productive ways in the elaboration of the nature of civic responsibility.

Another challenging topic for planners of social change in Africa has been the field of health science and preventive health practices. In the Northern Province of Zambia, Lindiwe Makubalo (forthcoming) reports that elderly women with experience as traditional birth attendants proved to be more effective and acceptable as Community Health Workers than younger men and women with many more years of formal schooling to their credit. Moreover, given an appropriate context, these elderly, largely illiterate adults were willing and able to assimilate new technical information in the course of their very brief training.

We tried in some of our family interviews to explore the idea of pooling knowledge and expertise with respect to public affairs and traditional healing practices, but with little success. The abstract terms we chose to broach the subject carried very particular connotations for most of our respondents, and their juxtaposition with the topic of the school curriculum evoked explicit resistance. When we enquired what parents thought about the idea of including some treatment of *za-ndale* or of *za-ung'anga* in what their children learned at school, most of them responded as if we had mooted the idea of recruiting school pupils to participate in organised local or national politics (*ndale*) or of recruiting traditional healing specialists (*ng'anga*) as part-time instructors. These concrete versions of how the topics of public affairs or traditional healing practices might be introduced into the curriculum were strongly rejected, the first on the grounds that it would get the youngsters into trouble, the latter on the grounds that the knowledge of specialists was either too private to be shared (cf. Gay and Cole 1967) or suspect.

Parents conspire with teachers to perpetuate their own exclusion from the kind of discourse which would be most productive by insisting on only discussing school success in terms of its external facets as a mode of access to secondary school, which in turn is construed instrumentally as a route for obtaining credentials to deploy in the formal-sector labour market. This elitist view excludes from consideration any of the young people who do not proceed to secondary school, who constitute the great majority of all those who enter primary school.

The teachers whose situation I have described in this chapter are faced with an extraordinarily difficult version of the challenge confronting all teachers everywhere: to interpret the world for other people's children in ways which will expand their horizons and enrich their understanding without alienating them from the culture of their home community. I believe their own biculturation equips them uniquely well to address this challenge as mediators between the two cultures they straddle. This optimistic view presupposes that the perspectives of those two cultures, although quite different, are not irredeemably closed to one another. In chapter 6, for instance, I describe an insightful and effective theatrical portrayal by one of the school teachers, Mr Banda, of a village elder who was adamantly opposed to his niece's continuation of her schooling now that she had reached a marriageable age. The theoretical basis for supposing that the cognitive systems of different cultures are mutually penetrable is discussed in the Appendix.

5

Life-journeys and the significance
of schooling

1   Introduction

Construing the significance of schooling in the lives of individuals
growing up in Kondwelani community has been the principal motivation for this study. The overwhelming impression given by the data we
have collected for this purpose over fourteen years is one of immense
diversity. Not only do individuals differ from one another in their
interpretations of events and opportunities, but a given individual's
perspective also tends to change over time. An important dimension of
the significance attributed to schooling is defined by the position in
one's own life-journey from which one is looking at it. Although
several members of our cohort have migrated out of Kondwelani, the
main dimension of these life-journeys is a temporal one. Progress
along the journey reflects a number of types of change: a developmental progression of the individual's social status and a cumulative
sequence of experiences, decisions and shifts of priorities in the
individual's personal agenda.

Some individuals developed a commitment to schooling over the
course of this journey and came to accept its narrow staircase definition as a channel for their career. For others the school remained a
marginal resource, a place they visited at one time (somewhat as one
visits a shop to sample its wares) but which had little to offer them, a
club which they briefly expressed an interest in joining but which
rejected them. The channelling interpretation of schooling fits well
with the official ideology discussed in chapters 3 and 4. Not only is this
technological perspective product-orientated but it also implies a stratified and compartmentalised view of society: you either make it into
the upper class (*apamwamba*) world of the 'educated' or you don't. The
cut-off points for class membership are defined by the hierarchical
selection system. Completing Grade 7 defines one tier, completing
Form 3 (or Form 2) another, completing Form 5 yet a further tier, and
tertiary education a final upper crust.

Many of the young men started out, adopting the extractive definition of success, with the opinion that schooling is primarily a way of gaining access to formal-sector employment. Later in their lives, as the limited effectiveness of schooling for the attainment of this limited, practical end became apparent to this generation, their initial view of schooling as a passport to success gave way for many of them to a more relativistic appraisal. Thus one young man of 19 who never went to school was asked in 1983 to look back over his youth and compare himself to two of his childhood playmates from the same village, who were now in Grades 6 and 7 of the local school. He replied:

Tonse tilibwino . . . Ine ndili ndi ng'ombe. Zuze ndi Mavuto ali pasukulu ndipo akhoza kupeza nchito yabwino.

'We're all doing fine – I've got my cattle. Zuze and Mavuto[1] are at school and so they'll be able to find a good job.'[2]

Note behind this optimistic statement the implicit assumption that if they don't find a 'good job' then Zuze and Mavuto will have wasted their time at school. This line of reasoning is more explicit in the following exchange with another young man who left school after Grade 4 several years ago:

Q. *Kodi unachita bwino kusiya sukulu?*
A. *Koma, ee, ndachita bwino.*
Q. *Chifukwa chiani?*
A. *Chifukwa olo amene analikutsiliza Grade 7 ndipo uphasa sapeza nchito.*
Q. *Mukamba zoona?*
A. *Eee, kweni-kweni olekeza muForm 3, sapeza nchito ndipo tilinayo m'midzi mumuno kulima sunflower ndi ladyo.*

Q. 'Was it a good move for you to leave school?'
A. 'Well, yes, it was a good move for me.'
Q. 'Why?'
A. 'Because even those who completed Grade 7 and passed still don't find jobs.'
Q. 'Is that really true?'
A. 'Yes, in fact even some Form 3 school-leavers don't find jobs, and they're here in the fields with us, growing sunflower and garlic.'[3]

The idea that life in the city is a natural outcome of schooling was often expressed by parents at the point where their sons completed primary school. In one of our family discussions I asked the mother of a young man who had completed Grade 7 and was currently enrolled in a private, fee-paying secondary day school on the Copperbelt, some 500 miles away, if it didn't bother her that he might find a job in town so far away from her. On the contrary, she replied:

Ndiliokondwela ngati azikhala kutauni chifukwa kuno kulibe phindu kuti angakhalile kuno. Ngati akhala ku midzi ndingabvutike chabe.

'I'll be happy if he stays in town, because here – there's no use him hanging around here. If he stayed in the village, that might bother me.'[4]

A quite different interpretation of schooling derives from the humanistic ideals of education as a fundamental right and as a resource for personal and social development. In terms of the metaphor of travel, the focus is on the intrinsic value of the journey, rather than on arriving at a particular destination. In public discussions of education in Zambian society this interpretation seldom gets a hearing. It tends to be dismissed as a 'soft-sell' with no tangible pay-off in the race for economic growth and indeed with little consumer appeal except to a privileged and complacent class of wishy-washy liberals protected from the cut and thrust of the real world market by their privileged economic status. But what then are the benefits to be derived by members of a humble rural community from a period of schooling too short by the standards of the technological perspective to make them truly 'educated'? Is the memory of having tried and failed all that a terminal basic education has to offer to its graduates? I will return to this question later in the chapter.

2   Benchmarks for the description of life-journeys

As our trace study of children born into the Kondwelani community in the 1960s evolved between 1973 and 1988 we sought to establish a number of benchmarks for the description of their life-journeys and for documenting their interaction with the process of schooling. Ratings of individuals on each of these benchmarks were based on our initial round of tests and adult interviews in 1973–4; on tape-recorded interviews with some of their families in 1980; on periodic enquiries from the local school; and on interviews with the individuals themselves in 1983, and again in 1987–8, reflecting on their childhood experiences and their plans for the future. These various databases, although incompletely replicated across all members of the cohort, provide a rich network of information about family child-rearing agendas, parental expectations, formal educational opportunities, attitudes of pupils and graduates of the local school, and the patterning of life-journeys across time.

About one-third of our cohort of forty-six young people, although resident within easy daily walking distance of the local school, never enrolled in it; less than a third completed the full, seven-year primary course and the remainder spent varying amounts of time in school. We have been able to examine the life-journeys of these young people from a variety of angles. The first two come from a phase of their early pre-adolescence before almost any of them were enrolled in school.[5]

2.1   *Home Village Ratings (HVR)*

We have an account of their abilities and dispositions as seen through the eyes of elders in their village communities, elicited in 1973–4 through the structured interviews described in chapter 2. A summary index of this perspective was coded as the Aggregate Adult Ranking. At the end of some of the interviews, and in other cases on a follow-up visit three to six months later, each adult informant was asked to rank the children about whom she or he had been interviewed with respect to the attribute the informant had cited most frequently to justify his or her choices of one child above the rest for our imaginary tasks.[6] The psychometric properties of this index have been discussed elsewhere (Serpell 1977a, 1982a; Dasen *et al.* 1985). On the one hand, rankings of the same set of children by different adults living in the same village showed only rather low positive concordance.[7] On the other hand, each individual adult displayed quite a high level of consistency even when the original interview was separated from the follow-up ranking by several months.[8]

For the purpose of examining the relation between these assessments of the children, by adults who knew them well in their home villages using indigenous criteria and other indices, the aggregate rank position of each child relative to his or her peers was converted to a stanine Home Village Rating score.[9]

2.2   *Early Childhood Test Scores (ECTS)*

At the same point in time we also have each child's performance scores on three specially developed cognitive tests: the General Verbal Test, the Hand Positions Test and the Panga Munthu Test. The detailed rationale for each of these tests and the experience derived from their subsequent application to a range of Zambian samples have been described elsewhere (Serpell 1977a, 1989a). Each was based on an eclectic synthesis of concepts and measurement principles derived from Western developmental and educational psychology, together with intuitions derived from observation of some of the cultural practices and opportunities for development described in section 5 of chapter 2.

The Hand Positions Test (HPT) takes the form of the tester and subject sitting face to face across a table; the tester places his hands (all the children were tested by men in this part of the study) in a standardised position relative to one another, thus constituting a pattern or configuration of fingers, and the subject is required to imitate the pattern by positioning his or her own hands in the same way.[10] The Panga Munthu[11] Test (PMT) ('Make-a-Person Test') took the following form. In this early version of the test, the child was shown for about 30 seconds a crude model of a person made either from a strip of wire or from plasticine modelling clay, and was then asked, in the absence of the standard, to build his or her own model of a person in the same medium.[12] The General Verbal Test (GVT) comprises a varied set of twenty verbal items, ranging from pointing to named objects and carrying out simple commands to supplying quite complex information about the physical and cultural environment. Some of the items involve performing simple manipulative operations on familiar types of object, such as threading beads and handling rough blocks of wood.

Within our Kondwelani sample, the pattern of scores on these tests displayed a number of features which may be taken as indications of local validity. They showed the expected improvement with age even when children without schooling were considered, and the two non-verbal tests (HPT and PMT) correlated more highly with one another than with the verbal test. But no significant association was found between the rank order of test scores within each group of peers and the Home Village Ratings discussed above. Yet, as we saw in chapter 2, not only were those adult assessments backed up with convincing justifications using appropriate terminolgy, but they were also quite consistently repeated several months later in follow-up interviews with the same adults.

The puzzle of why these two approaches to assessing the intelligence of children growing up in Kondwelani were so discrepant provided the initial stimulus to follow their subsequent development, in the hope of finding out more about the significance of these different assessments in the light of their correlations with measures of various cognitive and behavioural characteristics later in their lives.

2.3   *Level of schooling completed*

Only eight boys in our sample were enrolled in school before 1973, the year in which we began our testing, while five more boys were enrolled in the First Grade that year. Because of the difficulty of establishing precise ages, and our uncertainty about the likely distribution of ages at initial enrolment in this population, we were inclined at that stage to think of those children who were not enrolled as 'pre-schoolers'. Looking back, we can now distinguish three broad categories of response to the local schooling on offer.

(a) Fourteen individuals (six men and eight women) reached adulthood[13] without ever enrolling in school at all. One young man told us that he was enrolled in Grade 1 at another near-by school but never continued with any schooling beyond that point. Including him in this group yields a total of fifteen, or 33 per cent of the total cohort who effectively ignored the school system.

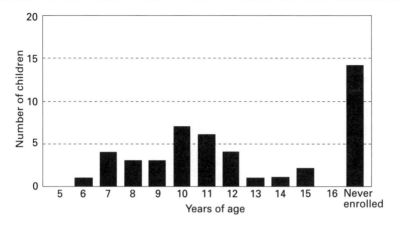

Fig. 5.1 Age of enrolment in Grade 1.

(b) At the other extreme, twelve individuals (all boys), comprising 26 per cent of the cohort, completed the entire seven-year primary school curriculum. Seven of these young men proceeded to some form of secondary schooling, two of them completing the full five-year secondary curriculum. One of these last two was admitted to the Copperbelt University and, at the age of 24, was entering the final year of a four-year degree programme in 1988, while the other obtained passing grades in eight subjects in the final Grade 12 examination that year, and appeared likely to qualify for admission to a university or other tertiary-level institution with effect from 1989 at the age of 25.

(c) In between these two contrasting groups lies a third group comprising 41 per cent of the cohort, who enrolled in one of the primary schools in the neighbourhood but withdrew without completing the full seven-year curriculum. Eleven of these subjects were girls and eight were boys. One more boy would have been included in this group if the trace study had stopped between 1977 and 1982, since he withdrew from Grade 6 in the former year, but five years later he re-enrolled in Grade 5 at the same school and in due course proceeded to complete the sixth and seventh years of the curriculum. The life-journey of this young man, Shamba, is presented in more detail below.

2.4   *Age at first enrolment in school (GD1AGE)*

Figure 5.1 shows the distribution of ages at which members of our cohort enrolled in the First Grade. It is noteworthy that the modal age was 10 years, and that only five out of thirty-two (or 16 per cent of those who enrolled) did so, as prescribed by official policy, before the age of 8. The mean age at initial enrolment for the eleven girls who went to school was 10.09 years (standard deviation 1.38), much the same as for the thirteen boys who completed no more than seven years of formal schooling for whom the mean was 10.38 years, but with a much greater variance (sd 3.15). When we combine this index with the preceding one, years of schooling, to consider the ages at which these two groups of students ended their schooling, one factor contributing to the generally longer school careers among the men than among the women of this community begins to emerge. The mean age when withdrawing from school for the young women was 14.82 (sd 2.27), while for the young men who did not proceed beyond Grade 7 the mean age was 16.31 (sd 3.66).[14] Evidently, if we were to include in the masculine sample those who proceeded with schooling at the post-primary level, the mean age at which they stopped schooling would rise much higher than this.

One reason for taking an interest in the age at which individuals were first enrolled in school was that it might be considered an indirect index of a family's support for their child's schooling. Every year, the Headmaster of the local school (like many of his counterparts at other rural Zambian schools) used to tour the neighbourhood visiting families whose children were not enrolled to urge them to do so once they reached the age of 7. Parents who postponed or avoided complying with this advice could therefore be construed as taking a public stand against the value of schooling for their child. This issue will be discussed further below.

2.5   *Class Teacher Ratings (CTR)*

Public examinations which are set and graded centrally are confined in the Zambian school system to three nodes: Grade 7, Grade 9 (for a number of years this was moved to Grade 10) and Grade 12. Only two of our cohort reached Grade 12, seven reached Grade 9 and twelve reached Grade 7, all of them male. In order to assess the quality of academic performance by the other nineteen members of our cohort who enrolled in school, we were forced to rely on the unstandardised class examinations conducted by teachers. Inspection of the distributions of grades on these internal exams showed that they varied greatly in their level of difficulty relative to the populations for which they were designed. Under these circumstances, the most reasonable index for comparing the academic performance of students who were taught and examined by different teachers at a given grade level seemed to be their overall ranked position in class. In order to include a maximum number of students in the analysis, three levels of schooling were selected as units of analysis for this variable: Grades 1 and 2 combined, Grades 3 and 4 and Grades 5 and 6. The school records for the period

1974–9 yielded interpretable class rankings for a total of fifty-three cases of a student in one of these two-grade intervals.[15] These rankings were converted to stanine scores in the same manner as the Home Village Ratings discussed above.[16]

2.6   *Secondary School Selection Examination*

Because of the high level of publicity and anxiety attached to this public examination set at the end of Grade 7, we did not consider it socially acceptable to ask members of the cohort to provide us with their own results. The information is, however, a matter of official record in the files of the Ministry of Education, and we were able to trace the grades for six of the twelve individuals in our cohort who claimed to have sat for the examination between 1979 and 1985. The nature of the examination and the socio-political character of its interpretation in various fora of Zambian society will be discussed in chapter 7. For the present it will be sufficient to note that the Total Scores used for selection purposes are composed of the sum of the standardised scores on each of six papers (English, Mathematics, Science, Social Studies, Special Paper I, Special Paper II). Each paper is composed entirely of multiple-choice items and candidates are required to answer these on machine-readable answer sheets. Special Paper I is conceived as a test of verbal reasoning and Special Paper II as a test of non-verbal reasoning. Illustrative examples of items from the two tests are shown in Fig. 5.2.

2.7   *Adult literacy ratings*

Our tests of adult literacy were presented informally and covered three aspects of literacy: ability to read and write in English (English Literacy); ability to read and write in Chi-Chewa/Chi-Nyanja (Nyanja Literacy); and ability to carry out arithmetical computation (Numeracy).

English Literacy (ELT). After the trace study interview had settled down with a series of demographic questions and questions about the respondent's current and past economic activities, we asked what were his or her ambitions for the future. Following on the response to this question we said, 'I've got a list here of various jobs people do in Zambia. Suppose you were given a chance to do any one of them, which would be your first choice?' And casually we handed the respondent a sheet of paper on which were typed a list of ten occupations, including farmer, garage mechanic, school teacher and domestic servant. Some respondents took the list and read it silently, others demurred, glanced hesitantly at the list and explained that they could

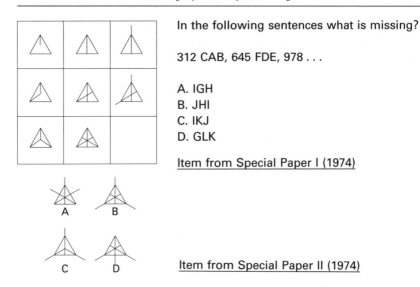

In the following sentences what is missing?

312 CAB, 645 FDE, 978 . . .

A. IGH
B. JHI
C. IKJ
D. GLK

Item from Special Paper I (1974)

Item from Special Paper II (1974)

Fig. 5.2 Some examples of verbal and non-verbal items from Special Papers I and II of the national Secondary Schools Selection Examination (reproduced with the permission of the Ministry of General Education and Culture, Government of the Republic of Zambia).

not read, others never even touched the page and when we persisted merely observed it as if it contained no information. When we knew that the respondent had spent some years at school we tried sitting next to them and pointing to selected words such as school and encouraging them to try. Later in the interview, a series of focussed questions was addressed to the respondent concerning what she or he reads and with what frequency. Details of these questions are presented below in section 5.4 (cf. Fig. 2.2, p. 52).

The ELT score was computed as follows. A zero score was recorded in cases where we could observe no sign of any vestigial literacy, a score of 1 when a little reading and or writing was observed, 2 when the respondent could read our sample of text and write adequately, 3 when the subject indicated that she/he reads regularly and showed that she/he can write competently, and 4 if she/he reads extensively.

Nyanja Literacy (NLT). A list of Chi-Chewa words was presented at the very end of the interview. It comprised the abstract words for ten evaluative attributes (including *nzelu, u-chenjela* and *chi-khulupililo*), all probably rather lower in frequency of usage than the occupations in the English list. The cognate adjectival terms had been used orally in the immediately preceding exercise described in chapter 2: requesting the respondent to rank his or her contemporaries with respect to each attribute. The written material was now presented for ranking of the attributes in terms of general desirability. Once again, we first observed the respondent's reaction to our matter-of-fact request that she read through the list. Then, if the respondent was reluctant, we tried to persuade her to try and read a few selected words. The more highly literate respondents often asked for a pencil and wrote out the words in their rank order of importance. The numerical scale for NLT was scored by the same criteria as those specified above for ELT. But none of the respondents was judged to read extensively enough in Nyanja to warrant a score of 4.

Numeracy (NUM) was assessed in the context of a series of questions about the subject's current economic activity. After the occupational ranking exercise on which our assessment of English reading was based, we selected a topic about which we could expect the individual to be quantitatively informed and elicited a first number from that repertoire of active knowledge. In the case of those in formal wage employment, this was the individual's current monthly rate of pay. We then specified a second number, in this case related to the period of time the individual said she or he had been employed at this rate. Then we asked a question which required the respondent to compute the arithmetic operation of multiplication, e.g. 'So how much have you earned altogether in this job over the past year?' If the individual was engaged in family agriculture, the first number we elicited was often the unit price at which she or he was currently selling a particular variety of vegetables produced in the dry-season garden. The second number was the respondent's estimate of how many units she or he usually sells in a day or in a week. Then we asked, 'So, how much do you earn from the sale of this product in a week (day)?' Young men engaged in small-scale commercial agriculture were asked about the price per sack at which they had marketed their crop, the number of sacks sold in the previous year and then their total earnings from sale of that crop.

Some respondents immediately looked around for a pencil and paper to work out the sums we set them in this way, while others figured out the answers in their head, often using their fingers to help them count. The NUM scale was scored as follows:

0 No computational skills at all
1 Some computation observed, but minimal and/or incompetent
2 Accurate computation observed
3 In addition to (2), Subject reports doing quite a lot of computation as part of her/his daily routine
4 Subject has passed the Grade 12 public examination in mathematics

Table 5.1 summarises the distribution of scores on these three measures of adult literacy across the categories of economic activity

Table 5.1 *Domicile and estimated literacy and numeracy as a function of gender and years of schooling*

Men		Literacy score		Numeracy
		English/4	Chewa/4	score/3
	(N)			
Full primary (N = 11 + 1 deceased)				
	Urban (3 + 2#)	2.3/4.0#	2.7/2.0#	1.7/3.0#
	Rural (6)	2.7	2.8	1.8
Less than full primary (N = 8; mean yrs of schooling = 5.3)				
	Urban (8)	2.0	2.3	1.3
	Rural (0)			
No schooling (N = 6 + 1 not traced, rural domicile)				
	Urban (2)	0.5	1.0	0.5
	Rural (4)	0.0	0.0	1.8

Women		Literacy score		Numeracy
		English/4	Chewa/4	score/3
	(N)			

Full primary (N = 0)
Less than full primary (N = 10; mean yrs of schooling = 4.8; + 1 not traced, urban domicile)

| | Urban (3) | 0.7 | 1.3 | 1.7 |
| | Rural (7) | 0.3 | 0.6 | 1.3 |

No schooling (N = 5 + 1 deceased + 2 not traced, rural domicile)

| | Urban (3) | 0.0 | 0.0 | 1.0 |
| | Rural (2) | 0.0 | 0.0 | 1.5 |

Correlations among the three measures of literacy

Men (N = 25)		Women (N = 16)	
NLT	ELT	NLT	ELT
NUM + .53*	+ .74**	NUM + .06	− .14
ELT + .83**		ELT + .83**	

#Two subjects with full secondary schooling, currently still enrolled in full-time studies
*p<.01
**p<.001

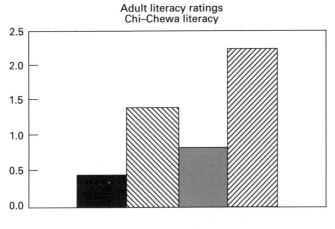

Adult literacy ratings
Chi–Chewa literacy

■ Women Trad. ▨ Men Trad. ▥ Women Mod. ▨ Men Mod.

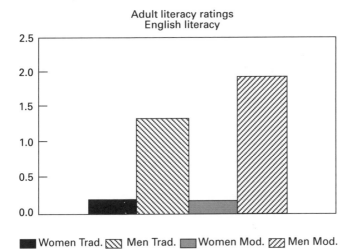

Adult literacy ratings
English literacy

■ Women Trad. ▨ Men Trad. ▥ Women Mod. ▨ Men Mod.

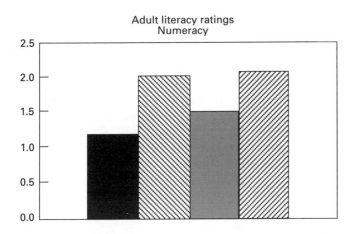

Adult literacy ratings
Numeracy

■ Women Trad. ▨ Men Trad. ▥ Women Mod. ▨ Men Mod.

Fig. 5.3 Adult literacy ratings.

discussed in the next section, and shows how they were intercorrelated among men and among women (see Fig. 5.3).

2.8   *Economic activity*

Table 5.1 also provides a summary account of the current domicile and years of schooling completed for the forty-one members of our cohort we were able to trace during 1987–8. Their economic occupations in young adulthood now included farming (N=21) and trading (N=7), both on a small scale; various kinds of wage employment (N=12), mainly unskilled; two cases of full-time study, two cases of unemployment and one case of full-time home-keeping.[17] In order to facilitate group comparisons, two relatively homogeneous categories of economic activity were defined: modern urban activity (comprising petty trading in peri-urban areas, unskilled and semi-skilled work in urban industries, and domestic service in urban households); and small-scale, rural farming. Excluding those whose current pattern of life did not fall clearly into either of these categories or whom we were unable to contact for interview yielded four subsamples: seven women and five men engaged in rural farming and five women and seven men engaged in modern urban economic activities.

2.9   *Marriage and procreation*

By 1987, eleven of the twenty-five men we traced from our cohort (or 44 per cent) were married and eight of these acknowledged having children. Nine of the sixteen women we traced were married, two were divorced and three of the other five who had not married acknowledged having borne one or more children. Thus all but two of the sixteen women (or 88 per cent) had either been married, borne a child or both. The mean age at marriage of the nine women for whom that information was recorded was 19 years (range 17–21), while for the eleven men the mean age was 21.8 years (range 18–25). This statistic was clearly likely to rise, as more of the men in the cohort got married. Seventeen of the twenty-two marriages in which members of our cohort were involved had lasted for two or more years, and only two of these were as yet without a child.[18] Fertility is a very highly prized aspect of life in Zambian society, and this is especially true of women. According to many of the adult men of the community with whom this topic was discussed,[19] concern over their prospects of getting married and starting a family of their own was probably a major consideration leading many of the girls of fifteen, sixteen and seventeen to decide against continuing with their schooling.

3   Interrelationships among the benchmark variables

One approach to the analysis of variables such as those described above is to try and show a causal influence of certain antecedent variables on individual differences in participation and performance in the activities of schooling. Another approach is to try and document a causal influence of schooling on various outcome variables. The following are the prime candidates for such designation in an analysis of this kind:

Antecedent variables	*Outcome variables*
Gender	Marital status, parenthood
Home Village Ratings	Adult Literacy Ratings
	English literacy
	Nyanja literacy
	Numeracy
Early Childhood Test Scores	Economic activity
Panga Munthu Test	
Hand Positions Test	
General Verbal Test	
Family support for enrolment	Domicile

Figure 5.4 presents a speculative model of how these variables might be interrelated in a causal framework. Consideration of the variable 'family support for enrolment' (FSE) illustrates the analytical weakness of this causative approach. On the one hand, we cannot overlook the influence of the child's family on the decision whether and, if so, when

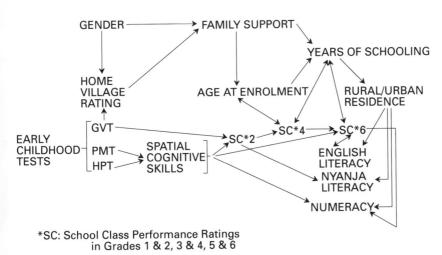

*SC: School Class Performance Ratings
in Grades 1 & 2, 3 & 4, 5 & 6

Fig. 5.4 A general causative model for the relations among variables.

155

the child should be enrolled in school. On the other hand, clearly the attitudes expressed towards this topic are dynamically related to the gender of the child, to her age, to her demonstrated aptitudes, to the community's perception of her aptitudes and dispositions, to her obligations towards the family in which she is being raised and to her prospects of fulfilment as an adult member of the community, including marriage and child-bearing. Which of the multiple arrows between FSE and these other variables should point in which direction, and how should we interpret correlations among such variables? Such a complex defies causal analysis.[20]

Narrowing the focus of our attention, however, the following patterns of correlation illustrate some of the interdependencies among sets of variables.

3.1   Early Childhood Test Scores (ECTS)

The raw scores on our three tests were converted to standard scores relative to the distribution within two age-groups, an older group of nineteen subjects, and a younger group of twenty-seven subjects.[21] When the resulting z-scores were entered into a correlation analysis all three tests showed moderate-sized and statistically reliable[22] intercorrelations for both boys and girls. These are shown in Table 5.2. Unlike the earlier analysis of these data (Serpell 1977a), the present analysis does not show the expected tendency for the two non-verbal tests to be more closely correlated with each other than with the verbal test.

For purposes of some of the further analyses reported below an Aggregate ECTS was computed by summing the standardised scores on GVT, HPT and PMT. Consistent with the analysis conducted on a village-by-village basis in 1974, no significant association was found between the Aggregate Early Childhood Test Scores and the Aggregate Home Village Rating scores either for boys or for girls.[23]

Table 5.2 *Correlations among scores on the three Early Childhood Tests*

	Boys (N = 27)			Girls (N = 19)	
	HPT	GVT		HPT	GVT
PMT	.44**	.45**	PMT	.44**	.31
GVT	.49**		GVT	.61**	

*p<.05
**p<.01

Table 5.3 *Correlations among Class Teacher Ratings at different grade levels*

| | Boys (N = 7–10) | | Girls (N = 7) |
	CTR Gds 1–2	CTR Gds 5–6	CTR Gds 1–2
CTR Gds 3–4	+ .56	+ .70*	CTR Gds 3–4 + .93**
CTR Gds 5–6	– .38		

*p<.05
**p<.01

3.2   Class Teacher Ratings (CTR)

The sample size was drastically reduced for this analysis because of (a) the large number of children who did not enrol in school and (b) the incompleteness of the school records of past examination results to which we had access. Wherever possible a stanine class rating was computed for the pairs of Grades 1 and 2, 3 and 4, and 5 and 6. An insufficient number of CTR scores were available for girls in Grades 5 and 6, but their ratings in Grades 1 and 2 were highly correlated with those in Grades 3 and 4. Intercorrelations among these scores are presented in Table 5.3. Even with this small sample the result is statistically reliable. In the case of boys, ratings in Grades 3 and 4 showed a significant positive correlation with those in the lower grades and also with those in the higher grades. But, paradoxically, the ratings in Grades 1 and 2 were negatively correlated with those in Grades 5 and 6.

3.3   Family Support for Enrolment (FSE)

A review of the transcripts of family discussions in 1980 and retrospective interviews with members of the cohort themselves in 1983 generated firm indications of the degree of support available to twenty-three individuals from their families in respect of enrolment in school. These indications ranged from four situations where the parents of a child of school-going age explicitly opposed either the child's enrolment or his/her continuation in school, and, at the other extreme, one family where, beyond enrolling the child and supporting him with school necessities, the parents had actively encouraged the child to persist with his schooling.

There was considerable variation across cases in the nature of the evidence for the degree of family support and in the particular family members who played a key positive or negative role: uncles, grandparents and elder siblings sometimes featured as much as, or more than, fathers and mothers. It is thus questionable whether it was appropriate to construct a single quantitative index to represent family support as a unidimensional variable. For the sake of exploration, however, a 6-point scale was devised with the two extremes above as its end-points (-2 and $+3$). In between a score of -1 was assigned in cases where the parents were said to have been short of money as a reason for non-enrolment; a score of 0 in cases where the child enrolled himself in school; $+1$ when another family member such as an elder sibling enrolled the child; and $+2$ when the child's mother and/or father enrolled the child.

Among the eighteen children who did attend school for some time and for whom this FSE index was available, no significant correlation was found with age at the time of enrolment in Grade 1 ($r=0.16$). Furthermore, no significant correlation obtained between the FSE index and the Home Village Ratings ($r=0.13$, $N=18$), nor with the Aggregate Early Childhood Test Scores ($r=0.14$, $N=23$). The FSE index did, however, correlate quite highly and reliably with the level of schooling completed by the child ($r=+0.68$, $N=23$). It should be noted in this regard that some of the evidence contributing to the determination of the FSE index was collected from cohort members in retrospective interviews. Individuals who had withdrawn at an early level of schooling may have been more likely to refer explicitly to a lack of family support than those who were continuing in school, and this interpretative bias could have increased the strength of the apparent association between FSE and Years of Schooling above the degree warranted by any direct causal influence of the former on the latter.

3.4   *Prediction of the level of schooling attained*

We are now in a position to consider a number of possible statistical predictors of the level of schooling attained by different individuals within our cohort. Since it is already clear that boys proceeded much more often than girls to higher levels of schooling, the correlations of level attained with other variables will be presented separately for each gender.

The rather large positive correlation between age at enrolment and level of schooling attained among girls, which approaches statistical significance, is not consistent with other aspects of our data, and should be interpreted with caution in view of the small number of cases on which it is based.[24] The one young woman who embarked on her schooling at the age of 13, whom I shall call Ngosa, was interviewed by Peter Phiri in 1983, just after she stopped schooling, following the birth of her first child. During the interview she indicated that she would have liked to go to secondary school, and felt that primary schooling is of little use nowadays. Peter then challenged her to explain the anomaly that she herself had not continued with her primary schooling or sat for the secondary school selection examination.[25] Ngosa replied:

Siningapitilize chifukwa nakula ngako kuti nizipita ku sukulu. Icho nchofunika ang'ono ang'ono.

'I can't continue because I'm much too big now to go to school. That's for little kids.'

Later in the same interview, when she asserted that she planned to enrol her own children in school, Peter once again pressed Ngosa to justify her position:

P: *Kodi iwonso sadzathawa monga m'mene munachitila inu?*
    'Won't they drop out too just the way you have?'
N: *Ai; ine nali m'kulu kuti nzipita ku sukulu. Lomba mwana wanga nizamulembetsa sukulu akali mn'gono kuti akhulile pa sukulu.*
    'No; I was big for starting school. But I'll enrol my son when he's small so that he can grow up while he's at school.'

She went on to confirm that she felt her parents had left it too late by enrolling her at the age of 13, and that she intended to enrol her own children at the age of 7 or 8.

The remaining correlations in Table 5.4 form a pattern suggesting that persistence with schooling is related among boys, but not among girls, to the aptitudes indexed by our Early Childhood Tests and to performance in class as rated by the teacher. Persistence with schooling

Table 5.4 *Correlations with level of schooling completed*

	Female subjects	(N)	Male subjects	(N)
Age at Gd 1 enrolment	+ .57	(11)	+ .14	(21)
Family support for enrolment	+ .93*	(10)	+ .74*	(13)
Home Village Ratings	+ .83*	(8)	− .27	(19)
Early Childhood Test Scores				
Aggregate ECTS	− .15	(19)	+ .46*	(27)
GVT	− .25	(19)	+ .28	(27)
HPT	− .28	(19)	+ .37	(27)
PMT	+ .19	(19)	+ .44*	(27)
Aggregate ECTS (scholars only)	− .35	(11)	+ .57*	(20)
Class Teacher Ratings, Gds 1&2	− .08	(9)	+ .53	(8)
Gds 3&4	− .46	(9)	+ .72*	(12)
Gds 5&6			+ .50*	(10)

*p<.05

among the few girls who enrolled at all, although clearly overall much less than among boys, was positively correlated with Home Village Ratings, whereas this was not the case for boys.

3.5   *Correlates of Adult Literacy Ratings*

Table 5.5 shows the correlation between each of the Adult Literacy Ratings and various other indices. For both genders, as one might expect, the number of years of schooling completed was positively and significantly correlated with adult literacy. Noteworthy in this respect is the fact that these correlations are equally high for the Nyanja Literacy Rating as for literacy in English, the medium of instruction in school. Also striking is the finding that the correlation of numeracy with level of schooling completed was only significant in the case of men. Only a weak and non-significant association was found with schooling in the case of the women.

Still more striking is the difference between the genders in the association between adult numeracy and teachers' class ratings in Grades 3 and 4. For men the association is highly and reliably positive, indicating as one might expect that students identified in Grades 3 and 4 as high achievers by their class examinations were destined to have relatively high levels of numeracy in adulthood. But for women the association is somewhat but unreliably negative, suggesting that their performance on class tests at this stage was inversely related to their numeracy in adulthood. This finding should be interpreted with caution in the light of the dissociation between the numeracy and literacy ratings for women noted in Table 5.1.

Table 5.5 *Correlations with Adult Literacy Scores*

	Women (n = 8–16)			Men (n = 11–24)		
	NUM	NLT	ELT	NUM	NLT	ELT
Home Village Ratings	− .31	+ .42	+ .75*	+ .09	− .07	− .05
Early Childhood Test Scores						
Aggregate ECTS	− .20	− .07	− .01	+ .07	+ .57*	+ .45*
GVT	− .26	− .24	− .24	− .14	+ .48*	+ .28
HPT	− .15	− .23	− .14	+ .06	+ .49*	+ .48*
PMT	− .08	+ .29	+ .34	+ .23	+ .43*	+ .35*
Level of schooling completed	+ .20	+ .46	+ .51*	+. 63*	+ .72*	+. 78*
Class Teacher Rating in Gds. 3 & 4	− .39	+ .47	+ .47	+ .85*	+ .25	+ .49*

*p<.05

Regarding the Early Childhood Test Scores, since our General Verbal Test was couched in Chi-Chewa (Nyanja), it is not surprising to find that in the case of boys it correlated more highly with the Nyanja Literacy Rating later in life than with the English Literacy Rating. Nor is it surprising to find that the Panga Munthu Test was a somewhat better predictor of adult numeracy than the General Verbal Test. But it is striking to note that both of the non-verbal tests at this age correlated more highly with the verbal literacy ratings in adulthood than with the numeracy rating, suggesting that the effect is mediated by some intervening variable such as scholastic aptitude or general ability. None of the Early Childhood Test Scores were significantly related to any of the Adult Literacy Ratings among the women.

The last gender contrast to note in Table 5.5 concerns the correlations with Home Village Ratings. These are all close to zero for the men, whereas they reach a high and reliable positive value for women in the case of English literacy, a moderate positive level for Nyanja literacy and (the same anomaly noted earlier) a moderate negative level for numeracy.

3.6   Gender differences in the correlates of schooling and adult literacy

The overall pattern of the correlations discussed above together suggest that, among those boys who enrolled, the school curriculum latched on to certain aptitudes which were indexed by our Early Childhood Tests but not by the Home Village Ratings, and generated predictable levels of skills, especially in English literacy and numeracy as a function of the level of schooling to which individuals proceeded. Among girls, on the other hand, the school curriculum seems to have captured little or none of the same aptitudes. In their case, the Home Village Ratings, rather than our Early Childhood Test Scores (with the possible exception of the PMT), were the only variable other than years of school experience which predicted the level of functional literacy displayed by young women later in life. A plausible causal route for the mediation of such a relationship between the Home Village Ratings and later adult literacy would be that (a) Home Village Ratings (HVR) influenced Family Support for Enrolment (FSE), which in turn (b) influenced the level of schooling attained, which eventually (c) influenced the level of adult literacy. Unfortunately, the range of available data concerning HVR and FSE for our female subjects is too small to warrant a comparative analysis to test the hypothesis of a higher correlation at step (a) in the case of girls than boys.

The present data set is not ideal for exploring issues of this nature since too many descriptive variables are deployed across too small a sample of individuals. The data points are too few to warrant a path analysis or a log–linear modelling analysis. As for multivariate multiple regression–correlation analyses, when gender is included as one of the predictors of the level of schooling attained or when schooling is included as one of the predictors of adult literacy scores, they over-whelm all other variables, and the cases are too few to warrant analysis by that technique for separate subgroups of men and women. Aggre-gating the data at the level of the individual's profile, the technique of configural frequency analysis (von Eye 1988; von Eye and Nesselroade 1989) was applied to the full sample of subjects in our trace study cohort for whom various categories of data were available. Using the categories of gender, level of schooling completed and literacy (coded dichotomously as high or low in accordance with an unweighted sum of their scores on the NLT, ELT and NUM scales) yielded the only statistically reliable outcome among several alternative matrices of three-way cross-classification. A disproportionate number of subjects (ten out of forty) fell into the following category: masculine, com-pleted more than six years of schooling, and scored high on the measures of adult literacy. The detailed patterning of individual characteristics and experiences lying behind this bald fact are evoked rather than captured by the qualitative analysis presented in sections 5 and 6 of this chapter. However, a complementary sample of data col-lected in the same area on a more restricted set of variables provides some quantitative support for the interpretation proposed at the begin-ning of this section. All of the pupils attending class on a particular day in October 1979 in Grades 2, 3, 4, 5 and 6 at Kondwelani School were administered the Panga Munthu Test (PMT), and then the Goodenough-Harris Draw-a-Person Test (DPT). The same procedure was repeated in March 1980 in a random selection of the correspond-ing grades at a large primary school in a low-income suburb of the capital city of Lusaka.[26]

Table 5.6 shows the correlations among scores on the two tests and the variables of age and teacher ratings on a five-point scale of scholastic attainment for boys and girls separately at each of the schools. Three features of the pattern are of particular interest. (1) Correlations among scores on the two tests were highest among urban boys and lowest among rural girls. (2) Age was less highly correlated with scores on the DPT than with scores on the PMT in all the samples except for the urban boys, was more highly correlated with PMT scores among rural than urban children, and was only reliably correlated with DPT scores for the male samples. (3) In both the rural and urban samples, performance on the DPT was more highly correlated with teacher ratings of school attainment among boys than among girls.

Each of these findings is consistent with the notion that the worlds of

Table 5.6 *Correlations among scores on the Pangu Munthu Test, the Draw-a-Person Test, age and teacher ratings of school attainment among rural and urban girls and boys*

	Girls	Boys
(a) *PMT × DPT*		
Rural	− .04	+ .24
	(N = 34)	(N = 42)
Urban	+ .35*	+ .40**
	(N = 43)	(N = 41)
(b) *Age × PMT*		
Rural	+ .66***	+ .65***
Urban	+ .47***	+ .24
Age × DPT		
Rural	+ .13	+ .31*
Urban	+ .13	+ .37**
(c) *Teacher rating × PMT*	+ .04	− .06
Rural	+ .26*	+ .18
Urban		
Teacher rating × DPT		
Rural	+ .23	+ .46***
Urban	+ .15	+ .51***

*p<.05
**p<.01
***p<.001

home and school are least well integrated psychologically for rural girls and best integrated (in relative terms) for urban boys. (1) The drawing skills required for scoring high on the DPT could theoretically build on a cognitive infrastructure which also feeds the skills tapped by the PMT. The extent to which scores on the two tests are correlated can thus be interpreted as an index of the extent to which the school curriculum has effectively latched on to the child's pre-existing aptitudes. Given the many factors militating against girls, especially rural girls, taking their participation in schooling seriously, it is understandable that evidence of such psychological integration is least apparent in the case of rural girls and most apparent in the case of urban boys. (2) The PMT taps a set of skills which are actively cultivated in the everyday lives of all the children, especially rural children who are not yet at school. Rural children who enrol in school continue to practise this skill in their play activities, whereas urban school children, especially boys, tend to leave it behind as they grow up. Thus skill in this domain continues to develop with age in rural school children but less so among urban school children, yielding significant correlations of PMT scores with age among rural but not among urban children.[27] (3) The DPT taps a set of skills which are theoretically closely related to the school curriculum, and this theoretical connection is most apparent in the sample with the best prospects of success at higher levels of the school system. Hence the higher correlation of DPT scores with teacher ratings of school attainment among boys than among girls.

A major factor constraining my enthusiasm for undertaking elaborate, integrative forms of multivariate analysis on the data of our trace study has been a sense that it accords excessive prominence to those outcome variables which are susceptible to simple quantification. If we were to give serious attention to the psychological variables emphasised by the adults who made the Village Ratings, we would need to consider their 'predictive' power in respect of such subtle outcomes as loyalty, compassion, personal integrity, social responsibility, community respect, etc. While these may not be essentially intangible human qualities, they would require a set of observations and interviews extending well beyond the scope of what we have been able to conduct in this trace study.

The nearest we have come so far to a systematic attempt to broaden the definition of 'quality of adult life' beyond practical efficacy in materially rewarding economic activities is an exploratory analysis of peer ratings as an index of interpersonal respect on the basis of our trace interviews. We computed a Weighted Peer Rating Index[28] for each member of the cohort from the responses of those of his or her childhood village neighbourhood peers we were able to contact and who felt sufficiently in touch with them to rate them in terms of personal characteristics. We were dependent for these ratings on the ability of the young adults to remember their peers, and those who had migrated to the city were often so out of touch with those in the village that they felt unable to give a meaningful rating of one another. As a result of these additional constraints, index values based on ratings by two or more peers were only available for twenty-eight of the forty-one young adults traced.

Table 5.7 shows the coefficients of correlation between this index and four of the benchmark variables discussed above. For neither men nor women was there any significant correlation between this index of esteem by one's peers and either the Home Village Ratings or the aggregate Early Childhood Test Scores. Among the young men both the level of schooling completed and the aggregate Adult Literacy Ratings were significantly, positively correlated with the level of esteem expressed for them by their peers. Among the young women,

Table 5.7 *Correlation of Weighted Peer Ratings with other indices*

	Men	(N)	Women	(N)
Home Village Ratings	.27	(12)	.26	(8)
Early Childhood Test Scores (Aggregate)	.25	(16)	.43	(12)
Level of schooling completed	.61**	(16)	− .16	(12)
Adult Literacy Ratings (Aggregate)	.54*	(15)	.33	(12)

*p<.05
**p<.01

however, neither of these variables was significantly related to our measure of peer esteem, and the coefficient of correlation with level of schooling completed was actually negative.

Incomplete though they are, these data seem to confirm, from the perspective of their peers, that the significance of schooling in the lives of women in our cohort was systematically less than in the lives of men. In chapter 6, we will see that, on the plane of fictional narrative at least, it is culturally plausible to advance the hypothesis that for young women in this community ambitions in the domain of formal education run against the current of public opinion and may militate against the chances of contracting a stable and harmonious marriage.

4   Literacy in adult life

The measures of adult literacy considered in sections 2 and 3 constitute a very bare, schematic index of the skills and activities represented by that expression. In this section, I will try to flesh out that schema with an account of the intellectual environment within which members of this cohort can deploy the skills of literacy and numeracy. As researchers in several parts of the world have been at pains to point out in recent years (Scribner and Cole 1981; Levine 1982; Heath 1983; Street 1984; Cook-Gumperz 1987), literacy is not adequately characterised as a set of cognitive skills without reference to the social and cultural practices in which they are deployed.

Among the Vai people of Liberia, Sylvia Scribner and Michael Cole (1981) explored in great detail the cognitive consequences of becoming literate in each of three different scripts used in that society. The pattern of skills they found was closely tied to the particular social practices for which each script is used. The indigenous Vai script is learned by tutorial from a friend or neighbour and is used primarily for letter writing. The Arabic script by contrast is learned and used in Vai society almost exclusively in the context of Koranic study, which places a heavy emphasis on recitation of religious texts from memory.

Those Vai individuals who learn the Roman script do so in the context of Western-type schools similar in many respects to rural Zambian primary schools. Scribner and Cole devised a variety of tests which they administered to individuals literate in none, one, two or all of these three scripts. The cognitive skills displayed by those who were literate only in Vai or Arabic tended to be closely confined to the particular contexts in which the script was learned and used. Literacy in the Roman script, on the other hand, was associated with a different and somewhat broader range of school-related cognitive skills.

This apparently more extensive cognitive utility of English literacy seems, on the basis of Scribner and Cole's detailed findings, to be due not to any special feature of the Roman script itself but to the wider range of contexts in which it is deployed in that society. Each type of literacy comprises, in addition to a particular technology and system of knowledge, a 'socially developed and patterned' practice which dictates how the technology and knowledge is used to accomplish tasks. Jack Goody (1987), who collaborated with Scribner and Cole on a case study of one individual who used the Vai script for an exceptionally ambitious set of social purposes (Goody, Cole and Scribner 1987), has emphasised that the crucial factors determining the cognitive scope of literacy are cultural and historical phenomena extended to the individual. When mastering the technology of reading and writing, the learner acquires a focus of interest on the potential of that technology. That potential is structured historically in the form of a cultural practice, and the ways in which literate individuals deploy their cognitive skills are intrinsically bound up with that practice.

In the United States, Shirley Brice Heath (1983) has presented compelling evidence that the uses of English literacy are likewise socially differentiated. She studied three communities residing in close geographical proximity within the Piedmont Carolinas, each of which displayed a distinctive 'literate tradition' which was embedded in other aspects of social organisation. The uses of writing in the everyday life of each community were related in different ways to the dominant patterns of language usage and to parents' socialisation goals and practices. Those children who grow up in middle-class urban homes arrive at school with a set of skills and attitudes towards the organisation of time and space, the telling of stories and the uses of written materials which mesh effortlessly with the design of the school curriculum.[29] Children raised in the two non-'mainstream', working-class communities of 'Trackton' and 'Roadville' arrive with two systematically different sets of presuppositions about the nature of literacy which are embedded in the different home cultures in which their cognitive competencies have developed, neither of which matches the design of the curriculum.

As American society evolves new forms of child socialisation and new patterns of industrial work interface with technology, the forms of literate practice institutionalised in the academic curriculum are liable to become obsolete, and as Heath (1989) has pointed out, some of the non-'mainstream' alternatives may acquire a new relevance to the design of public policy. But the weight of the establishment has tended to focus exclusively on the need for individuals from disempowered, marginalised subcultural groups to adapt to the 'mainstream'. As a result, the literate practices of non-mainstream communities seldom receive serious attention and when they do are generally characterised as both socially deviant and cognitively restricted.

Relative to the status quo in the society as a whole (or what Bronfenbrenner (1979) would term the macrosystem), this characterisation is often accurate in many respects. But the explanation offered by these studies of multiple literacies in Vai and Piedmont society is that the restrictiveness of a particular form of literacy arises from the concrete nature of its instantiation as a social practice rather than from any abstract limitation of its potential as a technology, or from any enduring intellectual limitations of the people who practise it. Historical changes in the culture shared by the population, whether planned or not, are capable of transforming a restricted literacy into a much more powerful and empowering one.

Brian Street has described within the context of a rural Iranian community how the literacy practices engaged in by economically productive local entrepreneurs differed from those of returning high-school students visiting their homes briefly for holidays:

The shift to 'commercial' from 'maktab' [traditional Koranic] literacy for the older generation had taken place within a shared context, with communal interests in and perceptions of literacy. The situation within which literacy was acquired and took on meaning for high-school students was quite alien from this environment and from both the 'maktab' and 'commercial' ideology...

The villagers were quite acutely aware of these differences and were fairly confident in ascribing relative value to the various literacies. (Street 1984, pp. 178–8)

Describing the literate environment of our cohort is quite a challenge. Zambian society generates a good deal of printed material, and the British administration left a number of institutional patterns in place which guarantee accessibility of a fair amount of literature free of charge in the urban centres. But only a narrow band of the population actually utilizes this stock of printed material.

In our trace interview, a series of questions was designed to reveal the scope of what the respondent was reading in this phase of his or her life, as follows:

21. Do you have any calculations/sums to do at work?
22. Do you have any writing to do at work?
23. Any reading at work?
24. What else do you read these days?
25. Do you receive letters from friends or relatives? How often?
26. Do you go to church? (regularly/occasionally/only for special occasions, e.g. weddings/funerals/never)
27. Do you ever read: the Bible; religious pamphlets; newspapers (in English; in Chi-Nyanja); books (in English; in Chi-Nyanja; in other languages); political pamphlets; other documents?
28. What have you read yesterday and/or today?
29. What else have you read in the past week?
30. (if nothing in the past week) When did you last read something? What was it? For how long did you read?[30]

Table 5.8 provides an overview of the literature cited in response to questions 24, 28 and 29 by the literate members of the two contrasting occupational groups. The Traditional Rural Economy group (T/R) comprised individuals engaged in traditional farming in the rural neighbourhood of their childhood origins in Katete District (three men and two women); while the Modern Urban Economy group (M/U) comprised individuals residing in low-income housing in the capital city of Lusaka,[31] and engaged in one of the following types of work: unskilled or semi-skilled wage employment in industry or as domestic helpers, petty retail trading (five men and two women). (When reading the table, it will be useful to remember that the more general question 'What do you read these days?' (TD) was asked at an earlier stage of the interview than the two more focussed questions 'What have you read yesterday and/or today?' (YT) and 'What else have you read in the past week?' (PW).)

Table 5.8 *What various individuals had read yesterday or today (YD), in the past week (PW), and what they read these days (TD)*

Rural farming sector: men

Maganizo (Grade 7)
 YD: a novel in English about a Dutch boat-maker; a book in Chi-Chewa
 PW: the Bible, and other literature
 TD: novels; primary schoolbooks; the Bible

Mavuto (Grade 7)
 YD: one paragraph of a school exercise in science
 PW: eight chapters of St Matthew's Gospel
 TD: just exercise books

Shamba (Grade 7)
    YD: some English schoolbooks
    PW: an Oxford Book 4
    TD: school notes, little books like novels and so on

Rural farming sector: women

Mpeza (Grade 6)
    YD: nothing
    PW: some Chi-Nyanja books lent by a friend: *Lima; Tiyeni Kumudzi; Idesi*
    TD: nothing

Gillian (Grade 5)
    YD: a religious booklet
    PW: another one of the same
    TD: not asked

Modern urban sector: men

Kekerani (Grade 10)
    YD: a newspaper
    PW: a Chase novel; 'I usually buy newspapers when I am well up.'
    TD: newspapers, magazines and novels

Langison (Grade 7)
    YD: a religious booklet
    PW: the same kind of religious booklets
    TD: religious booklets

Esau (Grade 6)
    YD: nothing
    PW: the Bible
    TD: English and Nyanja – like the Bible

Modern urban sector: men

Matthew (Grade 4)
    YD: nothing
    PW: nothing
    TD: 'It's been a while: I used to read the Bible in church but because of travelling to and from the village to collect garlic . . .'

Kamwendo (no schooling; learned to read at church)
    YD: the Bible; *Son of God* magazine
    PW: one or two pages per day
    TD: letters, always in Chi-Nyanja

Modern urban sector: women

Tisiyenji (Grade 6)
    YD: some words of God
    PW: the same, here at home and in church
    TD: 'I don't like reading these days.'

Table 5.8 *(cont.)*

Miriam (Grade 3)
    YD: a booklet on *Nsanja Yolonda*
    PW: nothing else
    TD: 'I don't read these days.'

Only three of the items listed in question 27 were read by all twelve of these respondents: the Bible, religious pamphlets and books in Chi-Nyanja. Religious pamphlets were read frequently by more of the rural respondents (five out of six) than by those living in town (one out of seven). Most of these would have been in Chi-Nyanja.

As I indicated in chapter 2, the total range of literature published in book form in Chi-Nyanja is very limited, comprising mainly novelettes and a few brief treatises on the nature of Chewa traditional wisdom and practices.

Newspapers were read only occasionally, even by those resident in town, and not at all by three of the four women. Zambia Information Services, the Government news agency, used to publish a Chi-Nyanja medium newspaper *Tsopano* fortnightly, with Eastern Province as its main 'target area', but even in 1971 its readership in Eastern Province included only 9 per cent of the adult respondents to a mass media audience survey, whereas 22 per cent of that sample had completed five or more years of schooling, and 'distribution was a major problem' (Mytton 1974, p. 60). In recent years it has ceased to appear regularly, largely because of financial constraints, with the result that reading about the news is necessarily confined to the medium of English. Two English-language newspapers are published daily and have a large circulation in the cities. But they are primarily addressed to people with at least two years of secondary schooling, and much of the vocabulary used in their editorials and feature articles is demanding even for university students.

All the respondents said they received letters from friends or relatives, but none of them as frequently as once a month.

Only two respondents acknowledged having ever read a political pamphlet. Although the national government publishes a fair number of political documents in English, only a small subset are translated into the Zambian languages, and the distribution of these local-language versions tends to be confined to widely separated episodes of electioneering or canvassing of public opinion. It may be that the generic expressions we used to enquire about them failed to bring such documents to our respondents' minds.

Three respondents (all men, two living in the city) said they occasionally read material in another Zambian language. In two cases

this was Ichi-Bemba, the lingua franca of the Copperbelt, while the
third (Kamwendo) claimed that he occasionally reads books in Ichi-
Bemba, Chi-Tonga and Ki-Kaonde.

The answers to our questions about work showed that those
engaged in agriculture all made calculations and kept records, but only
one of them considered that anything he read was pertinent to his
work. This was Mavuto, who stated that he makes frequent reference
to his school notes on science and finds them useful.

The pattern which emerges from this survey suggests that the epi-
stemic scope of the literacy within the reach of this population,
whether living and working in a rural or an urban area, is largely
confined to the Bible and interpretations of it, plus a small dose of
recreational literature in Nyanja.

By contrast, the following responses by our two cohort members
who were engaged in full-time study will be more familiar to many
readers of this book:

John (reflecting on the scope of his reading while at University studying for a
      degree in Business Administration)
      'I read so much. I haven't stopped reading Chemistry, Physics, Mathe-
      matics, stories about new discoveries – a lot more things, that is, outside
      my curriculum.'

Richard (while at home for the last school holiday before sitting for the Grade
         12 examination)
         YT: 'Notes in Physics. I was reading Abbot.'
         PW: 'Chemistry and Geography.'
         TD: 'Revising what I do in School and reading some novels like *River
              between* and *No longer at ease*.'[32]

It is clear that a domain of reading was open to these two young men
which is different in kind from that in which the other members of our
cohort were deploying their literacy skills. Both of them indicated that
their reading was orientated towards the acquisition of new information, and both demonstrated an awareness of subject domains and
types of literature which was missing from the responses of the other
respondents.

5   Contemporary cultural themes informing the pattern of life-journeys

Although the uniquely individualised nature of these experiences
defies any simple form of comprehensive aggregation, certain recurrent themes emerge which have a relevance to the lives of almost all of
our cohort, and which in a sense define the cultural framework of their

generation. In this section of the chapter, I will illustrate each of these themes in terms of contrasts between selected pairs of individuals in the cohort. The contrasts are largely phenomenological. The variables at issue are the subject of ongoing interpretation in relation to as-yet-unresolved dilemmas in these individuals' lives. As they reach decisions and compromises between their personal aspirations and the demands of their immediate situation their perspectives on schooling continue to change in an open-ended process of continuous reinterpretation.

5.1   *Production versus trading*

For many of these young people a tension exists between the demands of two alternative ways of acquiring wealth. As they search for a way of thriving in Zambia's fragmented and unsettled economy the one resource they can be sure of is the land: the subsistence agricultural economy continues to provide adequate food and shelter for survival. But a general consensus now prevails that this way of life constitutes poverty, and the young all want to improve on it. At the minimum they need cash to buy clothes and agricultural tools; many feel a strong desire to acquire other industrial products such as a bicycle and a radio.

The standard solution is to produce more and different crops. This particular area has begun during the period of our research to special-ise in growing garlic, which is informally transported by the producer to the cities, by passenger bus or by negotiating 'lifts' on commercial lorries carrying other goods, and sold with a high profit margin to the Indian-origin community who use it extensively in their cuisine. Other cash crops are sunflower, groundnuts and maize,[33] the latter being also grown as a staple food for the local diet. Only the five-month rainy season is devoted to the production of these crops once per year. Part of the cash they generate is used for the purchase of fertiliser. Veg-etable gardens are cultivated in the dry season and the produce marketed locally, mainly for cash but also occasionally bartered for seed.

For one of our young Grade 7 school leavers (Mavuto) this cycle of production and sale had been the sole focus of his economic activity during the four years since his last year at school. He had produced a sizeable crop in 1987 and declared himself very satisfied with his cur-rent occupation. He got married to a Grade 6 school leaver from the same school in a near-by village three years after leaving school and his ambition is to learn to drive a big lorry so that he can earn better money to help his family. His longer-term ambition is to be a businessman.

His friend and age-mate (Zuze) who grew up with him in the same village, completed Grade 7 one year later and had produced a smaller but quite substantial crop in 1987. He declared himself dissatisfied with his occupation and was in fact quite heavily involved in a parallel activity of trading, travelling to the city to buy washing powder and digital watches for resale in the rural area. He saw his future as a member of a local farming cooperative and concurrently as a trader living in the same rural area. The tension between the labour demands of production and the attraction of opportunities for quick profits in trading seems likely to increase in his life ahead.

Both these young men felt the main value of their schooling for their present occupations related to the keeping of financial records and budgeting. But they also felt they had learned something about agriculture from the School Production Unit, and Mavuto claimed that he sometimes reads his class notes on science and finds them useful.

5.2   *What technical applications does schooling have in agriculture?*

Both Peter and Maganizo are a little older and sat for the Grade 7 selection exam about four years earlier. They both repeated, Maganizo at the same school, Peter at an urban school, and both eventually spent a year or two in one of the less well-endowed private secondary schools in the city. They both tried their luck looking for work in town but eventually gave up and by 1987 were back in Katete District working on the land. Maganizo was articulately enthusiastic about the relevance of his schooling to his current occupation. He stated (in English, in an interview with me) that he had learned at school:

how to plant the seeds; what time you can prepare land, what time you can plant your seeds ... that you should not throw away grass but let it go down and fertilise your land; ... that where you see water destroying your crops you should make some trenches.[34]

In response to my probing he assured me that the old people who did not go to school do not know this. He also attributed his awareness of the value of agriculture to his learning at school:

that when you grow more food around your house there will be no suffering: children will always be happy; ... that it's the most important job around Zambia; ... the need to put effort into farming to improve your country; ... that when you grow more food you'll also help those who suffer in other countries.[35]

By contrast he felt that his schooling had taught him nothing of use for the jobs he tried in town, tailoring and electrical repairs.

Peter, on the other hand, bluntly informed my colleague, Peter Phiri: 'what I have learnt at school is no longer useful to me now.

Maybe when I get a job in future.' Whereas Maganizo is farming independently and supporting his young wife and baby, Peter is still single and helping his father to farm. Maganizo expressed frustration because he lacked the capital to employ labour and expand his production, but he was determined to make a success of it and to become established as a commercial farmer within ten years. Peter feels 'it is tiring to be here at home ... I want to go to town and look for employment.' In five years' time he expects to 'be working somewhere in town' and in ten years 'doing the same type of job'. But 'if I don't get a job I'll continue farming with the help of a loan of fertiliser from the government. In that way I will get the money to take me back to town to look for a job.'[36]

The same division of opinion is echoed in the sentiments expressed by the two members of our cohort who completed the longest periods of schooling, John and Richard. John was a classmate of Maganizo in Grade 7 but scored much higher on the secondary school selection exam. He went on to complete Form 3 and Form 5 at two different secondary schools in the Eastern Province and qualified for a place at the University of Zambia where he completed his second year of studies in 1987. I have already quoted his views (in chapter 4) about the necessity of leaving the village in 'one's quest for advancement'. His career plans are irrevocably urban, and he envisages fulfilling his obligations towards a family which has been very supportive of his long period of full-time study by bringing his parents out of the village too:

for – as they are growing old – at least easy access to medical facilities. *Pali nchito kumunda, anso kuli ... mvula* ('there's work to be done in the fields, and sometimes it's raining') – there's no way they are going to get warm enough, and you know asthma: it's really terrible ... each time I go back and see the same, there are moments when Dad and Mum have horrible nights ... I really feel bad about them.[37]

This passage, which is transcribed verbatim from a tape-recorded interview in which John conversed freely with Chikomeni Banda and myself, illustrates the code-switching discussed in chapter 4. The metaphorical connotation of rural life was probably the semiotic factor motivating the shift into Chi-Chewa at this particular juncture.

But not all secondary school graduates take such a gloomy view of rural life. When Richard was asked in his last term of Form 5 studies about his ambitions he stipulated 'securing employment in the agricultural sector' and, when asked for his reasons, he cited the quality of accommodation in rural areas. Although he hoped to go for further studies beyond Form 5, he saw himself in ten years' time 'working in an agricultural environment, if possible'.

5.3   *Does primary schooling make its students literate?*

The statistics presented in Table 5.1 show the expected pattern of higher degrees of literacy among primary school graduates than among those who do not complete the course. Another comparison, however, is less straightforward to interpret. Among those who experienced less than full primary schooling, literacy scores in Chi-Chewa were consistently higher than in English. Yet throughout the period of our study the prescribed medium of instruction in all the grades was English. Before reporting this pattern of findings to teachers of the school, I used the opportunity of a meeting with them to pool their expectations. 'If a student leaves your school without completing the programme, which language would you expect him or her to be able to read most fluently?' One by one, each of the six teachers assembled in the Head's office explained why they would expect their former pupils to be more literate in English than in Chi-Chewa: far more time is devoted to teaching the children to read and write in English.

Nevertheless, the results on this question were unequivocally contrary to the teachers' expectations. Six members of our cohort were able to read aloud and even write the Chi-Chewa words but could read little or nothing of the English list. Four of these were young people (three of them women) who had attended the school for three to six years, one was a young man who had completed Grade 7 and one had never been to school. Moreover, these young people were fully aware of their greater degree of literacy in Chi-Chewa than in English and mentioned it as a matter of fact during their retrospective interviews with Peter Phiri four years earlier. The only cases where a higher score was assigned for literacy in English than in Chi-Chewa were the three young men with the longest periods of schooling, all of whom were literate in both languages but professed to read more extensively in English.

Very similar findings have been reported recently from Kenya, another country where English has been adopted as the principal medium of primary school instruction in rural areas despite the fact that it is rarely used outside the school context. Eisemon describes as follows the results of systematically varying the language of presentation and of questioning, when texts from the Koran and from a health science textbook were presented to a sample of primary school students in their local language, Ki-Swahili, in Arabic or in English:

comprehension declines when children are presented with texts and questions in a language used only for school instruction and examination ... Comprehension of the religion and science texts seriously declined when the texts were presented to the children in English and they were also questioned in English, despite the fact that all children received instruction in English for at least three years and were being prepared to take the school leaving examinations in English. (Eisemon 1988, pp. 95, 101)

We questioned the women in our sample who had young children about their children's health and asked to see their clinic cards. An interesting contrast emerged between two young mothers, who are close personal friends and neighbours. The elder, Mpeza, who completed five years of schooling, had a 4-year-old and a 1-month-old baby. Her friend, Yumba, who is younger by a year completed one year less of schooling and had just one child aged 3 months. Mpeza responded to my request with a clear account of the meaning of the graph showing the child's weight including both the level and the slope. Her friend, however, stated that she didn't know what the graph meant. Unable to read at all, she thought the card was only for recording immunisations.[38] Yet this young woman correctly calculated in her head the total of 20 times 20n as K4.00, whereas her more literate friend decided to work out K4.00×7 in writing and eventually gave up without having found an answer. Situational factors may have influenced this particular failure, but several of the young women who were unable to read showed themselves able to perform mental arithmetic quite rapidly.

Another striking aspect of the relation between schooling and literacy emerges from the case of Gillian, who was a year ahead of Mpeza at school in Grade 5 in 1979 but refused to re-register in 1980. One of our family discussions that year focussed on the reasons for her withdrawal and she publicly endorsed her parents' contention that the decision was her own. Her reason:

Ndinaona kuti kuwelenga sindidziwa kuwelenga koma ndili Grade 5. Lomba chifukwa chache ndinanena kuti sukulu ndileka sindidzapitakonso ... ndalama zingopita ku sukulu ... ndikapumule ku mudzi.

'I could see I didn't know how to read and yet I'm in Grade 5. So that's why I said "I'm leaving school, I won't go back" ... money could just be wasted on me going to school ... I decided I could just as well take a rest at home.'[39]

Three years later she reiterated in an interview with Peter Phiri:

Linandikanga sukulu ... Ine ku sukulu palibe chimene ndinaphunzilako.

'School was too tough for me ... personally I didn't learn anything at school.'

Then, as an afterthought:

Amene anandiphunziwa uwelenga Chi-Nyanja ndi Amai.

'The one who taught me how to read Chi-Nyanja (=Chi-Chewa) is my Mum.'[40]

It was not until five years later that we secured an interview with

Gillian's mother,[41] who confirmed that she had indeed taught her daughter to read at home some time between 1980 and 1983, using Chi-Nyanja books that she had kept from her own school days. She herself had learned to read and write in Chi-Nyanja in a matter of two years, back in the mid-fifties at a local school (now closed down); and it seems her daughter, Gillian, likewise picked it up rather quickly, having failed to learn anything about reading and writing throughout five years of English-medium schooling. When we assessed her literacy in 1987 the only English word that Gillian could recognise on our list was 'school', whereas she was able to read aloud correctly the full list of Chi-Chewa words. She also wrote one of them and a number in a shaky but legible script. She told us that she reads the Bible and Prayer Book occasionally, that she reads her own letters herself but gets her husband (a Grade 6 school leaver) to write her replies.

5.4 *Is marriage a career for women?*

All three of these young women were married and actively engaged in the family's agricultural production which appeared to be a genuinely joint project with their husbands. Only one of the sixteen women we interviewed described her work as that of housekeeping. Those living in a village always focussed immediately on their agricultural work. Some of the city-dwellers sell vegetables at the market and one works in a shop. One of our cohort (Ngosa) is raising two children alone and has ambitions to expand the scale of her farming, first with a scotch-cart, later by buying some cattle.

Only one (Jelita) is in paid employment as a salesperson in a small shop in a peri-urban market. She is the most literate of the women in our cohort. She dropped out of Grade 6 in the same year as Gillian and claimed three years later that she had stopped for similar reasons. But she had in fact learned to read in Chi-Chewa by that time and by 1987 was even able to read our list of English occupations. The more probable reason for her discontinuing her schooling is that she gave birth to a child in that year.[42] Later she was married for two years to another man but they divorced without having any children together. Her first and only child is being raised in the village by his maternal grandmother while his mother is working in town.

5.5 *Where is home?*

I have deliberately used the bureaucratic term 'domicile' in Table 5.1 because the concept of home is subjectively complex for these young people. Even our university student (John), so committed to the city life, will probably continue throughout his life to refer to Kondwelani as 'home'. The ambivalence which this usage symbolises is reflected in many other ways. One of the young men we interviewed in 1987, Mbulande, informed us that he was visiting his parental village for the purpose of documenting his place of birth for registration as an adult citizen.[43]

He was hoping to find a wife also during this visit, and seemed in fact uncertain whether he would go back to his job in the provincial town or remain 'at home' and resume farming. He explained:

Ndiona kuti kuja nditailako chabe nthawi yanga.

'I can see I'm just wasting my time there.'[44]

This was because he was earning a pittance for working as a delivery hand for a grocery shop – although with free food and accommodation this had enabled him to buy a rather smart set of clothes which made him quite conspicuous in the village.

This young man had left school in Grade 4 or Grade 6 but denied he had ever been to school. He claimed he was now learning to read in Chi-Nyanja from a friend with secondary schooling, who was tutoring him along with another young man in the evenings at his house in town. All he was able to read of our English list were two words: 'school' and 'teacher', and his performance on the Chi-Chewa list was no better. He tried to calculate his annual salary from the monthly rate of K70 by writing down 140 six times and then 280 four times. The result was wildly inaccurate.

5.6   *What future lies in the city?*

Another of our Grade 6 school leavers (Esau) was living in the capital city in 1987, married with three children. He was now with his fourth employer as a house-servant, the previous jobs having lasted for three months, four months and eighteen months. He ranked his present occupation highest in the preference ratings, but expressed a long-term ambition to become a businessman in town. His reason:

Kumudzi kuli usiwa ndichifukwa chache ndifuna usewenza kuno ku tauni.

'In the rural areas there is poverty – that's why I want to work here in town.'[45]

He has occasion to use his literacy for recording telephone messages in his boss' house but reads little for pleasure, and never reads the newspaper.

One of the town-dwellers who was the object of envious admiration by his contemporaries still living in Kondwelani was Kamwendo, who never went to school but managed to get a driving licence and was employed as a driver-cum-general-assistant in a city shop. Yet, despite this economically advantageous position, Kamwendo informed us that he 'would like to go back home to do farming after two or three years'. Why?

'Because nowadays in Lusaka food is very expensive – I'm sweating to feed one child and my wife. What if God agrees for me to have four or five children? I can be suffer. That's why I want to go back.'

In five years' time he is 'planning to be back to the land farming'.[46]

5.7   *How much schooling is enough?*

During the 1983 retrospective interviews, most of those six who had pursued their studies up to Grade 7 or at secondary school were strongly committed to a continuation of their education, mentioning private schools and correspondence classes as alternatives in the event of exclusion from the mainstream of government secondary schools. A similar commitment was expressed by the one boy who was still continuing in Grade 6. Only one of them, a young man who dropped out in the second term of Form 2, expressed some hesitation, as follows: 'I am thinking of sitting for Form 3 examinations through correspondence. If I do well, I will proceed to studying GCE O-Levels if chances allow.'[47] By 1987 these plans had largely disappeared and the school leavers had settled down to try and earn a living.

Among thirteen individuals whose schooling was interrupted before the end of Grade 6, eight (six women and two men) were quite definite by 1983 that they had no intention of pursuing any further education. Only one young man, Shamba, had a firm intention of resuming school. He had reached Grade 6 when his maternal uncle (a very influential relative according to Chewa matrilineal custom) prevailed over his father's wishes for him to continue in school and he was withdrawn to keep his uncle's cattle with a promise, as yet unfulfilled, that some of them would be passed on to him. This young man was still planning (seven years after being withdrawn from Grade 6) to re-enrol as a full-time pupil in Grade 5. He had discussed the idea some time back with the Deputy Headmaster of the school and had been encouraged to come back at the beginning of the year. This apparent 'pipe-dream' turned out to be a genuine plan. Six years later we found he had indeed resumed his schooling in Grade 5 later that year, and had continued up to Grade 7 in 1985, at an age of about 22. Like so many others, however, he did not qualify for a place in Form 1. He was therefore now farming at home and, as he put it, helping his parents.

During the preparatory discussion for the popular theatre workshop in 1988 (described in chapter 6) a group of us had occasion in 1988 to quiz Shamba a little more intensively about his motives and attitudes towards schooling. When we asked him what benefit he felt he had derived from school he emphasised literacy. 'But just how', one of us asked, 'does that relate to the help you now say you are rendering to your parents, since you say you are just farming here in the village?'

Oo, thandizo yake ndikuti: nga kuno ku mudzi pali ulandila kalata apa mudzi, andiuza kuti 'welengako'. Olo kwamfumu komwe ati 'welengako kalata': ndawelengela. Also, nga amai andituma, ati 'ndilembako kalata', ndalemba.

'I see. Well the way it helps is: suppose a letter arrives here in the village, they tell me "read it". Even if it's for the Headman himself, he says "read the letter": so I read it for him. Also, if my mother asks me "write a letter for me", I write it.'

Proudly though this dramatic little account was delivered, one of the outsiders was not satisfied, and asked in Chi-Chewa:

'You tell us you started school, you left off half way through, you stayed for some years, then you came back to school again. That time when you left in Grade 6, didn't you already know how to write?' He did. 'So, why did you go back to school again after you had been herding?'
'I wanted to go further.'
'Why did you want to go further since you'd already got the benefit of reading and writing the way you help with these days?'
'Well, my hope was that my studies would go further. Because Grade 6 and Grade 7 are much the same. I thought if I continued, maybe I could go to secondary. That's the reason why I went on with my schooling.'[48]

There was quite an audience for this exchange. Did we, I wonder pressure Shamba into producing the stock reason for wanting to continue his schooling? Did we coax him into revealing a consideration he had suppressed, or was his initial explanation what he really felt?

5.8   *The next generation*

Many of our cohort are now parents themselves. We asked them whether they would in due course send these children to school. The answer was unanimously affirmative. Even those who were sceptical of the value of schooling in their own lives, nevertheless insisted that their children should be 'given the chance'. They attributed their own 'failure' to benefit to lack of *nzelu* or to not having started early enough in life or to some other accident. None of them was ready to question the fundamental appropriateness or intrinsic value of schooling, however much it seemed to an outside observer to have let them down. Time will tell whether this endorsement is backed up in practice, or whether like many of their parents' generation they will find that other matters acquire higher priority.

6 Intellectual, social and cultural connotations of school failure and success

At the moment of initial enrolment, many parents, teachers and children in Kondwelani seem to agree on the premise that any child can make a success of it. Yet by the time they reach Grade 4 or 5, around the age of 12 to 15, most of the girls have decided that school is not the place for them. Their explanation is twofold: (1) 'girls in general, and I in particular, do not have the intellectual ability to cope with the curriculum'; (2) 'the most important challenge at this stage in my life is to get married and start a family, and further schooling will contribute little or nothing to my attainment of those goals: indeed it may even impede it'.

This sexist view of schooling as an intrinsically masculine enterprise is so widely endorsed that one member of our cohort, Tisiyenji, enunciated it quite casually during an interview with Peter Phiri, three years after she had left school at the end of Grade 6. She was now recently married at the age of 19.

PP: *Kodi munachita bwino kuchoka sukulu?*
T: *Chilekelenji ukhala chabwino? Uphunzila kufunika inu anzathu azimuna. Ife akazi sitikutha kwathu kuno.*
PP: *Chifukwa chiani atsikana akudza kwathu simukonda kukhala pa sukulu?*
T: *Pali zifukwa zambili – ukhuta mimba, upanda nzelu pasukulu, ndiponso olo apite ku Secondary sapasa Form 3.*[49]

PP: Did you make a good move to leave school?
T: Why shouldn't it be a good move? Schooling is useful for you menfolk from back home. We womenfolk from home aren't up to it.
PP: Why is it that you girls from our area don't like to stay on at school?
T: There are lots of reasons – getting pregnant; lack of *nzelu* at school; and then again, even if they go to secondary, they don't pass in Form 3.

For boys the credibility of schooling is threatened by its weak linkage with economic opportunities. They see around them examples of relatively wealthy and respected men who did not go to secondary school, and increasingly they also see young men returning to the village after secondary school with no apparent gains beyond some symbols of participation in a prestigious, but also alien culture. Those who withdraw from school before Grade 7 also subscribe to a twofold explanation: (1) 'I lacked the ability to climb that crucial last step up into the secondary school'; and (2) 'it is very doubtful whether further schooling would have brought me the wealth and status I aspire to as a young man: it might well have slowed me down'. Among those who stop schooling at the end of Grade 7, some of the young men explain their situation in the same way. Others, given the growing number of private secondary schools in the cities which accept students who completed Grade 7 but did not obtain high enough marks on the secondary school selection exam to qualify for a place in a government secondary school, while subscribing to reason (2), give as their first reason that (1) 'I couldn't find a sponsor to pay my fees for continuing my education.'

In all these lines of explanation, the same ambivalence about schooling is apparent. The agenda specified by the curriculum was accepted to the point where non-completion of the primary course, and indeed of the secondary course for which the primary currriculum is so explicitly geared as a preparation, is construed as a personal failure. A complementary shift in attitude towards the school curriculum devalues it as lacking relevance and power within the framework of local cultural values. The pain of failure is softened by the discovery that one didn't really need to succeed. For the young women, a new phase of personal development with its own rewards provides a convincing rationale for putting the disappointment of school failure behind them, but its relevance to economic success is kept alive by shifting it across to a gender-segregated domain. For the young men, distancing themselves from schooling requires a different categorical distinction. For some this purpose is served by social class, based on wealth, residence and cultural style: schooling is good for (and accessible to) the *apamwamba*, the 'upper class'.

Two conversations illustrate the tensions underlying these compartmentalisation strategies. The first is between a university-educated woman and the mother of Gillian, whose contrasting experience with English and Chi-Chewa literacy was described above in Section 5.3. Tamika Kaluwa, whose role in the participatory popular theatre will be described in chapter 6, accompanied me and two other urban-based members of the theatre team to the home of Gillian's mother to follow up our documentation of how it came about that Gillian, having left school in Grade 5 without learning how to read or write in English, was later able to learn how to read and write Chi-Nyanja under the tutelage of her mother at home:

Tamika Kaluwa: *Iwo A-Gillian anatani? Anati ndiwo ekha analiufuna uleka?*
Amake Gillian: *Sukulu ka? Ee. Analeka iye ekha, ee.*
TK: *Alibe umufotokozelani chifukwa chikulu ichi analeka? Sanakambe?*
AG: *Koma analikufeluka-feluka kawili kawili. Lomba anakana kupita. Kuyetsa kuchichiliza kuti: 'pitani kusukulu, mukaphunzile'. Anakana.*
TK: *Mm.*
AG: *Ee.*
TK: *Bwanji? Sanali uphunzitsa bwino maticha, mwina sanali umvetsa bwino Gillian?*

AG: *Kaya: sindinadziwe bwino bwino kapena sanaliumvela za analiukamba aticha, kaya, kaya ndikufa kwamutu iye, kaya.*

TK: *Koma 'kufa kwamutu'! Mwina simungathe kukamba kuti ndi kufa kwamutu, pakuti imwe apa munaliuwaphunzitsa AGillian ulemba mu Chi-Chewa, uwelenga Chi-Chewa. AGillian anaphunzila: ndiye kuti mutu wao unali bwino bwino chabe, ka!*

(laughter)

AG: *Koma usafuna sukulu: avimba mu moyo wake.*

TK: *Koma m'tima ofuna uphunzila unalipo . . .*

AG: *Ee, unalipo.*

TK: *. . . chifukwa anaphunzila Chi-Chewa.*

AG: *Ee.*

TK: What did Gillian say? Did she say she wanted to leave of her own accord?

AG: School, you mean? Yes, she left of her own accord.

TK: She didn't let you know what was the main reason why she left? Didn't she say?

AG: Well, she kept failing again and again. And then she refused to go. I tried to reason with her and say: "go to school, so you can learn". She refused.

TK: Mm.

AG: Yes.

TK: How come? Were the teachers not teaching well, or was it that Gillian wasn't paying attention?[50]

AG: I don't know. I really didn't know for sure: maybe she wasn't listening to what the teachers said, maybe; or maybe she was just thick-headed,[51] I don't know!

(laughter)

TK: What? 'Thick-headed'? But you can't say she was thick-headed, because you yourself taught Gillian to write in Chi-Chewa and to read Chi-Chewa. And Gillian learned: which means her head was just fine, you know!

AG: Well, it was a case of not wanting school – something deep down inside her.[52]

TK: But the urge to learn was there in her heart . . .

AG: 'Yes, it was there.'

TK: . . . because she did learn Chi-Chewa.

AG: Yes.

Clearly, Tamika put quite a lot of pressure on Gillian's mother in this exchange. But her agreement seemed genuine, and she went on to explain with enthusiasm how she had set about teaching her daughter to read using old Nyanja textbooks and demonstrating writing. The strategy of blaming her daughter's school failure on inadequate intelligence was transparently inadequate once it was pointed out to her. And in fact the hesitant manner in which she first advanced the hypothesis suggests that her heart was not in it from the outset. It has become almost a cliché in contemporary Zambian discourse about one's educational career to attribute one's failures to 'thick-headedness'. Since none of the interviewing team were known to Gillian's mother in advance of this interview, and we were all evidently from the city and presumably highly educated (in the school-based sense of that term), it may well have seemed appropriate to her to concede the possibility that her daughter's lack of ability was the problem. But it would not be wise to conclude from this that all of the self-deprecatory comments made by our cohort in interviews about their school failure were merely superficial, rhetorical gambits. Many of these remarks were embedded in conversations among people well known to one another, and the sentiments they expressed are widely echoed in Zambian society.

A quite different conversation took place in my house in Lusaka among Chikomeni Banda, myself and the member of our cohort named Richard, who was on his way back, after a visit to his parents in Kondwelani, to the University of the Copperbelt where he was about to embark on his third year of studies in Business Administration. After discussing Richard's career plans, which were focussed on setting up as an independent businessman, I asked:

RS: What else do you think you've got out of the education you've received? I mean, do you find yourself reading for pleasure? Do you read outside your curriculum at all?

Richard's initial response concerning his reading habits was cited above in Section 5.2. Next he went on to say:

R: From going to school I've also met a lot of friends, and it's just interesting. It's really interesting. I wouldn't have met them if I'd stayed at home. I've met a lot of friends; some are really good to me. And we have a lot of nice times together, which I wouldn't have got if I was just staying at home.

As the conversation progressed, it turned out that one of Richard's closest friendships was formed at secondary school, with a young man who grew up in a rural area adjacent to Kondwelani. Later I asked:

RS: Do you find that ... the friendships you have with people who've been to secondary school, or even to campus, with you are very different from the friendships you have with people who you grew up with, but they didn't go beyond Grade 7?

R: Yes. If I go to the village. You must have seen some of the shoes I wear? ... When I go away, I try by all means to be simple, and really mix with them, but it's real difficult: they will always try to get busy ... There are very few people who can be real mates ... And most of them, you'd be simple, don't talk English, talk Nyanja throughout − still somehow they'll try to find a mistake and say 'Ah, look! Why, that one? That one is from the University.' And, OK, they associate University education with riches, which you may not have ... So, OK, style of life has changed. But you may try and (*)[53] them and be with them, ask for their company, understanding. But it's difficult. There's just one person who, I feel, is quite a blessing, Zuze: he's been a good friend all through. He's been so nice. He doesn't ...

CB: No hang-ups.

R: No hang-ups. You won't find him in a (*) and then he says 'he has come here, let me run away from him!' We will always be together. If he has his own programme, he'll say 'This is my programme. Can we do this, this?' We do it together ... Otherwise the rest will look onto you with that kind of 'Yeah, look this is a nice, educated man. Just leave him be...'

CB: 'Leave him alone.'

R: '...leave him alone.' So, some people don't really understand, no matter how simple I try to be. It's difficult. Some do understand, but they are very few.

I asked for examples of the kind of issue around which Kondwelani residents would tend to rationalise their unwillingness to treat a University-educated person as part of the in-group, and both Richard and Chikomeni cited cases of being excluded from participation in routine manual chores, which they themselves were confident of being able and willing to perform. Not only their age-mates but also their parents tend to be overprotective. The attitudes lying behind this alienating set of barriers which both of them had encountered during their visits 'back home', beginning when they embarked on a secondary education and with increasing intensity over the years, were summarised as follows:

CB: I think that's what education meant to those people. I mean that is the definition: sending me to school, I have to be a *bwana*.

R: Yes. You have to be more than just what they are.

CB: You have to be a *muzungu*. And the moment you want to disappoint them, they say 'Look...'

R: They say 'Now what did we send this kid for?'

CB: 'What's wrong with him?'

In this discussion, two of the most educationally successful sons of Kondwelani community seemed to concur that they had been required to sacrifice any possibility of real social integration as adult members of their natal community. Neither of them felt this was a price they should have been required to pay for their education. Neither thinks of himself, nor wants to be perceived by others as a replica of the colonial *bwana* (master), or as a *muzungu*, a person with the cultural values of Europeans. Viewed from the inside, the experience of living in the big city, while bringing many material and social benefits, is impoverished by a loss of continuity as a full member of the community into which they were born. Whereas the experience of Gillian shows the inadequacy of the notion that only those without intelligence are unable to benefit from school education, the experience of Richard belies the notion that successful mastery of the curriculum will confer all of the rewards of personal fulfilment.

If, as I have been suggesting, we should reject as inadequate the compartmentalised view of schooling as only valuable as a preparation for upper-class, city-dwelling men, what should we put in its place? Many of the young people whose life-journeys have been discussed in this chapter fall into neither of the extreme categories of abject failure or unqualified success. They emerge as relatively autonomous students who charted their own course through a few grades of the school system. Within the context of school activities they complied superficially with the directives of a rigid and often inhospitable curriculum. But they displayed an autonomous eclecticism with respect to schooling, seeking to use the system to their personal advantage, opting in and out of attendance in accordance with a private agenda which was only partly accessible to either their parents or their teachers. Rather than 'trajectories' into which they were propelled by an external impetus, I have therefore preferred to describe the developmental sequences in this chapter as life-journeys.

6

Dialogue and accountability: the school as a community resource

1   Local accountability of schooling and research

Schooling in Kondwelani community, as we saw in chapter 5, carries a variety of meanings in the lives of different individuals and contributes in various strikingly different ways to their life-journeys. These findings are somewhat at variance with the official ideology of education described in chapters 3 and 4, which informs the design of the school curriculum and the training of teachers, as well as many other aspects of public decision-making in contemporary Zambian society. That ideology construes the impact of schooling as more homogeneous, discontinuous and mechanistic than we found it to be in the actual experiences of our cohort. The account of those experiences given in chapter 5 suggests that young people who enrolled in school did so with a sense of purpose and made eclectic use of it as a resource in the pursuit of their personal life-journey's independent agenda. They and their families seem to share as agreed premises with the school authorities some aspects of the official ideology but not others.

Such discrepancies in understanding of the schooling process may constitute at least a partial explanation for the failure of public education programmes in Zambia and many other Third World countries to attain more than a small fraction of their objectives. This chapter will describe two different attempts made at different stages of the project to explore this possibility through the confrontation of certain contradictory opinions in the presence of local professionals and their clients. Although the initiative for this part of the project was my own, it took shape gradually in close consultation, and eventually in active collaboration, with a number of colleagues. Chikomeni Banda has already featured in chapter 2 as the undergraduate student at UNZA who first introduced me to Kondwelani School, to his home village near by, and thus also to the whole community in 1973. At the time this feedback phase of the research began in 1980, Chikomeni Banda, BA (with Education) had completed a period of service as a secondary school teacher in Zambia's Luapula Province, was enrolled in the second year of UNZA's postgraduate study programme and had begun to collect data for his dissertation (Banda 1981) leading to the Master's degree in Education. As our plan evolved, Chikomeni introduced me to two undergraduate students at UNZA who had grown up in the Kondwelani community and, like Chikomeni himself, had received part of their primary education at Kondwelani School. Godfrey Banda was studying for a BA degree in Economics, and Peter Phiri was studying for a BSc (with Education) degree in Mathematics.

Our purpose in the activities described in this chapter was to feed back and share with the community what we felt we had learned from them in our research, with the ultimate objective of empowering the actors whose activities and situations had been documented to use that information in socially productive ways. The very fact that such a deliberate, planned process of feedback appeared to be necessary reflects the degree to which our understanding as researchers was experienced as alienated from the self-understanding of community members themselves. Often the process of theorising in social science is construed as transcending or 'rising above' everyday understanding. The principles of abstraction and generalisation are construed as generating a set of concepts, relations and regularities which are superordinate to those accessible to actors from the flow of down-to-earth, daily experience. Yet, as I have argued in the Appendix, this 'superordinacy' is obtained at a price: it entails a loss of that immediacy and certainty which characterises the 'primary theory' (Horton 1982) and 'emergent structure' (Lakoff and Johnson 1980) informing people's everyday understanding. And, more often than not, it requires a detachment from the fine-grain detail which imparts to our real-world experiences their uniqueness and intensity. In defending abstract generalisations against the charge of a consequent loss of contact with reality, theorists sometimes describe themselves as 'retreating to high ground', a metaphor which connotes not only the 'bird's-eye view' of Mount Olympus,[1] but also its godly elitism. The attempts described in this chapter to share the results of research with members of the community were motivated by a desire to escape from both of these traps for the professional theorist: the loss of contact with reality and the illusion of moral superiority.

2 Public debate: the village discussions

2.1 *Rationale*

Our first attempt was organised along the lines of a public policy debate, focussing on specific arguments about the appropriateness of selected aspects of the school's activities and their behavioural consequences in relation to agreed community goals. A deliberate effort was made in the planning of this exercise to redress the imbalance of power between non-literate members of the client community and representatives of the educational bureaucracy. The discussions were held in the medium of their local language, on the villagers' home territory, and were preceded by the distribution in writing of selected statements, some critical of the school's activities, some supportive, by various adult relatives of children currently enrolled in the local school.

In the course of our family discussions concerning specific decisions on school enrolment and withdrawal, we had placed considerable emphasis on eliciting from parents and other influential adult relatives their explicit evaluations of what their children could, should and did in fact derive from schooling. A selection of arguments stated in their own words by village elders in the context of these conversations with the research team was made as follows. The tape-recordings of the family discussions were transcribed, translated and analysed by Godfrey Banda and Peter Phiri, the two university students mentioned above, both of whom had grown up in this community and, in an earlier generation, attended the same primary school. These transcripts were then reviewed by myself and by Chikomeni Banda, who had assisted in conducting some of the discussions during the preceding year.

2.1.1   *Agricultural production*

One of the striking features of the protocols was the intensity and conviction with which many of the discussants addressed the topic of the School Production Unit. This was the official designation for a small farming plot allocated to the school, in which pupils received on-the-job training in basic agricultural techniques as part of their curriculum and from which the produce was sold commercially to raise funds for various school requirements and activities. Unlike many of the other topics we had raised, this one seemed to make an immediate connection with local people's current preoccupations, and to elicit clearly articulated value judgements, some positive, others negative. Moreover, a complementary preoccupation with this topic was also current among educational planners in Lusaka. The concept was still relatively new at this time and had been reaffirmed as part of the national primary curriculum in the latest major policy document, the *Educational reform proposals and recommendations*.[2]

The conventional wisdom of the branch of academic research known as Development Studies identifies agricultural production and primary health care (discussed below) as two of the key domains of

---

Box 6.1 Opinions expressed by village elders on the value of current practices at their local primary school concerning agriculture (*za-malimidwe*)*

When Mr Serpell and Mr Chikomeni Banda from the University of Zambia came to Chief Kathumba's area, they asked many of the elders about the value of the school children having an agricultural plot. And this is what they found.

Some people said 'it's useful to have a ... "production unit" at the school',

> because it'll be helpful to them when they have their own plots if they drop out of school.

From the school plot children:

> learn how to farm and they will be able to teach agricultural methods to their fellows.

> They sell their produce and use the income to pay for transport to go and play football at other schools, and when they have matches here they buy their fellows food and make snacks ...

Others, however, said that what the children do in their plot is not useful, because:

> they don't see the use to which the income is put which they earn at the production unit.

On the topic of modern agricultural methods, some said

> they are not teaching them to the schoolchildren, and what they do at the school plot aren't things which would be useful to them if they stop in Grade 7 and don't go to secondary school.

Others said the schoolchildren learn about modern agricultural methods through the Agricultural Extension Assistants.

*Translated excerpts from Peter Z. Phiri (June 1981) Maganizo yamakolo a m'midzi pa zamalimidwe ya ana a sukulu. Lusaka: University of Zambia, Institute for African Studies (mimeo).

---

knowledge and skills in which progress is required if impoverished rural communities in the Third World are to take responsibility at a local level for efforts to improve their quality of life. Zambia's national educational planners were doubtless influenced by this literature and by Julius Nyerere's ideals of education for self-reliance (1968) in justifying the concept of school production units which was formally announced in the mid-1970s and has received fluctuating emphasis since then. In 1981 the fifty-two schools of Katete District harvested crops worth K13,700,[3] which is an average of nearly K270 per school. The exact figure for our Friendly school is not available but in the preceding year they sold their production unit's crop of nineteen bags of sunflower for K310; and the year before that they harvested twenty-eight bags of maize which earned them K260, a great improvement on their 1978 crop of seven bags which fetched only K50.[4]

The attitudes expressed towards the School Production Unit among the parents we interviewed were quite varied (cf. Box 6.1). One sceptical comment from a father who never went to school himself was: 'What's needed at school is lessons about writing. We're very pleased with that, 'cos our children become bosses ... but when it comes to farming that's our speciality from long ago' (*ndi zathu zakale*). The unstated implication (which emerged also in other transcripts) was that the teachers were out of their depth when it comes to farming or, if not out their depth, then trespassing on the prerogatives of parents. Many parents complained about their children borrowing the home's farming tools for work in the Production Unit. This was seen as adding insult to injury, following the phasing out by government of the free provision of pencils and paper in schools. Some parents voiced suspicion about where the profits went to (although our independent enquiries suggested there was no misappropriation). Several expressed the view that teachers were exploiting the school children by making them work on their private vegetable gardens.

The issue of how earnings from the Production Unit should be spent is a vexed one, as are all transactions involving that rare commodity – hard cash – in this area. The three university-educated 'sons' of the area, however, felt that the Production Unit was one line of positive development worth pursuing, in the light of at least some positive responses from parents in the family discussions (see Box 6.1). Thus the topic of agricultural production was identified as holding some promise for convergence between the concerns of pupils' families and those of the teachers and curriculum developers, and was selected as a theme around which we might hope to promote a constructive discourse in the community related to one aspect of the significance of schooling.

2.1.2   *Primary health care*

Another theme on which we decided to focus was that of health. Research by Wim Hoppers (1980) in another rural district of Zambia had shown that Grade 7 school leavers tended to place a high priority on maintaining their personal and domestic hygiene, so that these served as conspicuous symbolic indicators within their communtiy setting of their educational attainment. We noted what appeared to be

Box 6.2 Opinions expressed by village elders on the value of current practices at their local primary school concerning health and hygiene (*za-ukhondo*)*

Mr Chikomeni Banda and Professor Robert Serpell ... wanted to find out whether the elders find it useful for children to learn about health at school even if they don't continue their studies beyond Grade 6 ... On the topic of health (the prevention of illness) there are traditional medicines (*mankhwala yaung'anga*) and there is education about hygiene which is often learned at school ... When they were asked about the teaching of hygiene at school, the elders replied that it's a useful thing to teach, because:

> We see that they're nice and clean, both in taking baths and in looking after their clothes.

> She comes home and tells me 'Mother, at school they tell us we should boil drinking water, then pour in into a clay pot and keep it in a nice cool place, so that all the germs in the water die.

> They also know how to sweep the house.

> Schoolboys are different from those who herd cattle: they are hygienic.

One thing many people were opposed to was the idea of teaching traditional medicine at the school. Here are some of the reasons given:

> Traditional healers don't like revealing their medicines.

> Some traditional healers just talk bunkum, and there's no use teaching children bunkum. Different traditional healers give you different diagnoses for the same condition.

So it's better to go to the clinic, because traditional healers could just suck people dry of money.

> It's not desirable to teach children about our village medicines over there at the school.

Because the teaching of our village medicines is adapted to the child's particular behaviour. At school there are mentally disturbed children and clear-headed children all mixed in together; so they couldn't teach them this kind of medicine.

Those who gave a bit of support to the idea said it's useful for children just to know about their elders' practices, but not for them to become traditional healers themselves.

*Translated excerpts from Godfrey Banda (June 1981) Maganizo yamakolo am'midzi pa zaukhondo wa ana asukulu. Lusaka: University of Zambia, Institute for African Studies (mimeo).

an appreciative acknowledgement of the same phenomenon in some of the remarks by parents on the subject of health in our family discussions (see Box 6.2).

Here too, we reasoned, was a potential consequence of schooling which might be appreciated by the client population as having a direct and positive bearing on their quality of life. Moreover, the Zambian government had not only endorsed the Alma Ata declaration on Primary Health Care (WHO/UNICEF 1978) but had also recently launched a vigorous nationwide development programme to lay the foundations for such an approach to the delivery of affordable, decentralised health services with an emphasis on preventive health education. Primary schools appeared to be an ideal institutional channel for dissemination of such ideas to a broad slice of the population at a formative stage in their intellectual and moral development. Paul Freund and Katele Kalumba (1984) have described the results of some exploratory experimentation with ways in which this practical disposition and parental receptiveness could be harnessed to PHC efforts at some other rural primary schools in Zambia's Western Province. Earlier efforts along similar lines have been reported by Hall (1980) in the Mwacisompola Health demonstration zone. More recently the Child-to-Child programme promoted by the Institute of Child Health in London has revived interest in Zambia in this approach.

These two themes were thus adopted as the framework of a purposive search through the transcripts for clearly articulated value judgements by local community elders and parents on the value of current practices at their local primary school. The collections of statements eventually printed for distribution are reproduced, in translation, in Boxes 6.1 and 6.2. A deliberate attempt was made to include statements which were to a certain extent mutually contradictory, or at least opposite in tone. This feature of the selection was designed to highlight the legitimacy of differences of opinion within the same community, in the hope of thus encouraging individuals to express their own opinions freely without feeling obliged to conform with views previously expressed by others.

2.2   *Planning*

Equipped with these focussed selections of local opinion, we next turned our attention to the project of animating participation in a series of community discussions by the professional personnel of relevant local services. The school itself had been apprised of several of the major themes reflected in our family discussions, immediately following the period of 'fieldwork' in which they were conducted. This was a normal courtesy extended to the staff of the school in appreciation of the supportive interest they had shown in the project over the years, but on this occasion we took advantage of having taken a tape-recorder with us, to record the discussion which ensued among the staff of the school. Analysis of this recording indicated that the Head-master held definite views about what his school should and could realistically hope to do in the way of enhancing the impact of its programme on the client community, but that he was also willing to consider new ideas, and was interested to learn more of what parents had told us about their expectations of the school and their evaluation of its performance. We therefore approached him about the possibility of liaison with the local health centre, the local agricultural extension service and the local community development programme. He gladly agreed to hold some planning sessions at the school, together with the personnel of these other three arms of Government and the research team.

A guiding principle of the introduction to these sessions was to 'hand over' the knowledge generated by the research to date and to relinquish control of how it should be used. The problem focus which had first inspired the project back in 1973 was briefly reviewed, fol-lowed by an account of how its terms of reference had shifted and widened, from the elicitation and systematisation of indigenous con-cepts of intellectual functioning, to an exploration of the circumstances impinging on families' decisions on whether to enrol children in school and subsequently on whether to withdraw them before completion of the seven-year primary programme.

I then explained that, in consultation with my colleagues, two of whom (Godfrey Banda and Peter Phiri, both offspring of the local community) were with us now, we had identified two areas in which local elders seemed to recognise the potential of the local primary school to make a positive impact on the development of their children, above and beyond the conventionally acknowledged goals of literacy, numeracy and credentials for entry into secondary school. (This par-ticular audience needed little reminding that a Grade 7 certificate no longer carried any significant weight as a credential for entry into formal sector employment.) These two selected foci for our attention were (1) preventive health and hygiene (*zaukhondo*), and (2) agri-cultural knowledge and skills (*zamalimidwe*). Hence the presence at our meeting of the local experts in these two domains, the Medical Assistant[5] in charge of the nearest Rural Health Centre at M'tandaza, and his neighbour, the Agricultural Assistant responsible for demonstration and promotion of modern agricultural methods in this part of the District, along with the local Community Development Assistant.[6] Each of these three professional-service workers readily acknowledged the relevance to the duties prescribed in their existing job description of trying to promote the effectiveness of the school in one or the other of the designated areas. Indeed, both the Medical Assistant and the Agricultural Assistant had in the past visited the school at the Headmaster's invitation to give talks to the pupils in his particular area of expertise.

The meetings (which were held in the Headmaster's office on two successive days due to the non-availability of the Agricultural Assistant on the first day) were then invited to discuss ways in which the potential of the school curriculum in these two areas could be realised more effectively, and how best a series of community discussions might be organised at which such prospects could be discussed in public with a view to mobilising community participation. In retrospect, it seems the obvious question – 'participation in what?' – was left remarkably ill defined in these planning discussions. Our rationale for this omission, had it been pointed out at the time, would probably have been that our research team had no mandate to define such action goals, and that full-time agents of public-service programmes in education, health, agriculture and community development could only reasonably be requested to pay attention to such an exercise if they were able to locate it in relation to their existing responsibilities. No definite action outcomes were therefore specified as targets for the community discussions which we were planning. It was assumed that since the topic was so intimately related to their ongoing activities, the discussions could not fail to be useful to the service personnel, while our focus on prioritising the concerns and value judgements of the client population would afford them a welcome opportunity to influence the form of any such service activities. To attempt to predetermine the outcomes of the discussions would have seemed incompatible with our conception of the primary goal of empowerment, that the actors themselves should decide how best to use the information generated by the research.

The first concrete question addressed at these planning sessions was where the community discussions should be held. A consensus was quickly reached that the best place would be within the actual villages, since all members of the community could participate freely in that setting. The Headmaster therefore undertook to notify the Headman of each of the seven villages where family discussions had been held that a series of meetings would take place over the following two weeks. These would start around four o'clock in the afternoon, by which time most people could be expected to be back from their dry-season gardens. Godfrey Banda and Peter Phiri would act as recorders (in long-hand) at the meetings. I would not be present. This was a deliberate personal decision motivated by a concern to demonstrate unequivocally that these meetings 'belonged' to the community, of which Godfrey and Peter were a part at least by descent even if they were now full-time students at the University in Lusaka.

2.3   Implementation

Two somewhat different records arose from these meetings: a written transcript made on the spot at each of the five meetings which actually took place; and two personal impressionistic essays[7] which Godfrey and Peter each prepared as a complementary, more interpretive record following their return to Lusaka after completing their translations of the transcripts into English. The transcripts doubtless provide an incomplete account of what was said at them, although the recorders assured me that whenever they had difficulty keeping up with the flow of talk, participants agreed to slow down and/or repeat what they had said. Certain aspects of the information they contain are unlikely to have been distorted by the technical constraints of hand-written recording. First, it is clear that a rather small number of persons actually contributed at all to these discussions: forty adults in all, comprising a range of two to five men and two to six women in each of the villages. Possibly as many again attended but remained silent. However, the overall impression is that the exercise attracted only a limited amount of attention from the adults of the community, who at that time would have constituted a total of about 200 to 300.

Now participation by a small sample of the population might perhaps have been an advantage if they were well briefed, perceptive and enthusiastic, in that a small gathering can sometimes achieve a sharper focus on the discussion topic and exchange views in a more directly responsive fashion than is possible for a larger gathering. However, an examination of the form and content of the discussions reveals that they were a far remove from the intense and productive kind of dialogue we had hoped to stimulate. The transcripts comprise a mix of two types of communications: (1) somewhat stilted elicitation of information from the villagers by the Headmaster and/or the 'recorder'; and (2) criticism and exhortation of parents by the school Headmaster and Health Officer. Moreover, women villagers, who in the context of intimate family conversations had supplied many of the arguments pre-circulated in writing, remained essentially passive in these more public discussions.

2.4   Evaluation

While I was reflecting on this far from satisfactory outcome, my attention was caught by discussions of a somewhat similar impasse which seemed to have frustrated a much more intensive and prolonged attempt in another part of the world to promote a sense of greater accountability among the personnel of primary schools towards the communities they aspired to serve. The Cambridge Accountability Project discussed briefly in chapter 4 describes how, even in a society where twelve years of schooling is virtually universal, many parents find the negotiation with teachers of a basis for discussion of their children's educational needs and problems problematic. Four of the six categories of reason cited by David Bridges for parents' not availing themselves of the opportunities provided by the Cambridgeshire schools for them to meet with teachers seem equally relevant in Katete (Elliott *et al.* 1981)[8]: deference to teachers as experts, not infrequently fostered by the tone and the topics set by teachers ('I don't really know enough about education basically to feel that I have any right to comment on it', 'if there was something you didn't understand you didn't really like to attract him and ask him to explain'); cynicism about the value of such discussion ('schools do what they want to do anyway, regardless of what parents think. That's why I don't bother...'); perception of the meetings as a culturally alien type of social event; and sheer dread of entering the school building because of its connotations of their own inadequacy or past failures.

Teachers tend to expect as an entitlement that parents will trust them, yet their professionalism often intimidates parents rather than inspiring confidence, and few of them ever engage in discussion of schooling with parents outside their territorial domain. Even when they genuinely try to be approachable, as John Elliott argues:

there is a kind of approachability which the expert may possess in relation to the layperson who is perceived to be in need of enlightenment. The experts are sympathetic to the concerns of the laymen and listen to their questions, but they are the ones who 'know best'. They see their role in terms of enlightening others but not being enlightened by others. Their 'knowledge' is not open to question. The communications of the 'approachable' expert, although responsive to laypersons' questions, are paternalistic. The exchange is not one of dialogue. (Elliott *et al.* 1981, p. 102)

Perhaps the deepest of the problems which this analysis reveals is that the very existence in society of a cadre of 'experts' to whom responsibility for education of other people's children (cf. Delpit 1988) is assigned by tradition seems to create a communicative context which legitimates a denial on the part of parents themselves of their own competence to make prescriptive judgements on issues regarding their children's education. This undermining of moral self-confidence in such an intensely personal domain by the institutionalisation of education as schooling constitutes the central problem of the present study.

Returning to our Zambian primary school it seems clear that although they were brought together on the home territory of the parents, primed with a number of fairly critical appraisals of the school's programme elicited from parents in private interviews, the participants never really engaged in an exchange of views in the context of public debate. With the wisdom of hindsight, perhaps it was unrealistic to expect them to do so. Some years later we conducted the survey of opinions and attitudes among Eastern Province primary school teachers discussed in chapter 4, which sought among other things to get a feel for the teachers' attitudes towards their pupils' parents in relation to their professional responsibilities. In one part of the questionnaire we asked the teachers to rate the degree to which they feel professionally accountable to various categories of interested party. The responses reported in chapter 4 indicate that they definitely do not feel accountable in respect of their professional work either to their pupils or to their pupils' parents. The openness with which the teachers were willing to profess these attitudes suggested that part of the publicly shared interpretation of what it means to be a teacher is that you are an authority figure who represents the Ministry. And if anybody is in a position to tell you whether you are doing the job properly it's the Inspector or the Head of the school. But it is regarded as beyond the competence of parents to assess whether you are doing your job as a teacher properly.

Another part of the questionnaire concerned the teachers' conception of the functions of the PTA (the Parent Teachers Association). Table 6.1 shows some of the functions which were listed by the respondents. These responses are of particular interest as a source of information about the pre-existing relationship between staff of the school and parents of the pupils. The PTA stands out as one of the few existing institutional resources for a rural primary school to promote communication among the various groups and individuals with different perspectives on its psychological, social and economic potential. We can see in the table that many of the higher-priority functions are construed as making the school system work the way the teachers would like it to work: enlisting the parents' support in whatever the school wants to do; getting a school administration working properly; mobilising projects. Parent participation in school decisions receives much lower priority; and recognising parents' concerns receives rank no. 11, even after informing parents. In sum, teachers seem to perceive PTA meetings principally as an opportunity to tell the parents what they need to know, rather than for parents to express their own concerns.

Given this background of prior, regular interaction, one way of characterising what took place at our village discussion sessions would be that the participants, faced with an unfamiliar and unguided social

Table 6.1 *Most important functions attributed to the PTA by primary school teachers in Zambia's Eastern Province,* * *and frequency with which their own PTA was seen as fulfilling these functions in practice*

	Aggregate importance attached to function (0–153)		Mean estimated frequency of fulfilment (0–4)	
		(N mention)	Rank	
Recognition of parents' concerns	6	(3)	11	1.5
Parent participation in school decision-making	25	(14)	5	2.1
Parent information about school activities	7	(4)	10	2.8
Bringing school closer to community	9	(3)	9	1.7
Partnership between parents and teachers	68	(27)	1	2.8
Dispute or problem resolution among parents and teachers	23	(12)	6	2.6
Improving quality of school as a learning environment	20	(8)	7	2.5
Enlisting parent support in solving teachers' problems	55	(33)	2	2.6
Mobilising projects	33	(16)	4	2.4
Fund-raising	14	(6)	8	2.3
School Administration	40	(19)	3	2.4
Across all items				2.4
(Heads and Deputy Heads)				2.8

*scored as for Table 4.2(a)

situation, 'imported [their] expectations from [a] well-known script onto [the] novel situation' (Nelson 1981, p. 109). This metaphorical application by Katherine Nelson of the concept of a theatrical 'script' provides an illuminating theoretical link between the domains of cognitive and social organisation:

Scripts ... serve social encounters ... by providing a shared knowledge base within which interactions take place. Although some negotiation between participants usually is necessary, without shared scripts every social act would need to be negotiated afresh, effectively prohibiting action. Indeed one can think of script knowledge as precisely cultural knowledge that enables people within a given culture to operate effectively together. (p. 109)

The comparison of life with performance on a stage is an old idiom in Western culture. Indeed, Harre suggests that it is 'perhaps the oldest analytical model of all. We see and hear a simulacrum of life on the stage. Perhaps the way that simulacrum is created and the illusion sustained can be a guide to our understanding of how real life is created' (Harre 1979, p. 190). William Shakespeare, for instance, wrote:

> All the world's a stage,
> And all the men and women merely players:
> They have their exits and their entrances;
> And one man in his time plays many parts...
> *(As you like it,* II. vii, 139)

Erving Goffman has advanced an influential elaboration of this idea in his seminal book *The presentation of self in everyday life* and a rich series of subsequent studies (Goffman 1956, 1974). More recently, Rom Harre has given this 'dramaturgical' account of social action a new lease of life in what he has termed an 'ethogenic' social psychology, arguing with abundant examples that, in most societies and at most times in history:

the major human preoccupation in the complex interweaving of practical and expressive activities is the presentation of an acceptable persona, appropriate to the scene and the part in the action ... associated with worth and dignity. (Harre 1979, p. 207)

These ideas also find a place in Jurgen Habermas' theory (1984) of communicative action. Habermas distinguishes three types of world-concept, each of which has different implications for the interpretation and evaluation of action. (1) In relation to an objective world, action is construed 'teleologically' in terms of decisions by a solitary actor among alternative courses of action with a view to the realisation of an end, guided by maxims and based on an interpretation of the situation. This is the model advanced by game theory and decision theory. (2) In relation to a social world, action is construed as 'normatively regulated', with the actor fulfilling a generalised expectation of behaviour which members of the social group to which she or he belongs are entitled to hold in the light of a shared body of common values. This is the model underlying role theory. (3) In relation to a subjective world, action is construed 'dramaturgically' in terms of self-presentation, the actor stylising his or her own experiences with a view to an audience, purposively disclosing her subjectivity and monitoring public access to the system of her own thoughts and feelings. This is the model advanced by Goffman and elaborated by Harre.

The communicative model of action proposed by Habermas focusses on the actor's reflective stance in relation to these three worlds.

Speakers integrate the three formal world-concepts ... either singly or in pairs, into a system and presuppose this system in common as a framework of interpretation within which they can reach an understanding ... A speaker puts forward a criticisable claim in relating with his utterance to at least one 'world'; he thereby uses the fact that this relation between actor and world is in principle open to objective appraisal in order to call upon his opposite number to take a rationally motivated position ... an actor who is oriented to understanding in this sense must raise at least three validity claims with his utterance (Habermas 1984, p. 98)

(1) that it fits with the objective world (propositional truth, effectiveness or instrumental success); (2) that it is right in the sense of according with social norms or expectations given the context of its utterance; and (3) that it genuinely expresses the subjective state of mind of the actor, i.e. is sincere or authentic.

In these theoretical terms the professional and non-professional participants in our village discussions may be regarded as having attached greatest importance to negotiating (or reaffirming a pre-existing) consensus on the definition of the social life-world they cohabit. This was achieved dramaturgically by presenting mutually acceptable personae in accordance with generalised expectations of their behaviour as members of a complex social group with sharply differentiated social roles. Not only did this agenda of impression management and role performance eclipse in importance any disagreements there may have been in respect of the rational-instrumental efficacy of the school curriculum for empowering its graduates in relation to the physical world domains of agriculture and health; but it probably conflicted directly with the possibility of their engaging in an egalitarian, argumentative discussion of such issues.

In an earlier version of the theory (cf. McCarthy 1978), Habermas argued that the possibility of reaching either a genuine understanding or a valid consensus is guaranteed in ordinary language by certain types of validity claim implicit in the pragmatics (cf. Austin 1962; Searle 1965) of conversation. The nature of those claims was reconstituted in Habermas' model of pure communicative action. According to his analysis an ideal speech situation was one in which there is a symmetrical distribution of chances to select and employ the various kinds of speech act (communicatives, constatives, self-representatives and regulatives). This in turn guarantees an effective equality of chances for the assumption of various dialogue roles, so that the outcome of the discussion will be simply the result of the force of the better argument and not of accidental or systematic constraints on the discussion. In practice, he noted, the conditions he defined as ideal are seldom if ever realised. 'Systematic barriers to will-forming communication' are institutionalised in such a way that one party is not really accountable to the other, in the sense of being able and willing to justify discursively the beliefs and norms informing his or her position. Moreover, these same barriers 'support at the same time the belief in legitimacy which sustains the fiction and prevents it from being found out' (cited by McCarthy 1976, pp. 477–8).

Now I have been arguing that the relations prevailing between teachers and their students' parents in Kondwelani community were characterised by just such an absence of full accountability combined with a legitimating ideology. Under the terms of that ideology, teachers have privileged access via a body of technical knowledge to an understanding of those aspects of children's mental functioning which in turn are pertinent to the determination of their capacity to benefit from schooling. According to the earlier version of the theory we could have thus described the public debates as an instance of what Habermas called 'systematically distorted communication'. How should we proceed philosophically from such an analysis? A key step in Habermas' argument is that although the ideal speech situation is not an empirical phenomenon it is more than a mere theoretical construct. It is a shared supposition unavoidable in discourse which is reciprocally imputed by all interlocutors. Whether counterfactual or not, it is its 'anticipation' which permits us to join the claim of rationality to any consensus attained in practice. It also serves as a critical standard against which any actually realised consensus can be questioned and checked. Thus if a full transcript of our village discussions were available, we would expect to find within it episodes or exchanges in which (1) the views of the politically privileged were imposed without any genuine opportunity having occurred to challenge them or (2) criticisms by weaker participants were overruled without any reasoned rebuttal having been advanced.

In a sympathetic critique of this early version of Habermas' theory, McCarthy (1976) identified two problems with the notion that symmetry of the type described is a necessary and sufficient condition of rational discourse. First, at the level of theoretical explanation what counts as rational discourse does not seem to require any particular psychological, moral or political attitudes of the participants, 'so long as these do not occasion a departure from the standards accepted within the discipline' (p. 491). Indeed, a pedagogical kind of domination often pervades theoretical discourse and this does not seem to be counterproductive. Perhaps, though, this pedagogical orientation is useful only in the phase of establishing what Thomas Kuhn (1962) has called 'scientific paradigms', and is necessarily subject to challenge in the course of 'scientific revolutions'. Hence the symmetry assumption might be said to hold over a longer period of time. Second, it is unclear how the symmetry requirement ensures 'the freedom to move from level to level of discourse. The freedom, for example, to consider alternative conceptual schemata or to reflect upon the conditions of knowledge seems to require presuppositions about the reflective capacities of the participants and about the cultural traditions to which they belong' (McCarthy 1976, p. 492).

In the introduction to his more recent enunciation of the theory, Habermas reflects on the various criticisms published against his theory of truth, and still 'view[s] as correct [his] intention to reconstruct the general symmetry conditions that every competent speaker must presuppose are sufficiently satisfied insofar as he intends to enter into argumentation at all' (Habermas 1984, p. 25). But this intention may be just what was missing from our village discussions. Neither party perhaps entertained a serious intention of entering into argumentation: the villagers at best intended to praise or to complain; the professionals to sympathise or to teach. Regarding themselves as experts, invested with authoritative, technical knowledge of agriculture, health and education, respectively, the professionals construed the agenda we had agreed at our planning meetings as an opportunity primarily to impart to an audience of laypersons some of that technical knowledge, and secondarily to enlist the cooperation of laypersons in the implementation and development of their service programmes. The notion that such cooperation would be more likely to grow from an authentic, negotiated, common understanding of the problems at issue was obscured by the professionals' intense commitment to the goal of replacing existing practices with what they believed to be more effective cognitive-instrumental methods of control over the physical world.

3   Participatory drama: the popular theatre workshop

3.1   *Rationale*

Reflecting on the apparent failure of our public debate format to provide the conditions for a pattern of discourse which approximates the validity criteria outlined by Habermas, I found myself attracted by a qualitatively very different approach to communication concerning issues of community development. Penina Mlama (1988) has reviewed the often troubled history of the popular theatre, or 'theatre for development' movement in Africa. The cultural resources on which this movement has drawn include two major rivers of ideas, one indigenous to Africa, the other originating from Europe. Within each river, however, literary and cultural historians distinguish many streams, cross-currents and eddies. As the two great rivers have converged and flowed into one another over time it has become increasingly difficult to attribute particular pools or currents of the present to a single traditional origin.[9] Rather, what remain are streaks of colour or odours[10] reminiscent by analogy of earlier episodes which have been recreated through a complex set of historical processes.

The African cultural river included *rites de passage*, festivities held to mark changes in the seasons, military victories, etc., religious and secret society rituals, royal praise poetry, and in at least some parts of the continent activities with an explicit entertainment or educational function, as well as folk songs of protest, and the incorporation of song in everyday activities such as fetching water, pounding grain, children's games, etc. (cf. Traore 1972; Schipper 1982). By the time its systematic contact with these indigenous African forms began in the nineteenth century, European theatre had become institutionalised as an organised activity as separate and professionalised in its own way as the institution of schooling, with a strong emphasis on artistic entertainment. During the first part of the twentieth century, various experimental attempts were made in Europe to break away from the established forms and to deploy drama as a medium of political protest or reform (e.g. the drama of George Bernard Shaw and Bertolt Brecht). From the confluence of these two complex and turbulent rivers of cultural tradition there emerged in the period of revolution against colonialism a number of new forms which were then subjected to various transformations in the period following constitutional independence.

Lewis Nkosi (1981, chapter 2) has described how the European philosophical and aesthetic debates emanating from the various challenges mounted (by the theories of Sigmund Freud and Karl Marx and by the Romantic and Surrealist movements in literature and art) against the eighteenth-century Enlightenment were appropriated with varying degrees of self-consciousness by the pioneers of the *négritude* perspective in Afro-Caribbean, francophone literature in the 1930s. Yet many of the proponents of that perspective have preferred to minimise those connections and instead to emphasise its authenticity as an expression of indigenous African cultural tradition. In similar fashion both the new establishment and the political radicals in post-colonial African states have often tended to exaggerate the exclusively African characteristics of their contemporary uses of dramatic forms.

Cutting across the cultural divide, albeit not in a simple orthogonal transection which would allow us to construct a neat classification matrix, a number of contrastive dichotomies emerge.

1. Was the drama designed to proclaim, celebrate and reinforce the status quo or was it designed to question, criticise and challenge the validity of establishment values?
2. Was the communicative stance primarily one of entertainment or one of instruction?
3. Was the drama conceived by, and addressed to an audience comprising members of a powerful elite, or by/to members of a disempowered or oppressed section of society?

Combining these features in various ways, Mlama describes various episodes in the evolution of theatrical forms in Africa during the twentieth century.

In the colonial period, directly exported European drama in the racially exclusive theatres and clubs was 'used to entertain the European community in the colonies' (Mlama 1988, p. 62); while in the colonial schools for a select group of Africans, the same form was deployed 'to inculcate European values and attitudes among the colonized as part of the cultural domination crucial to the colonization process' (p. 62). In opposition to these various uses of drama to sustain or promote the interests of the politically dominant classes, several liberation movements (including Mau-Mau in Kenya, FRELIMO in Mozambique and ZANU in Zimbabwe) 'used indigenous theatre forms not only to keep up the morale of their fighters but also to mobilize popular support among the masses' (p. 63).

Less clearly polarised on this political landscape were the activities of missionaries and development workers. Some Christian missionaries borrowed and adapted indigenous local cultural forms and 'used storytelling forms to preach Christianity by substituting the African mores with Christian teachings' (p. 62). Concurrently, extension education on the 'developmentalist' model began, as early as the 1930s, to use popular theatre forms 'to carry development messages to an audience which is expected to translate those messages into action[11] ... Field workers travelled from village to village organising drama performances, discussions and demonstrations based on such topics as cash crop production, taxation and disease eradication. The theatrical programmes were planned, messages chosen and scripts prepared by government extension workers' (p. 74). On a political-ideological plane Mlama suggests that in such contexts drama was used by liberal allies of the colonial/evangelical enterprise 'to brighten the lives of the people and thus distract them from the mounting opposition to colonial domination' (p. 62). An alternative view might be that such efforts were essentially benign in their motivation and contained the seeds of later efforts to mobilise and empower disadvantaged sections of the population, but lacked an adequately articulated philosophical rationale to recognise that they were inconsistent with the over-whelming central thrust of the colonial scheme of economic exploi-tation and political domination.

In post-colonial African states, 'many regimes ... have found theatre, especially traditional dance, a convenient tool for trumpeting praises, often undeserved, for the leader and ruling parties' and as a 'vehicle of blunt political propaganda' (p. 29). In parallel, 'develop-mentalist' extension programmes have rediscovered and elaborated the approach of staging dramatic performances in local languages designed to educate the public in rural areas about the efficacy of 'modern' techniques in the fields of agriculture, health and community development. Mlama remarks:

Even though one could mistake this type of theatrical venture for Popular Theatre because of its preoccupation with the grassroots people and its use of theatrical forms popular with the people, it is important to note that such theatre is not truly popular. It is, in fact, an invasion from above. The villagers are treated as depositories, or to use Freire's term 'empty pots', for propaganda containing messages which exclude their viewpoint. (p. 75)

Three themes converged to precipitate the latest phase in the evolu-tion of what is now known as popular theatre for development in Africa: a sense of cultural alienation among professional dramatists based in cities and/or universities which pointed to the need to return to their cultural roots; a political reaction against the growth of a pattern of conspicuous consumption by the urban elite; and a preoccu-pation in development circles with the essential contribution of popular participation in the design and management of projects. The metaphor of returning to one's roots has in practice often been used to conflate linguistic, geographical and economic dimensions: African authors and actors resorting to their mother-tongue, travelling with their ideas back to their ancestral villages and projecting their messages towards an audience of the 'grassroots' masses.

Mlama distinguishes several phases in the recent history of popular theatre for development in Africa, each characterised by a somewhat different strategic orientation. In the late 1960s and early 1970s, travelling theatre was organised, notably by a group of drama lecturers and students from the University of Zambia, in an attempt to escape the stifling atmosphere of urban elite audiences and to reach out to the masses, both in poorer sections of the cities and in rural areas. The transition from urban theatre to popular theatre was perhaps most poignant in the domain of language. A vivid illustration occurred during a performance which I watched in the early 1970s. The play, composed in English by an African dramatist, was being staged in a low-income suburb of Lusaka, when a couple of actors departed from the script into an improvised aside in the local lingua franca, Chi-Nyanja. The previously subdued audience burst into roars of laughter, followed by a prolonged chatter of animated comments which soon provoked the actors to try the same gambit again. It was as if a veil had been lifted: no longer fascinated as detached observers, the audience were now deeply involved in the unfolding plot.

As Lewis Nkosi has observed, 'to speak of a crisis in this connection is not to be unduly alarmist' (1981, p. 1):

> Like other peoples, black Africans possess a rich and living heritage in philosophy, ethics, religion and artistic creation, the deepest roots of which are embedded in the rich soil of African languages. To re-possess that tradition means not only unlocking the caskets of syntax, disentangling metaphysics from poetry and proverb; it also means extracting social philosophy and habits from the rhythm, imagery, repetitiousness, sometimes the very circumlocution of native African speech ... Translating from an African language into a European one has grave risks; even in the hands of a sophisticated writer the undertaking can prove quite treacherous...
>
> In the face of these difficulties it would seem that the advantages of writing in the African languages would prove overwhelming: that the most sophisticated and articulate of modern African writers feel unable to do so has created, I suggest, both for the writer and his African audience, a situation of extreme cultural ambiguity. (p. 3)

A forceful expression of these sentiments was recently made by the Kenyan writer Ngugi Wa Thiongo, whose novels in the English language established him in the 1960s and 1970s as one of the continent's outstanding contributors to English literature. In what he terms a 'farewell to English as a vehicle for any of my writings', Ngugi Wa Thiongo traces the brief history of a popular theatre experiment at Kamiriithu, a farmstead located a few miles outside the capital city of Nairobi, where politically radical drama was staged in the local Gikuyu language until the government intervened, banning the plays, imprisoning Ngugi and eventually demolishing the theatre with bulldozers.

The project of composing drama in his mother-tongue occurred to Ngugi during an earlier period of imprisonment for political opposition to the national government:

> It was Kamiriithu which forced me to Gikuyu and hence to what for me has amounted to 'an epistemological break' with my past, particularly in the area of theatre. The question of audience settled the problem of language choice; and the language choice settled the question of audience. (Ngugi 1986, p. 44).

Impressed by such expositions of the potential of participatory drama and by the vibrant quality of audience response which I had witnessed at a number of such performances in Zambia over the years, I approached two Zambian colleagues to explore the possibilities of drawing on their experience with popular theatre in promoting a reflective dramatisation of some of the issues emerging from our research in Kondwelani. Rather than explicit presentation of issues in the form of abstracted principles and interpretations of actual occurrences for focussed debate, the strategy would be one of more indirect evocation of the issues through the medium of fictional dramatic narrative for unstructured reflection. My reasoning, reflected in notes made in preparation for this innovatory phase of the project, was that the unschooled adult members of our village community, especially the mothers of my cohort, whose ideas and behaviour had proved least accessible to influence through other media would have an opportunity in participatory drama to (a) define the idiom in which issues of social development are to be represented; (b) actively express their own views on those issues. Given my objectives of facilitating a more egalitarian dialogue which would evoke a more constructive response from the school system to the locally perceived educational needs of the community's youth, the strategic advantages I perceived were that (a) would reduce the chances of misunderstanding, while (b) would reduce the chances of people distancing themselves from the problems. Residual doubts which concerned me at that time concerned the feasibility of drawing on the community's aesthetic repertoire and the possibility that the form of reflection we might promote through drama would be too self-contained to serve as a stimulus for practical action to address the problems in a constructive manner.

My first contact was Dr Mapopa M'tonga, who grew up and went to school in Zambia's Eastern Province, received his first degree from the University of Zambia, completed a Master's degree at the University of Ghana in Legon and a Doctorate at Queen's University, Belfast, in Northern Ireland. Well known both nationally and internationally for his performing talents as a drummer, singer and dancer as well as for his skilful production of popular theatre workshops, Mapopa had the additional unique qualification of having made a special study of the Chewa performing art-form, *Nyau*.

My other contact was Ms Tamika Kaluwa, who also grew up and went to school in Zambia's Eastern Province, received her first degree from the University of Zambia and completed a Master's degree at a Canadian university. Tamika was singled out for me by Dr Mlama as an outstanding animator of popular theatre, whose participation she had admired at a number of national, regional and international workshops.

In August 1987, Mapopa M'tonga, Tamika Kaluwa, Chikomeni Banda and Peter Phiri met with me in the Psychology Department at the University of Zambia to discuss the potential of popular theatre for promoting a more equal dialogue in Kondwelani about the values of education and schooling. The advantages we noted were as follows:

> the use of fictional characters in drama allows the community to confront problem behaviour without 'pointing a finger' at any local individuals, which would violate social etiquette;
>
> the 'veil' of drama provides an excuse for the shy members of the community to express their real feelings;
>
> the pleasure element of theatre taps the affective culture (through laughter at satire, etc.) and deepens understanding, in a way which is not possible when issues are 'intellectualised' in a public debate.

Problems we recognised were:

> the most prestigious and sophisticated art-forms of Chewa culture are embedded in the activities of the *Nyau* cult which restricts participation to male initiates, and even spectatorship to initiates and women;
>
> adaptation of the *Nyau* art-form to create a theatrical performance including joint participation by women and men would probably not be acceptable in a rural community, since (a) it would carry connotations of 'outsiders coming in to tell us how to solve our problems', a reaction expressed by local residents to certain unsuccessful popular theatre projects in the past, and (b) such adaptations are often perceived as culturally inauthentic;
>
> the popular image of *Nyau* in rural Chewa society appeared to some of those present to be heavily laden with connotations of evil and fearsomeness, symbolised, for instance, by their initiates' practice of holding some of their secret activities in graveyards.

Later that month, I introduced the topic of drama at the end of a wide-ranging discussion at Kondwelani School with the Headmaster and four of his colleagues. Several teachers with some experience of using drama in schools expressed the view that it was a potentially beneficial element of the curriculum, provided that the theme arose from local issues and the text was composed extemporaneously by the student actors, rather than requiring them to commit to memory a script whose meaning they often found hard to grasp. One of the teachers, who was quite new to the school, indicated that she had organised a dramatic production with some of her pupils at another rural school in the Mumbwa District of Central Province, depicting themes related to 'witchdoctors' and *mashabe* (a form of spirit possession with comparable counterparts in several other parts of Zambia, associated with neurotic episodes especially in women). The school had taken it on tour around the neighbouring villages, but had not attempted to involve local residents as performers. When I floated the idea of using theatre as a medium for airing local issues concerned with the goals and consequences of schooling, the reaction of the meeting was less positive, with references to dangers of overloading the syllabus, which was already crowded with classwork, Production Unit activities, etc.

3.2   Nyau: *the indigenous theatrical form of Chewa culture*

The term *Nyau* is used to refer to several aspects of Chewa culture, some cosmological, some social organisational and some aesthetic. The following excerpts from a succinct account by Schoffeleers and Linden illustrate how these various cultural dimensions are interrelated:

Like the Catholic Church the *Nyau* is not only a system of beliefs but a society with all embracing claims on its membership. The name 'Nyau' refers to the societies themselves, their masks and other apparel in which the dancers perform...

If the analogy with the Catholic church can be pressed further the performances of the dancers make up a liturgical celebration. In cosmic terms they may be interpreted as a re-enactment of the primal co-existence of the three categories of men, animals and spirits in friendship, and their subsequent division by fire ... The spirits and animals come in from the bush and a temporary reconciliation with man is enacted as they associate with the people in the village around pots of beer, as in the Chewa creation myth they were first united around the waters which came with them from heaven.

Initiation into the society takes the form, as in Christian baptism, of a symbolic death with the neophyte protected by a sponsor, the *phungu*, who is already a member. The neophyte is introduced to the *Nyau* secret vocabulary, songs and the meaning of the masks and enjoined under pain of death not to divulge the secrets.

Performance of the *Nyau* used to take place at the major transition rites of death and at female circumcision ceremonies ... The characters portrayed by the *Nyau* are divided into diurnal and nocturnal representations; the former are mainly human figures in the form of masked persons while the nocturnal characters are all animals. In the course of the performance women are subjected to insults, obscenities and vituperative male behaviour ... This pronounced sexual antagonism plays an important role in the resolution of social conflict within the traditional matrilineal society of the Chewa peoples.

Active membership of the society requires that a person be either a leader, a drummer, a dancer or an assistant. Among the dancers and drummers there is further hierarchical distinction according to the degree of accomplishment; the more expert either play the major drums or wear the best masks. Initiates will spend a long period as assistants before rising in seniority. Nominal members of the society form a middle group between the active members and non-initiates. Formerly all villagers would be initiated, though this is, of course, no longer the case. By virtue of their initiation nominal members are allowed to go ... and watch the performances and they provide the clientele for the dances. It is an honour to have the *Nyau* performed at the funeral of one's kin and the lavishness of the performance serves as an indicator of social status; so the role of nominal members is not significant. However, there is considerable friction engendered between nominal and active members over finance ... Since the quality of the performance is largely a subjective judgement constant haggling can arise over the price, and on occasions the dances are broken off owing to disputes of this nature. (Schoffeleers and Linden 1972, pp. 257–8)

The cultural tradition of *Nyau* specifies the normal location for a public performance as *pa bwalo*,[12] in the open space at the centre of a village, as contrasted with *msitu*, the thicket or bush where rehearsals and some private performances are held (M'tonga 1980). This is clearly only a partial equivalent to the English concept of a stage which is based etymologically on the concept of a raised platform, built for the specific function of theatrical display.[13] On the other hand, the deliberate display of fictive characters to an audience is clearly a feature of *Nyau* shared with Western theatre, a term derived from the Ionic root-form *theaomai*, to view or to behold.

The characters of the *Nyau* repertory are identified by a complex of visible and audible characteristics: a mask, a costume and a style of dancing, as well as a particular name, certain vocal expressions and behavioural dispositions. Mapopa M'tonga, who was initiated as a member of a *Nyau* society in his youth and later wrote a Master's thesis on the subject of its dramatic characteristics, writes that:

while *nyau* is associated with the rites of passage and entails some form of real-life involvement, it has a lot to do with theatre and drama. For instance, it involves the use of imitation and make-believe. Man imitates man; man imitates animal; man tries to bring into the actuality all his imaginations about life, death, etc. Thus during the *nyau* performances depicting animal life or other forms of natural phenomena, it becomes known to those involved that whatever they are doing is not real even if it is aimed at helping them understand their very existence. (1980, p. 112)

In this respect *Nyau* performances are, according to M'tonga, systematically different from the phenomenon of spirit possession which 'entails a lot of real-life involvement', including subconscious 'communion with supernatural forces' and 'abnormal' behaviour (p. 112). M'tonga seems to differ on this point from Schoffeleers and Linden who explicitly state for the Malawi *Nyau* that: 'Fundamental to the religious significance of the cult is the belief that underneath his mask the dancer has undergone what might be called a "spiritual transubstantiation" to become a spirit' (Schoffeleers and Linden 1972, p. 257). Arguably, as an inititate himself, M'tonga would have had more reliable insight into the psychological *quale* of *nyau* performance for the actors. It is also, of course, possible that over time the emphasis on the religious significance of performance has declined, and/or that marked individual or group differences exist in the way in which performance is interpreted by initiates, just as different Christian denominations and individuals profess different interpretations of the ceremony of the Eucharist, ranging from pure symbolism to physical transubstantiation.

To many Zambians who have grown up far removed from the rural Chewa culture, the cosmological, quasi-religious aspects of the *Nyau* cult are obscure if not completely unknown. But the aesthetic aspect has received widespread recognition through the inclusion of *Nyau* performances in the repertoire of urban dance troupes. The striking and sometimes humorous masks and the vigorous style of dancing have combined to make *Nyau* one of the most popular spectacles at public functions such as Independence Day celebrations and agricultural shows. Many Eastern Province residents, especially A-Chewa, derive some vicarious pride from this public recognition of the aesthetic appeal of a dance-form which is distinctive to their home region. This ethnic/regional cultural pride is conspicuously celebrated on occasions when a prominent political figure visits the region from the capital, or when a provincial or district politician visits a local Chewa community. A somewhat similar context in which *Nyau* dancing has been adapted to the demands of the modern state is the self-consciously revived chief's ceremony among the neighbouring Ngoni people: *ncwala* (cf. Auslander 1989). A competition was held in Katete District during 1987 to select the best two local *Nyau* dance troupes to go and perform at that year's *ncwala* ceremony. On such occasions the traditional rules of who may watch *Nyau* performances are relaxed and the event takes on a form in which entertainment is a much more dominant theme than religion. We were able to capitalise on the existence of this established adaptation of the tradition in the context of the Participatory Theatre Workshop described below.

The social organisation aspects of *Nyau* have several features of special interest which were reflected in our Participatory Theatre Workshop: the tension with the matrilineage; the opposition between the religious ideologies of *Nyau* and Christianity; and the concept of *Nyau* membership as an exclusive kind of schooling. Those who enter the society, *olowa*, are instructed in its secrets, its regulations and its special skilled activities. According to M'tonga, the curriculum includes some philosophical orientation to the cosmological theory underpinning the cult's practices, a fiercely authoritarian approach to discipline, enforced by severe corporal punishment, and an apprentice-like induction into the skills of dancing and drumming. In Kondwelani, one middle-aged village resident (P.) who had been active in the local *Nyau* group in his youth and a young man (K.) who was still active in it shared with me some of their knowledge and experience during a lengthy private conversation in 1987.[14] They assured me that the *Nyau* society these days and in the days of my elder informant's youth did not try to discourage boys from going to school, nor even from going to church – though they were quick to point out that the church is very hostile to the *Nyau* society and tries to stop the boys from going to it.

We talked about the society's relationship with womenfolk, the connotations of graveyard activities, the criteria for admission and the curriculum. As evidence of the lack of confrontational hostility to women, P. pointed out that some women are admitted to certain of the sect's gatherings, albeit only to perform a restricted range of subsidiary activities, such as fetching food and cooking. The graveyard connotations, he insisted, are quite innocent. 'We only go there to hide our masks, because we know it's one place where womenfolk won't stumble on them while collecting firewood. There is nothing to do with the actual graves as such.'[15] Not every member is a dancer, and even a person with handicapped legs could enter the society if he wished. The curriculum includes skilled craftwork (presumably in connection with making the masks and the drums), and often those who seem *osachenjela*[16] (not clever) in other settings seem to blossom in the context of *Nyau*.

3.3   The emergent process of interpretation and representation

The theatre animation team which assembled in Kondwelani in April 1988 was composed of two actor-producers, Mapopa M'tonga and Tamika Kaluwa and three 'professional' actors. Two of the latter were resident in Lusaka, Saulos Njovu,[17] whose acting abilities had been demonstrated in a variety of popular theatre workshops in Lusaka and several different different rural areas in association with Mapopa M'tonga as well as other, independent drama groups, and Mary Ngwira, who had worked with Tamika Kaluwa in two recent 'theatre for development' workshops; while the third, Matthews Chirwa, who had recently completed a Master's degree at the University of Zambia, was currently employed in one of the Districts immediately adjacent to Katete as a teacher of English at Petauke Secondary School, where he was responsible for the school's drama programme. Mediating between this theatrical group and the host community were Peter Phiri, in whose parental village we took our meals, and myself. Peter acted as a bridge-person throughout the Workshop, a member of the community but no longer a permanent resident within it, negotiating and explaining the needs and concerns of the outsiders and insiders as the process was gradually set in motion. The six of us from outside the community were lodged for the week in some vacant buildings next to the Catholic church[18] at a distance of about 300 m from a rocky area surrounding a large *mugalilondo* tree, which is often used for public meetings addressed by the Chief, the District Governor and other visiting officials,[19] while about 200 m further on lay the village of Kam'tengo.

In contrast with the procedure followed in planning for the village discussions, where the transcription, selection and printing of statements by local residents was done independently of the prospective participants (albeit by people intimately familiar with the community), in the case of the play the plot and the cast were gradually and quite conspicuously assembled on the spot among members of the community. Issues identified from earlier data analysis were aired and redefined in the course of an open-ended brain-storming session among a group of potential actors (including members of the original study cohort), who reflected on their life experiences and thus substantiated the issues prior to their crystallisation in the form of a plot for the play.

Various documentary summaries of the research up to this stage of the project were distributed to all members of the animation team,[20] one in advance as part of their briefing when enlisting their participation, the remainder on arrival at the research/workshop site. On the first day following arrival of the theatre animation team, we split up into two groups to visit the more outlying villages of the locality from which the study's longitudinal cohort had been drawn. These visits afforded newcomers to the area (MC, TK, MM, MN and SN) an opportunity to 'concretise' the documentary information supplied to them and to 'test' their reading of it against the interpretations they were able to elicit in the course of unstructured conversations with several members of the study cohort, as well as a number of their contemporaries and elders living in the same communities. Reflections on this experience were shared among members of the theatre team in conversations among themselves in twos or threes during the evening and the following morning.

On the second day, early in the morning a team of schoolboys was detailed to clear a circular patch of ground at the site selected for our theatrical performance, directly in front of the *mugalilondo* tree. Then, under the direction of their teachers, some of the pupils of the local school presented a series of performances they had prepared for the Workshop. These included a number of traditional songs and dances (*chitelele* and *chimtali*) and some 'situation comedy' sketches, around the themes of responsibility, cooperation, trickery, lawlessness and prodigality (the last of these was taken directly from a school reader). A few talented performers were identified in this context by the visiting drama specialists, and recruited for participation in the play that was still to be composed, but little or none of the thematic material was deemed appropriate, apart from one of the dances.

Later that day, a much more intimate group discussion took place under the same *mugalilondo* tree, among a group of young adults who had responded to the invitation issued during our informal interviews the previous day.[21] In addition to the six outsiders to the community and Peter Phiri, there were eleven local residents present in this gathering (all below the age of 30), including five members of the study cohort, two relatives of Chikomeni Banda (one married to a cohort member) and two relatives of Peter Phiri (one a member of the cohort). Four of these local participants (two men and two women) had completed the full seven-year primary course at the local school. Three of the women had their youngest baby with them. Of the eighteen adults present, nine were women and nine men.

Mapopa M'tonga recounted in some detail the conversations he had held with several different people of the community during his group's exploratory visits on the previous day, and outlined several themes which had struck them as pertinent to the play we planned to put on, including the reasons cited by some youth for their non-enrolment in school, and the ambivalence expressed by some elders about the benefits of schooling. Tamika Kaluwa reported on our interview with the mother of Gillian described at the end of chapter 5, highlighting the paradox of her successful acquisition of literacy in Chi-Chewa under her mother's tuition following her 'failure' at school. And I emphasised the diversity of ways in which different individuals in the community had experienced the impact of schooling on their life-journeys.

The first few contributions to the discussion by local residents tended to take the form of brief personal histories, with a focus on their disappointment with the interruption of their school careers. The group became increasingly supportive of speakers as the day wore on, urging them on with sounds of approval, agreement or empathy, and not infrequently inserting words of clarification or expansion of the main speaker's intended meaning. Mavuto, one of our cohort who had sat for the secondary school selection exam four years ago but had not been selected for a place in secondary school, was recently married and was working hard at making a success of farming locally. But the focus of his remarks centred on his disappointment with not proceeding to secondary school. Shamba, another Grade 7 school leaver told the story of his protracted efforts to complete the curriculum in the face of competing responsibilities as a herdsman.[22] Mpeza volunteered that she had learned to read all right in Chi-Chewa, but had found the English part of the school curriculum too tough (*nzelu zinali zopelewela*

... *Chizungu ndi chimene chinasowa*). There ensued an animated discussion designed to clarify the practice of the school in respect of language use in the classroom. It was apparent that teachers at the local school had varied considerably among themselves in the extent to which the use of Chi-Chewa was tolerated or even encouraged in the lower grades. A similar variability has been reported by MacAdam (1973) and Sekeleti (1987) among the much larger samples of Zambian primary school teachers they surveyed in their studies.

I then asked one of the young women to express her preference as a parental consumer with respect to the next generation. Pointing to the child on her lap, I asked if she planned to send him to school when he grew up (to which she assented) and then asked, supposing she could choose for him to learn in Chi-Chewa or in English, which she would wish him to learn. Her first reply was 'both'; but when pressed, she chose Chi-Chewa. When I then referred the same consumer preference question to two other young mothers they expressed the same preference. After some elaboration, we asked the young men present for their views on the subject. One after another, three of them replied '*Chizungu*', and proceeded to justify their preference in terms of the greater utility of English in finding paid employment in town. I drew attention to this striking gender difference, and Mapopa M'tonga observed that it probably reflected a difference between local social definitions of the world of men and the world of women, the latter being much more narrowly restricted to the rural areas than the former. When Tamika Kaluwa put the question to the group, a lively burst of discussion ensued, mixed with a lot of laughter around the issue of whether women would like to explore the wider world if they were not tied down with family responsibilities. At least one young mother acknowledged that she had never been to town.

The next phase of the discussion took up the proposition cited earlier by Mapopa M'tonga from some local elders, that young people who go far with their formal schooling do not fully understand the traditional wisdom of village culture. Those who addressed this topic, by and large, interpreted the concept of the traditional wisdom of village culture (*mambo wa m'mudzi*) as constituting social norms of respect (*ulemu*), especially for one's elders. One woman felt that boarding schools expose youngsters to corrupting influences from children who have been badly brought up. But others insisted that if one's original upbringing at home was adequate no amount of such exposure would change one's basic character, and pointed out that disrespectful children are also found among those who have not been enrolled in school.

Linking this topic to the preceding one, I enquired what those present felt about the adverse reaction of some elders to their children addressing them in English. One young man felt that such behaviour by school children was indeed a serious mark of disrespect. But three of the more highly educated participants defended it as a legitimate way for a school child to try to share with his or her parents some of what they were learning at school, and recalled that their own parents had always taken visible pride in their child's precocious use of the language of scholarship.

Finally, I asked participants to react to the stereotyped view expressed by a number of our local informants over the years that while it was good to send one's boys to school, there was much less point (*phindu*) in doing so with girls. This elicited some forceful opposition from the two young women living locally who had completed some secondary schooling, who acknowledged that such views were indeed widespread, despite the fact that a basic education brings significant intrinsic benefits, such as being able to read and write one's own personal mail.[23] They attributed the popular stereotype to a somewhat mercenary attitude which construes paid employment as the only tangible benefit to be derived from schooling and pointed to the scarcity of such job opportunities for women: *Aona kuti sitilikusewenza: sono ati kulibe phindu.* ('They see we're not working: so they say there's no point.') Moreover, if a young woman after completing Grade 7 were to take a job as a waitress in a neighbourhood tavern, she would most probably be reviled by many people in the community as being morally compromised. One of the women present then courageously intimated that she had indeed had just that experience.

Prior to the next meeting with local residents, the visiting theatre team now began to specify some of the ingredients of the play (*masewela*) which we had been promising to our hosts over the preceding two days.

(a) *Cast.* Given the diversity of the life-journeys documented by earlier stages of the project and the different perspectives on the value of schooling which they revealed, it was agreed that central characters of the play should include both young men and young women with at least three levels of school experience.

(b) *Time-span.* The story should extend over a period of several years so that changes in the perception of schooling held by an individual over time could be represented.

(c) *Personal relationships.* Familial and romantic relationships should be featured, including both attraction and conflict.

(d) *Economic correlates* of schooling should be represented.

(e) *Technical advantages of literacy* and their relationship to the medium of instruction should be represented.

(f) The potential conflict between *indigenous cultural values* and those promoted by school and church should be represented.

(g)   The special *difficulties faced by young women* in putting their education
      to effective use should be represented.

The first three of these ingredients were explicitly articulated and
agreed by the group, while the others emerged somewhat less themati-
cally as the elements of a drama were tentatively outlined. That evening Mapopa M'tonga and I created a full story segmented into a series
of sixteen scenes which is summarised in Box 6.3. We took care in this
process to avoid exact replication in the plot of any of the case material
collected by the researchers or presented in the preparatory brain-
storming session under the *mugalilondo* tree.

Casting was undertaken by Mapopa M'tonga and Tamika Kaluwa
with a professional eye to the talents displayed by each individual in
the course of the rehearsal. By and large, people were cast in roles
which were very different from their everyday occupations, and we
were careful to avoid re-enacting in the play the one love-triangle of
which we were aware among the people who made up our cast. Thus a
Grade 6 schoolboy played the part of an elderly father, a Form II school
leaver the part of an elderly mother, a secondary school teacher the
part of a boy who proceeds from Grade 7 to Form I, a university
graduate the part of a girl who left school after Grade 7, and so on.

3.4   *Performance*

As we saw in chapter 5, one reason why women have such difficulty
internalising the objectives of schooling in rural Zambian society is that
the dimension of amount of education is so closely aligned in public
discourse with the dimension of power that it is very difficult for a
woman to see herself as advancing her own personal development in a
socially acceptable way as she progresses in school. This may explain
why it was self-evident to us as producers of the play that Tionenji
should be played by Tamika, an outsider to the local community,
whose elevated social status was apparent to our hosts, and whose
family origins were unknown to them, and thus whose family dignity
could not be impugned by her acting in public the ethically fraught role
of a waitress.

The role of Anastasia, on the other hand, seemed open to Enelia, a
young woman of local upbringing, whose father was a highly successful local businessman, and who had already set herself further apart
from local norms by completing primary school and two years of further education at a provincial secondary school. Thus her performance
of the part of Anastasia engaged in a confrontation with her family
over her claim to the right to continue her schooling against their
wishes would not arouse uncomfortable connotations of an actual

Box 6.3
Kasinja and Anastasia:
a dramatisation of young people's life-journeys in rural Zambia

Developed and performed by the popular participatory theatre workshop
in Nshingilizya Ward of Katete District, April 1988, co-produced by
Robert Serpell, Mapopa M'tonga and Tamika Kaluwa, with the
assistance of Matthews Chirwa, Mary Ngwira, Saulos Njovu and Peter
Phiri and local community residents.

The plot

There are two central families in the play. Two brothers of one family
feature along with their father and mother. Masautso has completed his
primary schooling but did not get a place in secondary school: he is
working hard to make a success of farming locally, growing garlic for
cash sale in the city as well as a wide variety of vegetables for local
consumption. His younger brother, Ganizani,[1] has just completed Grade
7 and is awaiting the results of his Secondary School Selection Exam.

In the other family, Kasinja[2] is a herdsman and an enthusiastic initiate
of the local *Nyau* society: he has never been to school. His sister, Tionenji, is a class-mate of Ganizani, also waiting for her exam results.

The play begins with an encounter between Kasinja, the herdsman,
and his contemporary, Ganizani, the schoolboy. They tease each other
about their different careers. Kasinja hopes to earn a share of his uncle's
herd of cattle for himself, Ganizani to pass the selection exam and go on
to secondary school. Each is sceptical of the other's chances of success.
Just then two teachers from the local school arrive, Mr and Mrs Sakala.
They announce to Ganizani that he has passed and congratulate him. Mr
Sakala and Ganizani go off to break the good news to his parents. Mrs
Sakala asks Kasinja why he has never been to school. '*Nyau* is my
school', he replies. As she begins to protest, he points out that his family
is represented in the school by his sister, Tionenji. The teacher asks him
to lead her to where Tionenji is, since she has news for her.

Scene 2 opens with the mothers of Ganizani and Tionenji pounding grain
together. As they speculate about their children's prospects of success in
the selection exam, Ganizani rushes up with his good news. His mother
congratulates him and sends him to tell his father who is sharpening an

[1]Ganizani is quite a common, conventional name in Chewa society.
Literally it expresses an injunction to 'think', and it carried connotations
of intellectual reflection.
[2]Kasinja is the name of one of the characters in the *Nyau* society's great
dance (*gule wamkulu*) repertory. Kasinja is not used as a personal name
in Chewa society, and its use in this way in the play was an innovative
metaphor.

axe in the *mphala*[3]: his father is amazed and overjoyed. As they leave, Tionenji arrives in tears: she has just been told that she failed to qualify for a place in secondary school. Her mother tries to comfort her.

Scene 3. Mrs Sakala visits Tionenji's home and tries to persuade her to re-enrol in school to repeat Grade 7: she narrowly missed qualifying for a secondary school place, and she was such a promising student. Tionenji's mother is supportive of the idea, but Tionenji is sulky and adamant: she's had her chance; now she must start helping the family to finance the schooling of her younger sister, Malita. She herself will leave home to look for a job.

Scene 4. Masautso is talking to his father and mother before going off to work in his garlic field. The family will need to raise money for Ganizani's secondary schooling. Masautso explains that he is planning a new irrigation scheme for the garlic and that he has been checking the accounts from last year's sales and plans to share transport costs with some of his friends. His father shows little interest, and as Masautso goes off his father reverts to singing Ganizani's praises to his mother: Masautso, he says, will never achieve anything.

Enter the uncle of Kasinja, who has come to seek advice from Ganizani's father. He would like his nephew Kasinja to marry into a good family, and wonders how to approach the uncle of Anastasia, that schoolfriend of his niece Malita. They agree to enlist the help of Lumbwe (the leader of the *Nyau* society) as an emissary (*m'tenga* or *Kazembe wa ukwati*): he's known as a good negotiator in setting up marriages.

Scene 5. Anastasia's mother and uncle are at home receiving Lumbwe and agreeing to his proposal for Anastasia to marry Kasinja.

Enter Anastasia with her schoolbooks. She is sent to the kitchen to bring refreshment (*thobwa*) for the visitor. After he's left, they tell her she'll have to stop school, since she's been promised in marriage. She protests, but they insist.

Scene 6. Kasinja and Lumbwe meet to discuss the programme for their next *Nyau* meeting of *gule wamkulu* (the great dance) and fix a day for it. Lumbwe instructs Kasinja to inform the others, but then reflects that maybe he'll be very busy with preparations for his marriage, now that Anastasia's uncle has agreed to the match. This is the first Kasinja has heard of his uncle's plan and he is shocked. He goes off to confront his uncle.

He finds his uncle at his mother's house already discussing the match. He expresses his preference for another girl, Misozi. But his uncle tells him he must accept what has been arranged, and threatens to disinherit him if he disobeys.

[3]The *mphala* is a place identified in every village for gatherings of adult men in the evening, especially for discussion of important topics. In the daytime it is often used for craftwork or repairs.

Kasinja runs off upset and declares his love to Misozi while explaining that he will have to marry Anastasia.

ACT II

(Six months has passed. It is now the end of the second school term, the beginning of the August holidays)

Scene 7. A group of young women are dancing the *chimtali*. Ganizani has just returned home from secondary school, carrying a suitcase, and stops to watch the dance. Masautso greets him and starts to escort him to their parents' home. On the way they meet Kasinja who announces that he is now married, and invites Ganizani to visit his new home. To Ganizani's surprise he reveals that he is married, not to Misozi but to Anastasia.

When the two brothers reach home, Ganizani shows off with a bit of English.[4] Masautso reports on the proceeds of his sale of garlic (three whole sacks). Father is unimpressed and boasts that Ganizani will earn much more than that when he's completed his secondary schooling. He remarks that Ganizani is already a member of the upper class (*akhala muzungu tsopano . . . ali mupamwamba*).

Scene 8. Kasinja is at home with Anastasia who is trying to persuade him to come to church with her. He has other (*gule*) plans related to the *Nyau* society and proclaims the virtues of the indigenous traditional culture (*mwambo wathu*). Anastasia denounces the *Nyau* practices as wicked and uncivilised. Kasinja retorts that this disparaging attitude towards *Nyau* propagated by the Church reflects a lack of understanding.

Ganizani arrives to pay a social visit and finds the argument in full swing. He wonders if he should leave, but Kasinja persuades him to stay. He retains a diplomatic distance from their quarrel. Anastasia asks him about school, and he in turn asks after Tionenji. Kasinja says she's found a job in Katete township at a certain restaurant. Ganizani remarks that in that case she must have turned into a whore. After he takes his leave, the domestic quarrel starts up again.

Scene 9. Ganizani is preparing to leave the village to return to school. He is advised by his mother and father to concentrate in his studies and avoid escapades like going to bars. 'Oh yes', exclaims Ganizani, 'I wouldn't want to meet the likes of Tionenji.' His brother, Masautso protests Tionenji's innocence: 'She's just doing a job; Tionenji is all right'.

Scene 10. In the bar in Katete town. Tionenji is selling beers, and being pestered by customers. She preserves her dignity, and complains about the way customers take it for granted that a waitress is available for prostitution.

[4]This kind of behaviour is often cited by village elders as a sign that a schoolboy or schoolgirl is lacking in proper respect of their elders (*alibe ulemu*).

Act III
(2 years later)

Scene 11. Tionenji returns home, smartly dressed with a bag, and is met by her young sister, Malita. She unpacks a new uniform for Malita, a *chitenge* wrap for mother and an electric torch for uncle, who are all delighted with their gifts.

Misozi comes to the house to welcome Tionenji home. She asks her for help with reading a letter she has just received through the mail from her brother who is in Lusaka. She explains she never went to school. When Tionenji asks why not, she says didn't see the need for a simple village girl like herself to learn the ways of the *a-zungu* (Europeans). Tionenji points out that the letter is in fact not in English (*Chi-zungu*) but in Chi-Chewa. She reads the letter out loud to Misozi. Near the end, the letter mentions that he's heard that Kasinja (Tionenji's brother) plans to take Misozi as his second (co-)wife. Both parties try to conceal their embarrassment about the revelation of this confidential information.

Scene 12. Tionenji visits her brother's house and finds his wife Anastasia at home. She reveals the contents of Misozi's letter. Anastasia is appalled. Kasinja comes home and Tionenji takes her leave. As soon as she is gone, Anastasia confronts her husband, and he confirms that he is planning to establish Misozi as his second wife. Anastasia is furious and insists that her religion will not allow her to accept such an arrangement. If he marries Misozi, she will leave home.

Scene 13. Tionenji goes to the gardens (*madimba*) to shop for vegetables. When she meets Masautso he declares his love for her. He explains that he has saved enough to start a new home. She asks after his brother and he explains that Ganizani is now working as a security guard – not at all an upper class (*mupamwamba*) occupation! – in Lusaka, having failed to secure a place in Form III. When they had written suggesting that his mother might go to Lusaka for medical treatment, Ganizani had replied advising against it on the grounds that life is just too expensive in the city. 'I make a better living here with my vegetable-growing in the *madimba* than he can manage as a security guard in Lusaka!' Ganizani has promised to send their mother some medicine by post, and they are hoping the parcel will arrive soon. They decide to get married by elopement, since Tionenji's reputation has been spoiled by the rumours that went round about her work in Katete.

Scene 14. Anastasia is trekking, with a bag on her head and her baby on her back. She expresses her unhappiness and worries to the audience: should she go back to school? She can't read properly because she left school when she was still in Grade 4. At least Tionenji was able to get a job and earn some money. She wanders off uncertainly.

Scene 15. Masautso's mother is coughing and vomiting. Tionenji's mother is nearby and is unable to help. Tionenji arrives with some vegetables for her mother and asks what is Masautso's mother's problem. Her mother explains that the old lady has been sick for some time, but just recently she received some medicine by mail from Ganizani. Tionenji goes to ask her mother-in-law if the medicine has helped at all. 'Not really, I've been drinking it after each meal since it arrived the day before yesterday, but I feel so sick today!' When she is shown the bottle, Tionenji reads the label which says: 'for external use only'. She explains to the old lady that she was supposed only to rub the medicine on her skin, and that it is poisonous to drink. She wishes she'd learned more at school about how to deal with such problems. 'Let's take you to the clinic.'

Scene 16 Epilogue. The father Masautso and Ganizani, meeting Tionenji's uncle, asks:

> *Kodi ndani pa anyamata athu awili amene anatithandiza kwambili, Ganizani, amene apasa mayeso mu Grade 7 ndipo anapita kusekondari, ndipo tsopano asewenza kutauni, kapena Masautso amene sanapase mayeso, koma akhala pamene apa pa mudzi ndipo alima pali pathu, anso agulitsa ladyo, ndipo akwatila mtsikana amene anathandiza choncho ndi mabvuto amankhwala?*

'Who has helped us most, Ganizani with all his schooling or Masautso who stayed here with us and worked in the *madimba?'*

The uncle reciprocates:

> *Kodi ndachita bwino kusankha mkazi wa Kasinja ndipo kumukamiza kuti akwatile ndi Anastasia, ngakhale anandiuza kuti akonda Misozi?*

'Did I do right to insist on Kasinja's marriage to Anastasia?'

Anastasia's uncle:

> *Kodi ndachita bwino kubvomela kuti Anastasia akwatiwe ndi aKasinja? Kodi ndachita bwino kumuletsa Anastasia kuti apitilile musukulu?*

'Did I do right to make Anastasia leave school?

Mr Sakala, the Teacher:

> *Kodi ndachita bwino kutokoza Ganizani kwambili ndipo kuitana Masautso 'wofeluka'? Ndani pali anyamata awo awili anali ndi ulemu ndipo ndi nzelu kwambili?*

'Was I right to praise Ganizani so much? Masautso seems to be doing more for his family and yet I called him a failure.'

Mrs Sakala, the Teacher:

> *Kodi ndachita bwino kunyengelela Tionenji kuti achiterepeat pamene sanapase mayeso? Kodi sanathandize akumudzi?*

'Did I do right to try and persuade Tionenji to repeat? Look what a valuable member of the community she has become.'

Imwe amphunzitsi ndi makolo, kodi tichite bwanji kuti sukulu yathu ithandize onse akumudzi? Kodi chifukwa chiani timathokoza ana amene apasa mayeso ya Grade 7 chabe, ndipo sitithokoza amene atsiliza Grade 7 koma sapitilila ku Sekondari? Kodi tichite bwanji kuti tialimbikitsa amene atsiliza maphunzilo akuPrimari ndipo akhalila pamene apa pa mudzi, kuti adziwe kuti tiakonda ndipo tiakhulupilila?

'Teachers and parents, what should we do so that our school could help the whole community? Why do we only praise the pupils who pass the Grade 7 exams and never praise those who complete Grade 7 but don't go on to secondary school. What could we do to give these young school-leavers greater confidence?'

experience in her real life. We later learned that other, less immediately apparent aspects of Enelia's life-journey coincided rather closely with the story of Anastasia: in her private life she too was a devout Catholic and like Anastasia she was having to bring up her children alone – a coincidence which may have caused her a certain degree of social embarrassment, but which also imparted an exhilarating intensity of passion to her performance.

Despite some initial shyness, Shamba seemed to enjoy playing the part of Masautso, a role quite close to his own life, and devoted some effort to elaborating the garden scenes, laying out small plants on the ground as props to represent the vegetables. But in the second performance he introduced a somewhat anomalous element into his performance by donning a pair of spectacles – perhaps to symbolise some kind of intellectual attribute the conspicuous absence of which from his part may have caused him some embarrassment among his peers.[24]

Kamuzu rose comfortably to the part of A-Lumbwe, a piece of casting which evoked an amused comment during one of the rehearsals from the real-life A-Lumbwe of the local *Nyau* society to which Kamuzu belonged. I had not seen this real A-Lumbwe since the previous year, when he had graciously agreed for me to take some photographs of his group's performances at their regular stage (*pa bwalo*) near an adjacent village. I showed him some prints which I had brought along with me, and he complained somewhat legitimately about the delay in receiving the copies I had promised him. He had heard, meanwhile, of our approach to the other *Nyau* society, whose leader was also present among the audience, and was evidently a little piqued at his own group not having been chosen. 'I see there are three A-Lumbwe here today', he said with a wry smile.

Mavuto, on the other hand, was plainly delighted with the role of school teacher, and like the real-life school teacher, Mr Banda, who was cast in the role of an 'anti-school' uncle, he clowned quite a bit, gently satirising his portrayal of the part. A young schoolboy, Jonas, was cast as Masautso's elderly father because he had shown a special talent at portraying an old man in the skits prepared by the school before we arrived. Donning an old miner's helmet, a home-made false beard and a stick, he clowned hilariously to the great delight of the audience.

Kasinja, the *Nyau* character whose name we borrowed for one of the central characters in our play, is one of the most accessible characters in the society's great dance (*gule wamkulu*) repertory. Although, like all of the *Nyau* stage characters, he represents a mystical spirit, he is one of the more human subset among them, and rejoices in a humorous, teasing relationship with the women of the Chewa community. Literally the name denotes an object for pounding and when the *Nyau* society is encamped he is one of the two characters regularly sent to beg for food from the womenfolk of the villages, whom he finds at their pounding places. In the course of these collecting rounds he addresses sexually seductive and insulting remarks to the women, which are sometimes echoed in the banter exchanged between the audience and the character when he appears on stage (*pa bwalo*). Here he actually responds verbally to questions from the audience, dances in a sexually suggestive fashion when taunted and demands payment for his performance as is the custom among human dancers. When the idea occurred to Mapopa M'tonga, he gave a mischievous chuckle, which I later realised was provoked by the fact that the situation we had created for this character was such that he would be torn between two women, an apt misfortune for the sexually playful *Nyau* character called Kasinja.

Thus the choice of this particular name was a happy one in several different ways: it provided a link between our locally unfamiliar dramatic form and the indigenous *Nyau* dramatic form already implanted in the aesthetic-symbolic repertoire of the audience; it enriched the presuppositional implications of traditionalism with which we had endowed the character of the non-school-going young herdsman by underlining his membership of the *Nyau* society; and it laid the ground for a dramatic situation which formed part of the narrative plot of our play, legitimating in a sense this character's plight with reference to a presupposed reputation of licentiousness. The casting of Saulos Njovu to play this part also meshed elegantly with this 'planned syncretism' (LCHC 1986), since his dreadlocks hairstyle provided a faint imaginal allusion to the traditional costume of Kasinja, the *Nyau* character, who wears a mysterious layer of feathers completely covering his face (see Fig. 6.1).

The location of the play was carefully planned. We chose it as the

Fig. 6.1 This photograph, taken by the author at a special performance with the permission of the secret society's leader (A-Lumbwe), shows dynamic portrayal of the mythical character Kasinja by a young *Nyau* dancer in the traditional performance arena (*pa bwalo*) near one of the villages in the Kondwelani neighbourhood.

least partial of several possible venues. The staff of the school offered and even encouraged us to mount the play on the 'stage' in their grounds; but we felt, whatever the content of the play and the range of its participants, this would have distanced the event from those members of the community who were not comfortable with the school's style of discourse. On the other hand, we could have sought permission from the local *Nyau* society and the village headman to use the 'stage' regularly used for *Nyau* dances. This, however, we felt would have distanced the event from those members of the community who were openly hostile to the *Nyau* cult. The *mugalilondo* tree seemed to be an ideal compromise; since it had some of the physical characteristics of a typical *pa bwalo* 'stage', yet was clearly public property with no alignment with one particular political constituency.

The only change we made to this setting to define it as a stage was to arrange for some schoolboys to clear the short wild grass with hoes from a circle of about 10 m in diameter immediately to the southeast of the rocks. The resulting patch of dry, brown soil was almost undetectable from a distance between performances. But during the play it was framed by a ring of standing adults from two to five or more people deep, with a number of children seated on the ground at their feet ranging from about 5 to 15 years old. On the side of the rocks, the audience extended back to a depth of ten or fifteen people, standing or sitting in 'tiers' formed by the sloping surface of the rocks. Directly facing the rocks and tree across the *bwalo*, Mapopa M'tonga stationed himself with a team of drummers, all young men and boys recruited from local residents. The drums burst into life to mark each change of scene, as well as providing an accompaniment to the dance performed at the beginning of Act II. Actors entered from either side (northeast or southwest), often needing to push their way through that section of the audience (see Fig. 6.2).

Two performances of the play were staged for quite large audiences, the first at about four o'clock on the Friday afternoon. The second performance was 'prefaced' by a lengthy *Nyau* production mounted at our invitation, for a fee which was negotiated for us by the Headmaster of the school in consultation with Peter Phiri. I was little more than an assistant stage manager in the first production and for the second production was released from even those minor duties in order to record as much as possible on video-tape. Audience reactions to the play were intense and attention was sustained. Several of the actors drawn from the community elaborated their roles well beyond the script initially rehearsed and did so in relevant ways. One of the striking contrasts with village discussions was that the women actors expressed themselves with very little inhibition on stage and some of the distinctive problems encountered by young women in relation to schooling were clearly projected. Standing in their midst, I gained a very strong impression, which was shared by Mapopa M'tonga,[25] that the audience was genuinely captivated by the play. There were times at the beginning when Peter Phiri and one or two other people felt it was necessary to hush the audience. But in fact whenever an important development of the plot was being presented the audience fell quiet of their own accord, manifesting a keen interest in the story.

3.5   *Audience reactions*

The pertinence of the narrative as a representation of local social reality was explicitly acknowledged by many observers from contrasting constituencies within the local community. We can distinguish at least eight such constituencies whose reactions to the themes of the play might be expected to be systematically different: (1) *Nyau* society members; (2) church members; (3) school teachers; (4) school pupils; (5) parents; (6) school leavers farming locally; (7) secondary school graduates living locally; and (8) women. Each group, to the extent that we were able to assess their reaction, seems to have derived some satisfaction from the theatrical event, if only that it stimulated some reflection on issues affecting their own lives.

3.5.1   Nyau *society members*

Right after the first performance, a group of *Nyau* initiates from Kalinda approached me to inspect an album of photographs I had taken of their *Nyau* dancing the previous year. After a brief chat about the photos, I asked them what they felt about the play. The following remarks were partly captured on my concealed microphone, and transcribed with the assistance of interpretations by Saulos Njovu and Matthews Chirwa who were with us during the brief informal conversation:[26]

ndi yokomeza maningi masewelo!
'The play is really wonderful!'[27]

ndi yabwino: tichezerako[28] *tere!*
'It's good: we really enjoyed it!'

zamene zija zimachitika!
'Those things do happen!'

This last remark was echoed enthusiastically by two or three other members of the group:

ee, zicitikadi!
'Yes, they sure do happen!'

They then proceeded to elaborate, each building on the other's story:

(A)   *Ee, ati ndipita kugula ndiwo bas, ayamba ku kamba zina . . .*
(B)   *Ati: 'bwanji?' Ati: 'amuna apita kutali, apita ku Sinda'. Afuna so, ati bene zija . . .*
(C)   *Mwambo wa nkani iyi ndi osagula ndiwo . . .*
(B)   *Amupatsa chabe ndiwo. Ati: 'no, mukaphike; ndalama tengani, mugaiwe'.*

(A)   'Yeah, she says "I'm just going to buy some vegetables" and then she starts talking about other things . . .'
(B)   'He says "how are you?" She says "my husband's off on a long trip; he's gone to Sinda". She wants you know what, and one things leads to another . . .'
(C)   'The moral of this story is "don't buy vegetables!" '
(B)   'He just gives her the vegetables. He says "no, go and cook them; keep the money, you'll need it for milling the flour".'

This allusion to the romantic liaison struck up by Tionenji and Masautso in the *madimba* (vegetable gardens) gave rise to uproarious laughter. During a post mortem on the first performance that evening the theatre animation team[29] concluded that we had not achieved the right balance in that scene, and that it should be corrected in the next performance of the play following some extra rehearsal. This episode illustrates one of the dangers of improvisation: the thematic purpose of a scene may be distorted by quite minor deviations whose entertainment value gives them considerable prominence in the overall dramatic impact of the play.

On the other hand, I think it is important to acknowledge that the 'damaged virtue' of Tionenji was perceived as a significant theme of the play for several members of the audience. Another indirect allusion to this fact was cited by Mapopa M'tonga who overheard one of the audience reacting to Anastasia's rhetorical reflections on Tionenji's economic self-reliance in scene 14, following the break-up of her marriage, as follows:

Ungapite pa njila iyo, naiwe?
'O-oh, you'd consider following that route too would you?'

The implication of moral disapproval was clear.

Another message derived from the play by members of the *Nyau* society concerned certain difficulties in maintaining social relations with non-initiates or people who actively disapproved of *Nyau*:

...zinacitika apo: ena ndi osapita, ena aGule. Aline: 'church? ine Gule siningaleke!...'
'That's what was happening there: some don't go and some are members of the Dance. He said: "Church? Me, I couldn't give up the Dance!..."' (citing words used by Kasinja in his argument with Anastasia).

Then someone else chipped in with a theme which was taken up by several of those present with much animation and laughter:

(A) *Koma chikwati chingakhale bwanji ichi? ... wina waNyau, wina wak-waChurch. Wina ayenda ku Nyau; wina akonda kupita ku church.*

(B) *Ee: achita choncho, apita ku Gule; ati 'siningaleke!'...*

(C) *Wina a tere; wina a tere!*

(A) 'But what would it be like this marriage? ... one is a *Nyau*-member, the other a church-member. One goes to *Nyau*, the other likes to go to church.

(B) 'Yeah, he does just that, he goes to the Dance; he says "I couldn't give it up!"'

(C) 'One's like this; one's like that!'

Saulos Njovu, who may have caught some of the words which were obscure on the tape, interpreted this part of the discussion as follows: 'the *Nyau* guys also were impressed, the guys from Kalinda. They were saying: "It can happen where a guy who goes to *Nyau* gets married to a lady who goes to the church. I don't think you can go very far with that with the marriage, because of the problems." It was a good example to the young guys who have just entered it to watch out.'

Saulos, the actor, made a strong impression on the *Nyau* members who watched the play. They crowded round him after the performances, and sought him out in the evenings, some even asking for his autograph. The fact that this part was played by one of the outsiders to the community seems to have been perceived by members as providing a boost to the legitimacy of their perspective. However, it was not only members of the *Nyau* society who felt in tune with the traditionalist perspective which Kasinja projected. From his position among the drums, Mapopa M'tonga overheard one of the older women loudly expressing from afar her agreement with what Kasinja was saying about *mwambo* (traditional wisdom).[30]

3.5.2   Church members

Church members, on the other hand, sought out Mary Njovu, who played the part of Anastasia in the second performance, and Tamika Kaluwa, to share their appreciation of the point of view projected by Anastasia. For many of the women with whom they spoke after the performances, the feature of the play which had made the greatest impact was the polarisation between Kasinja (masculine, unschooled, un-Christian, *Nyau*-member) and Anastasia (feminine, committed to school and to the church). They saw this as an authentic portrayal of an important tension in the community.

Unfortunately, it was not feasible in the context of these informal follow-up discussions with local residents to keep track systematically of the social, religious and educational background of each individual who articulated a particular interpretation. Many of the most illuminating discussions were held in loosely constituted, spontaneous gatherings, and the flow of the conversation tended to branch off in tangential and reactive fashion with various speakers elaborating one another's points, so that a collective point of view was generated without much sense of individual authorship of ideas or ownership of opinions. The available evidence therefore is insufficient to permit a clear decision between two interpretations. Modestly we might infer that the association in Anastasia's dramatic role between schooling and Christianity caught the imagination of an articulate minority for whom it reflected a significant strand of their personal intellectual synthesis.[31] Or, more ambitiously, we might conclude that it reverberated with a widely held sense among women in the community that their struggle for enfranchisement through education was connected with a struggle for power against the social dominance of men, which derives support from the opposition of the Catholic Church to the *Nyau* cult.

One unanticipated manifestation of these political undercurrents occurred in response to the invited performance of *Nyau* dances on the morning preceding our second performance of the play. The first level of spatial organisation which came to our attention was an imaginary barrier created by the *Nyau* performers, beyond which they forbade uninitiated men to proceed (see Fig. 6.2). The crowd of spectators which assembled behind this line of prohibition was mainly composed of schoolboys (including the sixth-grader who played a major role as the father of Ganizani and Masautso in our play). Initiated men, any women and members of the theatre animation team were exempted from this restriction, and formed a circle around the *bwalo* ('stage'), which on one side coincided with rocks in the shade of the *mugalilondo* tree. Unlike the actors in our play, the *Nyau* dancers performed with their backs towards the tree, facing the drummers who were lined up on the other side, surrounded by a group of singing women. The uninitiated boys and men watched from a distance of about 50 m behind and to the south. From time to time a boy from this group would sneak into the crowd close to the stage, and when discovered would be chased away with threats of physical violence which were sometimes quite serious. The invisible line demarcating the border beyond which non-initiates were forbidden to trespass was patrolled by one or two young *Nyau* initiates.

While I was filming the *Nyau* dancing, I found that I had left part of my equipment at the church office in which we were housed, and wandered off to collect it. As I approached the church, I became aware of voices singing hymns and then noticed a row of churchwomen standing with their backs to the church facing the *Nyau* dancing arena from a distance of about 200 m, and singing hymns if not of actual exorcism, at least of commitment to fight against the evil spirits of the *Nyau*:

Tiyeni tialangize zoona
'Come let us show them the truth.'

This resulted in the configuration shown in Fig. 6.2, with church-women lined up against *Nyau* men and uninitiated men in the middle distance. Later our popular theatre re-enacted this confrontation on stage: with Anastasia, a woman with a Christian name and an avowed member of the church in moral confrontation against Kasinja, a man with a *Nyau* name and an avowed devotee of the *Nyau* cult. The spatial configuration with which community residents expressed their polaris-ation thus symbolised the theme which was later taken up by women from the audience of our play. Which of these confrontations was a reflection of the other is perhaps a futile question.[32] But the parallelism

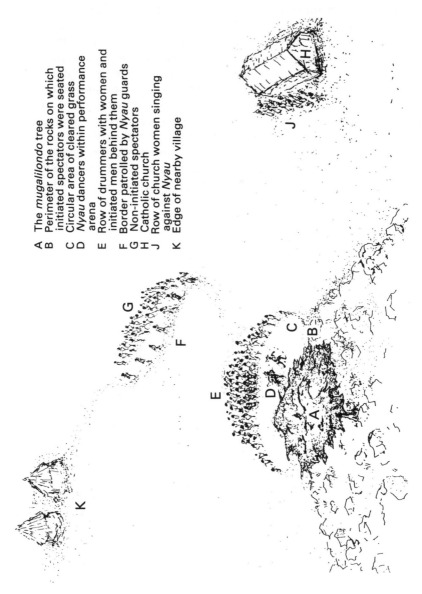

A The *mugaliondo* tree
B Perimeter of the rocks on which
   initiated spectators were seated
C Circular area of cleared grass
D *Nyau* dancers within performance
   arena
E Row of drummers with women and
   initiated men behind them
F Border patrolled by *Nyau* guards
G Non-initiated spectators
H Catholic church
J Row of church women singing
   against *Nyau*
K Edge of nearby village

Fig. 6.2 Diagram of the *Nyau* performance at the *mugaliondo* tree.

illustrates what, following Cole and his colleagues, we might call the 'planned syncretism' (LCHC 1986) which characterised our use of *Nyau* symbolism in a play which was really about much more modern issues, and which arose from a research project in which the *Nyau* cult had featured only very marginally.

There may appear to be an element of arbitrariness about the emphasis of our drama on *Nyau*, particularly in view of the assurances by our various informants, cited above, that the *Nyau* authorities do not see their activities as in direct competition with contemporary schooling. Moreover, the government primary school is explicit in offering a lay curriculum and in separating itself from the Christian religion under whose guise its intellectual precursors first entered Chewa society. But although my original motivation for looking at *Nyau* was primarily aesthetic and representational, it does seem on reflection that the explicit conflict between the Catholic Church and the *Nyau* cult[33] which characterised an earlier historical era retains a residual relevance as a symbolic representation of the contemporary confrontation between the extractive goals of the state's educational system and the indigenous socialisation goals of local families and communities.

Mapopa M'tonga considers that the Catholic Church's hostility to *Nyau* is related to their awareness of close parallels between the rituals of the two creeds.[34] There are several elements to this. Schoffeleers and Linden point out that even at the moment of initial contact the Catholic Church's practices such as baptism and liturgy bore sufficient similarity to aspects of the indigenous religion that 'its idiom could hardly be considered as totally alien to the culture of the Chewa peoples' (Schoffeleers and Linden 1972, p. 259).

In the context of the open conflict which developed in the early decades of the twentieth century, new connections were forged of a more deliberately threatening nature:

> In order to reduce the mystique of the Catholic cult [*Nyau* dance] costumes were invented for key Christian figures such as the Virgin Mary, Joseph and St Peter. 'Maliya' portrayed a white woman with pronounced breasts, made of 'magwebe' (fruit of a type of palm), an animal tail for hair and red complexion, carrying a baby. The figures 'Josephe' and 'Simon' also imitated Europeans with red faces. The *Nyau* song 'Wagona, wagona, wagona ndi gojo' – 'she slept, she slept, slept with an impotent one', which was formerly a reference to the test of manhood faced by a fiancé after a girl's final rites of initiation, came to be associated with 'Maliya' and 'Josephe'. (p. 261)

'Maliya' and 'Josephe' featured in the *Nyau* production mounted as a prelude to our second performance, and evoked an enthusiastic audience response. It is likely that their continued popularity as elements of the *Nyau* repertoire, even at public performances like this, constitutes a source of grievous embarrassment to devotees of the Catholic Church.

3.5.3   *School teachers*

Despite the reservations expressed in the meeting I held with them the previous year in August, the staff of the local school had shown by their preparation of the skits and dances on the Thursday morning that they were willing to cooperate with the animation team in mounting the theatre workshop. We had, however, deliberately distanced ourselves somewhat from the institution by declining their invitation to use the school 'stage' as our venue. Moreover, the message of the play was certainly not an uncritical celebration of the virtues of the school's existing practices. However, we secured a powerful logistical advantage for earning the trust of the teachers by involving the member of their staff directly responsible for the Ministry of Education's 'cultural programme' as a member of our cast. After the first performance I was able to report to other members of the team that Mr Banda, the school teacher, enjoyed acting in the play and he told me he felt it was very well balanced: 'it really shows the good side and the bad side'. This was a welcome tribute from a school teacher given the danger I had anticipated that we might come across as very negative about school. It suggests that the drama managed to portray enough of the positive contributions of schooling for this committed professional not to feel under attack.

When we lost the services of one of our most talented locally resident actresses (because she had to attend a relative's funeral in a neighbouring village), we were again graciously assisted by another teacher, who stepped in to fill a small part left vacant by the transfer of Mary Njovu to the part of Anastasia. This was Mrs Phiri, the teacher who had told me the previous year of her experience with taking a school drama group on tour around villages in Mumbwa District.

The Headmaster was unable to attend either of the performances because of duties which called him away from the area for a couple of days. But his wife, Mrs Chisi, also a teacher at the school, made a point of attending and of calling on the animation team during one of our evenings in the village. I asked her: 'Did you feel the play was fair to the school?' She replied: 'Yes, very good.'[35] When we congratulated her on representing the Headmaster's family on this occasion, she pointed out that in addition to herself as a member of the audience, two of their children had participated as drummers in Mapopa's team.

3.5.4   School pupils

The two actors recruited to the cast from the school drama group evidently enjoyed their participation in the play. The boy, in particular, put on an outstanding performance. Mapopa M'tonga and Matthews Chirwa speculated that the play would be likely to inspire a new range of themes and activities for the school drama group. But to date no follow-up has been made to investigate whether this has actually taken place.

3.5.5   Parents

Many parents, of course, concurrently belonged to one or more of the other constituencies I have described. One evaluative-interpretive discussion overheard by Mapopa M'tonga as he was walking in the dusk illustrates the potential of the drama to stimulate debate:

...people [four men] were heatedly talking about the play ... analysing the play and what kind of lessons it [taught] ... each one was giving a different point of view, saying that this play – you see – what it teaches us here is that (1) we should not curtail our girls' education because of marriage. The other one said: 'no, no, that play after all it was telling us that even if a girl fails in grade 7, that's not the only success in life going further than that, because they can do other things, like these other girls did, the other one who was working as a barmaid' ... So you see it was a mixed bag ... another person said: 'you see those are the many sides of education, that it is not only going very far to secondary school, but even the little knowledge that you have in primary school once you use it usefully it can really be of service to the community'.

Later I invited a mixed group of younger and older parents who all knew me well to debate some of the rhetorical questions addressed to the audience at the end of the play. Several of them had evidently already given several of the questions some thought and voiced their opinions without hesitation. Others seemed either not to have heard the questions or to have misunderstood their thrust, but there was no need for me to intervene, since other local participants were at hand to help them focus more precisely. It is tempting to speculate that many such discussions may have taken place as people wandered back in groups towards their villages, and even on subsequent days as a naturally occurring situation provided an opportunity for a jocular or more serious allusion to one of the characters or situations in the play.

3.5.6   School leavers farming locally

This constituency was well represented in the cast and contributed significantly to the contents of the play. Those who acted certainly seemed to enjoy the opportunity of reflecting on their situation and subsequently sharing those reflections with the community at large through the medium of the play. One of them made the intriguing comment to Mapopa M'tonga: 'the way this play is constructed is very mathematical'; which I take to mean that he was impressed by the way the various characters' life-journeys were interdigitated.

Two rather shy young women members of our cohort (Yumba, Ngosa) who attended the discussion under the *mugalilondo* tree were eventually not cast in speaking roles. They did, however, join in the *chimtali* dancing at the beginning of Act II. One of them quietly told me after the first performance that it was 'wonderful' (*ndi okomezya*), a term also used independently by someone else to describe the play. Together with two of their contemporaries who did have speaking parts these young mothers, who had all been at school together for some years, formed a small clique within the theatre group. Shortly after the second performance when they were gathered at my house before dispersing to return to their homes, they expressed a strong consensus that the second performance had been an improvement over the first. They clearly felt somewhat proprietorial about the drama by this time and were comfortable with the idea that the performance could be evaluated without detracting from the fun of participation.

It occurred to me as I reflected on the dynamics of this small group of neighbourhood peers that there are probably intrinsic benefits in a workshop of this nature to mounting several performances by/for/in a single community, maybe with some casting rotation. The only rotation in our case was done out of necessity, when Enelia was unable to be present on the second day, and was experienced by the cast as a somewhat threatening change. But it is arguable that the subjunctivisation discussed below would be facilitated and extended by the process, which could doubtless be made less threatening by letting it be known in advance that it would occur.

Following the second performance I met Zuze, a member of our cohort, who had come over to watch the play. He remarked:

Makhalidwe a anthu a pano adzayamba kusintha cifukwa ca masewela anu.
'The behaviour of people around here is going to start changing because of your play.'

The next morning I saw him again and asked him to amplify what he had said:

Enanga alinanzelu[36] *adzayamba kutengerako makhalidwe abwino.*
'Some people, those who have *nzelu*, will start to learn some good behaviour from it.'

3.5.7 *Women*

A dimension of the experience offered by the popular theatre work-shop which seems to have been quite salient for several local partici-pants was the social recognition they earned by coming out on to the stage. This was perhaps particularly salient for the women. Mapopa M'tonga sensed from the remarks of the audience standing close to him that:

some of the women were really envious of their fellow young women on stage – even the oldest, because, to them, it gave them some pride that they could be able to participate: it was something they had never done in their lives ... they thought it was quite brave ... to go on stage with children on their back ... and talking very freely about things in real life which actually confront them: about being married to a polygamous husband and ... stopping school because it was an arranged marriage ... And these other girls were using that as a platform to speak on behalf of women.[37]

3.5.8 *Secondary school graduates*

This constituency was also well represented, and most explicitly strad-dled the different worlds of rural and city life, including as it did three young women living locally, Peter Phiri, a university graduate, whose local roots are strong but who lives and works in the capital city, and all five of the professional dramatists in the animation team, whose formal education ranged from partial secondary schooling to a doctoral degree, and four of whom live and work in the capital, but who all shared with the local participants memories of a rural childhood in the Eastern Province. In addition, two secondary school boys who were on holiday visiting their families in their home villages in the neighbour-hood attended the play and approached me afterwards to enquire whether they might obtain a copy of the script, since they would like to mount a production at their schools (both in other Districts of the Eastern Province). We had, of course, to explain that at this point in time there was no script as such in existence, but we agreed to send them copies if and when one were to be produced. The outsiders all expressed a sense of excitement about the intensity of the communica-tion they had achieved with the local community.

Matthews Chirwa, who lives and works in the Eastern Province at a secondary school and produces drama there, said to me after the first performance: 'I've really come down to the reality of popular theatre.' Mapopa M'tonga has told me that he feels more of the objectives of popular theatre, as he understands it, were achieved in this workshop than in any in which he had participated previously. Tamika Kaluwa was also impressed by the experience and in discussion agreed with me that a key factor contributing to our success in mobilising participation and in striking a convincing note was the fact of knowing on a long-term trusting basis several grassroots members of the community. As I see it, the fact that the group we recruited to discuss the project under the *mugalilondo* tree knew from previous contact over many years that they could trust Peter Phiri and me enabled them to focus their attention wholeheartedly and without hesitation on the process of creating the drama, without any misgivings about what the outsiders' motives might be in coming here.

3.5.9   Longer-term impressions

Peter Phiri returned to his teaching post in Lusaka shortly after the popular theatre workshop, but had occasion to return to his home village for a family visit about three weeks later. When he returned to Lusaka again, he shared with me the following account of the impressions various people had retained of the drama.

   Most of the people he met asked questions in the form:

Mudzabwelanso liti mutichezela[38] ndi magule[39] anu?
'When are you coming back again to entertain us with your dances?'

He felt that most people had seen the play as basically entertainment and failed to appreciate its 'enlightening' significance. In contrast with this interpretation, however, he cited the following specific discussions about the play which he had with people during his brief visit. One young man, a resident of one of the adjacent villages, whose name and educational background were not known to me, had recalled the disappointment of Kasinja over the inheritance he felt he had earned by herding his uncle's cattle, and Ganizani's success in getting a place at secondary school and later a job. The chaplain of the local church had recalled the incident of the misuse of the medicine by Ganizani's mother as illustrating the kind of misunderstanding common among rural people and the value of schooling. At the school, Mr Chisi, the Headmaster, and Mr Banda had both expressed the view that the play had been highly 'educational'. Four of the five people Peter recalled meeting among those who had acted with speaking parts in the play had recalled the event enthusiastically, and one was keen, as were the school teachers, to read our written account of the workshop.

3.6   Evaluation

The stated purpose of our workshop was to feed back and share with the community what we felt we had learned from them in our research, with the ultimate objective of empowering the people whose activities and situations had been documented to use that information in socially productive ways. One measure of our success is the number of relevant people we reached. Another is the clarity with which our central themes were communicated. And a third is the extent to which what we communicated was empowering and socially productive.

The theatre was watched by a large number of people, probably more than 500 in all over the two performances. Most of those whom we were able to ask about it seemed to have understood at least some of the themes represented. Moreover, one of the immediate conse- quences seems to have been some debate among members of the community. Whether they will deploy the information in socially pro- ductive ways is much more difficult to determine. Certainly the direc- tion of social change implicitly advocated by the drama was extremely vaguely defined. But this may be construed as a strength of the approach rather than a weakness. In order to justify this paradoxical proposition it will be necessary to examine in some detail the ways in which this type of communication gets its message across.

One of the paradoxical strengths of the theatre workshop was its capacity to represent conflict within the community without taking sides. If the play had a message it was a multidimensional one which offered opportunities for self-expression, and a kind of authentication if not actual legitimation for members of the community with very varied points of view. Thus, at one extreme, members of the Catholic Church were able to identify with the plight of Anastasia and to con- strue the play as a condemnation of *Nyau* traditionalism as represented by Kasinja. On the other hand, *Nyau* members seem to have found a way of interpreting the image of their society portrayed in the play as a source of pride rather than shame. As Mapopa M'tonga put it, the *Nyau* society sees itself as playing a

police role ... in safeguarding this kind of cultural values [*mwambo*] by making almost all the young males able to join the society and learn certain things which have to do with their cosmology, deeper religious beliefs ... also that magical world ... of day-to-day reality in the village ... The seriousness with which they approach their art [suggests] that they are quite committed: they think that their existence, their world of secrecy [helps to maintain the wisdom] of their elders.[40]

Thus the fact that it is Kasinja in the play who affirms the importance of traditional wisdom, and that he explicitly equates the *Nyau* activities with a form of schooling (*Ine, sukulu langa ndi lija* – 'As for me, my school is over there') was interpreted by this constituency as an auth- entication of their positive role in the life of the community as a whole.

Apart from the various interpretations open for the events that occur in the plot, this ambivalent potential of the play was enhanced by the ambiguous configuration of several of the key parts: Kasinja, whose name evoked an image (already embedded in the imagination of the audience) imbued with connotations of mysterious and slightly ominous power, is at the same time, as a herdsboy, a marginal figure in terms of the orthodoxy of the modern state. Ganizani, a model of success in terms of that orthodoxy, is also a figure of fun when he shows off his English in the village, and perhaps something of a failure in terms of the low-status job he secures, leading him to complain in his letter of the unaffordable cost of living in town. Anastasia, as a young woman, is a low-power, low-prestige figure, but is associated with a high-power, high-prestige institution in the Catholic Church. Tionenji's search for paid employment (a high-prestige concept) lands her in a social slot which is an object of public contempt. The tragedies of Anastasia and Ganizani are respectively products of excessive antagonism towards the agenda of schooling and excessive enthusiasm for it. Tionenji and Masautso, on the other hand, emerge as heroic figures who triumph over adversity, transcending their initial definition as 'school failures' to demonstrate the compatibility of basic schooling with productive membership of the local community. The thematic significance of the life-journeys of Kasinja and Misozi is less sharply defined. Misozi is a vulnerable character, Kasinja a forceful one whose freedom is nevertheless constrained. The sources of their weaknesses are respectively lack of schooling and dependence on the traditional pattern of avuncular patronage. The details of these thematic meanings were not explicitly recognised at the time of construction of the narrative. If they served as guides to the plot's evolving pattern, they did so without the benefit of theoretical formulation.

The communicative strategy through which our play lent itself to such diverse interpretations is akin to what Jerome Bruner calls 'subjunctivising reality'.[41] In his analysis of the differences between the narrative mode of thought and the 'paradigmatic' (or 'logico-scientific') mode, Bruner identifies three features of discourse as crucial to the process of recruiting the imagination of each member of the audience and thus enlisting her in what Wolfgang Iser calls 'the performance of meaning under the guidance of the text' (Iser 1978, cited by Bruner 1986, p. 25):

1. "the triggering of ... a presuppositional background in terms of which stories may be interpreted."
2. "subjectification: the depiction of reality ... through the filter of the consciousness of the protagonists in the story."
3. "multiple perspective: beholding the world ... through a set of prisms each of which catches some part of it." (Bruner 1986, chapter 2)

In our popular theatre, the common background which we were able to rely on was a set of parameters which are familiar to the society and to the community in which the theatre was performed: parameters to do with power relations between generations, role differentiation between genders and the symbolic confrontation between the Christian and *Nyau* cosmologies. The issues raised by the research described in earlier chapters of this book were 'projected' through a set of fictional, symbolically representative case studies rather than objectively classified and expounded logically. And within the context of the participatory drama the subjunctivisation of these themes occurred at several levels. First, within the 'text' of the play where situations and the emotions which they evoked in the play's characters were sketched rather than concretely defined; second, in the form of drama employed, where actors are assigned the responsibility for creating their own dialogue by improvisation, so that, as Mapopa M'tonga puts it, they are required to think creatively about the content of the play; third, in the interactive format of the performance which precipitates an implicit (sometimes even explicit) dialogue between actors and audience, such that the actors play up to and resonate with the audience's tone of response.

This kind of audience interaction with the performers was easy to elicit, given the community's pre-existing cultural repertoire of women teasing the *Nyau* dancers and children echoing refrains in *nthano*, the traditional Chewa story form. A nice example was reported by Mapopa M'tonga: certain 'very critical' members of the audience seized on Anastasia's rhetorical speculation that maybe she should now follow Tionenji's example, go back to school and then find a job and shouted: 'Oho, you mean you would follow that route?' Their interpretation was that here was a new irony: the indignantly self-righteous Christian girl who could not tolerate what she saw as a humiliating affront to her virtue by Kasinja's bringing home a second wife would risk the far greater dishonour, as they saw it, of working as a bar-girl where she would be perceived by society as a prostitute.

Another dimension of the communicative style employed in our play was metaphorical. We were able to capture, mobilise and, theoretically, exploit metaphorical dimensions of thought in a Chewa audience, such that they incorporated within their value system, at least for the purpose of reflective analysis, a set of issues which were only implicitly accessible to them previously. The first element of this communicative strategy is the expository use of analogy with the lives of individual characters in this society. The audience is invited to generalise from these particular life histories to more general principles in trying to understand the significance of schooling in their society and its relation to *nzelu*. Second, the analogies represented metaphorically are covert, rather than explicit. This relieves the authors and the actors, who share the 'author' role of communication in this project, of the obligation to justify strictly the details of the analogy. If the lives of these individual characters were presented formally as models, e.g. with a justification of the form 'this is what will happen if your child does or doesn't go to school, or leaves school at such or such an age ...', the resistance by some members of the audience to the explicit analogy would be so strong that it would probably defeat the communicative goal of persuading them to consider a new way of interpreting their experience. The covert analogies embedded in the metaphors sustaining the drama are less likely to provoke such defensive resistance.

A third feature of metaphor which seems to be important as a communicative device is the succinctness with which the analogy is represented within a single character or a single scene. Kasinja and Anastasia's unhappy forced marriage constitutes an epitome of a whole set of issues: their relationship summarises the tension between the generations which leads to unsatisfactory selection of spouses by the older generation for the younger generation; it symbolises the conflict between church and traditional Chewa society; it symbolises the ambivalence of Chewa society about schooling in which a young woman's four years of schooling are regarded as less important than her marriage prospects. On the other hand, Kasinja's amiable rivalry with his contemporary, Ganizani, defines another facet of his character in terms of his deliberate choice not to go to school. The juxtaposition of the contemporaneous unfolding of these two boys' unhappy life-journeys thus evokes a theme of ambivalence with respect to the occupational and economic advantages attached to schooling.

Mlama's evaluation (1988) of previous popular theatre projects in Africa goes beyond the questions of communicative effectiveness and authenticity on which I have dwelt so far, into the domain of impact on developmental processes. She points out that in most cases the demonstrable consequences of the dramatic performances in the lives of community residents are quite minor and short lived, and seems to regard this as a shortcoming. My own feeling is that the issue of the magnitude and durability of the impact is problematically intertwined with the issue of demonstrability. To the extent that the philosophy of this type of 'intervention' attaches priority to the autonomy of community residents in determining what problems to address and how to address them, evaluation of the impact of the intervention faces a dilemma: the more directly the intervention can be shown to have caused social change, the more it tends to undermine the appearance of autonomy of the community residents. Conversely, if the drama is appropriated by the community as part of its own repertoire of interpretative resources and construed as adding little that is new, the

Table 6.2 *Theoretical differences between debate and drama as media for communication*

	debate	drama
objectives	1 analysis 2 policy change 3 policy implementation	1 empathy 2 conscientisation 3 adoption of responsibility
rerquirements	1 categories 2 authority of source 3 collaboration 4 balanced appraisal	1 images 2 credibility of source 3 involvement 4 intense appreciation

drama team may claim greater success in the attainment of their goal of resonating with local concerns.

Michael Etherton, who played a pioneering role in the development of popular theatre in Zambia, and later in Nigeria, has recently articulated his views on the special properties of this medium in somewhat similar terms:

the form of 'plays' of the popular theatre ... is 'incompleteness'. By developing thought through the dramatic processes, activists and their audiences can discover the key contradictions. Laying bare one contradiction through modes of drama raises others, either in rehearsals or in an actual performance, which then have to be brought out through discussion ... Peeling off the layers of contradiction becomes the shared activity of the theatre activists and their audiences; and therein lies the process of acquiring true consciousness, no matter what level of formal education one has reached. (Etherton 1982, p. 350)

4   Implications for the future

There were several indications that the popular theatre was more successful in communicating essential insights from the study than the village discussions. Why was this so? Was it that the two undertakings were implemented with different degrees of skill and efficiency? Or was it that the strategic approach was more appropriate in theoretically significant ways? The two strategies of public debate and participatory drama differed in so many respects that it is difficult to apply a common yardstick of evaluation. Qualitative comparison may, however, prove illuminating. Several points of contrast are summarised in Table 6.2.

Beyond their initial shared objective of feeding back research results to the community, the goals of the two enterprises diverged significantly. This divergence was responsible for the decisions to adopt different procedures and to recruit different external resource personnel. Another important factor seems to have been the legitimate opportunities afforded by the play context for individuals to adopt certain expressive roles. In the context of the village discussions, participants defined their roles in relation to one another as part of an ongoing relationship structured by pre-existing reciprocal obligations. Conflict is barely admissible in such a context, since social decorum requires all parties to avoid hurting each other's feelings. In the play, however, the shared premise of unreality (which underlies 'the willing suspension of disbelief' (Coleridge 1817, chapter 14) required for the appreciation of fiction and more generally of representational art[42]) permits the expression of emotions and attitudes which are taboo, or at least strictly controlled, in 'real-life', down-to-earth, accountable social interactions.

Whereas participants in the discussion entered through separate and opposing doors poised for confrontation, the drama was composed collectively and the role reversals represented by the pattern of casting served to underline that the participants were engaged in a joint enterprise with a common goal. The confrontations in the plot were a step removed from the personal feelings and concerns of the participants whose mandate required them to suppress those in favour of a fictitious role displayed not mendaciously as their own but for the shared purpose of representing a collective predicament: the problem of the community's relations with schooling.

Jennifer Nias (1980, p. 88) reports in her account of parent–teacher association activities in England that 'meetings tended ... to be run in ways which hindered parents from filling in the gaps in their understanding by asking questions. Forms of organisation and layout which ensured that information was conveyed clearly by their very success discouraged parents from discussion...' It may seem paradoxical to suggest that teachers can be too clear in their presentation of issues for discussion with parents; but clarity is only functional for communication within a particular framework defining the limits of what are appropriate topics for discussion. If, for instance, the agenda is sharply focussed on (1) the educational needs of an individual child, it may seem quite legitimate to broaden the discussion to include some consideration of (2) parental responsibilities, of (3) disciplinary methods in the school and even of (4) priorities in the allocation of teacher time and efforts. But the last of these topics can only be systematically addressed in the light of some premises regarding (5) curriculum content, which in turn rests on (6) a theory of educational objectives. Because professional teachers regard themselves as holding specialised technical knowledge of foundational topics such as (5) and (6), they tend to exclude them from their discussions with parents, and therefore to be defensive about topics such as (4).

The obliqueness with which such issues are evoked in the narrative format of drama makes it easier for parents to focus their appraisal of the topic in terms which reflect their own priorities. The cognitive impact of the participatory drama was thus not so much explanatory as 'maieutic' – facilitatory of creative performance by the client. The strategic character of this maieutic activity is reflected first in the relatively open-ended formulation of dramatic roles which the actors could develop into something of their own, and secondly of underdetermined representations of local life which invited the audience subjunctively to formulate their own reflective interpretations.

The participatory theatre workshop was an attempt, in Andrew Turton's words, to 'restore agency to people who are denied agency in theories, policies and practice of the most varied kinds' (Turton 1988). Viewed from this perspective, the principle of not scripting the dialogue but rather inviting the actors to extemporise holds a significance much deeper than that of facilitating 'natural' performances and promoting the use of a locally intelligible linguistic medium. It was also a way of enticing the actors, in their capacity as members of the local community, to take responsibility for articulating the themes lying behind and beneath the plot.

Jerome Bruner concludes his discussion of the implications of a hermeneutical analysis for the language of education as follows:

a culture is as much a *forum* for negotiating and renegotiating meaning and for explicating action as it is a set of rules or specifications for action. Indeed, every culture maintains specialized institutions or occasions for intensifying this 'forum-like' feature. Storytelling, theater, science, even jurisprudence are all techniques for intensifying this function – ways of exploring possible worlds out of the context of immediate need. Education is (or should be) one of the principal forums for performing this function – though it is often timid in doing so. It is the forum aspect of a culture that gives its participants a role in constantly making and remaking the culture – an *active* role as participants rather than as performing spectators who play out their canonical roles according to rule when appropriate cues occur. (Bruner 1986, p. 123)

7

Perspectivist reflections on educational planning

1   Introduction

The challenge posed in earlier chapters of this book has been how to reformulate the nature of schooling in such a way that its approach to cultivating children's intellectual and moral development contributes harmoniously both to the transmission of culture across generations and to the promotion of economic progress. The focus of my analysis has been on a set of paradoxes. I have argued that the particular form in which the Western educational tradition has been institutionalised in Zambia's system of primary schooling is often dysfunctional in its consequences for the young people who enrol in it, as well as for the rural communities it purports to serve. Many young people emerge from school with a sense of frustration and lowered self-esteem. Some of those who experience 'success' as defined by the system become estranged from their indigenous culture. Many parents doubt the value of the system as a preparation for life in the community.

On the other hand, substantial numbers of those graduating from the system feel a continuing loyalty to its agenda, so that they are sure they will enrol their own children. Moreover, tangible benefits may be seen to accrue to the community when some of the school leavers decide to apply technical knowledge acquired from the curriculum locally to activities such as health care and agricultural production. The perspective on schooling shared by most of the local villagers construes it as a unique community resource, somewhat marginal to the economic and cultural life of the community,[1] specialising in matters pertaining to children and adolescents, constrained by its official terms of reference to use the English language, and committed to a set of values which are somewhat alien, and associated for the vast majority of its students with an experience of failure.

These paradoxes arise from the coexistence of multiple and sometimes incompatible perspectives on the nature of human development. In chapter 4 I discussed the challenge for teachers of trying to coordinate or mediate between the perspective of Western educational theory embedded in the institutions of the Zambian school system and the perspective of Chewa cultural traditions. In this final chapter I wish to consider a related set of integrative challenges for educational planners. The bird's-eye view of educational planning represents (as I have argued in more detail in the Appendix) only one of many possible perspectives for guiding how to assess the significance of schooling. The rationale for such a central, Olympian perspective is that it is the only way to take account of, and coordinate impartially, all the claims of various client groups or electoral constituencies. A plan (often called a 'blueprint' or 'programme') is drawn up by 'experts', ratified by 'representatives' of the various client groups and then entrusted for implementation to 'professionals'. If any evaluation is attempted, it consists mainly of central monitoring of quantitative indicators of progress in the implementation of the plan. Because the conception of the plan and its evaluation are conducted centrally, it is the perspective of centrally placed bureaucrats on what constitutes education that determines the criteria guiding the evaluation.

2   Scales of analysis

One of the problems with the bureaucratic mechanisms used to select primary school leavers for secondary school in Zambia is that they operate in terms of a locally invisible (or at least unseen and largely inscrutable) set of principles. Their logic is characterised by adherence to the dictates of a macrosystem which only has reality for those few people who familiarise themselves with the national-level statistics. These statistics are so remote from the everyday reality in which any of us lives that even the seasoned 'expert' tends to think about them in a manner which is excessively detached from the rest of his or her experience.

One of the major attractions for planners of statistical summaries such as Fig. 1.3 (p. 11) is that they are designed to facilitate cross-national and/or diachronic comparative analyses. Because formulations such as 'the shape of the educational pyramid' represent higher-order abstractions from the raw data, they are in principle more readily open to comparison across contexts than lower-order summaries which are biased by local, case-specific factors. It is, for instance, difficult to make sense of a comparison between (a) the absolute numbers of children enrolled in school in two cases (which might be two countries, or profiles of the same country at two different moments in history), since we would need to know about the size of the child population, or (b) between the percentage of 6-year-olds enrolled, since we would need to know the age at which enrolment is mandated by law. But it seems more straightforward to interpret a comparison (c) between the two cases' patterns of enrolment ratios by gender and age.

Thus one of the attractions of this type of analysis is that it appears to permit comparison across countries and continents – on a hologeistic scale. Many planners unfamiliar with Zambia will have wondered not only whether the particular cohort studied in this book was representative of the population of the school, and the school of rural Zambian schools in general, but also how representative Zambia is of the continent of Africa.

In broad economic and demographic terms relative to the rest of Africa, Zambia is a middle-income, oil-importing country with a low overall density of population, a high level of urbanisation (48 per cent) and a high population growth rate (3.2 per cent p.a.). The statistical profile of Zambia's primary schooling system in 1983 presented in the World Bank's (1988) report on Education in sub-Saharan Africa is of a high gross enrolment ratio (100 per cent), a relatively high proportion of female students (47 per cent), a very low proportion of repeaters (1 per cent), a high, but acceptable pupil–teacher ratio (46), allocating an average proportion of its total public expenditures to the education sector (15 per cent) and an average proportion of that education budget to the primary sector (48 per cent). Other facets of Zambia's educational profile in 1983 included relatively high levels of schooling (an average of 4.27 years) and literacy (76 per cent) in the adult population, a medium gross secondary schooling enrolment ratio of 17 per cent, a low progression rate of 21 per cent from primary to secondary schooling (the median for the continent being 40 per cent) and a low ratio of secondary to primary enrolments (1:10 as against a continental median of 1:5). For secondary schooling, the proportion of the public education budget was average (34 per cent), the proportion of GNP somewhat above average at 5.5 per cent and the proportion of female students about average at 36 per cent.

Such comparisons may sometimes appear helpful in the context of international or cross-cultural communication, but they also tend to obscure important singularities arising from a given society's particular configuration of circumstances. Inspection of Fig. 1.3 reveals that the overall enrolment ratio of 100 per cent was unevenly distributed across grade levels, dropping as low as 80 per cent in Grade 7 and rising to a meaningless 108 per cent in Grade 1. Indeed, the enrolment ratio was greater than 100 per cent for boys at six of the seven grade levels. This anomaly arises from the fact that the categories into which children are classified as enrolled represent nominal ages (i.e. the ages prescribed as normal by the country in question for a given grade level of their school system), whereas the categories used to specify the base on which the percentage enrolment ratios are calculated are actual chronological ages reported by the respondents to a national census of population (or projected from such data on the basis of population growth indices derived from successive censuses). The logic of the enrolment ratio is therefore premised on the supposition that all of the children enrolled in schools at a given grade level fall within the age-range prescribed by policy. Thus the hatched portion of the left-hand bottom bar in Fig. 1.3 is supposed to represent boys aged 7 enrolled in Grade 1. In fact, however, the number which it represents is derived from the school returns specifying the total number of pupils enrolled in Grade 1, some of whom were aged 7 while others were aged 6 or 8 or 9 or 10, etc.

The complexity of interpreting such data is illustrated by Kenneth King in an analysis of the progress towards the stated national goal of universal primary education in Tanzania. He presents Ministry of Education statistics showing that in 1980 there were a total of some 425,000 11-year-olds enrolled in school, of whom only 10 per cent were in the 'correct' grade (Standard 5), while 23 per cent were in Standard 4, 43 per cent in Standard 3, 18 per cent in Standard 2 and 5 per cent in Standard 1, and another 1 per cent in Standard 6 or 7. From this he concludes: 'if this pattern continues to the present, then it is meaningless to talk of 95 per cent of the children between the ages of 7 and 14 being in school' (as claimed in a 1982 government report). It would be more appropriate, I think, to call such an assertion false and misleading, since the actual situation was that about 90 per cent of 11-year-olds were in school, while a much lower proportion of 7-year-olds were – 'in some areas less than 20%' (King 1983, p. 19).

This particular conceptual difficulty is understood by many planners and need not in itself be held to invalidate the use of aggregated statistics about school enrolment for planning purposes. For instance, gradual progress towards higher gross enrolment ratios might be accompanied by analyses of the age-distribution within grades and increasing stringency in restricting school entry to the prescribed age-range. Some planners would argue that the imprecision of such approximations is a small price to pay for the convenience of the bird's-eye view which they afford of the school system as a whole, allowing, for instance, comparison across Districts and over time as broad measures of equity and progress. Often, however, the mere fact of approaching the topic from the perspective of a central overview tends to obscure certain parameters which are salient at a level closer to the raw data.

Politicians and administrators, for instance, understandably would like us to believe that the situation represented by the educational pyramid of Figure 1.3 is changing for the better. The official position is that the upper section of the pyramid is expanding, and that eventually the wider base will extend right up to Grade 9 as the new pattern of nine years of basic education replaces the seven-year primary course. The form in which statistics are released to the mass media each year by the Ministry of Education manages to make it sound as if the situation is improving. For instance, if last year x thousand young people 'got in' to Grade 8, this year x thousand plus 200 or plus 500 'got in'. Thus between 1977 and 1978, the number of students selected to Grade 8 in Eastern Province rose from 1042 to 1203; while the corresponding figures for the nation as a whole were 21,308 and 21,406.[2] Of course, what these statistics omit to mention is that the number of children competing for the places was larger (since primary school enrolments are continuously growing), so that the percentage success rate tends to change rather little and indeed often goes down from one year to the next. In 1977–8, for instance, the number of candidates for the Secondary School Selection Examination rose from about 107,000 to about 115,000, yielding a slight decline in progression rate from 19.9 per cent to 18.6 per cent. Comparison among the educational pyramids of successive years would seem to be an appropriate way of focussing attention on proportional changes over time in the progression ratio from primary to secondary school.

But the problem goes deeper. Analysis of local, regional and national statistics on progression from Grade 7 to Grade 8 reveals quite striking contrasts between the impressions of major trends that emerge at different levels of aggregation. Dramatic fluctuations from one year to the next in the number of Grade 7 pupils selected for progression, which dominate the picture at the level of an individual school, disappear from sight when the data are pooled for a whole District or Province – an effect which statisticians call 'averaging out'. Conversely, the slow but steady expansion in the number of places available in Grade 8 on a national scale is imperceptible at the District level.

Figures 7.1 to 7.5 provide progressively closer and closer views of the Grade 7 to Grade 8 progression rate data for the period 1975–81. In Fig. 7.1 the national picture shows a steady rise in the number of candidates per year from 100,000 in 1975 to more than 125,000 in 1981. This rise is fairly similar for boys and girls, but note how few the girls are by comparison with the boys (about 2:3). The number of candidates selected for admission to secondary school, on the other hand, remained rather constant over this period, increasingly by only 200–300 each year. Thus the percentage of the total number of candidates accounted for by this fairly stable 21,000 secondary school places inevitably dropped from year to year (from about 21 per cent in 1975 to less than 16 per cent in 1981).

Figure 7.2 magnifies the scale by a factor of 10, and thus enables us to see the gentle rise in the number of students selected nationwide. At

Number of students

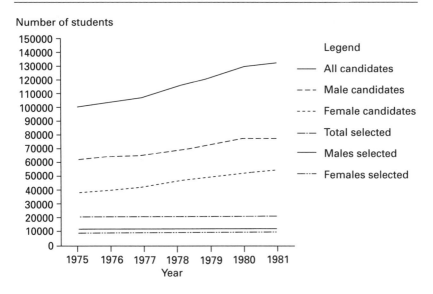

Fig. 7.1 Selection for admission to secondary school: nationwide perspective.

Number selected

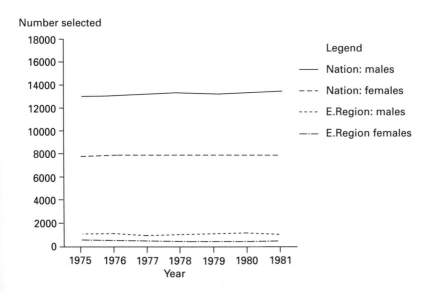

Fig. 7.2 Selection for admission to secondary school: nation vs. Eastern
Region.

the bottom of the graph we see the pattern for the 7 or 8 per cent drawn from Zambia's Eastern Region, which houses around 12 per cent of the nation's population. This inequity reflects principally the greater number of day secondary schools in the major cities of the Central and Copperbelt Regions which take in more candidates from urban areas.

Figure 7.3, multiplying the scale by 10 again, enables us to see a slight rise in the number of places for Eastern Province candidates and to see the pattern for Katete District. Figure 7.4, multiplying yet again by 10 (i.e. by 1000 relative to the national picture presented in Fig. 7.1), enables us to see the very uneven pattern across these seven years for Katete District. Not only is the general rise minimal so that by the end of the period the total number selected (206) was only very slightly higher than the number selected in 1975 (184), although the District had increased the number of classes presenting candidates by a third from twenty-five to thirty-three, but the year 1979 in particular was a 'disastrous' one for the District. Even at this level, then, we can see the negative impact of the falling national percentage on a peripheral sector of the population. But the scale is still too gross to reveal the pattern at the level of the individual school where the realities are confronted by members of the general public.

Figure 7.5 multiplies the scale again by 4 (i.e. ×4000 relative to the national picture) and shows the track record over these seven years from Kondwelani School and two of its nearest neighbours, labelled Helpful and Neighbourhood Schools. All three of these schools show the 1979 plunge, and none of them shows the slight recovery which was experienced in 1980–1 by the District as a whole. Small wonder that so many parents complained to us in 1980–1 about 'falling standards' at their local school! Note that this is the first of our graphs where the trends actually depict numerical patterns which can be psychologically apprehended by most of us. Thus we can appreciate the impact on the Grade 7 teacher at Kondwelani School of an increase in the size of his class from forty-three to forty-eight in 1979, still more the rise in Grade 7 enrolment at Neighbourhood School from twenty-eight in its first year of operation as a full upper primary school in 1975 to forty-five in the year following. The gaps also now acquire psychological reality. The thirteen children selected at Friendly School in 1978 knew that they left behind the rest of their class of forty-three as 'Grade 7 drop-outs' or 'failures'. They also knew of the twenty-eight pupils selected at Helpful School just 10 miles down the road, having played football against them at interschool matches and probably including a number of kinspeople among them.[3]

Of particular interest is the phenomenon of zero selection which has no counterpart at the District, Provincial or National level and yet has a

Number selected

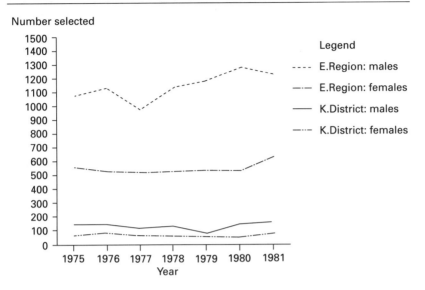

Fig. 7.3 Selection for admission to secondary school: Eastern Region vs. Katete District.

Number selected

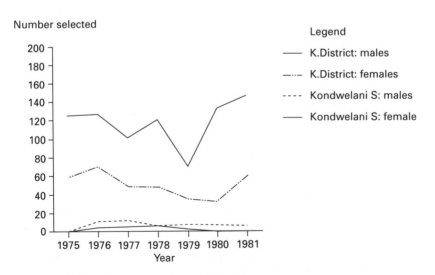

Fig. 7.4 Selection for admission to secondary school: Katete District perspective.

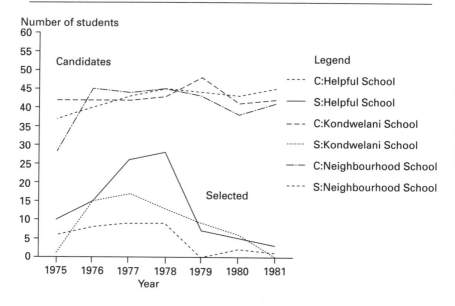

Fig. 7.5 Selection for admission to secondary school: local perspective.

devastating impact on the image of a single school in the community it serves. No less than 40 per cent of the Grade 7 classes in Katete District (with an average size of forty-two) presenting themselves for the national selection exam over the nine-year period 1974 to 1984 achieved a selection rate of nought, one or two pupils. Moreover, none of the twenty-three primary schools in the District[4] escaped having this demoralising experience at least once within that period. Statistically speaking, it is not at all surprising. A small rural upper primary school will typically present a single class of about forty candidates, and the average progression rate for the 207 classes over this period was about 15 per cent. Fifteen per cent of forty is six. On a purely random basis, we would expect a value of 2 or less to occur under these circumstances with a probability of about 1 time out of 4. But none of the families we interviewed understood this. What they perceived was a total failure of their local school.

Comparison among these various statistical profiles illustrates the fact that although a single primary school is from one perspective a very small cog in a large machine its impact on the catchment community from which it draws its pupils is primarily interpreted in a more parochial framework. By comparison with the fairly smooth curves of Figs. 7.1 to 7.4, if we focus the zoom-lens of our Olympian overview[5] on the profiles of individual schools across time, what we see are dramatically wide fluctuations. Statistically, this is a perfectly normal phenomenon. In Eastern Province there are 454 primary schools (ERIP 1986), with an average of some 200 Grade 7 classes sitting each year for the national selection exam. So the 18–24 per cent going forward each year comprises children some of whom come from schools which got 50 per cent of their candidates through, while others come from schools which got 0 per cent through. To a statistician examining trends over time within the province (still more so if the interest is in national trends) these variations across individual schools are merely random error or 'noise' to be ignored: hence the attraction of 'averaging them out'. But if you are concerned about the dialogue discussed in chapter 6, and with the relationship between the teachers and the community they serve, statistical trends at the provincial level are of little relevance. These parties are not interested in what is happening in Eastern Province; they are interested in what is happening in *this* school *here*. And every time there are zero children going through, there is a major crisis. The school has to come up with an answer to the charge: 'How come not even one? You teachers must be totally incompetent. How could you fail to get even one child through?'

It requires something of a feat of divided attention to hold both of these perspectives in mind simultaneously. The fluctuations from year to year disappear from view at the higher levels of abstraction. As a result, the problems faced at the level of a local school in maintaining its credibility in the eyes of the community it serves may be ironed out of view from the Olympian vantage-point of the national planner. How should policy-makers deal with these different perspectives? The policy-makers in Lusaka deal with aggregated statistics, and if a parent or a Member of Parliament comes to complain about the results from one particular school, the predictable reaction is dismissive. I recall that the first Ministry official to whom I presented statistics about Kondwelani School, in 1976, started by assuring me that I must be mistaken, and then retreated to the position that it must be a very unusual school. The data presented in this chapter show that it was in fact quite normal in this respect relative to other schools in the District, and I have received clear confirmation of essentially the same pattern of enrolment from anthropologists working in rural areas of North-Western and Southern Provinces.

When central planners overlook the fact that teachers and school heads are as a matter of course accountable to the community on the basis of school X, of just one school, they neglect an important part of the analysis required for effective educational planning and management. Even for urban communities, the effect of planning constraints is often to distort the image of the school in the eyes of its clientele. By holding the number of secondary school places constant and marking centrally, a compelling illusion of declining standards is created, which in reality probably reflects nothing more than increasing competition. Parents and pupils who have internalised the extractive definition of success are invited to blame for a pedagogical failure teachers who have no say in how success shall be defined or distributed among their pupils.

Concepts such as 'national manpower development' and 'raising the level of mass literacy' derive their meaning from the bird's-eye perspective and bear a very unclear relation to the issues explored in chapters 6 and 7: the contributions of schooling to an individual's life-journey, and the value of the school as a community resource. It is not just that laypeople are ignorant of this level of discourse: even if it were opened up to them, they would more than likely have little use for it. The common ground we seem to need to mediate between the authentic concerns of the local community and the (in their own way) authentic concerns of the central planners is a set of ordered principles for connecting their two domains of reasoning. These principles may include a certain amount of quantitative aggregation, but a more important requirement is a logic which faces in both directions, which makes sense on the plane of everyday discourse and local knowledge and also makes sense (or can be made sense of) at a macrosystematic level.

3   Pseudo-quantification

An influential set of studies often-cited by the World Bank (e.g. 1988) have sought to demonstrate the economic rationality of public investment in the education sector. From one angle these studies can be construed as a liberalising influence on market-economy-orientated development planning. The authors are concerned to make a case that the provision of free or subsidised schooling is a wise step which can reliably be expected to yield measurable social benefits such as higher rates of child survival, lower levels of reproduction, increased economic productivity and more equitable income distribution. On the other hand, the very attempt to estimate the costs and benefits of schooling in such a way can be considered counterproductive in relation to the more ambitious philosophical goal of injecting into public policy debates a recognition that physical survival and material production are only two among many desirable societal goals. Peaceful coexistence and cooperation, honesty and trust in interpersonal relations are social goods which do not lend themselves to quantification, nor arguably does the central educational goal of promoting optimal personal development. As Ivan Illich put it succinctly, 'personal growth is not a measurable entity' (1973, p. 45).

The argument advanced in a seminal World Bank discussion paper by Colclough (1980)[6] seeks to make a case for foreign financial aid investment in primary schooling in low-income, Third World countries. The strategic context is thus primarily economic, comparing this 'sector' of the economy to others such as 'industry', 'infra-structure' (p. 19), and also comparing the primary education sector with the secondary- and tertiary-level educational sectors (pp. 8–11). The goal of his review is to show that the experience of primary schooling alone (i.e. in the absence of further formal education) leads in poor countries to significant changes in the productivity and quality of life of those who receive it.

The evidence is weak on several grounds. First, it is all correlational, based on one-time surveys of populations in which participation in schooling is uneven. This means that any inferred causal influence of schooling on a particular benefit is open to various alternative interpretations. Consider, for example, the one case in which Colclough explicitly addresses the issue of how to choose among various causal explanations of observed correlation. Unpublished analyses of data relating to several Third World countries by O'Hara cited by Colclough apparently show that 'infant and child mortality are lower, the higher the mother's level of schooling' (p. 15). Now it is certainly more plausible to infer that what mothers learned at school helped to keep their babies alive than that the survival of their babies caused some mothers to extend the duration of their schooling. Colclough proudly asserts 'a causal relation could not in this case work the other way around' (p. 15). But it is also quite plausible to support that other antecedent variables mediated the correlation between maternal schooling and child health.

For instance, it is likely that the economic status of the household in which the mother was raised would be positively correlated with a willingness to enrol her in school for several years, as well as with a highly nutritious diet which in turn would be likely to protect her against certain obstetric accidents and probably to be correlated with a good diet for her children. Moreover, mothers who stay in school longer are less likely to give birth to children in their early teens (and vice versa) which is known to be a significant risk factor for premature and low-birth-weight babies. My concern here is not to deny the plausibility of the idea that some primary schooling may lead to improvements in the pattern of young mothers' care for their infants, but merely to illustrate the complexity of drawing causal inferences from correlational data and to question whether the evidence Colclough reviewed is generally strong, this particular case being one of the strongest cases in the set.

A second weakness in these studies relates to the measures of productivity used to calculate the 'returns' on investment in education.

Part of Colclough's argument centres on the finding 'that both the private and social returns to primary schooling appear to be considerably greater than those at higher educational levels. This is one of the most consistent findings of rate-of-return studies...' (pp. 8–9).

The concept of a private rate-of-return is straightforward. It compares 'the privately incurred costs of attending a particular programme' (including uniforms and expected earnings foregone) with 'the post-tax earnings stream associated with graduates from this level of education and the similar stream that could be expected by the individual if the programme were not undertaken' (p. 8). One might even suppose that this calculation is roughly made by some young men and women when deciding whether or not to enrol (or continue) in school.

But the concept of a *social* rate-of-return is based on a much less straightforward analogy. Here private costs are combined with public expenditures and subsidies (including teachers' salaries, school buildings, etc.) and 'pre-tax earnings differentials' are taken as 'a measure of benefits'. These differentials are, of course, based on the existing labour market situation, in which people without schooling compete for the same jobs in the formal sector with those holding schooling credentials. But, whereas for any one individual it may be quite reasonable over a short time-span to calculate that he can improve his future earning power by going to school, it does not follow that if all those of an age to enrol were to go to school, they would all stand to increase their earnings by that amount. Indeed, in countries like Zambia (where the number of formal-sector jobs has steadily declined concurrently with a steady growth in the annual number of graduates from each level of schooling) there are good grounds for believing that enrolling more people in school will have either no effect, or more probably a negative effect on the real wages associated with a given level of schooling. In fact recent research in Kenya using the same basic paradigm found that 'credential inflation' in the job market has reduced the marginal, private rate-of-return on primary schooling to a level where it no longer exceeds the rate for secondary schooling (World Bank 1988, p. 23).

The underlying problem is that a rate of earnings cannot be taken as a measure of social benefits unless it is assumed that it can be aggregated. In a situation of unlimited land and agricultural inputs and a large, industrial market for agricultural produce this assumption might be warranted, but in a small, competitive, and either static or contracting, formal-sector job market the assumption clearly will not hold.[7]

In the case of self-employed, small-scale farmers, some studies have examined the correlation of schooling with measures of agricultural production, thus apparently circumventing the problem of the relativity of formal-sector wages to the labour market situation. Both Colclough and the more recent World Bank report appear to rely heavily on a meta-analysis by Lockheed, Jamison and Lau (1980)[8] of thirty-one data sets collected in ten low-income countries between 1963 and 1975. Each of these studies computed the correlation between the number of years of schooling completed by working members of a household and the quantity or value of the household's output of crops. The relationship was found to depend on whether or not the environment in which farming was undertaken was 'modern' or at least 'modernising'. This variable was assessed for twenty-three of the thirty-one data sets in terms of whether the report indicated the 'availability of new crop varieties, innovative planting methods, erosion control, and the availability of capital inputs such as insecticides, fertilizers, and tractors or machines' (p. 56). Only in those studies which reported that such conditions were in place was a consistent positive correlation found between the level of schooling completed and households' level of agricultural productivity.

Here again, a serious difficulty arises with drawing causal inferences. The interpretation proposed by Colclough is that skills, knowledge and attitudes acquired at school enable young school leavers to put these development project opportunities to good effect. In our Katete case study, however, it was clear that this hypothesis was shared by the Agricultural Extension Officer, who therefore actively recruited school leavers. This is likely to be the case quite generally. Being themselves graduates of the formal educational system, project personnel in decision-making positions are likely to discriminate in favour of any small amount of schooling when selecting farmers to demonstrate the effectiveness of their new approach.[9] Thus, if we assume that the extension services which provide such 'modernising' inputs place the recipients at an advantage in respect of agricultural productivity, this policy could account for any observed correlation between productivity and level of schooling.

Finally, Colclough notes the well-known evidence that those who spend some time at school in rural areas of Third World countries are prone to migrate to town for economic motives. Yet little evidence exists on whether modest amounts of schooling are correlated among these migrants with economic success within the urban 'informal sector'. In sum, the 'strong theoretical and empirical basis' which Colclough claims 'for believing that primary schooling helps to make people more productive at work' (1980, p. 13) falls into three main categories of study, all of them based on strictly correlational data. The first category misleadingly equates higher productivity with earning differentials in formal-sector jobs, the second finds increases in agricultural output only when innovatory agricultural projects are in place and the third documents migration into town without evidence of increased productivity or earnings.

A subsequent multi-authored elaboration of Colclough's arguments (Lewin, Little and Colclough 1983) acknowledges the weakness that 'every study in this review has regarded education as a linear variable', but excuses this on the grounds that 'this indicator is better than no indicator at all'. However, the misleading consequences of mis-representing education as the number of years spent in school are considerable. For, to the extent that policy-makers conclude that education measured in this way enhances economic productivity, they are encouraged to construe any policy measure designed to increase school enrolment as a rational step towards increasing production and thus the welfare of the general population.

The psychological model underlying the advocacy of this strategy is one in which teachers administer a curriculum (an enriching treat-ment) which enhances the cognitive development of their students, as a result of which they become more productive citizens. But, as we have seen in earlier chapters, the measurement of cognitive develop-ment is a subtle and elusive task. Understandably, therefore, analyses by economists and educational planners tend to remain at a high level of abstraction where numerical indices can be manipulated without close examination of the measurement procedures on which they are based.

One notable example is these authors' uncritical acceptance of Bloom's aphoristic proposition that: 'the "half development" of intelli-gence occurs at age 4, the "half development" of sight occurs at age $2\frac{1}{4}$ ... and of general school achievement at grade 3 or age 8' (Bloom 1964, cited by Lewin, Little and Colclough 1983). While recognising that Bloom's thesis is based only on relative measures, these authors claim that 'it is not unreasonable' to extrapolate to the development of psychological characteristics on some hypothetical absolute scales. And on the basis of that extrapolation they proceed to infer that educational interventions 'designed to help the poor groups in society are best implemented at an early age'. Still more concretely, they then interpret statistical evidence on the intercorrelations among measures of school achievement at various ages in different populations as suggesting that 'the "half-life" for the development of school-achievement character-istics may be later in Third World countries than in North America', so that in the Third World 'the quality of the school experience can still affect significantly differences between student outcomes' (p. 420). The authors thus appear to impute what they perceive as greater opportunities for educational intervention to redress social inequities in opportunity for intellectual development and/or academic achieve-ment to a generally slower rate of cognitive development in the population of Third World countries than in North American populations.

In order to appreciate the remoteness of these speculations from the data on which they are based we need first to distinguish what McCall (1981) has termed 'the two realms of development' delineated by two different methodological strategies. Bloom's aphorism is in fact not about developmental growth as such, but about the stability of individual differences over time. A more correct formulation of his thesis is that, within the North American populations studied longitudinally, half of the variance among individuals in IQ test scores at the age of 18 is accounted for by their IQ scores at age 4. There is no question here of asserting that the knowledge and understanding of these individuals at age 4 represented half of their endowment in those domains at age 18.[10] The 50 per cent computed is of a technical index ('variance') which represents a statistical property of the distribution of scores within a given group. The other 'half' is not a quantity of knowledge and understanding still to be acquired (from schooling or any other source): it is merely the proportion of the variance in the scores obtained by that particular group of 18-year-olds which remains unexplained when the 'predictive' power of their scores at an earlier age has been taken into account.

Returning now to the cross-cultural comparison, the data from which the hypothesis of a 'later ... "half-life" for the development of school-achievement' is based are once again correlations between test scores at various ages. The finding of interest is more correctly phrased as follows: correlations between earlier tests scores and those at age 18 of a sufficient magnitude (i.e. above $r=0.70$) to account for half of the latter's variance in Third World student populations are only found when the earlier scores are obtained at ages later than 8 years and/or at levels of schooling higher than Grade 3. This, of course, may reflect a wide variety of factors which differentiate Third World student populations from those of North America, such as later average age of enrolment, greater heterogeneity of age-grade correspondence, lower validity and hence lower reliability of tests, etc.

The level of conceptualisation at which this type of argumentation is conducted is very remote from the perspectives open to these young people themselves and their families. The planner takes the theme of certainty of pedagogical method (discussed in chapter 3) a step further than the practising teacher and construes the pedagogical process as the relatively mechanical transfer of a commodity from books and other curricular elements to the minds of the students. Successful transfer is indexed by performance in examinations, and is judged to depend on a minimal level of skill among teachers, a minimal level of health among pupils and certain minimal material conditions such as shelter, availability of textbooks and writing materials, etc. Focussing on the 'total picture', i.e. the bird's-eye view, the principal criterion of adequacy of the educational system is its 'coverage', followed by its efficiency measured in terms of throughput and unit costs.

This formulation represents a convergence of three principles informing a great deal of economic planning in the modern world: packaging, quantification and commoditisation. Labelling a package of ideas as pedagogical theory in this context affords an opportunity to construe it as a finite entity which is susceptible to quantification, and thus amenable to inclusion in a formula for computing its value as a commodity in the marketplace. A specifiable amount of this neatly packaged and labelled commodity can then be determined as 'cost-effective':

The increasing body of evidence on the payoff of various amounts and kinds of training indicates that for primary school teachers preservice training that consists of more than general secondary education and a minimum exposure to pedagogical theory is not cost-effective. Long residential courses tend to be expensive to produce, and teachers' salaries are usually closely tied to the amount of such training received. (World Bank 1988, p. 40)

Thus, with a touch of the economic wand, the entire substance of the preceding chapters of this book are dubbed irrelevant to the process of educational planning, because affording teachers more than a minimum exposure to this kind of subject matter is not a 'cost-effective' strategy. Yet, conversely, one might cite Philip Foster's observation in a critique of the World Bank report, that a comparison of educational plans and targets in Africa formulated in 1961 with the prevailing situation in the early 1980s reveals that: 'the dynamics of educational growth have largely been the result of factors exogenous to educational systems themselves rather than of the efforts of educational planners'.

Economics is not the only discipline within the social sciences to engage in the pseudo-quantification of human attributes. The phenomenon is also widespread in the branch of applied psychology known as psychometrics. The fictitious notions of social distribution of intellectual capacity, heritability, etc., with which some scientists and policy-makers operate in discussions of educational policy are rendered intelligible to those who use them by means of simplistic metaphors (often of a spatial and/or mechanistic kind) which bear only superficial inspection and break down as technical explanations of the real world once we embark on a serious, detailed discussion.

The reification of intelligence, for instance, lends plausibility to questions of the form 'how much of it has a person got?' and 'how much of it is heritable?' The notion of heritability in my view only has valid application as a capsule summary of a statistical issue: how much of the variance in scores indexing intelligence is predictable from variation in scores indexing the genetic material passed on to children from their parents? This legitimate statistical question is often translated into a pseudo-question of the form 'how much of a child's intelligence was passed on to her from her parents?' There are many reasons why this question is not equivalent to the legitimate one. One reason why people seem to make the transition so easily is that intelligence is conceptualised as an entity (reification) which is measurable (quantification), like cortical matter, cranial capacity, etc.

The word 'intelligence', as the discussion of *nzelu* and other related terms in Chi-Chewa in chapter 2 should have made clear, does not stand for a thing: it is an abstract noun representing a quality of behaviour: how people behave, not something they have. Once we stop thinking of intelligence as a concrete entity, the absurdity of asking how much of it someone has got or how much of it was passed on to them by their parents becomes apparent. The 'language-games' (Wittgenstein 1958) in which the notion of intelligence is used in ordinary discourse have no provision for its quantification or measurement. A specialised language-game has arisen in the community of psychometricians for the deployment of the term in ways which derive their justification from highly abstract, technical theoretical formulations. The casual insertion of segments of this 'artificial', specialised usage into ordinary discourse is often misleading, and may even be responsible for misleading scientists into ridiculous channels of research. For instance, the metaphor of locating mental activity 'inside a person's head' (which is not nearly as much of a step forward from locating it in the heart or the liver as many "modern" Western laypersons imagine it to be) led on from the artificial reification of intelligence to such absurdities as the measurement of great men's skulls (cf. Gould 1981).

Aside from the mystification introduced by the use of potentially misleading, packaged concepts such as the 'half-life' of a developmental variable or the 'heritability' of a psychological attribute, this type of conceptualisation of 'human resources' has become a driving force behind a tradition of research on educational measurement, which has begun to dominate bureaucratic perceptions of the utility of applied psychology in Africa in a manner similar to that which emerged in North America in the first half of the twentieth century. This 'economically driven' type of research seeks its legitimacy in the domain of public policy, often at the expense of its credibility in the community of psychological scientists.

Michael Durojaiye, for instance, writes in a symposium on the impact of psychology on Third World development, that:

selection of students for educational purposes is very necessary in most developing countries in Africa ... For this reason the best testing apparatus has got to be devised for selecting students who will benefit from their education, and later meet the high demand for man- and brain-power requirements of these countries. (Durojaiye 1984, p. 135)

Approaching the topic from this perspective, Durojaiye finds no inconsistency in stating in two succeeding paragraphs, first that

using Western tests is unsuitable for Africans, especially those least westernised ... because of their cultural and environmental bias (pp. 135–6)

and next that

their continued usage is justified on the grounds that most African nations are developing towards Western technology and culture and it is important to assess individuals in terms of the abilities that have foundations for this development. (p. 136)

This argument, which echoes the position adopted by Philip Vernon in the 1960s (Vernon 1967, 1969), justifies the use for educational administration of measures which are known to psychologists to be unsuitable for the task of assessing intellectual potential in the population in question, on the grounds that what they measure is appropriate for a politically defined macroeconomic objective. Yet it is precisely the equation of 'modernisation' with 'Westernisation' that has been repeatedly challenged by the political leaders of the continent. Rather than addressing the implications of this challenge for the elaboration of a more appropriate science of psychology for Africa, the technocratic approach endorsed by Durojaiye advocates the cross-cultural transfer of a packaged psychometric technology.

4   The experienced significance of schooling

Educational planners tend to express a deep commitment to the logical-scientific or paradigmatic mode of thought. The intellectual tradition of manpower planning relies on quantifying the educational process, and this requires that units be identified which can be treated as equivalent. The obvious candidates have been the individual pupil and the annual module of curricular activity. Inspired perhaps in part by some sort of democratic feeling, the notion has become established on the ground floor of educational planners' intellectual constructions that each pupil is a unit commensurate with every other pupil. And derived from the institutionalisation of graduated progression through the curriculum, we find the parallel notion that every year of schooling constitutes a commensurate unit of 'education'. From these twin assumptions it follows by logical deduction that the enrolment of more pupils in school is evidence of wider participation, that a greater number of years of schooling is evidence of higher education, and that these two variables can be multiplied to generate a global measure of the social impact of education: $P \times L = SI$, where P represents participation rate, L represents level of education and SI represents the social impact of education. In the case of the ideal consequences of an individual's progression through and mastery of an appropriate curriculum, the logic seems impeccable. But when it is projected on to the mass of students, in practice what can be measured at this global level is merely the number of heads sitting in classrooms (reflected in the class registers, which form the basis of the statistical returns which are used for aggregated analysis).

Yet if we dare to look behind the register at the individuals whose names it lists and enquire as to the impact of the experience of schooling on their lives, it is immediately apparent that these are in no sense commensurable units. Consider, for instance, the fictional cases of Kasinja, Misozi, Anastasia, Tionenji, Masautso and Ganizani in the play summarised in Box 6.3. According to the statistical criterion I have been describing, we could order these individuals in terms of the impact of schooling on society as follows: $K=0$; $Mi=0$; $A=3$; $T=7$; $Ma=7$; $G=9$. But what index of social benefit could be constructed to order these individuals in this way? The significance of schooling in their lives changed over time in such a way that the audience at times felt that Kasinja (0) had greater economic opportunities at his disposal than Ganizani (7–9), that the opportunities for marriage and social integration were better for Anastasia (3) than for Tionenji (7), and at the end of the play we may well conclude that the impact of Masauto (7) on society has been more positive than that of Ganizani (9). Such reversals are, of course, only a small part of the story, and other interpreters can point to concrete advantages derived by certain individuals from schooling, such as Tionenji's (7) deployment of her literacy to read a letter which Misozi (0) would have preferred to read for herself, and Masauto's (7) use of his knowledge of environmental science to irrigate his garden and produce more food than some of his neighbours.

But in each of these cases the individual-level focus requires a much more subtly differentiated set of criteria for social impact, in which the interpreted impact of school experience on the individual must be mediated through complex interactions with other persons before society's benefits can be assessed. A given number of grades completed holds a different significance depending on the individual's interpretation of what she or he has learned in school, its connections with other life activities and the perceptions of other members of society. To multiply numbers of pupils by numbers of grades completed ignores these well-known complexities and focusses instead on the implementation of a plan, irrespective of its real impact on people's lives.

One of the paradoxes of this economic line of reasoning (a strand within the grand Western, taxonomic-scientific tradition) is the way in which it depersonalises the individual. As Michael Ignatieff (1984, p. 52) puts it, 'the doctrine of universal human rights' is based on the plausible equation: 'if we all have the same needs, we all have the same rights'. Yet 'we recognise our mutual humanity in our differences, in our individuality, in our history, in the faithful discharge of our particular culture of obligations. There is no identity we can recognise in our universality. There is no such thing as love of the human race, only the love of this person for that, in this time and not in any other' (p. 52).

The project of universal education is conceived from the perspective of the central planner as too grand to allow itself to be swayed by considerations of particularity. The students are conceived as victims of ignorance, as recipients of knowledge and skills (commodities which are handed out in measured doses or packages) or as targets of a prestructured intervention, symbolised by 'millions upon millions of hands outstretched' (p. 51). Yet:

these abstract subjects created by our century of tyranny and terror cannot be protected by abstract doctrines of universal human needs and universal human rights, and not merely because these doctrines are words, and whips are things. The problem is not to defend universality, but to give these abstract individuals the chance to become real, historical individuals again, with the social relations and the power to protect themselves. (p. 53)

5   Policy implications

The bird's-eye view from which policy is generally formulated has certain strategic advantages, but these are gained at a price which should not be regarded as inevitable. The criteria for monitoring and evaluation of a school's performance need to be expanded to include accountability to its local clientele, if the cycle of disempowerment of marginal communities is to be broken.

5.1   *Schools as nodes*

Part of the solution to this dilemma, it seems to me, may come from developing alternative methods of aggregation which recognise the integrity of individual persons over time and the salience of the individual school as a pivot around which the accountability of the educational system to consumers must be negotiated. Rather than the centrally constructed and imposed 'blueprint approach' which has informed educational planning in the past, what is required is a 'learning process approach', which emphasises the primacy of impact at the small-scale level. Korten has argued with impressive supporting evidence that such a learning process has been a crucial factor in the success of several rural development projects in Asia which have succeeded from small beginnings as pilot projects in 'coming of age' and 'going to scale' as national or regional programmes (Korten 1980; Myers 1984).

If educational planning is to take account of this finding, greater prominence will need to be given to the individual school as a node in the planning process. As Tom Eisemon has noted, the planning strategies advocated by the World Bank centre on the mass production and distribution of

key qualitative inputs: teacher training, opportunities for in-service teacher education, textbook availability, school inspection, national examinations and so on ... [Yet] school-effectiveness research in developed and developing countries suggests that *schools*, rather than individual school inputs, must be the object of reform ... What matters, insofar as classroom instruction is concerned, is not just how much of various kinds of resources schools have but how they combine and use them. (1989, p. 113)[11]

In my view an essential part of the analysis of how a school combines and uses the resources at its disposal is the pattern of local accountability it maintains towards the community from which it draws its students. I suggested in chapter 4 that the reluctance of Zambian teachers to extend the scope of their identification with the life of the community to include a moral, informally negotiated answerability to parents in respect of their pedagogical activities arises from a technological perspective on schools shared by teachers and parents, which stresses product criteria, i.e. examination results. If, as I have argued, the impediments to their construing their responsibilities in these terms are institutional rather than personal, administrative reforms could in principle bring about a real improvement in the relations between schools and their client communities. Changes in both policy and training could effectively reorientate the pattern of regular activities of the school towards performing tangible services with a constructive rather than extractive impact on the local community. Some examples of this type of activity are briefly discussed below.

The analysis of our attempts to explore this domain in chapter 6 showed that the promotion of negotiated, local accountability is a demanding and sometimes elusive goal, but there are both theoretical and empirical grounds for believing that it is not unattainable. The idea that the alternative cultural systems of meaning described in chapters 2 and 3 are not inexorably sealed off from one another but are mutually penetrable is explored in the Appendix, and in the second half of chapter 6 the popular participatory theatre workshop was presented as an instance of productive communication across that interface.

Some readers may feel that the focus on responsiveness to local community needs advocated in this book is somewhat parochial and old-fashioned. Is not Africa now a continent of modern nations with supra-ethnic ideals and objectives? Would not a focus on local pre-occupations be counterproductive in the march towards nation-hood and economic progress? I have two reasons for rejecting this view, one fundamentally philosophical, the other more immediately pragmatic.

Fundamentally, I believe that the notion of national identity can only claim validity at a certain level of abstraction quite far removed from people's emotional lives. When it is elevated in importance above our personal, family and community commitments, it ceases to be a noble ideal and instead becomes depersonalising and profoundly threatening to our humanity.

At the more immediate level of political pragmatism, we have only to look at the kinds of solutions being proposed by African statesmen for 'the problem of the urban youth' to realise that a crisis of credibility of nationhood lies barely below the surface. For some time now, politi-cians who profess to endorse the ideology of Zambian Humanism have been openly canvassing an amendment to the constitution which would allow the state compulsorily to 'repatriate' to rural areas young people 'found' living in town 'unproductively'! An ominous rhetorical allusion to this 'new right' trend was made by President Kaunda in his address to a public rally on Youth Day in March 1988: 'Do not force me to change the constitution and force people to go back to the land. The Party and its government wants people to do this voluntarily with a clean heart and not by force.'[12] The constitutional amendment being contemplated would remove from the list of guaranteed basic rights the freedom of movement and residence within the nation's borders. Yet the very foundation of the new society rests on this freedom, which was denied to Africans in the colonial regime of Northern Rhodesia and continued to be denied to Africans in the racist Republic of South Africa. Rather than resorting to intimidation to chase the graduates of a necessarily 'terminal' primary schooling out of the over-crowded cities, surely a more constructive and more viable strategy would be to reorientate the schools in such a way that their graduates perceive themselves as both equipped and motivated to engage in productive activities within the rural economy.

The much publicised failures of some very explicit attempts to build the curriculum around productive activities should not, in my view, be interpreted too narrowly. Certainly, basic education should not be confused with vocational training. But the strong adverse reactions to the attempts by missionary and colonial educators to build a commitment to productive work into the primary curriculum in rural African schools were part of a wider critique of political and economic inequality between different racial groups in colonial society (Ball 1983), just as the criticisms of the Brigades in post-independence Botswana were premised on the coexistence of another, more privileged stream of educational opportunity (cf. van Rensburg 1984).

To explore in detail the implications of this line of reasoning would require another book, and expertise in the field of agriculture which lies beyond my competence. But it seems clear that the formulation of an intellectually coherent link between a rural community's economically productive activities and the content of the primary school curriculum is an essential area of curriculum development for the future of basic education in large parts of Africa.

5.2   *Focus on curriculum content*

One of the paradoxes of the 'rate-of-return' research reviewed above has been its neglect of content issues which, as Eisemon states,

are central to educational policy and decision making and ... figure prominently ... both in African educational research and in public debate ... It cannot be assumed that interventions that promote internal efficiency in terms of optimal utilization of available instructional inputs necessarily enable schools to be more effective in accomplishing what educational decision-makers and many parents expect schools to do ... Achievement test results indicate what a student should know based on what someone has determined a student should have been taught. They do not provide many insights into the knowledge students may possess or into the cognitive strategies they use or into the quality of instruction they may have received. (1989, pp. 113–14)

Significant economies of scale are bound to militate against decentralising all aspects of educational planning. The basic selection, segmentation and ordering of the content of the curriculum and the training of teachers will always call for some degree of centralisation. In these contexts, I have suggested in chapters 2 and 3 a need for greater emphasis on moral aspects of the curriculum, rather than the current reliance on a 'value-free' conceptualisation of the goals of pedagogy in terms of technological mastery. Although the scope for political and religious manipulation of this dimension of education is awesome, the responsibility to address it within the framework of schooling cannot be evaded.

Given the contrast drawn in earlier chapters between the cultural meaning-systems informing the school curriculum and the practices of many students' homes, it would appear that adult members of their families would need to be consulted as part of such a curriculum development process. In the USA, Heath (1983) has described productive ways in which primary school students can engage in local ethnographic research involving two-way communication with their elders, resulting in both a deeper appreciation by the students of their cultural heritage and a recognition of opportunities to provide local services to their community. Another factor which appears to contribute very significantly to the credibility gap for schooling in Kondwelani (and in many other communities in Zambia and indeed elsewhere in Africa) is its overwhelming reliance on a linguistic medium which is scarcely heard by students outside the walls of their classrooms. The arguments in favour and against the use of English in the Zambian educational system have been reviewed in chapter 4 and will not be repeated here. Probably most child psychologists in Africa would agree with the proposition that the current policy of immersing rural children in such an exogenous medium in the first grade is pedagogically unsound. Whatever the merits of the economic and political arguments available to defend the emphasis on English at the more advanced levels of the educational system, the insistence that children in monolingual rural communities such as Kondwelani should master a foreign language as a precondition to learning any part of the school curriculum seems pedagogically indefensible.

In addition to the domain of production mentioned above, a substantive topic within the curriculum which deserves much greater attention than it currently receives is that of health. Although biological topics bearing on health promotion feature in the existing curriculum, the continuing prevalence of behaviourally mediated hazards to public health in rural areas strongly suggests that only a small proportion of the behavioural implications of modern biological knowledge is understood or believed by young adults who have been to school for several years.

A striking example of a missed opportunity is the 'Road to Health' weight-monitoring chart printed on the health record card issued to the parents of every infant seen at a Zambian health centre. In chapter 5, I described the responses from two members of our cohort (Mpeza and Yumba) to questions about the significance of weight monitoring for the care of their infants. Both of these young women had spent more than four years at school and both were now young mothers responsible for raising a young child. One of them had learned from the local clinic how to interpret the weight chart and had clearly understood its significance; the other had not. It is standard policy for Rural Health centres in Zambia to try to familiarise the mothers who attend well-baby clinics with their infants with the meaning of the weight chart, and several mothers in our cohort with whom I discussed this topic showed either a partial or a full understanding. In all cases they assured me that their only knowledge on the subject came from the health centre: none of them remembered ever learning about it at school.

Yet this particular topic seems in several salient respects to be an ideal curriculum focus in terms of the theoretical principles informing the Zambian school curriculum. It has virtually universal relevance to the future lives of students. It is a clearly conceptualised topic, easy to present in a lucid fashion to young people. Its central concept, growth measured by weight, is quantifiable. It is supported by a strong scientific consensus in the modern world. And its behavioural implications have a high level of acceptance in political and administrative circles in Zambia and in many (if not all) other African countries.

Why, then, did such a straightforward topic not find its way into the basic school curriculum to which these young parents-to-be were exposed in their schooling? The most plausible explanation seems to be that it is considered an adult topic and one of exclusive relevance to women. Students in the lower grades of primary school are construed by curriculum developers as immature, and the mature cognitive tasks for which they are being prepared in the domain of Science are dominated by the technical requirements of income-generating activities. The care of infants with diarrhoea or malnutrition escapes this net under the guise of a domestic task for which mothers (as contrasted with children, students or economically productive citizens) are responsible.

The claims made by the United Nations Children's Fund (UNICEF) for the potential of growth charts to enhance the survival prospects of children in Africa and other parts of the Third World (Grant 1984; cf. Morley and Woodland 1979) suggest that every effort should be made to communicate the underlying concepts to parents of the next generation, both men and women. And schools are in a uniquely strong position to carry out this task. In rural communities in Zambia and elsewhere in Africa, girls are expected to participate from an early age in the care and nurturance of infants. There is therefore no danger of students in the lower grades failing to understand the relevance of this topic to their daily lives. It is also an unusually clear case of a simple item of knowledge they are unlikely to pick up informally at home and which could make a dramatic difference to their lives.

5.3   *Expansion of clientele*

5.3.1   *Adults*

A related area of practice requiring radical rethinking is the tight linkage of curriculum materials with age. In rural schools at least, provision needs to be made for a much closer linkage between adult education and the activities of primary schools. The literacy and other technical skills offered in schools will only have their full impact if young adults have access to continuing intellectual support for their application to the challenges of life in the community.

5.3.2   *Disabled children*

Orthogonal to the upward expansion of the designated clientele to include adult students, a strong case can be made for its horizontal expansion to recruit more actively those children living in its catchment zone who are born with, or acquire as a result of illness or injury, a significant impairment of sensory, motor or intellectual functions. This group of clients, who are known generically in Zambia as disabled children (Nabuzoka 1986; Serpell *et al.* 1988), pose a very provocative set of challenges to educational practice, against the background of the present study. The primary school teachers who responded to the survey described in chapter 4 recognised that their training and general professional outlook equips them uniquely well among the professional personnel available in rural areas to cater to the developmental needs of individuals falling into this category. When asked whether they would be willing to include a child with a severe disability in their regular classes, Table 7.1 shows the percentages of our respondents who indicated a willingness to do so under various conditions.

It is clear that expansion of the school's clientele in this direction would call for significant changes in the pattern of its service delivery, and of teacher training, as, of course, would its expansion to include more adult education. One such variation with respect to disabled children is discussed in the following section.

One significant consequence of contemplating the inclusion within a regular primary school of students with a severe intellectual disability is that it clearly rules out any conceivable relevance for the competitive orientation towards a selective, extractive definition of success. If the experience of schooling is to be useful for a child with such a disability, it must be able to offer tangible benefits irrespective of whether the student is able to proceed to a more advanced level. The nature of

Table 7.1 *Mainstream rural primary school-teachers' views on how they would react if requested by the Head Teacher to accept into the class they are currently teaching children with various types of disability*

(1) Accept this as a normal assignment which poses no serious problems for you?
(2) Accept this as a challenge which you feel you can tackle on your own?
(3) Accept the assignment, but request some special help in the form of guidance from the Inspectorate of Special Education?
(4) Refuse the assignment unless you are first promised some special in-service training to assist you to tackle it?
(5) Refuse the assignment as unreasonable, and insist on referring the child to a special class with specialist staff and specialised equipment?

	(1)	(2)	(3)	(4)	(5)
(a) walking disability	15	1	7	4	3
(b) hand movement disability	8	5	8	2	7
(c) vision disability	3	7	10	1	9
(d) hearing disability	0	5	6	7	12
(e) learning disability (mental retardation)	2	0	3	7	18

those benefits may range from strictly cognitive skills such as the use of Braille to socio-emotional assets such as acceptance by peers and participation in group activities (cf. Serpell 1982b, 1983b; Miles 1985).

I suggested in chapter 3 that the general claim that school-based literacy directly amplifies the cognition of those who go to school is probably an overstatement. But for many individuals with a severe disability in Africa, a strong case can be made that schooling will afford her or him opportunities which have no counterpart in the accessible out-of-school environment. Possibly even more important are the benefits of 'normalisation' which are expected to flow from a disabled person's inclusion in a 'mainstream' educational facility.

The strategy of community-based rehabilitation within which the idea of including disabled children in regular rural primary schools in Africa has been advanced (cf. Helander *et al.* 1980; Serpell 1986; Mariga and McConkey 1987) construes the role of professionals such as teachers as one of animation: to stimulate the flowering of potential, to provoke creative activity among members of the client family, neighbourhood, community. In this context pre-existing ideas, concepts and models derived from theory and based on accumulated empirical experience with other children, other families, other communities, will often have some potential relevance. But for its relevance to be grasped, its potential realised, the actors in the child's continuing network of caregivers, teachers and friends will have to appropriate those ideas as their own, as part of their cognitive repertoire. And here lies the communicative challenge for the professional: to negotiate with clients a shared interpretation of the child's problems and those of the other relevant actors which is both convincing and empowering to the clients (cf. Jardine 1988). In my view, this communicative challenge for teachers is also present in a less visible form for all of a rural primary school's students, in relation to the community by which they were raised, from which they commute to school and in which many of them may be expected to live in the future.

5.3.3   Pre-school age children

A different extension of the clientele of formal education in rural areas which has received considerable attention in 'Development Aid' circles is downwards to reach children of pre-school age. My attitude towards this proposal has generally been unfavourable, on the grounds that (a) it threatens to extend an already rampant pattern of culturally hegemonistic intervention characteristic of much of the existing primary schooling on offer in Africa, and thus to further undermine local confidence in indigenous socialisation practices, and (b) in the existing context of extreme competition for limited places in the formal school system, pre-school education is liable to be manipulated by privileged elites to divert public resources away from much needed reforms of the school system, with a view to merely providing a selection mechanism for those who enter school (Serpell 1983c).

If, however, pre-school age children were to be included along with their mothers in an expanded pattern of educational provision as outlined below, there might be valuable opportunities for women with partial primary schooling to deploy the skills which they have acquired in school in a socially productive way, to institutionalise in a publicly acknowledged way some of their commitment to the upbringing of their children, and thus to build bridges between their own cognitions and the curriculum of schooling. Such an arrangement might create a forum in which women could play a constructive role in the articulation of publicly agreed socialisation roles and activities.[13]

5.4   Expansion of local service functions

If rural primary schools are to become more accountable to their local communities and to cater to a more diverse clientele, as suggested above, they will have to engage in a wide variety of activities. Their use as libraries, as meeting places for clubs and discussion groups, as health education centres, etc., which already takes place informally and incidentally will need to be defined as part of their regular educational responsibilities and explicitly supported with financial and administrative inputs.

The library function could be one of the most important ways of realising and sustaining the unfulfilled promises of basic literacy discussed in chapters 3 and 6. The principle that there is little point in being literate if there is nothing available to read is both elementary and critical in Zambia's rural areas in the context of the economic recession which has persisted from the late 1970s and continued to accelerate throughout the 1980s. Every copy of a national newspaper reaching a school like Kondwelani is, typically, read by several individuals. A recent survey of four of Zambia's public libraries (two in cities and two in rural towns) by Juliano Kabamba (1988) revealed a very narrow pattern of utilisation. Most users were full-time enrolled students, many of them using the library as a quiet place to study. Less than 1 per cent of the users had completed less than seven years of schooling. A network of 160 rural-centre libraries launched in 1960, with collections ranging from twenty to a hundred volumes each, had expanded by 1965 to over 550 centres, mainly 'based in primary and secondary schools, agricultural camps, hospitals and National Service camps'. But by 1987 this service was effectively moribund (pp. 45–6).

For more than a decade, the national government has continued to invest substantially in the promotion of literacy through basic schooling, while doing nothing to ensure the availability of materials to read in rural areas. Assuming that the purpose is not to precipitate an immediate permanent exodus of all literate persons from the rural areas, it must be regarded as self-defeating not to commit at least some resources to making available a selection of reading materials which go beyond the textbooks prescribed for use in schools.

The establishment (or re-establishment) of school-based libraries catering to all of the local public would be a highly cost-effective strategy for tackling this problem. Moreover, coming to the school for the legitimate purpose of borrowing or returning a book would provide a natural way for school leavers to maintain contact with other cultural activities of the school. Other informational services which could be built around a basic book-loan system with a modest injection of additional resources would be broadcasting of selected radio programmes outside school hours and provision of access to an electronic calculator on a reference user basis. When economic conditions improve, and mains electricity supply and telephone lines become available, a further level of development of the service could eventually be planned to include information retrieval via computer search.

Meanwhile, other participatory opportunities for continuing education can be envisaged without any additional capital resources, including the use of the school as a forum for discussion by adults of current community and national events. In the case of children whose disabilities make it unrealistic for them to come to the school, the concept of a home visiting programme modelled along the lines of the Portage Project in the USA (Bluma et al. 1976) was floated in the survey of teacher opinions and attracted considerable interest. The question and the distribution of responses it elicited are presented in Table 7.2.

5.5   Increasing flexibility of access

A natural consequence of broadening the clientele of the school and the range of its activities would be to relax the pattern of access to the services it offers. Rather than the existing regimented and compartmentalised format, in which only children of a specified age are registered on an annual basis and required to follow a sharply predefined sequence of lessons in accordance with a strict time-table, the school would also become accessible over a wider range of times of day, periods of the week and seasons of the year to people of all ages who would be more selective of what information they receive, and in some cases the service offered by personnel of the school would be delivered to the community on an outreach basis.

Clearly this change of pattern would require considerable skill for its effective administration, but (as suggested in Table 7.2) many of the new activities could be combined with their existing duties by the current personnel. Moreover, financial incentives for performing extra work need not necessarily be part of such arrangements. Provided that these new functions of the school were accorded sufficiently high priority status as a matter of policy, they could be incorporated in the school's overall mandate in place of some of its current activities.

6   Mediation at the interface between cultures

Directly related to the feasibility of these various lines of curriculum development there will be a need to emphasise more strongly in the training of teachers the theme of moral accountability to the families of their pupils, rather than the current emphasis on professional efficiency. If a school is to perform a genuinely enlightening and empowering function in the community it aspires to serve, the school curriculum must be intelligible at least in its central thrust to the parents and other family members of pupils. In many communities this calls for a major effort of reinterpretation on several interrelated levels. The nature of social and economic opportunity needs to be understood as an open-ended adventure rather than a closed, narrow staircase.

Table 7.2 *Reactions of primary school teachers to suggested schemes for integrated classroom teaching and home visit teaching for disabled children*

If a short in-service course was offered to enable teachers to serve more effectively the special needs of disabled children in the context of a class integrated with other, able children, would you be interested to enrol in such a course?

(a) Yes, provided that the course was on full pay and did not require me to leave my family for more than 6 weeks.
(b) Yes, but only if the course was for a full year on full pay and would entitle me to an increase in my salary after completing it successfully.
(c) No, I would not be interested.

It has been suggested that in every primary school one teacher might be given a special responsibility for disabled children of school-age who are unable to attend school because of their disability. This teacher would be given time off from class-teaching duties in order to visit the disabled children at their homes, in order to discuss their education with their families and try to assist the family to promote the child's development in various ways.
If this scheme were to be introduced at your school, would you be interested in taking on this special responsiblity? yes/no
Please give your comments on the issue:

		Men teachers with *more* than 5 years teaching experience	Men teachers with *less* than 5 years	Women teachers with *more* than 5 years teaching experience	Women teachers with *less* than 5 years
interest in a (a) course on integrated class		4	1	3	0
teaching	(b)	18	9	9	4
No interest	(c)	0	0	1	0
(No answer)		(2)	(0)	(2)	(0)
Interest in special home visiting responsi-	Yes	21	7	7	3
bility	No	8	2	4	1

The goals of education should thus be construed not as qualifications for entry into specific occupational slots, but as resources for creative deployment on the social and economic stage. Pedagogy and instruction in turn should be construed, not as conditioning, moulding or transforming, but as cultivating, nurturing and feeding the learner's mind.

Such a wide-ranging reinterpretation is evidently a shared responsibility for society as a whole. However, primary school teachers are particularly well placed to take on the role of trail-blazers. To do so will present the challenge of combining with their professional expertise a new and reflective sense of accountability to the families and community they aspire to serve.

The evidence presented in chapter 4 shows that, in matters of teaching, teachers clearly regard themselves as primarily accountable to their professional and administrative constituency, rather than to the families of the children they teach. Under these circumstances, it becomes the responsibility of planners, administrators and trainers to 'represent' the interests of those primary clients, to gear the incentive system, the reward system and the disciplinary system of schooling in such a way as to maximise the responsiveness of serving teachers to the needs of the children they teach, of their families and of their local community. The measures outlined in Section 5 above are suggestions as to how such an administrative framework might begin to shift teachers' priorities in that direction.

The extent to which the project of the Enlightenment is appropriated by Africans for the promotion of a genuinely developmental form of education (developmental both for the individuals and for the society as a whole) will depend in large part on the extent to which the bicultural graduates of a largely alien curriculum are willing to share their critical understanding of Western culture with those of their fellow-citizens (be they grandparents, parents, contemporaries or children) who have not had the opportunity to sample it in depth. Out of such a sharing could arise a radical redefinition of what constitutes a modern education, incorporating the best of both cultures, a synthesis born of egalitarian discourse.

Appendix: Metaphors for schooling

1   Multiple perspectives on the cognitive development of children

The cognitive development of children is influenced by a multitude of thinking persons, including various audiences to whom this book is addressed: their parents and other elders in the local community, their teachers, the authors of the books they read, the designers of their school curriculum and the planners of the school system. The perspective on cognitive development adopted in each of chapters 2, 3 and 4 has more in common with the pre-existing concerns of some of those interested parties than others. In chapter 2, members of rural Chewa society in Katete District, as well as members of other rural African communities, will recognise particular features of the environment with which they deal on a daily basis. Chapter 3, on the other hand, deals mainly with concepts familiar to educational theorists and planners, and chapter 4 with issues of regular concern to teachers and planners. The purpose of this Appendix is to provide a linking framework for these various perspectives, which is grounded in philosophy.

A major premise of my approach to this topic is that there exists an intrinsic connection in the human sciences between theoretical validity and the audience to whom theoretical explanations are addressed. For a number of interrelated reasons, the authors of comparative studies across different cultural settings tend to project inappropriate ideas from their home culture on to the behaviour and experience of subjects whose cultural frame of reference they do not fit. This bias is neither a product of simple methodological errors nor an insuperable barrier to communication. It reflects the fact that every interpretation arises from a particular human perspective, which Lukes defines as 'a more or less closely related set of beliefs, attitudes and assumptions that specify how reality is to be understood' (1982, p. 301).

As I have argued in more detail elsewhere (Serpell 1990), culturally distinctive ideas can be construed as a system of dynamic rules which constitute the basis for a mutual understanding among those who share a given culture. Socially responsible psychologists are accountable to their subjects as self-conscious and autonomous agents. Any successful interpretation requires common ground between author, subject and audience. Different cultural perspectives share a common core of primary theory (Horton 1982) about immediate experience, which underwrites the possibility of cross-cultural communication. Translation between cultural perspectives hinges on what Gadamer (1975) has called 'a fusion of horizons'. For this a major resource is the semantic device of metaphor. Models which point the way for theoretical interpretation succeed in part by resonating with the pre-theoretical ideas of their audience.

My principal concern in this appendix is to explore the ways in which metaphors may help to integrate or at least coordinate various different perspectives on schooling, and thus to lay the basis for a shared understanding among the following audiences to whom this book is addressed:

1. Chewa society, centred around subsistence agricultural communities in Eastern Province and connecting out into subsistence agricultural communities in Malawi and Mozambique;
2. primary school teachers in the field and in training, with some diversification in relation to those three national, encapsulating state frameworks;
3. psychologists in Zambia, in other African Anglophone countries and in other Third World countries;
4. educational planners, branching out into the development planning community more generally;
5. theorists of developmental psychology, in relation to the growing interest in cultural and cross-cultural aspects of that discipline.

Although some of the themes of individual chapters are more familiar to one or more of these audiences than to others, I believe they are all intimately interconnected, and that a full understanding of the significance of schooling is only possible if they are somehow synthesised.

2   The reflexive triangle[1]

All forms of representation and intepretation are selective. The choice of which features to emphasise at the expense of others is motivated by the goals of communication. These goals vary even for a single individual depending on the situation. A psychological theory may be proposed as a guide to future research or as a frame of reference for interpreting individual acts of behaviour or events of experience. In each case we can identify three different roles which feature in the communication situation: the subject whose behaviour is to be

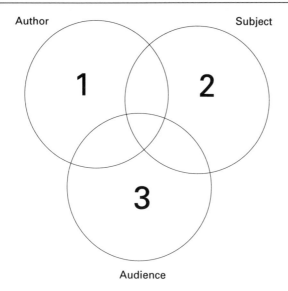

Fig. A.1 Cultures of interpretation (perspectives): the reflexive triangle.

explained, the author who proposes the explanation and the audience to whom the explanation is addressed (see Fig. A.1).

Sometimes two of the these roles may be played by the same individual. For instance, the audience may also be the subject, as when a clinician (as author) attempts to provide a client (as audience) with an explanation of the client's own experience (as subject). Or the subject may also take on the role of author, as when the client (as author) offers her own interpretation of her own behaviour (as subject) to the clinician (as audience). This potential for changing roles has been described as the challenge of reflexivity inherent in the enterprise of psychological theorising (e.g. Shotter 1975). An acid test, some would hold, of the adequacy of a psychological theory is whether it is satisfying to the subject who applies it to her own behaviour and experience, thus simultaneously playing the parts of subject, author and audience. But, of course, we also use such theories to explain the behaviour of others and not always to themselves. The interchangeable roles must also therefore remain separable so that, for instance, an educational psychologist may offer an explanation of a child's behaviour to other members of the family or to a school teacher, and an industrial/occupational psychologist may offer an interpretation of the experiences of workers and managers each to the other party.

The guiding paradigm of cross-cultural psychology has been the attempt by a researcher from a 'Western' cultural background to describe the behaviour or the mental life of people in cultures other than the one she shares with her audience. An important early insight of researchers following this paradigm was that some of their descriptions tended to miss the point of what they seek to interpret, because they failed to connect appropriately with the ways in which the people whose behaviour was described think about that behaviour themselves. Attempts to characterise this insight in ways which point ahead towards a solution of the problem have been beset with difficulties of a conceptual nature.[2] What I propose here is a reformulation of the original insight in terms of communication among the three essential participants in any psychological discourse: the person whose behaviour and/or mental life is to be interpreted, the author of the interpretation and the audience to whom the interpretation is addressed.

Paradoxically, when psychologists have explicitly set out to study cultural differences, this task of cross-cultural interpretation has often been neglected. Many 'Western' psychologists have not even appeared to be interested in whether their reports would be intelligible, let alone illuminating, for the people they studied. Indeed, they did not even acknowledge them as a potential audience: subjects were construed as objects of study but not as recipients of the wisdom generated by the study. Those cross-cultural researchers who have acknowledged an obligation to capture the meaning of behaviour and experience from the perspective of their subjects have most often construed this as a means of ensuring functional equivalence for the purpose of comparison. This concern emanates from the 'Olympian' (Berrien 1967) project of formulating a universalistic psychology.

Perhaps one of the hidden attractions of this metaphor has been the 'peculiar mixture of familiarity and strangeness' (Horton 1982) in Homer's account of the gods. In contemporary terms, we would say they were equipped with fantastic zoom-lenses and long-distance microphones so that from the great height of Mount Olympus they could listen to what people down below were saying and observe their behaviour at close range. In the real world, central government administrators and cosmopolitan social scientists do have a bird's-eye view of certain parameters of the total society and in this sense they may be regarded as privileged. But there is a high price to be paid for this privilege: loss of detail, loss of fine-grain texture, loss of contact with reality as it is experienced in the front line, with both feet on the ground.

And those researchers who seek to recover some of this lost detail must again pay a price, for we travel not by zoom-lens into the privacy of people's homes but as visitors, or at best as commuters between an alien and distant, powerful capital and the front doorstep of people's homes, where we must humbly ask them to share with us some of their experiences. Not only must we persuade them that this is an exercise worth their time, but we must also try to bear in mind how they interpret the task of communicating with us, what allowances they are making for our foreignness, what objectives they are pursuing in selecting what they choose to tell us, and so on.

Rather than explicit comparison between contrasting cultural groups or the construction of a universalistic psychology, the present study arises from an alternative set of concerns which warrant paying close attention to cultural issues in the psychology constructed in a Third World country. The focus of these concerns, in the light of the predominantly 'Western' cultural orientation of contemporary psychology, is on the question: what use can a socially responsible, Third World psychologist make of psychology (along with other, indigenous cultural resources) in explaining the behaviour and experience of a Third World subject to a Third World audience? If my analysis is correct, much will depend on whether the author succeeds in representing the central insights of his or her theoretical model in terms of metaphors which are intelligible to both subject and audience and which point the way towards a fusion of their various cognitive horizons.

The central insight which I wish to share with my various audiences, including the subjects whose lives I followed in arriving at this interpretation, is that schooling is just one resource among many for the enhancement of one's journey through life. It is a resource whose full potential for enriching that journey is realised by only a few. The reasons why so few of the ideals of the curriculum are attained by most of those who enter school must be sought at the point of interaction among a constellation of interested participants: the young person herself, the teachers and the young person's family. The significance of schooling in the life of this person will emerge from a shared interpretation which these three parties must negotiate.

3   Perspectivism, primary and secondary theory

The detailed analysis presented in chapter 2 showed that the notions of *-nzelu* and *-tumikila* in Chewa culture have no precise equivalents in English. Their nature is well summarised by Taylor's observation that 'the vocabulary . . . is grounded in the shape of social practice' (1971, p. 24). It is important to recognise that the problem runs deeper than sheer availability of terminology. It will not do, for instance, to say that the English and Chewa cultures merely have different vocabularies for describing intelligence, since the notion of intelligence is grounded in a different set of social practices. A culturally appropriate psychology for rural Chewa society needs a theory of -*nzelu*, not a theory of intelligence.

At the very least, in psychological theory 'interpretation and explanation must make reference to actors' perspectives' (Lukes 1982, p. 302). The logic, however, seems to point also towards a more fundamentally relativistic conclusion 'that there can be no perspective-neutral interpretation and explanation' (p. 302). This 'strong' version of perspectivism poses a number of difficulties for applied psychology. A practising psychologist has a professional obligation to formulate prescriptive statements based on the best evidence available. If inter-subjective meanings are construed as the primary defining criteria for social facts, what line of action should the practitioner prescribe in cases where her own interpretation of the relevant social facts differs significantly from that favoured by the subjects whose behaviour is involved? Prince, for instance, argued on the one hand that the type of explanation for mental illness proposed by psychoanalytic theory is qualitatively superior to the symbolic formulations of unconscious motivation indigenous to various non-Western cultures, and justifies his conclusion on scientific grounds. Yet he concludes that in the absence of 'a high degree of psychological mindedness' (Prince 1980, pp. 335–6) the psychoanalytic form of therapy is inapplicable, and that in many non-Western cultures 'trance states, religious experiences, and micropsychoses in the service of therapy have a much wider application' (p. 339). Behind the pragmatism which seems to justify such a decision lies an unstated value judgement which condemns those who adhere to certain cultural perspectives to a form of therapy which the therapist regards as technically inferior.

A similar dilemma confronts the educational practitioner in a still more poignant form when deciding what kind of education is best for the children of a rural African community. On the one hand, he or she may be convinced by arguments in favour of a number of crucial curriculum components and pedagogical principles developed in the context of a modern, industrialised society. Yet several of these ingredients of an ideal education may seem to be not only impracticable but also counterproductive as a preparation for life in the community into which these children were born. If she decides on relativistic grounds to eschew those ingredients as inappropriate, the objection can be raised that she is discounting the possibility of social change, and indeed neglecting her responsibility as a broker of technical knowledge to contribute to the guidance of such change in a 'progressive' direction.

A second kind of difficulty for perspectivism arises in the context of an egalitarian, multicultural, modern state like Zambia. Legislation to protect freedom of religious worship, choice of attire, diet, etc., may seem to be inspired by relativistic principles. But unless strict segregation between cultural groups is envisaged, provision has to be made for the resolution of conflicts between adherents of different cultural perspectives. Of course, as often happens in practice, the government could decide to impose the standards of one culture over those of others. But this appears philosophically arbitrary. What is required is some common ground on which an impartial resolution of conflict can be based. Also, in such a society public education is expected to cater within integrated schools for children from diverse cultural home backgrounds, and to cultivate mutual respect and tolerance among them. As Zec has pointed out, 'if inter-cultural understanding is to be an aim of multi-cultural education, it cannot develop solely on the basis of the notion – however well-meaning – that culturally different beliefs, practices, values and so on, are in principle incommensurable' (1980, p. 84).

Yet a further challenge for perspectivism is posed by the phenomena of individual biculturation discussed in chapter 4. Beliefs and practices which appear to 'belong' to two contrasting cultural systems often coexist within the cognitive and behavioural repertoire of a single, multicultural individual. Not only can different cultural perspectives coexist harmoniously within a multicultural community, but they are also amenable to various forms of psychological integration within a single person.

Finally, in addition to its morally unsatisfactory advocacy of double standards and its inability to account for certain social and psychological realities, the philosophical position of cultural relativism can be charged with a tendency towards paralysing investigators who wish to explore the application of existing theory beyond its present culturally narrow database. For there seems to be an infinite regress of relativistic questions which can be posed to undermine the validity of any research findings which purport to show substantive cross-cultural differences. For instance, when presenting to an audience of academic scholars some of the evidence (reviewed in chapter 2) that assessments of intelligence generated by Western-type tests do not conform with assessments by rural A-Chewa adults, I have been asked at various times:

> Do parents in that community normally assess or monitor the progress of their children towards certain goals?
> Do people in that community ever compare one individual to another in terms of capabilities, dispositions or other qualities of mind, as opposed to looking at the group's behaviour and products?
> Does the enterprise of assessment have any pertinence within that culture?

Each of these questions was posed by an experienced and thoughtful researcher of Western cultural origins, and I was tempted in each case to answer 'yes, of course'. But on a philosophical plane such an answer is no more adequate than Samuel Johnson's notorious attempt to refute Bishop Berkeley's arguments for the non-existence of matter by kicking a stone (Boswell 1799).

A very helpful approach to the resolution of these problems has been advanced by Horton (1982) in a reformulation of his earlier, much debated analysis of the similarities and differences between 'African traditional thought and Western science' (1967). He suggests that we should recognise two major levels of thought and discourse used by people to explain the world: primary and secondary theory. Primary theory constitutes an overall framework common to all humanity: it postulates a world filled with middle-sized, enduring, solid objects, interrelated in terms of a 'push–pull' conception of causality, and distinguishes sharply between the self, other human beings and other subjects. 'The entities and processes of primary thought are thought of as directly "given" to the human observer' (p. 229), but there is a great deal in everyone's experience which this level of theory cannot explain. And it is at the level of secondary theory that we encounter 'startling differences in kind' between cultures. In fact, 'the diversity of world-pictures presented by secondary-theoretical discourse ... is such that it almost defies any general characterization', except that the entities and processes it postulates 'are thought of as somehow "hidden" ... [and] present a peculiar mixture of familiarity and strangeness' (p. 229).

Because of its transcultural commonality, primary theory 'provides the cross-cultural voyager with his intellectual bridgehead' (p. 228) – that is, with some preliminary common ground which guarantees mutual intelligibility between two interlocutors with different cultural perspectives. Moreover, in all its diverse forms, secondary theory is derivative from its primary counterpart in several ways, notably that 'development of ideas as to the character of the "hidden" realm is based on the drawing of analogies with familiar everyday experiences as described in primary-theory terms' (p. 230). Thus in many cultures supernatural entities are conceptualised in terms analogous with human action and interaction, while the explanatory constructs of Newtonian physics were developed on the basis of analogies with colliding balls, water waves, etc. The importance of analogy in the comprehension and acceptance of psychological theories will be discussed in Section 5.

Thus a belief in the fundamental 'psychic unity of mankind'[3] can be reconciled with cultural perspectivism, through the recognition that despite their differences all peoples' conceptions of the world share a common core of universal primary theory. The defining properties of primary theory remain somewhat elusive: in addition to the sense of being directly 'given' these aspects of conceptualisation appear to 'emerge' from our experience with a sharply defined structure (Lakoff and Johnson 1980). This structure no doubt has to do with the biological structure of the human body as well as with the physical structure of the 'external' world. It may also reflect aspects of human communication which are universal across cultures. The spatial orientational concepts 'up–down', 'front–back' fit in obvious ways the human body's relationship with the physical environment. The coordination of gaze in early social interaction between infants and their primary caregivers lays the pragmatic foundations for deixis which in turn serves to anchor reference in linguistic communication (Bruner 1975; Trevarthen 1980). Children also appear by a very early age to have a mental model of what constitutes a person that includes assumptions of intentionality, of a capacity for adaptive learning, and for communication (Shields 1978). These assumptions remain available for adults as resources for cross-cultural communication and could be used to explain why the semiotic meaning of some manual signs are more 'transparent' than others, while others are merely 'translucent' (Kiernan 1985) in the sense that their meaning is easy to grasp once their rationale is explained.

Moreover, this shared theory bears a systematic relationship to the secondary theories which set cultures apart. For the teacher, as for the therapist, this formulation provides hope for negotiating a form of accountability consistent with the standards of both her client's culture and her own. For the social planner it provides hope for the harmonious coordination of multiple perspectives within a multi-cultural society. And for cross-cultural psychology it provides grounds for believing that the cognitive systems of different cultures are in some way mutually penetrable.

4   Fusion of horizons

If a psychological explanation is to contribute to the self-understanding of the person whose behaviour or experience it interprets, the author needs to penetrate that person's cultural perspective. Analysis of a perspective in terms of rule-constituted language games helps to explain how the indigenous participant in the culture acquired her competence. It is, however, unrealistic to expect every cross-cultural voyager, even if she is a committed researcher, to recapitulate that learning process. This is not just because of limited time: the adult who engages in research is no longer a naïve beginner but has been fully socialised into a different cultural perspective. As a result the interpreter is bound to begin with the projection of a set of concepts and rules derived from her own culture and which to some extent will prove to be inappropriate.

One field of enquiry which has paid a great deal of attention to this problem is that of translation. The tradition of classical European scholarship during the eighteenth and nineteenth centuries, of which traces are still alive, centres around the interpretation of a culture far removed in time, for which the main source of evidence is a body of literature in ancient Greek and Latin, which has influenced the form of the various contemporary European cultures in extremely complex ways over a period of some two thousand years. Gadamer's (1975) approach to the topic of translation emerges from that tradition and is therefore much preoccupied with the interpretation of texts. His analysis, however, includes a wide-ranging exploration of the foundations of meaning in all the human sciences, and has been taken up by a number of philosophers as offering important insights for the understanding of social action.

Central to Gadamer's analysis is the theme that human understanding is historically situated, a product of a particular set of social and cultural circumstances. In order to understand a text or statement by another person, the listener/reader must acknowledge the specificity of her own frame of reference, or as he terms it 'horizon': 'the range of vision that includes everything that can be seen from a particular vantage point' (p. 269). Acknowledging it includes recognising that it is historically and culturally specific, and therefore systematically different from that of the author whose text is to be interpreted, and that there is no way for the interpreter completely to escape her own horizon. The preconceptions and prejudices arising from the interpreter's own culture of primary socialisation are only objectionable to the extent that they are imposed unselfconsciously on the foreign material. It is in fact illogical to propose that the interpreter should detach herself completely from all preconceptions since there is no such thing as an interpreter without a perspective. 'Interpretation is always a hermeneutic mediation between different life-worlds', each of which is a product of particular socio-cultural conditions and is 'caught up in the movement of history' (McCarthy 1978, pp. 173–4).

The mark of a successful interpretation, then, is not that it constitutes some ultimately correct, detached explanation which stands outside the cultures of author, subject and audience, but rather that it has achieved what Gadamer terms 'a fusion of horizons':

The interpreter, like the translator, must capture the sense of his material in and through articulating it in a symbolic framework different from that in which it was originally constituted as meaningful. And as the translator must find a common language that preserves the rights of his mother tongue and at the same time respects the foreignness of his text, so too must the interpreter conceptualize his material in such a way that while its foreignness is preserved, it is nevertheless brought into intelligible relation with his own life-world. (McCarthy 1978, p. 173)

When applied to the interpretation of human action, this analysis appears to offer a resolution of the problems outlined above for the psychological interpretation either of behaviour in general within another culture or of the behaviour of an individual whose cultural presuppositions are different from those of the interpreter.

A Gadamerian perspective entails that ... understanding of the action is neither an appropriation of the actor's concepts nor the imposition of the interpreter's categories, but a fusion of the two into a distinct entity: the interpretation (Hekman 1986, p. 147)

One way of arriving at such a fusion may be construed as a form of negotiation in the course of dialogue (cf. Serpell 1977c; Gumperz 1982). Interlocutors can arrive at a consensus that they are mutually comprehensible through a variety of *ad hoc* discourse strategies. In the case of theory formulated for publication, the process may be likened to that of translating a text, which according to Gadamer has a 'hypothetical and circular character'. From the perspectives available to him, the interpreter makes a preliminary projection 'or sketch (*Vorentwurf*)' of the sense of the text as a whole. With further penetration into the details of his material, the preliminary projection is revised, alternative proposals are considered, and new projections are tested (McCarthy 1978, p. 172).

The end product of such a series of revisions has no pretensions to universal validity. Rather, it is akin to the outcome described by Gombrich in his analysis of 'visual discoveries' in the history of art: the painter 'enriches our experience because he offers us an equivalence within his medium that may also "work" for us'. And in the validation of this discovery process, a sceptical audience becomes the artist's 'partner in the game of equivalences' (Gombrich 1960, p. 276).

5   The use of metaphor in theoretical explanation

How should one begin this game? What kind of preliminary projection is most likely to stimulate a constructive dialogue in search of a negotiated fusion of horizons? In general it seems that for such a search, sharp formulations will be less useful at the outset than figurative sketches of hypothetical commonalities. In the design of such sketches the use of analogy is essential and this requires the theorist to exploit the metaphorical dimension of human thought.

An early formulation of the problem of innovative communication was phrased as follows by Barfield:

Every man, certainly every original man, has something new to say, something new to mean. Yet if he wants to express that meaning ... he must use language – a vehicle which presupposes that he must either mean what was meant before or talk nonsense! (Barfield 1947, p. 67)

Barfield went on to suggest that the semantic device of metaphor enables an author to transcend this dilemma by 'talk[ing] what is nonsense on the face of it, but in such a way that the recipient may have the meaning suggested to him' (p. 67). This potential has recently been explored in detail by Lakoff and Johnson (1980).

Metaphors are a somewhat mysterious resource for communication and their status has proved difficult to define. Some of their salient characteristics are as follows. 'Metaphor requires the establishment of an analogy for its interpretation' (Fraser 1979, p. 177). 'The hearer has to figure out what the speaker means ... by going through another and related semantic content from the one which is communicated' (Searle 1979, p. 123). 'Similarity is the principle of inference ... on the basis of which speakers produce and hearers understand metaphor' (p. 100). 'Although readers must take the metaphor as true in the world they are trying to synthesize from the text, they can only understand that world if they can find a basis in the real world that might have led the author to think of the metaphor (Miller 1979, p. 248).

Each of these properties is shared with the notion of an explicit model. Metaphors, however, are much less precise, and this imprecision may be a crucial strength in the process of expanding the audience's understanding of the topic represented. By evading the obligation to be precise, a metaphor can fix a new domain of reference without explicitly defining it. At the same time the partial focus achieved by this 'non-definitional reference-fixing' (Boyd 1979, p. 368) can serve to 'indicate a research direction' (p. 406).

This 'programmatic open-endedness' of scientific metaphors is construed by Boyd as a means to the objectivist end of eventually 'arranging our language so that our linguistic categories cut the world at its "joints"' (p. 358). Other philosophers doubt whether the 'real world' is ultimately knowable in this sense and hold that the most we can hope for is a progressive 'accommodation of language and experience' (Kuhn 1979, p. 419). Be that as it may, from a perspectivist position metaphors can be seen as helpful devices, once again because of their imprecision, for 'building a bridge' between alternative world views which could 'help to make the two views intelligible by emphasising, or even inducing, a similarity between them' (Pylyshyn 1979, p. 426).

The concept of metaphor is conventionally associated with literary rather than scientific activity. As Bruner has observed, when metaphors contribute to the process of model-making in science, there is a tendency to treat them as

crutches to get us up the abstract mountain. Once up, we throw them away (even hide them) in favor of a formal, logically consistent theory that (with luck) can be stated in mathematical or near-mathematical terms. The formal models that emerge are shared, carefully guarded against attack, and prescribe ways of life for their users. The metaphors that aided in this achievement are usually forgotten or, if the ascent turns out to be important, are made not part of science but part of the history of science. (Bruner 1986, p. 48)

Yet, as Lakoff and Johnson have shown with a wide range of examples, metaphor is conceptual in nature rather than a matter of 'pure language'. Metaphors are useful in cognition for enabling humans to 'get a handle on a concept' (1980, p. 116) which is 'not clearly enough delineated in its own terms to satisfy the purposes of our day-to-day functioning' (p. 118). Metaphors do this by highlighting certain correspondences between the slippery concept in question and other more clearly delineated concepts whose structure 'emerges' directly from our experience.

Against this background we can see that the intuitive appeal of a scientific theory arises partly from how well its metaphors fit one's experience. Psychological explanations of a certain sort seem perfectly natural to us because the metaphors that underlie them are an integral part of the model of the mind that we have in our culture. Formal scientific theories are attempts consistently to extend a set of 'ontological' and 'structural' metaphors already in current use in the culture. When the extension is experienced as illuminating, it is because a 'structural similarity' is defined between 'the entire range of experiences' to be explained and the characteristics of the proposed model to which they are likened (cf. Lakoff and Johnson 1980, chapter 22).

Theoretical models serve as focussing devices, narrowing our attention and thereby increasing our sensitivity to selected features of the world. They also thereby shut out information which they define as irrelevant, although an alternative model may be able to show that it is highly relevant to a superordinate goal shared by both of the models. (In Lakoff and Johnson's account of metaphor these complementary processes are referred to as 'highlighting' and 'hiding'.) In addition to selective focussing, a model contributes 'excess meaning', which Reese and Overton define as 'elements or relations that are only "accidentally" present' (1970, p. 120). This excess meaning arises from the concreteness of the ideas to which the target concept is compared in the presentation of the model. In some cases it may give additional heuristic power to a model, while in other cases it may be regarded as seriously misleading. (Lakoff and Johnson point out that this excess meaning is not completely random, but is constrained by the need for coherence among metaphors.)

Thus one way of conceptualising cultural validity would be a positive balance of benefits over costs for a given community at a given point in time engaged on a given task, where the sensitising and heuristic powers of a model outweigh the perceived narrowness of its focus and the extraneous connotations. Other factors influencing the acceptability of a model may include its compatibility with culturally prevalent 'pre-theoretical assumptions' (Reese and Overton), and the extent to which its key analogies are drawn from a domain in which the audience's 'primary theory' generates order, regularity and predictability in their daily lives (Horton 1982).

For these reasons, in addition to its theoretical fruitfulness and its empirically predictive power, a psychological theory will always be judged by its capacity to resonate with the broader cultural preoccupations of the society of which its audience are members.

6   Coordination of multiple perspectives

Even an indigenous Zambian psychologist can only expect, in his or her professional capacity, to make a marginal contribution to the design and implementation of the curriculum in rural Zambian primary schools. If any strands of psychological theory are to influence the actual practices of schooling, they will have to be appropriated by teachers.

In this regard, my conception of a primary school teacher is of an adult member of a community with special responsibility for addressing the developmental needs of children and young adults. The nature of those needs and of the teacher's responsibility is a matter for negotiated consensus between the teacher and other adults with special responsibilities towards those young people. In chapter 4 I suggested that teachers are in a uniquely powerful position to mediate between the disparate perspectives on child development encoded on the one hand in the culture of Chewa society and on the other in the Zambian institution of schooling. Much of their everyday thinking about social relationships is informed by the notions of *nzelu* articulated in chapter 2, and their professional training has orientated them towards the principles of explicit instruction geared to technological mastery over the environment, and embedded in the school's age-graded curriculum described in chapter 3.

In practice, however, the challenge of coordinating or integrating these perspectives seems to be evaded rather than confronted in Kondwelani community. Teachers, parents and students unselfconsciously

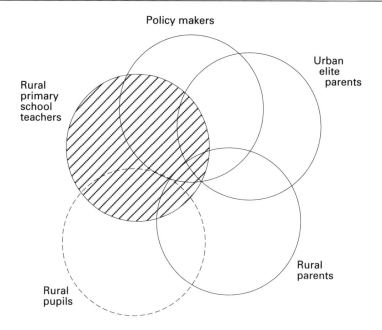

Fig. A.2 Multiple perspectives on the significance of schooling.

'conspire' to compartmentalise the domains of school and home socialisation, and to align them counterproductively with a series of contrasts beteeen masculine and feminine roles, literate and oral communication, English and Chi-Chewa language, modern and traditional values, high- and low-prestige occupations, urban and rural residence.

One way of representing the implications of this compartmentalisation is an elaboration of Fig. A.1 as shown in Fig. A.2. Each circle may be taken to represent the conceptual framework shared by a group of people for thinking about cognitive development and related issues. When engaging in discourse about the significance of schooling an urban, university-educated policy-maker (such as an official of the National Ministry of Education) and a rural primary school teacher would be warranted to assume a larger degree of common ground (in the form of shared concepts, lines of reasoning, values, etc.) than a policy-maker and a rural parent whose own experience of schooling did not extend beyond Grade 3 or 4.

According to the compartmentalised strategy, this difference of perspective is maintained by an impermeable barrier. But as I noted in chapter 2, a number of significant beliefs concerning the nature of children, parents and teachers appear to be shared by all of the adult groups represented in Fig. A.2. If, indeed, such premises are shared by rural parents, teachers and policy-makers, it should be possible to build on them to establish a secondary theoretical model of the process of schooling which is comprehensible to all parties. Such a model will, however, not emerge spontaneously in a vacuum. Rather, it will have to be constructed, elaborated and defended in competition with alternative pre-existing models in the minds and cultures of the various audiences.

In some respects the Venn diagram format of Fig. A.1 and A.2 is misleading since it implies the existence of definite borders around each person's (or group of persons') conceptualisation. Gadamer's (1975) metaphor of perspectives whose horizons may merge is superior in this respect. It allows us to think of Horton's primary theory (1982) as lying on the horizon, in the background, while the secondary theoretical constructs lie in the foreground. Participant members or bearers of different cultures are thus construed as gazing at similar or identical horizons from two different vantage points. Initially the differences between what they see in their respective foregrounds are so startling that they may be tempted to conclude that they are looking at radically incommensurable worlds. But by focussing their attention on a shared horizon they may be persuaded to work their way back to where each of them is standing, to understand how their different perspectives came about and even to empathise with one another's interpretations.

Yet a further complexity which is not represented in Fig. A.2 is the existence of a wide variety of alternative theoretical views within a single cultural tradition. Within Western psychological theory, for instance, we find the contrasting approaches of Skinner and Chomsky, Piaget and Vygotsky, psychodynamic, ethological, information-processing and hermeneutical approaches, to mention but a few major distinctive strands. Although acknowledging such diversity may seem overwhelming, it serves as a valuable reminder of the flexibility of cultural tradition. If such varied ideas could arise within the confines of Western society, surely we may hope to build some bridges between the Western institution of school and the concepts and values of other cultural meaning systems.

7   Metaphors for schooling

Kleibard, in a remarkably succinct contribution to a thick volume (1975), has articulated three metaphors which lie 'at the root of' much of modern Western theorising about the design of educational curricula: the metaphors of production, of growth and of travel. Table A.1 lays out schematically the implications of each of these different metaphors for how we conceptualise the student, the teacher and the

Table A1 *Alternative metaphors for schooling and their implications*

	Role of student	Educational process	School curriculum	Role of teachers	Educational goals
1. (Production)	Raw material	Transformation, production	Blueprint	Technician	Perfection, utility, efficiency
2. (Growth)	Plant	Growth, cultivation	Greenhouse	Gardener	Maturity, fruition, health
3. (Travel)	Traveller	Progress, guidance	Route	Guide, companion	Arrival, enjoyment, adaptation
4. (Enlightenment)	Prisoner	Enlightenment	Escape plan	Gatekeeper, liberator	Vision, freedom
5. (Staircase)	Climber	Ascent, elevation	Staircase	Anchorman	Reaching the top
6. (Amplifying tools)	Craftsman	Equipment, empowerment	Tool-kit	Expert	Task completion, competence
7. (Struggle)	Combatant	Armament, defence	Armoury	Armourer	Triumph, survival

process and goals of education. In addition I have sketched a similar account of four other metaphors which feature in the theoretical or ideological literature: the metaphors of enlightenment, of the staircase, of amplifying tools and of struggle.

A number of sociological and philosophical critiques of Western education have commented on its tendency to treat students as analogous with machines (e.g. Berger, Berger and Kellner 1973; Bowles and Gintis 1976). One of the major weaknesses of the metaphor of production in a country like Zambia is the uncertainty concerning whether the economic model which sets the criteria for determining the utility and efficiency of the output of the school system is applicable outside the framework of a highly industrialised, bureaucratised society. Planners and politicians with a firm commitment to a particular style of planned social change, however, may counter that this is merely a transitional problem which will be overcome once mass education has achieved its goal of modernisation. Another deeper problem is whether such a mechanistic view can ever do justice to the nature of mental experience.

Growth, on the other hand, seems an attractive metaphor in the context of communication with an agricultural audience, partly because it rests on an analogy with a domain in which, as Horton (1982) puts it, that audience's 'primary theory' generates order, regularity and predictability in their daily lives. In proverbs such as those cited in Box 2.1 in chapter 2 we see evidence of the willingness of Chewa-speaking adults to draw such analogies:

Mbeu poyamba. ('The harvest depends on the beginning.')

Kuongola m'tengo mpoyamba. ('A tree is straightened when it is young.')

Yet there is a certain imperviousness to social change about the horticultural metaphor which may reduce its credibility as a basis for the kind of education needed to prepare the next generation to confront new challenges and adversities. For representing this facet of the significance of schooling, the metaphors of amplifying tools and struggle may hold greater appeal.

The connection between education and human progress is perhaps most elegantly captured in the metaphor of travel. Unlike the first two metaphors, the image of the student here is clearly conscious and purposive. Attending school is construed as more than a passive experience. The main problem emphasised in earlier chapters in relation to the metaphor of travel is that it tends to be interpreted in terms of the image of the curriculum as a staircase up which the student must climb in a predetermined direction. By placing the teacher as an anchorman on the top flight of the staircase the metaphor constrains the teacher's contribution and students' options for success. Nothing short of the top will do, and in most societies the top is by definition attainable by only a few. It is arguable that directionality is inherent in the metaphor of travel since the dimension of time is unidirectional and is represented spatially in this metaphor. As Kleibard points out, however, the teacher can also construe her role as that of a companion exploring the world alongside her student, rather than a guide who knows in advance where the journey must end. In this interpretation the goal of the travel is to enjoy the journey in and of itself, in a spirit of companionable exploration, rather than treating it as a means to the end of arrival.

Katz and Kilner (1987) have described a model of human, personal development in terms of the straight path, based on an interpretation of indigenous Fijian ideas about the career progression of traditional healers, which they argue is not only more appropriate than existing Western psychological theories to the values and practices of rural Fijian society, but also has applicability to development in Western societies and holds potential for resolving some of the problems confronting Western theories because of their conceptual inadequacies.

The model has a number of attractive features, e.g. it is non-teleological and process-focussed, and claims to synthesise the often compartmentalised domains of cognitive, emotional, social and spiritual development. But to the present author the metaphor of the straight path seems curiously inapposite for some of the model's properties. For instance, the notion of development is said to be non-linear and non-directional. What could be more linear and directional than a straight path? Granted, the authors' use of straight to mean right is not without precedent, but surely it is a secondary meaning. It seems that we are being asked to ignore or suppress the primary meaning of straight in a context where it is already somewhat probable given the linear directionality of so many theories of development. One is left wondering what was the point of introducing the metaphor of cutting a way through the forest underbrush.

Perhaps a more apt metaphor for schooling as it functions in contemporary Zambian society is the wheelchair: a human artifact deliberately created for a particular purpose, designed to facilitate access to certain otherwise inaccessible places – related thus to the metaphor of travel and to the notion of life-journeys which has been developed in chapter 5.

A wheelchair has a truly dramatic affect on the mobility of someone without the use of legs and promises a corresponding increase of opportunities. But when we look at the practical implementation of plans people build around being equipped with a wheelchair, it turns out that very powerful constraints exist in the external environment outside the control of the individual. A person in a wheelchair theoretically could go anywhere. But much of the architecturally structured environment has been built on the presumption that we have feet and articulated knees. So we find that, as the people in wheelchairs have begun to define themselves as a political constituency and to articulate their own concerns, they express very considerable frustrations. Little has been heard about this particular self-advocacy movement in Africa. But in Europe and the United States it has succeeded in making a significant impact on legislation, so that the designers of buildings increasingly find themselves under pressure to construct ramps next to staircases, and so on. The University of Zambia, which includes a number of wheelchair-using students among its population, has very few elevators and only one ramp in the entire complex. The occupants of the wheelchairs therefore find themselves being lifted, with all the discomfort, dependency, infringement of personal autonomy and threat to their personal dignity which this involves, in order to be carried from one place to another. Under these circumstances the wheelchair loses much of its effectiveness as a result of an incompatibly designed environment.

This dependence of the technology's amplifying power on compatibility with the environment in which it is deployed is quite analogous to the amplifying power of literacy in a particular language. Becoming literate in the language of bureaucratic power may impart to an African primary school pupil a real competence to deal with many tasks within the bureaucratic domain, but it contributes little of direct use in the daily life of the rural community in which her family, friends and neighbours accomplish all their important tasks without the use of writing. If she goes to a bank in the District capital she will be better able than her unschooled peers to open an account, to write a cheque and to read a statement. If she has also learned to read Chi-Chewa she will be able to read the Bible and the Prayer Book of her local church. And if she can find a mobile library or a national newspaper, windows may be opened for her to explore many new horizons relevant to the practical affairs in which she is engaged, especially (as I discussed in chapter 6) in the domains of health and agriculture. But the realities of life in Katete District in the 1970s and 1980s were not encouraging in these respects. The wheels of the chair were liable to get bogged down in the mud long before these commanding heights of documentation were reached.

Another implication of the metaphor of schooling as the supply of a wheelchair is that the direction in which education propels its successful graduates is construed as 'horizontal', or 'down to earth'. A wheelchair may afford its owner access to certain resources which result in a significant increase of power. But it does not raise the person equipped in this way on to a different plane of existence, into some rarefied atmosphere away from the rest of humanity. The empowerment of the wheelchair, like that of education, is to enable its user to travel in a certain way over the same terrain (inclines, bumps and all) that confronts everyone in search of personal fulfilment, of rewarding lasting relationships with other people and of participation in the life of the community.

If the skills and knowledge of the school curriculum are merely a vehicle for the individual learner to deploy in the pursuit of her own personal life-goals, what is the role of the teacher? The analogy suggests that the teacher's efforts should be invested in familiarising students with the operational demands of the vehicle, with its potential in a wide range of situations and also with its limitations. In the case of an actual wheelchair, these are the responsibilities of a rehabilitation technician.

The metaphor of the wheelchair builds on both the metaphor of travel and the metaphor of amplifying tools. The latter was introduced by Jerome Bruner (1966) and elaborated in a seminal paper co-authored with Michael Cole on the relation between cultural variation and psychological processes (Cole and Bruner 1971). Originally inspired by Vygotsky's conception of language as a tool of thought, the idea is that education, like language and like the skills associated with a tool, faces both ways between an individual and a culture. On the one hand, it represents a historically accumulated stock of ideas passed down from one generation to the next and, on the other hand, it constitutes a body of knowledge to be internalised by the student. In a thoughtful reflection on how this image has been deployed in subsequent discussions of literacy and schooling, Cole, together with another colleague, Peg Griffin, reached the conclusion that 'the ambiguities of the amplifier metaphor mark a widespread ambivalence (or uncertainty) among scholars about the most fruitful way to conceive of culture's impact on cognition' (Cole and Griffin 1980, p. 350).

One crucial issue concerns whether the amplification of cognitive power imparted by cultural inventions such as writing and mathematics is anything more than the capacity to operate on the world through those technologies. In the case of an actual tool such as a hammer, an abacus or an electronic calculator, it is clear according to Cole and Griffin that 'the effect requires that the tool be in the user's hand' (p. 359). In the case of linguistic, mnemonic and other 'in the head' techniques, it is not quite clear how this condition should be interpreted. But it seems clear that every increase in the amplitude of cognitive power attributable to the mediation of cultural artifacts is constrained by the scope of these artifacts themselves. Thus we can know no more by virtue of literacy than is committed to writing. And

in this sense the metaphor of the wheelchair is quite apt: the wheelchair user's increase in mobility is strictly confined to the contexts in
which wheelchairs are available and usable.

Just as climbing up a staircase and moving in a wheelchair are
alternative forms of travel, so amplifying tools can be designed and
used for various skilled activities, one of the earliest of which in man's
prehistory was self-defence. If education and social change are viewed
in the context of the political and economic realities of the contemporary world, it is clear that those segments of society which receive the
smallest amounts of formal schooling are generally those facing the
greatest danger of exploitation and oppression. Disentangling cause
and effect from this correlation may pose certain problems. But the
hypothesis is widely entertained that education, of the right kind, is a
potentially empowering process – if only to defend oneself and one's
community against such dangers as unjust laws, and commercial trickery. Many would add to this list: natural disasters and preventable or
treatable diseases.

Liberation theorists of education tend to combine the thrust of the
metaphor of struggle under such captions as 'knowledge is power' with
that of the metaphor of enlightenment (cf. Freire 1972). 'Free a mind
behind those eyes: teach a person to read' is the caption on a billboard
displayed in central Baltimore as part of the campaign to increase the
prevalence of adult literacy among the inner city's predominantly Afri-
can-American population. It can indeed be argued that, in an American city with a well-stocked library system open to the public at no
charge, the acquisition of literacy would atuomatically open up for any
individual a wide range of new possibilities, at least for reflective consideration. By comparison, the range of literature available to any new
reader resident in a rural African community like Kondwelani is so
limited that the metaphor of liberation is far less convincing. In order
to reach a range of literature which would significantly add to the ideas
accessible to them locally through the medium of oral discourse,
graduates of the local primary school would need to travel to a distant
town. Only when the range of what is accessible to read is wide and
open-ended is it appropriate to construe a literacy-orientated education as liberating.

In practice, this metaphor has been deployed in Africa in recent
history mainly by the proponents of orthodox religious faiths. The
prison is construed by these proselytising missionaries as ignorance of a
particular truth, and the vision as access to a highly restricted body of
dogma. The role of the teacher in the implementation of this type of
escape plan is thus to open the gate from one enclosure to another. In
this guise, the conception of schooling as 'liberation' is well captured
by the metaphor of production: the goal is perfection by a set of

religious rather than industrial criteria. This is another illustration of the insufficiency of metaphors as resources for a complete explanation. By fixing the referent without defining it (Boyd 1979, p. 368), a metaphor opens the way for discourse, during which ambiguities are bound to emerge which call for more precise analysis and argumentation.

Notes

1   The multiple agenda of schooling

1 I hope I shall be forgiven for the linguistically cumbersome double
  pluralisation of agendas. The notion of 'an agenda' has come to be used in
  the modern world as more than a list of things to be done, drawn up for a
  committee. A person, for instance, may be said to 'have a different agenda'
  from her interlocutor, in cases where a conversation breaks down, on the
  supposition that her reasons for engaging in the conversation are such that
  they cannot be satisfied by a type of outcome which seems quite satisfactory to the other party. Each of the societal programmes I have described
  sets a different agenda for schooling, in the sense of formulating a set of
  logically interrelated goals for the activity. To call such a set an agendum
  would oversimplify my interpretation. Each programme has its own complex, but coherent agenda, and my purpose in this chapter is to compare
  and contrast these several agendas with each other.
2 In the remainder of this book I shall avoid the inelegance of acknowledging
  each time that a person may be masculine or feminine by using the
  feminine form to denote the general case. This may serve to counterbalance the fact that almost all the authors I have cited follow the opposite
  convention of using the masculine form for the general case.
3 This concept has been elaborated in enlightening ways by Super and Harkness (1986), under the title of the 'developmental niche'. Gallimore,
  Weisner, Kaufman and Bernheimer (1989) while accepting much of that
  analysis, use the expression 'eco-cultural niche' which I have adopted here,
  and add some further useful characterisation. One reason for preferring
  this expression is that it removes the ambiguity of 'developmental'.
  Although Super and Harkness do acknowledge the possibility that the
  niche itself may be subject to developmental change, this introduces a different branch of the meaning of the word development which threatens to
  cloud rather than clarify the nature of the relationship between the niche
  and the developing individual within it.
4 Within the Judaic culture, this problem is vividly illustrated in Barbara
  Streisand's film saga, *Yentl*.
5 E.g. Witkin 1967, Vernon 1967. Partly in response to my critique of Witkin's analysis (Serpell 1976), and the related critique by Cole and Scribner
  (1977), Berry later reformulated the theoretical relations among culture,

cognitive style and adaptation, in such a way as to allow the possibility of developmental progress along alternative, equally adaptive but culturally distinctive routes (Berry 1981). Vernon's views are discussed in chapter 2.

6 This view has been articulated in the field of development economics or political economy under the heading of dependency theory. Two recent analytical African reviews of the literature from widely different perspectives were presented by Claude Ake and Michael Chege at the Rockefeller Foundation's Reflections on Development Conference in Bellagio, Italy, July 1988.

7 I prefer this expression to other simplifying labels for the socio-political region of Africa extending from the Sahara desert in the north to the Limpopo river in the south, for reasons explained elsewhere (Serpell 1984b).

8 In addition to the University of Zambia in Lusaka, the Copperbelt University was established in 1987, formalising the autonomy of what was originally a sister campus under a federal structure.

9 Marwick also notes that: 'At present many agricultural reforms are being carried out among the A-Chewa, but most of these relate to soil conservation; and the need for them springs from overpopulation rather than from any fundamental defect in the native system of cultivation' (1965, p. 38).

10 Marwick 1965, p. 43. I have adjusted the spelling of A-Chewa to conform with my own usage throughout the rest of this book.

11 I count myself among these citizens, and recognise that it is difficult to resist the temptation to rely on such superficial indices of the sophistication and complexity of Zambian society, when one is confronted with the crass misconceptions about Africa which still prevail in many so-called 'educated' segments of the societies of industrialised countries.

12 The citations in Chi-Chewa (a central African language of the Bantu group, about which more details are provided in chapter 2) are as far as possible reproduced verbatim from taped or hand-written records made on the spot. My translations are deliberately free rather than literal, in the hope of capturing the spirit of the ideas expressed. In this particular passage and the one that follows, I have translated *nzelu* as 'brains', which seems to me the nearest equivalent in contemporary colloquial English for what these respondents were expressing in this context. However, as will be discussed in some depth in chapter 2, the word *nzelu* has a very wide range of meaning, closely connected but not coterminous with that of the English word 'intelligence'. The topic of translation and its relation to communication about theory is discussed in the Appendix.

13 Retrospective interview no. 30 with a young man aged about 20 who left school five years ago in Grade 6. April 1983.

14 Retrospective interview no. 34 with a young woman aged about 17 who left school two years ago. April 1983.

15 In the mid- to late 1970s, for instance, the national governments of nine sub-Saharan African countries (Botswana, Cameroon, Ethiopia, Ghana, Kenya, Nigeria, Senegal, Sierra Leone and Zambia) were committing between 12 and 26 per cent of their recurrent expenditure to the education

sector, and devoting about half of that amount to primary schooling (Cameron 1983; cf. also data cited by the World Bank 1988).

16 In the Gwembe District of Zambia's Southern Province, Haberat reports that a Tonga villager said to him: 'Education is only good for making an enemy of your son', which he interpreted as meaning that you will raise him to have certain expectations you cannot fulfil (Personal communication 1989).

17 Family discussion no. 26F, 1980.

18 These interviews were conducted by Peter Phiri, a University of Zambia graduate in his twenties, who had grown up in the same community and attended the same school. The excerpts cited here can therefore be regarded, to all intents and purposes, as samples of conversation between two youthful offspring of the local community, who have known one another's families since their childhood.

19 Retrospective interview no. 2, 1983. A longer segment of this interview is cited and discussed in chapter 5 (see p. 181).

20 Retrospective interview no. 3 with a young man aged about 20 who left school in Grade 6 five years ago. April 1983.

21 For instance, several of the young men in our cohort interviewed in 1987 who were stable residents of the area adjacent to our central school had sold two 90 kg bags of garlic this year at prices ranging from K3 to K7 per kg, while others had sold two or more bags of sunflower at K180 per bag. The Zambian Kwacha was pegged in May 1987 at an exchange value of K8=US$1. To give an idea of the perceived magnitude of these earnings, it is worth noting that some manual labourers and domestic workers in Lusaka at this period were earning monthly salaries of less than K100.

22 Barnum and Sabot 1976; Harbison and Myers 1964; cf. Clarke 1984. I am much indebted to Roy Clarke for clarifying for me the ideological focus of modernisation theory and several other aspects of political economic theories of development. Although we always seem to disagree, he has taught me more than I am wont to acknowledge in the course of our arguments.

23 Family discussion no. 8F, 1980.

24 Further details about this questionnaire and the sample of teachers who responded to it are presented in chapter 4.

25 The metaphor of schooling as some kind of industrial processing is caricatured by Berger, Berger and Kellner (1972).

26 This expression is a direct translation from one of the observations made by a parent, which is cited in context above on page 13, where it was translated as 'uplifting the nation' (family discussion no. 26F, 1980).

2   **Wanzelu ndani? A Chewa perspective on child development and intelligence**

1 Super and Harkness use the expression 'psychology of the caretaker', which has sometimes been misinterpreted as referring to the caregiver's psychological make-up, rather than her implicit psychological theory.

2 Joynson (1974) argues the case for a necessary connection between valid

psychology and common sense. Howarth (1980) has articulated the implications of this perspective for the use of psychology as a guide to intervention. The philosophical underpinnings of these ideas in hermeneutics and Habermas' (1984) critical theory of communicative action are discussed by Serpell (1990).

3 A fifth line of analysis has been embedded in the elaboration of practice in the field of action-orientated assessment. This has been discussed elsewhere (Serpell 1988, 1989a) and will be briefly touched on in chapter 7.

4 The particular situations we evoked in these interviews were generated through a series of informal brain-storming sessions which I held over a period of several months with various colleagues, friends and relations who had grown up and/or lived in Zambian village communities (Serpell 1977a, 1982a).

More recently Dasen and his colleagues (1985) in Côte d'Ivoire have shown the value of a more systematic, cyclic approach in which local residents are first asked to give examples of situations in which various qualities of mind are exemplified, and an edited list of such behaviours is then presented for elicitation of assessments and evaluative criteria. This approach is essentially analogous in the oral medium to that used by Sternberg and his colleagues (1981) in their investigation of lay ideas about intelligence among the American public.

5 Parkin (1974) and Pride (1970) have discussed the application of this concept of Goffman's (1964) to the deployment of linguistic varieties in multilingual communities, such as those of Kenya and Zambia. And Khubchandani (1983) has analysed the devastating effect this kind of ambivalence can have on the interpretability of census returns in India.

6 Orthography: Only in Malawi is the language used extensively for formal written communication, and the orthography favoured in that country is slightly different from that adopted by the Zambian government's Ministry of Education. I have as yet been able to locate only minimal documentation of Mozambique usage, where the preferred generic name appears to be Cinyanja, but it is quite likely to differ in respect of orthography, judging from what I have seen of the spelling conventions adopted in Angola and Zaire for some of the Bantu languages which straddle Zambia's borders with those countries. Such cross-national variations in orthography for the indigenous languages of Africa can be traced in large part to the orthographies of the national languages of the European missionaries, under whose auspices the first written documents were published in most of the African languages. Although the link between the work of the early missionary linguists and the colonising governments was often quite tenuous, the net result has been a pattern of Balkanisation which further compounds the detrimental effects of European cultural, educational and linguistic domination on the dissemination within the continent of literature in the African languages.

In choosing how to spell the speech samples reproduced in this book, I have been guided by several considerations. Within the political context of Zambian educational policy, it has seemed to me desirable to conform for the most part with the Ministry's guidelines. Thus I have elected to use the letter l consistently to represent the /l-r/ liquid sound which in other orthographies is variously represented by l, r or l(r).

With respect to the name of the language, however, I have opted for the version Chi-Chewa, since I believe it is less likely to be mispronounced by the majority of foreign readers familiar with the English language (in which the balance of the book's text is written) than Cewa, Cicewa, Tshi-Tsheoua, etc. Moreover, I am impressed by the argument of the Rwandan Bantu linguist, Alexis Kagame (1976), that writers should respect indigenous linguistic intuitions by preserving the prefix concord system, which is a shared characteristic of all the Bantu languages. For those unfamiliar with this system, it should be sufficient to illustrate it as follows. A member of the -Chewa tribe is Mu-Chewa. The people are the A-Chewa. Their language is Chi-Chewa. The root-form -Chewa is never used on its own in the language. I have therefore tried to ensure that whenever possible if the word appears embedded in a context of English words, an appropriate prefix is used. I have also inserted a hyphen in this and several words to draw the attention of non-Bantu-speakers to the lexical root-forms as distinct from their prefixes and/or suffixes.

7 Chongo 1972. A detailed study of the imagery of this series has been the subject of a doctoral dissertation by Wendland (1979).

8 I have in mind here remarks by the member of my study cohort with the longest period of formal education (trace interview no. 315, December 1987), and the rankings of attributes by various groups of cohort members, discussed below.

9 Serpell, R. and Banda, E. (1980) 'Wanzeru ndani?' Unpublished document, Institute for African Studies, University of Zambia (mimeo).

10 Trace interview no. 615. September 1987.

11 Sternberg, Conway and Ketron 1981. This study provides a clarification of some earlier studies (Asch 1946, cited by Bruner 1986; Bruner, Shapiro and Tagiuri 1958) in which the judgements by laypersons were treated as 'responses by subjects' rather than as alternative theoretical interpretations.

12 Even in the affluent, urban sector of the USA population sampled by Sternberg and his colleagues, members of the general public expect an 'ideally intelligent' person to display qualities not only of problem-solving ability but also of social competence. But theoretical and applied psychology in the Western tradition have tended to construe social responsibility as a quite separate dimension of personality, lying beyond the bounds of intelligence. It is not regarded as much of a paradox in English – at least in the discourse of psychologists – to say of someone: 'He's very intelligent, but he's a bad man.' The definition of intelligence emphasises a 'quick off the mark' ability to manipulate ideas. Whether the individual does so for the public good or for private, selfish purposes is irrelevant. But that is not irrelevant to *nzelu*. A person who does not use his or her intelligence in a socially productive way is not *wa-nzelu*.

13 This account of the origin of Brer Rabbit has been contested, but seems to me a very reasonable speculation.

14 The earlier, limited circulation, report of this study (Kingsley 1977) contains details of Ichi-Bemba terminology much of which is cited only in translation in the later, more widely accessible report (Kingsley 1985).

15 All of my citations are from the second edition, published by the Rhodesia Literature Bureau in 1974.

16 Indeed, such mismatches between the meaning in different languages of forms which are evidently linguistically cognate is a common source of jokes in multilingual central African society. An analogous source of misunderstandings and humour in Europe is the divergent meanings of the English verb 'become' and the German verb *bekommen*.

17 The French terms she uses are: 'maturité intellectuelle, capacité d'adaptation, perspicacité, mémoire, compréhension, raisonnement, habileté dans la résolution d'un problème, débrouillardise, connaissance, ruse'.

18 '...alors que la sagesse rwandiase bannit le mensonge et la malignité' (p. 100).

19 The French text for the numbered characteristics are as follows: (1) qui a de bonnes relations, (2) qui sait tirer profit de tout, (3) débrouillard, (4) qui sait prendre des initiatives, (5) poli, respectueux et obéissant, (6) prévoyant, (7) discret, (8) franc, (9) habile manuellement, (10) clairvoyant.

20 Cf. D'Andrade's (1984) account of cultural meaning systems.

21 This expression is borrowed from Halliday (1975).

22 Cf. Goffman (1956), Harre (1979) and the dramaturgical theme of Habermas' (1984) revised theory of communicative action, discussed in chapter 6.

23 The sample of adults who were interviewed in 1973–4 comprised twenty-seven men and twenty-four women. Only ten of the men had spent more than a year in school (and of these only three had spent more than four years in school), and only four of the women (none of whom had spent more than four years in school). Thus among this sample of the parental generation for our cohort, 27 per cent had some first-hand experience of school, 6 per cent of the upper primary grades and none of them of any secondary schooling.

24 The criterion adopted was reoccurrence of the same name or attribute across a given respondent's replies to three or more successive questions. In order to treat all respondents equivalently, this analysis was confined to Qs. 2, 3, 4 and 5. (N, in both cases=156).

25 Three components of a 'perfectly consistent' response were distinguished: (a) the child ranked no. 1 had received the highest or second highest frequency of citation in the basic interview; (b) the child ranked no. 2 had received the highest or second highest frequency of citation; (c) the child ranked last or lowest in respect of *-chenjela* or another relevant attribute had received a zero frequency of citation. Informants were rated highly consistent if they displayed all three of these components in an immediate follow-up ranking, or if they displayed at least two of the three in a delayed follow-up rating.

26 Ten displayed two of the three components in an immediate follow-up ranking and four displayed one of the three after a four-month delay.

27 I am indebted to Dr Keith Rennie for suggesting analysis along these lines, at a seminar held at the University of Zambia in 1975.
28 McNemar's test for the significance of changes yielded a value of the chi-squared statistic for each of these effects which was significant at or beyond the 0.05 level of confidence (chi-squared, d.f. 1, for Qs. 1–2=8.64; Qs. 2–3=7.10; Qs. 3–4=7.36; Qs. 4–5=4.45) (cf. Serpell 1989).
29 I have discussed this possible line of interpretation in greater depth elsewhere (Serpell 1989), and applied it to some of the results reported by Dasen *et al.* (1985).
30 Twenty-six of the twenty-nine respondents ranked *nzelu* higher than *uchenjela*, and the mean ranks assigned to these two attributes among a list of ten were 5.8 and 8.6, respectively. Cf. Table 2.6, and also chapter 5 for further discussion of how these young people rated one another in respect of various qualities when they were interviewed later in life.
31 The relevance of this application of developmental psychology in rural and urban African settings is discussed in chapter 5 (section 3) and chapter 7 (section 3).
32 This formulation is borrowed from the title and focus of an elegant and wide-ranging review of 'the cognitive consequences of cultural opportunity' by Nerlove and Snipper (1981).
33 The theoretical potential of metaphors is discussed in the Appendix.
34 On whether parents in rural Zambian communities regard games as a significant source of stimulation for their intellectual development, cf. Kingsley 1977; Serpell 1982b; Ng'andu 1986; Nabuzoka 1986. Cf. also Erchak (1976) on Kpelle parents' different attitudes towards play by boys and girls; and Ammar (1954) on the disdainful attitude towards play with children displayed by parents in the rural Egyptian community he studied.
35 M'tonga 1985; cf. also studies by Heath (1983) and by Opie and Opie (1959), as well as the autobiographical essays of Kenyatta (1938) and various other African intellectuals, e.g. the collection edited by Fox (1967). See also a well-illustrated account by Centner (1963) of children's traditional games in rural areas of Zaire's Shaba Province (formerly known as Katanga) which borders on the North-Western, Copperbelt and Luapula Provinces of Zambia.
36 Elizabeth Brooks (1980, pp. 57–8) makes a similar point with respect to the Luvale society of Zambia's North-Western Province.

3   The formal educational model of cognitive growth

1 I may have somewhat exaggerated the contrast between these two views at first for expository purposes, to highlight the nature of the crisis of compatibility confronting schooling in rural Chewa society. In the Appendix I return to some of the underlying commonalities, in search of ways to bridge what I believe to be a serious but not an unbridgeable gulf between them.
2 This formulation was first advanced by Vygotsky. It was eloquently articulated for American audiences by Cole and Bruner (1971). Powerful and productive though the metaphor has proven in the design of theory at the

interface among culture, cognition, development and instruction, I argue in the Appendix (Section 5) that there exists a significant danger of over-extending the analogy which underlies it. Ideas are only in some respects like tools or machines (cf. Lakoff and Johnson 1980).

This issue and some of its ramifications into the domains of political theory and history were discussed at some length on the computer-mediated conference, entitled 'xlchc', in February 1990. Participants in that discussion were Margaret Benson, Michael Cole, Arne Raeithel and myself.

3 A striking celebration of the potential of the metaphor of the distorting lens is a short story by Sylvain Bemba (1970) which describes the tormented thoughts of an African photographer living in Paris.

4 Cf. Serpell (1984a) for an overview of this issue in the wider context of 'the contribution of psychology to development in third world countries'.

5 To borrow Fortes' (1938) expression, which was introduced in chapter 2.

6 Consider: 'Know thyself'; 'In the beginning was the Word, and the Word was God.'

7 It is important to recognise that the transformation of Western culture known as the Renaissance was a very gradual process: 'The earlier renaissance of the 12th and 13th centuries was a much more unmistakable rebirth of the mind, while the forces at work in the Middle Ages, which in the 16th century were revealed as disruptive of the old order, did not produce their fundamental revolution in men's thinking until the 17th and 18th ... not till the turn of the 17th century did any man realise the nature of the new world [they were entering] and not till the 19th did its features impress the average man' (Randall 1926, pp. 111–12).

8 This notion, first clearly articulated by Descartes in the seventeenth century, has given rise to a dualistic contrast between the domains of physical and mental phenomena which has continued to perplex many modern psychologists.

9 Wilson (1980, p. 139), in a critical review from a historiological perspective that only came to my attention as this book was about to go to press, characterises Ariès' 'present-mindedness' as follows: 'What he has done is to search, in medieval and especially early-modern materials, for modern attitudes to the child, finding that these attitudes are absent, and it is this absence that he records.'

10 We may note in this context that interruptions in the historical continuity of the Western tradition of education (such as the period of European history known as the Dark Ages) are evidence of the capacity of a single generation to recapitulate a process which evolved over centuries, internalise and master it (e.g. in the European Renaissance). In psychological terms, these possibilities are articulated by the notions of recoding hierarchies in information-processing models of skilled performance. Grasping the essence of an end-product of a long period of thought as a capsule concept or theory does not require the individual to work through the long process of its discovery.

11 The punctuation of this passage in Sadler's book is unclear as to which parts of this set of related propositions are translated verbatim from *The great didactic* and which are paraphrased.

12 See Goody (1977) on the ubiquitous importance of lists in literate cultural practices.

13 Snelson (1974) cites (to the wry amusement of the Minister of Education in Zambia's independent government, Mr Wesley Nyirenda who wrote a preface to Snelson's book) a revealing statement by Cecil Rhodes that 'missionaries are better than policemen, and cheaper' (p. 19). For a powerful, albeit sometimes overstated, critique of the role of missionaries in the colonial exploitation of Africa, see Rodney (1972).

14 E.g. King 1988; but cf. also Brenner (1985) for a more optimistic view.

15 By contrast adult literacy materials in Zambia are at least designed to teach the techniques of reading, writing and numerical computation in the context of practically relevant adult activities such as agriculture, nutrition and health care.

16 In the light of more recent educational thinking, early stages of the curriculum are also designed to be attractive, to lure the child into the topic by making connections between the formal bodies of knowledge to be transmitted and the child's existing intuitions based on everyday experience. A lively discussion of this 'sense-making' approach in elementary education (including contributions by Goldenberg, Goodman, Wells, Minick, Hunt, Lampert, Benson, Dykstra and others) took place in the form of a computer-mediated conference entitled 'xclass' between January and June 1990.

17 Of course, the use of the term 'foreign' in this context is potentially controversial. In chapter 4, I discuss at some length the socio-linguistic status of English in Zambia generally and in Kondwelani in particular. Its foreignness is, however, historically and conceptually a primary distinguishing characteristic. Hence my decision to use the term at this point of my analysis.

18 Essentially similar considerations apply to the education systems in many of the 'francophone' African nations, where the language of the former colonial power (France or Belgium) has remained the major medium of instruction long after the termination of colonial rule. Likewise in Mozambique, the language of the former colonial power, Portuguese, is the principal medium of school instruction. Tanzania's experiment with the use of Swahili is probably the most famous attempt to break with the colonial linguistic heritage (cf. Mkilifi 1972; Polomé and Hill 1980).

19 Ngugi 1964; Akinasso in press. Sensitive cinematographic portrayals of this dimension of the experience of schooling have also been made in India (*Aparajito*, 1956, by Satyajit Ray) and in Martinique (*Sugarcane alley*, by Euzhan Palcy).

4   Bicultural mediation: local challenges for teachers

1 I am grateful to all of these teachers for the time and effort they invested in completing this rather lengthy questionnaire, and to Mr Jonas Phiri and Mr Edwin Sinjwala, Research Assistants of the Institute for African Studies, who delivered and collected the questionnaires.

2 The schools were selected on a semi-random basis primarily determined by convenience of access, and Heads were requested to arrange for as many teachers as possible to complete the questionnaire. At each school, typically responses were provided by the Head or Deputy Head, by two or three teachers with five or more years of service and by one or two teachers with less than five years of service (Serpell 1987).

3 Goffman's (1964) dramaturgical analysis from which this concept derives its meaning is expounded further below.

4 The conception of that role as maieutic (like that of the obstetrician or midwife) rather than directive, constructive or manipulative, tends to find its way more readily into higher education where a guiding premise is that the student has already acquired competence in foundation skills. Yet, even in Western universities it is not uncommon to find notions of expertise advanced as a rationale for the adoption of a condescending attitude on the part of professors, which is perhaps best illustrated by the endurance of the asymmetrical information flow of the lecture format and the rarity of student participation in academic assessment.

5 A wide range of contrasting views were expressed in the responses to our questionnaire about the value of corporal punishment in the enforcement of school discipline. But all the Heads endorsed the use of corporal punishment.

6 I am profoundly indebted to Mubanga Kashoki for alerting me to the importance of this topic. His extensive writing on the subject (e.g. Kashoki 1973, 1989, 1990) is exemplary in both its clarity and its courage.

7 The project of expanding the provision of schooling to enable all pupils to complete nine years of basic education, announced in the Educational Reforms proposals and recommendations (GRZ 1977) has been accompanied by a shift in terminology, with the former secondary schools and a new category of basic schools sharing the responsibility for providing Grade 8 and Grade 9 instruction. Basic schools began to appear in small numbers in Katete District in the early 1980s, by which time most of those in our study cohort who embarked on any primary schooling had stopped. Even on a national plane the notion that all children are entitled to progress as far as Grade 9 can scarcely be described as more than a blueprint at the time of writing (1990).

8 I am grateful for these opportunities to share ideas about the project, the first of which was organised by Dr Paul Acholla of the University of Zambia's Educational Research Bureau in March 1987, the second by Dr Wim Hoppers of the Ministry of General Education and Culture's SHAPE programme in December 1987. The suggestion of a connection in the thinking of our questionnaire respondents between a lack of honesty and the -*chenjela* dimension of *nzelu* was raised by Dr Paul Acholla, Dr Irene Maimbolwa-Sinyangwe and Dr Sichalwe Kasanda at the first seminar, and independently by Mr Clayton Sekeleti (personal communication) – all of them colleagues on the staff of the University of Zambia; it was also endorsed by several teachers at the second seminar.

9 A small number of weekly boarders are sometimes enrolled in rural upper primary schools which draw their pupils for Grades 5, 6 and 7 from the

Grade 4 graduates of two or three near-by lower primary schools as well as their own Grade 4.

10 Several commentators on the national debate on educational reform in Zambia and its outcome have drawn similar conclusions with respect to the collapse of the initially optimistic plans to extend access to secondary schooling and to reintroduce foundation teaching in the medium of indigenous languages. Roy Clarke (1978, 1985), for instance, argues that the proposals for these two major areas of reform were eventually defeated not as claimed by the policy document which proclaimed their demise because their implementation was technically impracticable, but primarily because they would have undermined the control of access to economic opportunity by a privileged elite class.

11 Family discussion no. 8, April 1980.

12 Note that the English term, wisdom, is used here in a different, albeit cognate sense from that which was used to translate one dimension of *nzelu* in chapter 2. *Mwambo* refers to an accumulated body of knowledge and moral tradition; *nzelu* refers to the capacity or tendency of an individual to behave in accordance with *mwambo*.

13 Family discussion no. 8, April 1980.

14 For accounts of similar views expressed in earlier historical periods, cf. King 1975 and Rogoff 1981.

15 Letter from cohort member no. 315, dated 18 December 1987.

5   **Life-journeys and the significance of school**

1 Pseudonyms have been assigned to each member of the cohort to protect their anonymity.

2 Retrospective interview no. 31, April 1983.

3 Retrospective interview no. 3, April 1983.

4 Family discussion no. 3, April 1980.

5 Note how the standard Western abbreviations pre-schoolers, or even children of pre-school age, subtly distort the perception of the audience and serve implicitly to evoke the expectation that the next stage in these individuals' life-journeys will be enrolment in school.

6 The tasks are specified in Table 2.1. Thus, if an informant used the term *wo-tumikila* to describe the child she selected for each of three tasks, the term *wo-chenjela* to describe the child selected for two tasks and the terms *wa-m-changu*, *wa-nzelu* and *wo-khulupilika* for one task each, she was asked, following the interview, to rank the children in terms of 'who is the most *wo-tumikila*?', etc.

7 The mean value of Kendall's coefficient of concordance across eight sets of 'mention scores' on the original interviews was 0.34 (range 0.21 to 0.59); and for the follow-up rankings it was 0.35 (range 0.12 to 0.64). The value of the coefficient was statistically significant at the 0.05 level for only four of the sixteen cases.

8 The proportion of questions in response to which a given child's name was cited was taken as the mention score for that child on each interview.

Among the eighteen informants requested to rank the children immediately, the mean mention score for the first-ranked child was 0.48 (range 0.12 to 0.75), for the second-ranked child 0.34 (range 0.00 to 0.88) and for the lowest-ranked child 0.04 (0.00 to 0.17). Among the twenty-two informants who ranked children during a follow-up interview three to six months later, the corresponding figures were first rank 0.34 (0.00 to 1.00), second rank 0.23 (0.00 to 0.50), lowest rank 0.10 (0.00 to 0.33).

9 For computation of these stanine HVR scores, an individual whose aggregate ranked position was higher than all the other members of a group of seven was assigned a score of 8 (higher than $\frac{8}{10}$ but not than $\frac{9}{10}$ of the sample), whereas an individual ranked highest in a group of four received a score of 7. Pairs of individuals who tied for the lowest aggregate ranking received a score of 0.

For the children of Village 4, this information was incomplete. Thus the index was available for only thirty-three of the total cohort of forty-six.

10 A total of twelve configurations are presented for imitation, and points amounting to a maximum of thirty-four are awarded for accuracy.

11 The expression Panga Munthu means 'make a person' in Chi-Chewa. By a happy accident of cognate root-forms, the title of the test has proved to be also intelligible in several other Zambian languages, such as Ichi-Bemba, although the spelling and pronunciation of an exact translation into those languages would be slightly different.

12 The current version of the test, on which Dr Bernice Ezeilo, Dr Ravinder Kathuria and others have conducted a certain amount of standardisation, differs from the early version we used in 1973–4 in three respects: 1. No standard is presented: the child is merely instructed verbally to make a model of a person. This was done because we felt that a very simple model might discourage more mature subjects from including in their own model as much detail as possible, while a complex model might have intimidated the less mature subjects. 2. Only plasticine modelling clay is used, because our research had shown that girls were less adept in the medium of wire than boys, whereas no significant gender differences emerged using the clay medium. 3. A more elaborate scoring system is now used which allows for up to 25 points, as compared with the 10-point scale we used in 1973–4. Bernice Ezeilo first developed a 20-point scoring system, and suggested a number of improvements based on her study in Lusaka in 1974–5 (Ezeilo 1975, 1978). These suggestions were incorporated along with her expanded scale in the present 25-point scoring system. Ravinder Kathuria (forthcoming) has compiled results from a sizeable sample of Lusaka school children as well as two samples of rural children from Western Province tested by Ms Lamping-Paffen and Ms Cosijn, who have made further suggestions for refinement of the scoring system.

13 The youngest member of our sample was more than 20 years old by 1988 when we last contacted her, and was married, with a 1-year-old child.

14 Because of the considerable variance, especially among the boys, the difference between these means is not statistically reliable (t=2.62, one-tailed p=0.07). The unusual case of Shamba was excluded from this analysis, since he completed Grade 7 at the age of 21.

15 The density of grades on which these rankings were based varied considerably across individuals.

16 Thus a student who was placed first, second or third in a class of thirty-four pupils was allocated a stanine score of 9, a student who was placed thirtieth in a class of thirty-eight a stanine score of 2, etc. Individuals for whom several class rankings were available within a given two-year period were assigned the arithmetic mean of the corresponding stanine scores, rounded to the nearest whole number.

17 Four cases were double coded, since the individual seemed to be alternating between two occupations: in two cases, farming and trading, and in two other cases, farming and unskilled wage employment.

18 One of these two 'infertile' marriages had already produced two miscarriages in its short history of three years.

19 This explanation for leaving school when they did was not advanced explicitly by any of the young women in the cohort when interviewed retrospectively by Peter Phiri in 1983. But this may simply reflect a certain shyness about acknowledging such considerations, especially to someone well acquainted with their husbands and other contemporaries.

20 Cf. Frijda and Jahoda (1966) for a similar comment on early conceptualisations of the relations between culture and personality.

21 The older group comprised seventeen boys and two girls aged 10–13 years at the time of testing, the younger group seventeen girls and ten boys aged 6–9 years.

22 For all statistical analyses reported in this chapter the criterion of statistical significance adopted, unless otherwise stated, was $p=0.05$, two-tailed.

23 The values of the product–moment correlation coefficient were $r=-0.28$ for boys ($N=22$), and $r=+0.09$ for girls ($N=10$).

24 It reflects the presence of two cases who were enrolled at the age of 8 among the five who completed less than five years of schooling, and of one case who was enrolled at the age of 13 among the six who completed five or six years of schooling. The remaining eight girls in our cohort who were ever enrolled in school all entered Grade 1 at the age of 10 or 11.

25 *Pakuti muganiza kuti maphunzilo yaku Primary School siyathandiza lomba muliko nalingolopitiliza maphunzilo yanu kuti mukafike ku Secondary School.*
   This, and the other citations in this passage of the text are transcribed verbatim from retrospective interview no. 25, 26 April 1983.

26 I am indebted to the Headmasters and staff of Kondwelani School and Kaunda Square Primary School for their excellent cooperation in the collection of these data, and to Mr Francis Simpanya for his assistance in scoring the Draw-a-Person Test protocols. I scored all of the Panga Munthu Test responses myself.

27 The very small sample of comparable data for children in the medium school-attainment category showed, as predicted, that rural girls scored higher on average on the PMT than their urban counterparts at both the Grade 3–4 level and the Grade 5–6 level, and lower on the DPT, while the differences were less clear-cut in the case of boys (Serpell 1980b, Table 3).

28 The Weighted Peer Rating Index used in this analysis was calculated as follows:

(a) The rank on each of the ten characteristics listed in chapter 2 (p. 57) was converted to a stanine value to take account of the size of the pool within which the person was ranked.

(b) A weight was entered to reflect the importance attached to each characteristic by the rater, by dividing the stanine value by the rank order of importance assigned by the rater to that characteristic.

(c) The weighted stanine values were then summed to yield a composite weighted rating.

(d) Finally, an arithmetic mean was computed of the composite weighted ratings by all those peers who rated a given individual to yield the aggregate index.

Index values were only used in those cases where two or more peers had rated the same individual. I am indebted to Chisha Serpell for assistance with these computations.

29 Although Heath presents the home culture of these families as representative of a substantial sector of the contemporary American middle class, it is noteworthy that her data on pre-schoolers' interactions with adults which constitute a key aspect of her account were derived from a small sample of 'primary-level school teachers whose families lived in suburbs around Gateway ... referred to as Maintown residents elsewhere' (Heath 1983, p. 392). The representativeness of this professional group of the middle class as a whole is therefore open to question. I am indebted to Maggie Lasaga for drawing this methodological weakness of the study to my attention.

30 Trace study interview guide, Qs. 22–30.

31 This includes informal housing structures in peri-urban settlements, as well as purpose-built, domestic servants' quarters in the back-yards of middle-class houses.

32 These are two of the best-known novels written in English by African authors, several of which are widely prescribed reading in the Zambian secondary school curriculum for the subject of English literature: Ngugi 1965; Achebe 1960.

33 The National Agricultural Marketing Board (Namboard) and the Eastern Cooperative Union (ECU) made arrangements to collect these cash crops by lorry from various collecting points in the District, which were accessible to local farmers by cattle-drawn *ngolo* or scotch-carts.

34 Trace interview no. 212, August 1987.

35 Trace interview no. 212, August 1987.

36 Trace interview no. 115, March 1988.

37 Trace interview no. 315, December 1987.

38 The significance of this observation in relation to the school curriculum is discussed further in chapters 6 and 7.

39 Family discussion no. 12, April 1980.

40 Retrospective interview no. 27, April 1983.

41 I am much obliged to Tamika Kaluwa, who used the occasion of her familiarisation visit in preparation for the Popular Theatre Workshop described in chapter 6, to conduct this interview while I tape-recorded it.

42 Like Ngosa, whose account of her reasons for leaving school was presented in Section 3.4 above.

43 Most members of the cohort had already completed this formality by that date. Although it was a legal requirement to register at the age of 18, the average age at which this was done by our cohort was over 20. Since very few parents register their children's birth, a parent is usually required to accompany the young person to swear an affidavit before a suitable authority such as the District Secretary confirming that the candidate for registration is their child and was born in a given place and year. Thumbprints in place of signatures on these cards served as further confirmation that many of those who had less than a full primary schooling were unable to write.

44 Trace interview no. 422, August 1987.

45 Trace interview no. 111, September 1987.

46 Trace interview no. 312, September 1987.

47 Retrospective interview no. 13, April 1983.

48 Popular theatre workshop tape no. 5, 067-130, April 1988.

49 Retrospective interview no. 2, April 1983.

50 Note that the term *(k)u-mvetsa* is systematically ambiguous in this context, meaning both to listen and to understand. Cf. chapter 2 where this polysemous character of the *-mva* family of words is discussed.

51 *Kufa kwamutu* means literally 'to be dead in the head'.

52 The recording is difficult to hear at this point, but AG appears to say *'avimba'*, meaning to cover up with thatch. I take her expression *avimba mu moyo wake* to mean literally 'she covered it up in her soul'.

53 * represents an inaudible passage on the tape.

6   **Dialogue and accountability: the school as a community resource**

1 Cf. Berrien 1967 and the discussion in the Appendix.

2 GRZ 1977, actually released only in 1979.

3 In 1981 the value of the Zambian Kwacha was equivalent to US $1.15. This was before the period of rapid decline in the national economy when the value plunged to $0.16 in 1986, and eventually to $0.10 in 1989, and about $0.02 in 1990.

4 These figures were supplied by the Headmaster of the school in interviews conducted in 1980.

5 This title has since been changed to the more appropriate designation of Clinical Officer. As Werner and Bower (1982) have pointed out, the role performed is anything but ancillary. Rather, despite the official hierarchy's definition of their relative status, these are the real professionals with continuing responsibility and accountability to the clientele of rural clinics, and the physicians who visit them from time to time are the para-professional, ancillary or back-up team. In recognition of this social reality, the persons appointed as Medical Assistant/Clinical Officer have long been addressed, and referred to, by the population of rural areas of Zambia as 'doctor'.

6 Like the concept of 'Medical Assistant' discussed in the preceding note, this

post is that of an assistant only in name. In practice the CDAs operate in rural areas as animateurs or resource-persons for various community development activities, with only minimal and intermittent supervision or guidance from a more highly trained superior officer.

7 My colleague Peter Phiri, at that time a university student, who took a special interest in the topic of agricultural production during 1981 and monitored the village discussions on it which were attended by the local Agricultural Assistant (Extension-Worker), emerged rather despondent about the prospects. The key factor in his interpretation which determines agricultural productivity among school leavers is motivation rather than technical skills or knowledge. Grade 7 leavers worked hard and produced a lot in their parents' fields because they expected this to influence their chances of raising financial support from their families for further education at the secondary level. Secondary school leavers at the Form 3 level, on the other hand, seemed to be less productive in the fields and to put on airs suggesting that such work was now beneath them.

8 The other two categories of reason seem to be less pertinent to the situation of our Katete parents: practical difficulties due to conflicting work obligations at the appointed time; and a resentful intimidation by the domineering approach adopted at meetings by a few highly educated parents.

9 I owe the idea for this image to the concluding chapter of Mallory Wober's book, *Psychology in Africa* (1975), where it is proposed as an alternative to the conflict or superimposition models of acculturation and modernisation.

10 A more conventional expression, which I have avoided here for fear of generating confusion with mixed metaphors, would be 'echoes'.

11 Mlama cites Kamlongera 1986 as tracing the current practices of Malawi's Ministry of Agriculture back to similar uses by the British colonial government in Malawi (Nyasaland) and Ghana (Gold Coast) in the 1930s: 'As early as the 1930s colonial health workers, secondary school teachers, agricultural and community extension workers were using drama to sell the virtues of modernisation, cash crop productivity and financial prudence' (p. 73).

12 Schoffeleers and Linden (1972, p. 258) refer to a tradition in the Chewa areas of what is now Malawi whereby 'heads of villages have to make an application to an area head of the *Nyau*, the *mfumu dziko*, for a piece of ground set aside – "consecrated" – for the performance, called the *mzinda*, which can cost up to twenty goats'. In our area of Zambia's Katete District, however, the place reserved for *Nyau* performances was referred to as *pa bwalo* (the same expression cited by M'tonga (1980) for the area of Zambia's Chipata District he studied), even though it was not located in the centre of a village.

13 In French, the root-meaning of the nearest equivalent is the backdrop rather than the platform. Scene is derived from the Latin *scena* and thence from the Greek *skene*, meaning originally a tent, of which some sort appears to have been used to 'house' the actors in Greek theatre – as opposed to the *thymele*, an altar-shaped platform on which the chorus stood. Thus whereas in English a play is 'staged', in French it is *mis en scène*.

14 Field-notes, 26 August 1987.

15 This translation features in my field-notes without a Chi-Chewa text.

16 Cf. the discussion of *u-chenjela* in chapter 2.

17 Also known as Brian Zanji wa Njovu, with his own company (entitled Zanji Roots, P.O. Box 33340, Lusaka).

18 Although these sleeping quarters belonged to the near-by Catholic church, our use of them was negotiated in advance by Peter Phiri strictly on a convenience basis, and we were at no time made to feel that we were thereby implicitly linked to the values or the local activities of the church.

19 Such functions were sometimes referred to collectively as *msonkhano*, a term originally used to describe tax collection.

During my stay in the area in August 1987, I witnessed the preparations there for a visit by an official of the national political party, UNIP, from the District capital, who eventually postponed her visit because of transport problems.

The Headmaster of the school described it as neutral territory for meetings to settle disputes among villages, even if the local UNIP branch is not involved. If Chief Kathumba is called to settle a dispute he would often preside there.

20 During the workshop we did not use the expression 'animation team', but contracted each individual as a 'resource person' for the popular theatre workshop. The team spirit forged during the workshop, however, was sufficiently strong to warrant this designation in retrospect.

21 I wore a concealed tape-recorder during this discussion as well as openly taking notes.

22 Part of this account is presented and discussed in chapter 5, p. 179.

23 This theme, which we built into the play, was also brought up to my wife, Namposya Serpell (1980, p. 82), time and again by women living in rural areas of Zambia's Central, Southern and Lusaka Provinces when she asked them to identify positive benefits of literacy. The wide dispersal of the extended network of kin in modern Zambia creates frequent occasions when relatives feel the need to communicate across long distances, and the prospect of depending on others to read one's mail, whatever Shamba's experience (chapter 5, p. 180), is evidently an uncomfortable one for many villagers.

24 Since on this occasion he had also taken a few beers, as he put it, 'to kill shyness' (*manyazi*) before appearing on stage, we opted not to confront him with this apparent departure from the agreed 'script' of the play.

25 Popular theatre, tape 7.

26 Popular theatre, tape 7.

27 It is difficult to capture the meaning of *komezya* in English. The term has connotations of admiration, but is not as strong as 'impressive' or 'wonderful', except perhaps as those terms are used informally sometimes as slang.

28 *Ku-cheza* is a polysemous term meaning to spend time, to keep company and to enjoy. Scott and Hetherwick (1929, p. 42) cite the following usages relevant to this comment by members of our drama's audience: '*Achezela masewela*, they dance all night, or spend the night in dancing. *Tikachezele nthanu ku bwalo kwa uje*, let us sit up telling stories at So-and-so's.'

29 Popular theatre, tape 7.

30 Popular theatre, tape 7.

31 The same question arises in the case of the philosophical rationalisations published by many African politicians, such as Kenneth Kaunda's theistic, liberal democratic 'Humanism' and Julius Nyerere's 'African Socialism'.

32 Since the *Nyau* dancing occurred only on the day of the second performance of our play, it is not clear whether the first performance in any way inspired the real-life confrontation. Certainly none of the actors with whom I discussed it were directly influenced by it in their stage performance, nor had any of them even noticed it.

33 Still later, the Catholic Church moved to assert the role of baptism on the death-bed as a route to salvation, 'and once baptised the mission claimed the right to undertake a Christian burial. Since death and mortuary rites were the principal occasion for dancing *Nyau* this represented a serious threat to the society. The Christian and *Nyau* transition rites were in direct confrontation and the macabre squabbles over corpses that took place in the '30s and '40s, both in the aptness of their symbolism and in their importance to both sides, were basic to the cultural struggle' (Schoffeleers and Linden 1972, p. 268).

34 Personal communication. He notes also that early Catholic schooling in Northern Rhodesia was more catechism-orientated, whereas Presbyterian schooling emphasised basic literacy. This was still true of the pattern of educational provision around Lundazi in the 1950s when he went to school.

35 Popular theatre, tape 13.

36 Consideration of the discussion of this term in chapter 2 will make it clear that it could be partially translated in this context as 'have some sense', partially by 'are smart enough', partially by 'are really wise'.

37 Popular theatre, tape 8.

38 Cf. note 32. Note that here the verb is used transitively, presumably with a causative meaning.

39 Peter Phiri's assessment was that the word *gule* was used here with its wider, general meaning of any dance, including *chimtali, chitelele* and also *Nyau* dances.

40 Popular theatre, tape 9.

41 Bruner (1986) refers throughout the discussion cited here to the readers of narrative texts, but his account applies even more forcefully to the audience of theatrical presentations.

42 Cf. the systematic ambiguity of perspective drawings and paintings, inside which we are invited to see depth while at the same time retaining an awareness that we are inspecting a flat surface (Gombrich 1960).

7   Perspectivist reflections on educational planning

1 In this respect I find Kenneth King's (1988) formulation of 'the ordinary rural primary school in Africa' as 'close to the primary socialization' and 'part of the local economy' to be unconvincing.

2 GRZ Ministry of General Education and Culture, unpublished statistics. GRZ/UNICEF (1986, p. 103) cite somewhat different figures to show the

national progression rate declining from 22 per cent in 1978 to 18.5 per cent in 1982.

3 The exceptionally high selection rate at Helpful School did not escape the attention of the authorities, who suspected a leakage of exam papers and required the whole school to resit the exam in at least one of these two years (1977 and 1978).

4 This analysis is confined to those schools (the more typical, small neighbourhood schools) presenting only one Grade 7 class. There were 181 such classes presenting themselves for the exam over the nine years from 1974 to 1982, with a median class size of forty-two, range thirty-three to forty-nine.

5 Cf. the Appendix for a discussion of this metaphor.

6 This paper is cited with approval by Court and Kinyanjui (1985), and evidently influenced the formulation of the World Bank's (1988) report on education in sub-Saharan Africa.

7 Colclough (1980) acknowledges this problem in passing on p. 10 but proceeds to disregard its implications.

8 Most of the countries in which these studies were conducted were in Asia, a few in Latin America and only two in Africa, both in Kenya.

9 Unpublished surveys by the Eastern Province Agricultural Development Project Research and Evaluation Unit found small but consistent differences in the number of years of schooling completed between 'contact' farmers receiving support/advice from the extension services and those not receiving such support. Likewise Honeybone and Marter (1975) concluded from a nationwide survey of ex-trainees at the Department of Agriculture's Farm Training Centres and Farm Institutes, that 'there seems to be a slight tendency for the more educated people to attend...' (p. 31).

10 This distinction is well explained by Applebaum and McCall (1983).

11 One major study with this message was conducted in secondary schools serving economically disadvantaged areas of Britain (Rutter *et al.* 1979).

12 *Times of Zambia*, March 1988.

13 My optimism about the potential of such a project was inspired by an illustrated presentation to the UNICEF Workshop in Florence, May 1990, by Cigdem Kagitcibasi of her pre-school project in Turkey. Cf. Kagitcibasi *et al.* (1988).

Appendix: Metaphors for schooling

1 This section and Sections 3, 4 and 5 of the Appendix draw heavily on the text of my paper entitled 'Audience, culture and psychological explanation', first drafted as a prolegomenon to this book, and published elsewhere (Serpell 1990).

2 In my detailed exposition of this argument (Serpell 1990) I have tried to show that certain elements of the classic distinction drawn by Pike (1954, 1967) beteeen 'emic' and 'etic' have an enduring relevance for cross-cultural psychology, while others can more profitably be replaced, in the light of subsequent advances in linguistics, psychology and epistemology, by a more dynamic conceptualisation.

3 See Jahoda (1982) for a discussion of this influential theme in anthropology.

Bibliography

Achebe, C. (1960). *No longer at ease*. London: Heinemann.

Akinasso, F. N. (in press). Literacy and individual consciousness. In A. C. Purves and E. M. Jennings (eds.), *Literate systems and individual lives*. Albany, NY: SUNY Press.

Ammar, H. M. (1954). *Growing up in an Egyptian village*. London: Kegan Paul.

Applebaum, M. I. and McCall, R. B. (1983). Design and analysis in developmental psychology. In W. Kessen and P. M. Mussen (eds.), *Handbook of child psychology*, vol. I: *History, theory and methods*. New York: Wiley, pp. 415–76.

Ariès, P. (1962). *Centuries of childhood* (trans. from the French by R. Baldick). London: Cape.

Asch, S. (1946). Forming impressions of personality. *Journal of Abnormal and Social Psychology* 41, 258–90.

Auslander, M. (1989). The reinvention of 'Tradition' and 'Culture' in the modern Ngoni Nc'wala ceremony. Unpublished seminar paper presented, March 29, 1989 at the Institute for African Studies. Lusaka: University of Zambia.

Austin, J. L. (1962). *How to do things with words*. Oxford: Oxford University Press.

Ball, S. J. (1983). Imperialism, social control and the colonial curriculum in Africa. *Journal of Curriculum Studies* 15(3), 237–63.

Banda, C. J. (1981). The primary-school leavers' problem in Zambia: official policies and attempted solutions. University of Zambia, Lusaka: unpublished MEd dissertation.

Banda, G. (1981). Maganizo yamakolo am'midzi pa zaukhondo wa ana asukulu. Lusaka: University of Zambia, Institute for African Studies (mimeo).

Barfield, O. (1947). Poetic diction and legal fiction. In M. Black (ed.), *The importance of language*. Englewood Cliffs, NJ; Prentice-Hall.

Barnum, H. N. and Sabot, R. H. (1976). *Migration, education and urban surplus labour: the case of Tanzania*. Paris: OECD, Development Centre Studies, Employment Series No. 13.

Bemba, S. (1970). The dark room. In C. R. Larson (ed.), *African short stories: a collection of contemporary African writing*. New York: Collier, pp. 85–100.

Berger, P. L., Berger, B. and Kellner, H. (1973). *The homeless mind*. New York: Random House.

Berlin, I. (1956). Introduction. In I. Berlin (ed.), *The age of enlightenment*. New York: Mentor.

Berrien, F. K. (1967). Methodological and related problems in cross-cultural research. *International Journal of Psychology* 2, 33–44.

Berry, J. W. (1981). Developmental issues in the comparative study of psychological differentiation. In R. L. Munroe, R. H. Munroe and B. B. Whiting (eds.), *Handbook of cross-cultural human development*. New York: Garland, pp. 475–99.

   (1984) Toward a universal psychology of cognitive competence. *International Journal of Psychology* 19(4/5), 335–61.

Bissiliat, J., Laya, D., Pierre, E. and Pidoux, C. (1967). La notion de *lakkal* dans la culture Djerma-Songhai. *Psychopathologie Africaine* 3, 207–64.

Bloom, B. (1964). *Stability and change in human characteristics*. New York: Wiley.

Bluma, S., Shearer, J., Frohman, A. and Hilliard, J. (1976). *Portage guide to early education*. Portage, WI: Cooperative Educational Service Agency No. 12.

Boswell, J. (1799). *The life of Samuel Johnson, LL.D.* London: Baldwin.

Bowles, S. and Gintis, H. (1976). *Schooling in capitalist America*. London: Routledge and Kegan Paul.

Boyd, R. (1979). Metaphor and theory change: what is 'metaphor' a metaphor for? In A. Ortony (ed.), *Metaphor and thought*. Cambridge: Cambridge University Press, pp. 356–408.

Brenner, M. E. (1985). The practice of arithmetic in Liberian schools. *Anthropology and Education Quarterly* 16(3), 177–213.

Brislin, R. W. (1976). Comparative research methodology; cross-cultural studies. *International Journal of Psychology* 11, 215–29.

   (1983). Comment. In J. B. Deregowski, S. Dziurawiec and R. C. Annis (eds.), *Expiscations in cross-cultural psychology*. Amsterdam: Swets and Zeitlinger, pp. 41–3.

Bronfenbrenner, J. (1979). *The ecology of human development*. Cambridge, MA: Harvard University Press.

Brooks, E. (1980). Social work intervention: a search for relevance in the Zambian context. University of Zambia, Lusaka: unpublished PhD dissertation.

Bruner, J. S. (1966). An overview. In J. S. Bruner, R. R. Olner and P. M. Greenfield *et al.* (eds.), *Studies in cognitive growth*. New York: Wiley, chapter 14.

   (1975). The ontogenesis of speech acts. *Journal of Child Language* 2, 1–19.

   (1986). *Actual minds, possible worlds*. Cambridge, MA: Harvard University Press.

Bruner, J. S., Shapiro, D. and Tagiuri, R. (1958). The meaning of traits in isolation and in combination. In R. Tagiuri and L. Petrullo (eds.), *Person perception and interpersonal behaviour*. Stanford, CA: Stanford University Press, pp. 277–88.

Brunswik, E. (1956). *Perception and the representative design of psychological experiments*. Berkeley, CA: University of California Press.

Bruwer, J. (1949). The composition of a Cewa village (mudzi). *African Studies* 8, 191–8.

Cameron, J. *et al.* (1983). *International handbook of education systems* (vol. II, Section A: *Sub-Saharan Africa*, ed. by J. Cameron).

Carby, H. (1982). Schooling in Babylon. In CCCS, *The empire strikes back: race and racism in 70s Britain*. London: Hutchinson.

Centner, Th. H. (1963). *L'enfant africain et ses jeux: dans le cadre de la vie traditionelle au Katanga*. CEPSI, Elizabethville, Katanga: collection memories CEPSI No. 17.

Central Statistical Office (1973). *Census of population and housing 1969: final report*, vol. I – *total Zambia*. Lusaka: Government Printer.

(1980). *National census of population and housing*. Lusaka: Government Printer.

(1984). *Country profile: Zambia 1984*. Lusaka: Central Statistical Office.

(1985). *1980 population and housing census of Zambia, Analytical Report*, vol. II. Lusaka: CSO.

Chafulumira, E. W. (1957). *Mfumu watsopano*. London: Macmillan.

Cherns, A. (1984). Contribution of social psychology to the nature and function of work and its relevance to societies of the Third World. *International Journal of Psychology* 19, 97–111.

Childs, C. P. and Greenfield, P. M. (1980). Informal modes of learning and teaching: the case of Zinacanteco weaving. In N. Warren (ed.), *Studies in cross-cultural psychology*, vol. II. London: Academic Press, pp. 269–316.

Chongo, J. (1972). *Fumbi Khoboo!* Lusaka: NECZAM.

Clanchy, M. T. (1979). *From memory to written record in England, 1066–1307*. Cambridge: Cambridge University Press.

Clarke, R. H. (1978). Policy and ideology in educational reform in Zambia. Lancaster University, UK: unpublished MEd dissertation.

(1984). School qualifications and the legitimation of inequality. University of Zambia, Lusaka: unpublished seminar paper (mimeo).

(1985). Schooling as an obstacle to development in Zambia. In R. Garrett (ed.), *Education and development*. London: Croom Helm.

Colclough, C. (1980). Primary schooling and economic development: a review of the evidence. *World Bank Staff Working Paper No. 339*. Washington, DC: World Books.

Cole, M. (1985). The zone of proximal development: where culture and cognition create each other. In J. V. Wertsch (ed.), *Culture, communication and cognition: Vygotskian perspectives*. Cambridge: Cambridge University Press, pp. 146–61.

(1990). Cognitive development and formal schooling: the evidence from cross-cultural research. In L. C. Moll (ed.), *Vygotsky and education: instructional implications and applications of sociohistorical psychology*. Cambridge: Cambridge University Press, pp. 89–110.

Cole, M. and Bruner, J. S. (1971). Cultural differences and inferences about psychological processes. *American Psychologist* 26, 867–76.

Cole, M. and Griffin, P. (1980). Cultural amplifiers reconsidered. In D. R. Olson (ed.), *The social foundation of language and thought*. New York: Norton, pp. 343–64.

Cole, M. and Scribner, S. (1977). Developmental theories applied to cross-cultural cognitive research. *Annals of the New York Academy of Sciences* 285, 366–73.

Coleridge, S. T. (1817). *Biographia Literaria; or biographical sketches of my literary life* (ed. by J. Shawcross, Oxford University Press, 1907).

Cook-Gumperz, J. (1986). Literacy and schooling: an unchanging equation? In J. Cook-Gumperz (ed.), *The social construction of literacy*. Cambridge: Cambridge University Press, pp. 16–44.

Coombe, T. (1967). The origins of secondary education in Zambia. *African Social Research* 3 and 4, 173–205, 283–315.

Court, D. (1985). Education and socio-economic development in Africa: the search for the missing link. Nairobi, Kenya: unpublished manuscript.

Court, D. and Kinyanjui, K. (1985). Education and development in sub-Saharan Africa: the operation and impact of education systems. Institute for Development Studies, Nairobi, Kenya: Working Paper No. 421.

D'Andrade, R. G. (1984). Cultural meaning systems. In R. A. Shweder and R. A. Levine (eds.), *Culture theory: essays on mind, self and emotion*. Cambridge: Cambridge University Press, pp. 88–119.

Dasen, P. R. (1984). The cross-cultural study of intelligence: Piaget and the Baoulé. *International Journal of Psychology* 19, 407–34.

(1987). Savoirs quotidiens et education informelle. Université de Génève, Faculté des Sciences et de l'Education (mimeo).

Dasen, P. R., Barthélémy, D., Kan, E., Kouamé, K., Daouda, K., Adjéi, K. K. and Assandé, N. (1985). N'glouele, l'intelligence chez les Baoulé. *Archives de Psychologie* 53, 295–324.

Dasen, P. R., Inhelder, B., Retschitzki, J. *et al.* (1978). *Naissance de l'intelligence chez l'enfant Baoulé de Côte d'Ivoire*. Berne: Huber.

Delpit, L. (1988). The silenced dialogue: power and pedagogy in educating other people's children. *Harvard Educational Review* 58, 280–98.

Diringer, D. (1948). *The alphabet: a key to the history of mankind*. New York: Philosophical Library.

Durojaiye, M. O. (1984). The impact of psychological testing on educational and personnel selection in Africa. *International Journal of Psychology* 19, 135–44.

Eisemon, T. O. (1988). *Benefiting from basic education, school quality and functional literacy in Kenya*. Oxford: Pergamon.

(1989). Educational reconstruction in Africa. *Comparative Education Review* 33(1), 110–16.

Elliott, J., Bridges, D., Ebbutt, D., Gibson, R. and Nias, J. (1981). *School accountability*. London: Grant MacIntyre.

Erchak, G. M. (1976). The nonsocial behaviour of young Kpelle children and the acquisition of sex roles. *Journal of Cross-Cultural Psychology* 7, 223–34.

ERIP (1986). *The provision of education for all: towards the implementation of Zambia's Educational Reforms under demographic and economic constraints, 1986–2000*. Lusaka, Zambia: University of Zambia, School of Education (interim report).

Etherton, M. (1982). *The development of African drama*. New York: Holmes and Meier/Africana.

Ezeilo, B. (1975). The performance of normal and mentally subnormal Zambian children on two intelligence tests and a conservation test. University of Zambia, Lusaka: unpublished MA dissertation.

(1978). Validing Danger Munthu Test and Porterns Maze Test in Zambia. *International Journal of Psychology* 13(4), 333–42.

Fellous, M. (1981). Socialisation de l'enfant bambara. *Journal des Africanistes* 51(1–2), 201–15.

Ferguson, C. A. (1959). Diglossia. *Word* 15, 325–40.

Fishman, J. A. (1960). A systematization of the Whorfian hypothesis. *Behavioral Science* 5, 323–9.

(1967). Bilingualism with and without diglossia; diglossia with and without bilingualism. *Journal of Social Issues* 23(2), 29–38.

Fortes, M. (1938). Social and psychological aspects of education in Taleland. *Africa* 11(4), 1–64 (Supplement).

Fox, L. K. (ed.) (1967). *East African childhood: three versions.* Nairobi: Oxford University Press.

Fraser, B. (1979). The interpretation of novel metaphors. In A. Ortony (ed.), *Metaphor and thought.* Cambridge: Cambridge University Press, pp. 172–85.

Freeman, N. H. (1972). Process and product in children's drawing. *Perception* 1, 123–40.

Freire, P. (1972). *Pedagogy of the oppressed* (trans. M. B. Ramos). London: Sheed and Ward.

Freund, P. J. and Kalumba, K. (1984). The UNICEF/GRZ monitoring and evaluation study of child health and nutrition in Western and Northern Provinces, Zambia: integrated report.

Frijda, V. and Jahoda, G. (1966). On the scope and methods of cross-cultural research. *International Journal of Psychology* 1, 109–27.

Gadamer, H. G. (1975). *Truth and method.* London: Sheed and Ward.

Gallimore, R., Weisner, T. S., Kaufman, S. Z. and Bernheimer, L. P. (198). The social construction of ecocultural niches: family accommodation of developmentally delayed children. *American Journal on Mental Retardation* 94(3), 216–30.

Gay, J. and Cole, M. (1967). *The new mathematics and an old culture.* New York: Holt, Rinehart and Winston.

Geertz, C. (1983). 'From the native's point of view.' On the nature of, anthropological understanding. In C. Geertz, *Local knowledge: further essays in interpretive anthropology.* New York: Basic Books, pp. 55–70.

Gibson, E. J. and Levin, H. (1975). *The psychology of reading.* Cambridge, MA: MIT Press.

Gibson, J. J. (1950). *The perception of the visual world.* Boston: Houghton Mifflin.

(1966). *The senses considered as perceptual systems.* Boston: Houghton Mifflin.

Goffman, E. (1956). *The presentation of self in everyday life.* Edinburgh: Edinburgh University Social Science Research Centre, Monograph No. 2.

(1964). The neglected situation. *American Anthropologist* 66(6), 133–6.

(1967). *Interaction ritual: essays in face-to-face behavior.* New York, Garden City: Anchor.

(1974). *Frame analysis.* New York: Harper and Row.

Gombrich, E. H. (1960). *Art and illusion.* London: Phaidon.

Goodnow, J. J. (1977). *Children's drawings.* Glasgow: Fontana.

Goody, J. (1968). Restricted literacy in Northern Ghana. In J. Goody (ed.),

Literacy in traditional societies. Cambridge: Cambridge University Press, pp. 199–264.

(1977). *The domestication of the savage mind.* Cambridge: Cambridge University Press.

(1986). *The logic of writing and the organization of society.* Cambridge: Cambridge University Press.

(1987). *The interface between the written and the oral.* Cambridge: Cambridge University Press.

Goody, J. and Watt, I. (1963). The consequences of literacy. *Comparative Studies in Society and History* 5, 304–26.

Goody, J., Cole, M. and Scribner, S. (1987). Writing and formal operations: a case study among the Vai. In J. Goody, *The interface between the written and the oral.* Cambridge: Cambridge University Press, pp. 191–208.

Gould, S. J. (1981). *The mismeasure of man.* New York: Norton.

Grant, J. P. (1984). *The state of the world's children.* Oxford: Oxford University Press.

Greenfield, P. and Lave, J. (1982). Cognitive aspects of informal education. In D. A. Wagner and H. W. Stevenson (eds.), *Cultural perspectives on child development.* San Francisco: Freeman, pp. 181–207.

Gregory, M. (1967). Aspects of varieties differentiation. *Journal of Linguistics* 3, 177–98.

GRZ (1977). *Educational reform: proposals and recommendations.* Lusaka: Government Printer.

GRZ/UNICEF (1986) *Situation analysis of children and women in Zambia.* Lusaka: UNICEF.

Gumperz, J. J. (1968). The speech community. In *International encyclopedia of the social sciences,* London: Macmillan, pp. 381–6. Reprinted in P. Giglioli (ed.), *Language and social context.* Harmondsworth: Penguin, 1972.

(1982). *Discourse strategies.* Cambridge: Cambridge University Press.

Guthrie, M. (1948). *The classification of the Bantu languages.* Oxford: Oxford University Press.

Habermas, J. (1984). *The theory of communicative action,* vol. I: *Reason and the rationalization of society* (trans. T. McCarthy). Boston: Beacon Press.

(1987). *The theory of communicative action,* vol. II. *Life-world and system* (trans. T. McCarthy). Boston: Beacon Press.

Hall, B. (1980). The primary school health education project in Mwacisonpola Health Demonstration zone. Lusaka: WHO (mimeo).

Halliday, M. A. K. (1975). *Learning how to mean: explorations in the development of language.* London: Arnold.

Hannan, M. (1974). *Standard Shona dictionary.* London: Rhodesia Literature Bureau. First published 1959.

Harbison, F. and Myers, C. A. (1964). *Education, manpower and economic growth.* New York: McGraw-Hill.

Hareven, T. (1986). Historical changes in the family and the life course: implications for child development. In SRCD Monograph No. 211, pp. 8–23.

Harre, R. (1979). *Social being.* Oxford: Blackwell.

Havelock, A. E. (1976). *Origins of eastern literacy.* Toronto: Ontario Institute for Studies in Education (Monograph Series, No. 4).

Heath, S. B. (1983). *Ways with words.* Cambridge: Cambridge University Press.

(1989). Oral and literate traditions among black Americans living in poverty. *American Psychologist* 44(2), 367–73.

Hekman, S. J. (1986). *Hermeneutics and the sociology of knowledge.* Notre Dame, IN: University of Notre Dame.

Helander, E., Mendis, P. and Nelson, G. (1980). *Training disabled people in the community: a manual on community-based rehabilitation for developing countries.* Geneva: WHO.

Higgs, P. L. (1978). Culture and Africanization in Zambian school literature. University of California, Los Angeles: unpublished PhD dissertation.

(1980). The introduction of English as the medium of instruction in Zambian schools. *Zambia Educational Review* 2(1), 21–31.

Honeybone, D. and Marter, A. (1975). An evaluation study of Zambia's Farm Training Institutes and Farmer Training Centres. Lusaka: University of Zambia, Rural Development Studies Bureau (mimeo).

Hoppers, W. (1980). The aftermath of failure: experiences of primary school-leavers in rural Zambia. *African Social Research* 29, 709–39.

(1981). Education in a rural society: primary pupils and school leavers in Munnilunga, Zambia. The Hague: CESO and Lusaka: Institute of African Studies.

Horton, R. (1967). African traditional thought and Western science. *Africa* 37(1–2), 50–71; 155–87.

(1982). Tradition and modernity revisited. In M. Hollis and S. Lukes (eds.), *Rationality and relativism.* Oxford: Blackwell.

Howard, A. and Scott, R. A. (1981). The study of minority groups in complex societies. In R. H. Munroe, R. L. Munroe and B. Whiting (eds.), *Handbook of cross-cultural human development.* New York: Garland/STPM Press, pp. 113–52.

Howarth, C. I. (1980). The structure of effective psychology. In A. J. Chapman and D. Jones (eds.), *Models of man.* Leicester: The British Psychological Society; Hillsdale, NJ: Erlbaum.

Hymes, D. (1972). On communicative competence. In J. B. Pride and J. Holmes (eds.), *Sociolinguistics.* Harmondsworth: Penguin.

Ignatieff, M. (1984). *The needs of strangers.* London: Chatto and Windus.

Illich, I. (1973). *Deschooling society.* Harmondsworth: Penguin Books.

Inagaki, T. (1986). School education: its history and contemporary status. In H. W. Stevenson, H. Azuma and K. Hakuta (eds.), *Child development and education in Japan.* New York: Freeman, pp. 75–92.

Inkeles, A. and Smith, D. H. (1974). *Becoming modern: individual change in six developing countries.* London: Heinemann.

I.P.A. (1949). The principles of the International Phonetic Association (University College, Gower Street, London WC1E 6BT).

Irvine, S. H. (1969a). Factor analysis of African abilities and attainments: cosntructs across cultures. *Psychological Bulletin* 71, 20–32.

(1969b). Contributions of ability and attainment testing in Africa to a general theory of intellect. *Journal of Biosocial Science*, Supplement 1, 91–102.

(1970). Affect and construct – a cross-cultural check on theories of intelligence. *Journal of Social Psychology* 80, 23–30.

Iser, W. (1978). *The act of reading*. Baltimore: Johns Hopkins University Press.

Jahoda, G. (1970). Supernatural beliefs and changing cognitive structures among Ghanaian university students. *Journal of Cross-Cultural Psychology* 1, 115–30.

(1980). Theoretical and systematic approaches in cross-cultural psychology. In H. C. Triandis and W. W. Lambert (eds.), *Handbook of cross-cultural psychology*, vol. I: *Perspectives*. Boston: Allyn and Bacon, pp. 69–141.

(1982). *Psychology and anthropology*. London: Academic Press.

Jardine, D. W. (1988). Piaget's clay and Descartes' wax. *Educational Theory* 38, 287–98.

Joynson, R. B. (1974). *Psychology and common sense*. London: Routledge and Kegan Paul.

Kabamba, J. M. (1988) Use studies of public libraries: the benefits of community based information services in Zambia. Preliminary report of a pilot study. Lusaka: University of Zambia, Institute for African Studies (mimeo).

Kaboré, O. (1981). Chants d'enfants Mossi. *Journal des Africanistes* 51(1–2), 183–200.

Kagame, A. (1976). *La philosophie bantu comparée*. Paris: Présence Africaine/UNESCO.

Kagitcibasi, C., Sunar, D. and Berkman, S. (1988). Comprehensive preschool education project: final report. Ottawa, Canada: IDRC, Manuscript LOGE.

Kandel, I. L. and Tate, W. E. (1966). History of education. In *Chambers's encyclopedia*, vol. IV, pp. 790–804.

Kashoki, M. E. (1973). Language: a blueprint for national integration. *Bulletin of the Zambia Language Group* 2(1), 21–49.

(1989). Language in Zambia: the lost battle on the frontline. Address presented to the Africa Centre, London: 20 May 1989. Kitwe, Zambia: Copperbelt University (mimeo).

(1990). *The factor of language in Zambia*. Lusaka: Kenneth Kaunda Foundation.

Katupha, J. M. M. (1984). The language situation of Mozambique, Paper presented at the SADCC conference on linguistics, Zomba, Malawi, November 1984. Eduardo Mondlane University, Faculty of Arts, Department of Linguistics (mimeo).

Katz, R. and Kilner, L. A. (1987). The straight path: A Fijian perspective on a transformational model of development. In C. M. Super (ed.), *The role of culture in developmental disorder*. San Diego: Academic Press.

Kaunda, K. D. (1974). *Humanism in Zambia and a guide to its implementation, Part II*. Lusaka, Zambia: GRZ Division of National Guidance.

Kavadias, G. (1966). The assimilation of the scientific and technological 'message'. *International Science Journal* 18, 362–75.

Kenyatta, J. (1938). *Facing Mount Kenya: the tribal life of the Gkikuyu*. London: Secker and Warburg.

Khubchandani, L. M. (1983). Plural languages, plural cultures: communication, identity and sociopolitical changes in contemporary India. Honolulu: East-Western Center, University of Hawaii.

Kibuuka, P. M. T. (1966). Traditional education of the Baganda tribe. Unpublished MS, National Institute of Education, Makerere University, Uganda.

Kidd, D. (1906). *Savage childhood*. London: A. and C. Black.

Kiernan, C. (1985). Communication. In A. M. Clarke, A. D. B. Clarke and J. M. Berg (eds.), *Mental deficiency: the changing outlook*, 4th edition. London: Methuen.

King, K. J. (1975). Nationalism, education and imperialism in the Southern Sudan (1920–70). In G. N. Brown and M. Hiskott (eds.), *Conflict and harmony in education in tropical Africa*. London: Allen and Unwin, pp. 296–318.

(1983). *The end of educational self-reliance in Tanzania?* Edinburgh: University of Edinburgh, Centre for African Studies, Occasional Paper.

(1988). Primary schooling and developmental knowledge in Africa: an issues paper. Unpublished MS presented at a Rockefeller Seminar on Science, Education and Developmental Knowledge in Africa, London: January 1988.

Kingsley, P. R. (1977). The measurement of intelligence in Africa: some conceptual issues and related research. *H.D.R.U. Reports, 28*. Lusaka: University of Zambia (mimeo).

(1985). Rural Zambian values and attitudes concerning cognitive competence. In I. R. Lagunes and Y. H. Poortinga (eds.), *From a different perspective: studies of behaviour across cultures*. Lisse: Swets and Zeitlinger, pp. 281–303.

Kleibard, W. (1975). Metaphorical roots of curriculum design. In W. Pinar (ed.), *Curriculum theorising: the reconceptualists*. Berkeley, CA: McCutchan.

Klein, R. E., Freeman, H. E., Spring, B., Nerlove, S. B. and Yarbrough, C. (1976). Cognitive test performance and indigenous conceptions of intelligence. *Journal of Psychology* 93, 273–9.

Korten, D. (1980). Community organisation and rural development: a learning process approach. *Public Administration Review* 40(5), 480–511.

Kuhn, T. S. (1962). *The structure of scientific revolutions*. Chicago: University of Chicago Press.

(1979). Metaphor in science. In A. Ortony (ed.), *Metaphor and thought*. Cambridge: Cambridge University Press, pp. 409–19.

Lakoff, G. and Johnson, M. (1980). *Metaphors we live by*. Chicago: University of Chicago Press.

Lambert, W. E. and Tucker, G. R. (1972). *Bilingual education of children: the St Lambert experiment*. Rowley, MA: Newbury House.

Lave, J. (1988). *Cognition in practice: mind, mathematics and culture in everyday life*. Cambridge: Cambridge University Press.

LCHC (Laboratory of Comparative Human Cognition) (1978). Cognition as a residual category in anthropology. *Annual Review of Anthropology* 7, 51–69.

(1979). What's cultural about cross-cultural psychology? *Annual Review of Psychology* 30, 145–72.

(1983). Culture and cognitive development. In W. Kessen and P. H. Mussen (eds.), *Handbook of child psychology*, vol. I: *History, theory and methods*. New York: Wiley, pp. 295–356.

(1986). Contributions of cross-cultural research to educational practice. *American Psychologist* 41, 1049–58.

Levine, K. (1982). Functional literacy: found illusions and false economies. *Harvard Educational Review* 52(3), 249–66.

Levine, R. and Levine, B. (1963). Nyansongo. In B. B. Whiting (ed.), *Six cultures: studies of child rearing*. New York: Wiley, pp. 15–202.

Lewin, K., Little, A. and Colclough, C. (1983). Effects of education on development objectives. *Prospects* 13(3), 299–311; (4), 413–25.

Lockheed, M., Jamison, D. and Lau, L. (1980). Farmer education and farmer efficiency: a survey. *Economic Development and Cultural Change* 29, 37–76.

Longwe, S. H. and Shakakata, R. (eds.) (1985). Women's rights in Zambia: proceedings of the second national women's conference held at Mindolo Ecumenical Foundation, Kitwe. Lusaka: Zambia Association for Research and Development.

Lukes, S. (1982). Relativism in its place. In M. Hollis and S. Lukes (eds.), *Rationality and relativism*. Oxford: Blackwell, pp. 261–305.

MacAdam, B. H. G. (1973). The effectiveness of the new English-medium primary school curriculum in Zambia. Manchester: University of Manchester, unpublished PhD thesis.

McCall, R. B. (1981). Nature–nurture and the two realms of development: a proposed integration with respect to mental development. *Child Development* 52, 1–12.

McCarthy, J. A. (1976) A theory of communicative competence. In P. Connerton (ed.) *Critical sociology*. Harmondsworth: Penguin, pp. 470–97.

McCarthy, T. (1978). *The critical theory of Juergen Habermas*. London: Hutchinson.

McClelland, D. C. (1961). *The achieving society*. Princeton, NJ: Van Nostrand.

Maimbolwa-Sinyangwe, I. M. (1987). Sex differences in progression in Zambian secondary schools. Seminar Paper No. 08/87. Lusaka: University of Zambia, Educational Research Bureau (mimeo).

Makubalo, E. L. (forthcoming). Psychological contributions to policy and practice in public health and primary health care. In R. Serpell (ed.), *Psychological theory, professional practice and public policy*.

Mariga, L. and McConkey, R. (1987). Home-based learning programmes for mentally handicapped people in rural areas of Zimbabwe. *International Journal of Rehabilitation Research* 10, 175–83.

Marwick, M. (1965). *Sorcery in its social setting: a study of the Northern Rhodesian Cewa*. Manchester: Manchester University Press.

Maslow, A. H. (1954). *Motivation and personality*. New York: Harper.

Miles, M. (1985). *Disabled children in ordinary schools*. Peshawan, NWFP, Pakistan: Mental Health Centre.

Milimo, J. T. (1972). *Bantu wisdom*. Lusaka: NECZAM.

Miller, G. A. (1979). Images and models, similes and metaphors. In A. Ortony (ed.), *Metaphor and thought*. Cambridge: Cambridge University Press, pp. 202–50.

Mitchell, C., Fortune, C. and Buchanan, R. (1964). *Map of African tribes and languages in Central Africa.* Lusaka, Zambia: Government Printer, reprinted under the title *Map of tribes and languages of Zambia, Malawi and Rhodesia.*

Mkilifi, M. H. A. (1972). Triglossia and Swahili–English bilingualism in Tanzamia. *Language in Society* 1, 197–213.

Mlama, P. (1988). Culture and development: the popular theater approach in Africa. Paper presented at the Reflections on Development Conference, Rockefeller Foundation, Bellagio, Italy: July 1988.

Morley, D. and Woodland, M. (1979). *See how they grow: monitoring child growth for appropriate health care in developing countries.* Macmillan Tropical Community Health Manuals.

M'tonga, M. (1980). The drama of Gule Wamkulu, Legon, Accra: University of Ghana, unpublished MA dissertation.

(1985). Children's games and plays in Zambia. Belfast: Queen's University, unpublished PhD thesis.

Mukamurama, D. (1985). La notion d'intelligence: ubwenge dans la culture rwandaise: essai d'une définition émique de l'intelligence dans sa conception intra-culturelle. Fribourg: Mémoire de licence.

Mvunga, M. P. (1979). Law and social change: a case study in the customary law of inheritance in Zambia. *African Social Research* 28, 643–54.

Mwanakatwe, J. M. (1976). Reflections on the use of English as a medium of instruction in schools. *Bulletin of the Zambia Language Group* 2(2), 1–21.

Myers, R. G. (1984). Going to scale. Paper presented at the Second Inter-Agency Meeting on Community-Based Child Development, New York, USA, September 1984. New York: UNICEF.

Mytton, G. (1974). *Listening, looking and learning: report on a national mass media audience survey in Zambia (1970–73).* Lusaka: University of Zambia, Institute for African Studies.

(1978). Language and the media in Zambia. In S. Ohannessian and M. E. Kashoki (eds.), *Language in Zambia.* London: International African Institute, pp. 207–27.

Nabuzoka, D. (1986). Child-rearing and management of childhood disabilities in Zambia. Lusaka: Institute for African Studies (mimeo).

Ndimurukundo, N. (1981). Les âges et les espaces de l'enfance dans le Burmoli traditionnel. *Journal des Africanistes* 51(1–2), 217–33.

Neisser, U. (1976). *Cognition and reality.* San Francisco: Freeman.

NELIMO (1988). Relatorio do i seminario sobre a padronizacao da ortografia de linguas Mocambicanas. Universidade Eduardo Mondlane, Faculdade de Letras, Maputo, Mozambique.

Nelson, K. (1981). Social cognition in a script framework. In J. H. Flavell and L. Ross (eds.), *Social cognitive development.* Cambridge: Cambridge University Press, pp. 97–118.

Nerlove, S. B. and Snipper, A. S. (1981). Cognitive consequences of cultural opportunity. In R. H. Munroe, R. L. Munroe and B. B. Whiting (eds.), *Handbook of cross-cultural human development.* New York: Garland/STPM Press, pp. 423–74.

Ng'andu, S. M. K. (1986). Aspects of the upbringing and education of children with special educational needs in a rural Zambian Bemba culture. University of London: unpublished MPhil dissertation.

Ngugi, Wa Thiongo (1964). *Weep not child.* London: Heinemann.

(1965). *The river between.* London: Heinemann.

(1986). *Decolonizing the mind: the politics of language in African Literature.* London: Currey/Heinemann.

Nias, J. (1981). Parent–teacher meetings. In J. Elliott, D. Bridges, D. Ebbutt, R. Gibson and J. Nias, *School accountability.* London: Grant McIntyre, pp. 82–95.

Nkosi, L. (1981). *Tasks and masks: themes and styles of African literature.* Harlow: Longman.

(1986). *Mating birds.* London: Constable.

Ntara, S. J. (1973). *The history of the Chewa.* University of Wiesbaden: Studien zu Kulturkunde.

Nyerere, J. K. (1968). Education for self-reliance. In J. K. Nyerere, *Ujamaa: essays on socialism.* Dar-es-Salaam, Tanzania: Oxford University Press, pp. 44–75.

Ogbu, J. U. (1978). *Minority education and caste: the American system in cross-cultural perspective.* New York: Academic Press.

Ohadike, P. (1981). *Demographic perspectives in Zambia: rural–urban growth and social change.* Zambian papers, No. 15. Lusaka: University of Zambia, Institute for African Studies.

Okonji, M. O. (1969). A grass root approach to revolution by education in Africa. *Mawazo* 2(1).

Olson, D. R. (1977). The languages of instruction: the literate bias of schooling. In R. C. Anderson, R. J. Spiro and W. E. Montague (eds.), *Schooling and the acquisition of knowledge.* Hillsdale, NJ: Erlbaum.

Opie, I. and Opie, P. (1959). *The lore and language of school children.* Oxford: Chancellor Press.

Parkin, D. J. (1974). Language switching in Nairobi. In W. H. Whiteley (ed.), *Language in Kenya.* Oxford: Oxford University Press, chapter 8.

Phiri, P. Z. (1981) Maganizo yamakolo a m'midzi pa zamalimidwe ya ana a sukulu. Lusaka: University of Zambia, Institute for African Studies (mimeo).

Pike, K. L. (1954, 1967). *Language in relation to a unified theory of the structure of human behavior.* The Hague: Mouton; enlarged edn, 1967.

Polomé, E. C. and Hill, P. C. (eds.) (1980). *Language in Tanzania.* London: International African Institute and Oxford University Press.

Poortinga, Y. H. (1986). Psychic unity versus cultural variation: an exploratory study of some basic personality variables in India and the Netherlands. University of Tilburg, Netherlands: Limited circulation report.

Pride, J. B. (1970). Sociolinguistics. In J. Lyons (ed.), *New horizons in linguistics.* Harmondsmounth: Penguin, chapter 16.

Pride, J. B. (ed.). (1982). *The new Englishes.* Rowley, MA: Newbury House.

Prince, R. (1980). Variations in psychotherapeutic procedures. In H. C. Triandis and J. G. Draguns (eds.), *Handbook of cross-cultural psychology,* vol. VI: *Psychopathology.* Boston, MA: Allyn and Bacon, pp. 291–349.

Pylyshyn, Z. W. (1979). Metaphorical imprecision and the 'top-down' research strategy. In A. Ortony (ed.), *Metaphor and thought*. Cambridge: Cambridge University Press, pp. 420–36.

Quinn, N. and Holland, D. (1987). Culture and cognition. In D. Holland and N. Quinn (eds.), *Cultural models in language and thought*. Cambridge: Cambridge University Press, pp. 3–40.

Randall, J. H. (1926). *The making of the modern mind: a survey of the intellectual background of the present age*. New York: Columbia University Press.

Read, M. (1959). *Children of their fathers*. London: Methuen.

Reese, W. H. and Overton, W. F. (1970). Models of development and theories of development. In L. R. Goulet and P. Baltes (eds.), *Life-span development psychology*. New York: Academic Press, pp. 116–45.

Resnick, D. and Resnick, L. (1977). The nature of literacy: an historical exploration. *Harvard Educational Review* 47, 370–85.

Retschitzki, J. (1990). *Stratégies des joueurs d'Awele*. Paris: Harmattan.

Retschitzki, J., Assandé, N'Guessan and Loesch-Berger, M.-C. (1986). Etude cognitive de jeu at des stratégies des joueurs d'Awele. *Archives de Psychologie* 54, 307–40.

Reyes, R. (1976). Studies in Chicano Spanish. Unpublished PhD dissertation, Harvard University.

Richards, A. I. (1956). *Chisungu: a girl's ceremony among the Bemba of Northern Rhodesia*. New York: Grove Press.

Riegel, K. and Freedle, R. (1976). What does it take to be bilingual or bidialectal? In D. S. Harrison and T. Trabasso (eds.), *Black English: a seminar*. Hillsdale, NJ: Erlbaum, pp. 25–44.

Roberts, J. I. and Akinsaya, S. K. (eds.) (1976). *Schooling in the cultural context: anthropological studies of education*. New York: David McKay.

Rodney, W. (1972). *How Europe underdeveloped Africa*. Dar-es-Salaam: Tanzania Publishing House.

Rogoff, B. (1981). Schooling and the development of cognitive skills. In H. C. Triandis and A. Heron (eds.), *Handbook of cross-cultural psychology*, vol. IV: *Developmental psychology*. Boston: Allyn and Bacon, pp. 233–94.

(1990). *Apprenticeship in thinking: cognitive development in social context*. New York: Oxford University Press.

Rogoff, B. and Lave, J. (eds.) (1984). *Everyday cognition*. Cambridge, MA: Harvard University Press.

Rutter, M., Maughan, B., Mortimore, P. and Ouston, J. (1979). *Fifteen thousand hours: secondary schools and their effects on children*. Cambridge, MA: Harvard University Press.

Sadler, J. E. (1966). *J. A. Comenius and the concept of universal education*. London: Allen and Unwin.

Schipper, M. (1982). *Theatre and society in Africa*. Johannesburg: Ravan Press.

Schoffeleers, M. and Linden, I. (1972). The resistance of the Nyau societies to the Roman Catholic missions in colonial Malawi. In T. O. Ranger and I. N. Kimambo (eds.), *The historical study of African religion*. Berkeley: University of California Press, pp. 252–73.

Scott, D. C. and Hetherwick, A. (1929). *Dictionary of the Nyanja language*. London: Lutterworth Press.

Scribner, S. and Cole, M. (1981). *The psychology of literacy.* Cambridge, MA: Harvard University Press.

Searle, J. R. (1965). What is a speech act? In M. Black (ed.), *Philosophy in America.* Ithaca, NY: Cornell University Press, pp. 221–39.

  (1979). Metaphor. In A. Ortony (ed.), *Metaphor and thought.* Cambridge: Cambridge University Press, pp. 92–123.

Segall, M. H., Campbell, D. T. and Herskovits, M. J. (1966). *The reference of culture on visual perception.* Indianapolis: Bobbs-Merrill.

Segall, M. H., Dasen, P. R., Berry, J. W. and Poortinga, Y. H. (1990). *Human behaviour in cross-cultural perspective: an introduction to cross-cultural psychology.* New York: Pergamon.

Sekeleti, C. (1985). The medium of instruction in Zambia's primary schools. University of Zambia, Lusaka: unpublished MA dissertation.

  (1987). The medium of instruction in Zambia primary schools. *Psychological Studies* 8(38). Lusaka: University of Zambia, Psychology Department (mimeo).

Selinker, L. (1972). Interlanguage. *International Review of Applied Linguistics* 10(3), 209–31.

Serpell, N. (1980). Women in Zambia: analysis of services in rural areas. Lusaka: UNICEF (mimeo).

Serpell, R. (1969). The influence of language, education and culture on attentional preference between colour and form. *International Journal of Psychology* 4, 183–94.

  (1971). Discrimination of orientation by Zambian children. *Journal of Comparative and Physiological Psychology* 75, 312–16.

  (1974). Aspects of intelligence in a developing country. *African Social Research* 17, 578–96.

  (1976). *Culture's influence on behaviour.* London: Methuen.

  (1977a). Estimates of intelligence in a rural community of Eastern Zambia. In F. M. Okatcha (ed.), *Modern psychology and cultural adaptation.* Nairobi: Swahili Language Consultants and Publishers, pp. 179–216.

  (1977b). Strategies for investigating intelligence in its cultural context. *Quarterly Newsletter of the Institute for Comparative Human Development* 1(3), 11–15.

  (1977c). Context and connotation: the negotiation of meaning in a multiple speech repertoire. *Quarterly Newsletter of the Institute for Comparative Human Development* 1,(4), 10–15.

  (1978a). Learning to say it better: a challenge for Zambian education. In L. N. Omondi and Y. T. Simukoko (eds.), *Language and education in Zambia* (Communication No. 14), pp. 29–57. Lusaka: Institute for African Studies (also reprinted in *Pride*, 1982).

  (1978b). Some developments in Zambia since 1971. In S. I. Ohannessian and M. E. Kashoki (eds.), *Language in Zambia.* London: International African Institute, pp. 424–47.

  (1979). How specific are perceptual skills? A cross-cultural study of pattern reproduction. *British Journal of Psychology* 70, 365–80.

  (1980a). Linguistic flexibility in urban Zambian school children. *Annals of the*

New York Academy of Sciences, vol. 345 (Studies in Child Language and Multilingualism, edited by V. Teller and S. J. White), pp. 97–119.

(1980b). Learning and transfer of special skills: some new evidence from Zambia. Paper presented at the 5th International Congress of the IACCP, Utkal University, Bhubaneswa, Orisssa, India, December 1980.

(1981). The cultural context of language learning: problems confronting English teachers in Zambia. *English Teachers' Journal* 5, 18–33.

(1982a). Measures of perception, skills and intelligence: the growth of a new perspective on children in a Third World country. In W. W. Hartup (ed.), *Review of child development research*, vol. VI. Chicago: University of Chicago Press, pp. 392–440.

(1982b). Intellectual handicap in a cross-cultural perspective. Inaugural lecture, University of Zambia, Lusaka. 9 July 1982.

(1983a). Social and psychological constructs in health records: the need for adaptation to different sociocultural environments. In M. Lipkin and K. Kupka (eds.), *Psychosocial factors affecting health*. New York: Praeger, pp. 243–74.

(1983b). *Mobilizing local resources in Africa for persons with learning difficulties or mental handicap*. Oslo: Norwegian Association for Mentally Retarded (NFPU); Brussels: International League of Societies for Persons with Mental Handicap (ILSMH).

(1983c). Why we do not need preschools in Africa. In *WHO-sponsored consultation on the applications of cross-cultural psychology to the promotion of healthy human development*. Geneva: WHO/.MNH/83-3, Appendix C.

(1984a). Commentary: the impact of psychology on Third World development. *International Journal of Psychology* 19, 179–92.

(1984b). Research on cognitive development in sub-Saharan Africa. *International Journal of Behavioural Development* 7, 111–27.

(1986). Specialized centres and the local home community: children with disabilities need them both. *International Journal of Special Education* 1(2), 107–27.

(1987). Teachers, pupils and parents in a rural area: experience and opinions of some primary school teachers in Zambia's Eastern Province. ERB Seminar Paper. Lusaka: Educational Research Bureau, University of Zambia (mimeo).

(1988). Childhood disability in sociocultural context: assessment and information needs for effective services. In P. R. Dasen, J. W. Berry and N. Sartorius (eds.), *Health and cross-cultural psychology: towards applications*. Newbury Park, CA: Sage, pp. 256–80.

(1989a). Psychological assessment as a guide to early intervention: reflections on the Zambian context of intellectual disability. In R. Serpell, D. Nabuzoka and F. Lesi (eds.), *Early intervention to prevent or ameliorate mental handicap and developmental disabilities in children of preschool age in Africa* (Report of a sub-regional workshop held in Lusaka, Zambia in June 1987). Lusaka: University of Zambia.

(1989b). Dimensions endogènes de l'intelligence chez les A-Chewa et autres peuples africains. In J. Retschitski, M. Bossel-Lagos and P. Dasen (eds.), *La recherche interculturelle*, vol. II. Paris: Harmattan, pp. 164–79.

(1990). Audience, culture and psychological explanation: a reformulation of the emic–etic problem in cultural psychology. *Quarterly Newsletter of the Laboratory of Comparative Human Cognition* 12(3), 99–132.

Serpell, R. and Mwanalushi, M. (1976). The impact of education and the information media on racism in Zambia since independence. Unpublished report prepared for UNESCO. University of Zambia, Lusaka (mimeo).

Serpell, R., Nabuzoka, D., Ng'andu, S. and Sinyangwe, I.M. (1988). The development of a community-based strategy for the habilitation of disabled children in Zambia: a case of action-oriented health systems research. *Disabilities and Impairments* 2(2), 117–29.

Shana, S.C.B. (1980). Which language? A brief history of the Medium of Instruction issue in Northern Rhodesia. *Zambia Educational Review* 2(1), 4–20.

Sharp, D., Cole, M. and Lave, C. (1979). Education and cognitive development: the evidence from experimental research. *Monographs of the Society for Research in Development* 44(1–2), Serial No. 178.

Shields, M.M. (1978). The child as psychologist: construing the social world. In A. Lock (ed.), *Action, gesture and symbol: the emergence of language*. London: Academic Press, pp. 529–81.

Shifferaw, M. (1982). Educational policy and practice affecting females in Zambian secondary schools. Milwaukee: University of Wisconsin, unpublished PhD dissertation.

Shotter, J. (1975). *Images of man in psychological research*. London: Methuen.

Snelson, P.D. (1974). *Educational development in Northern Rhodesia, 1883–1945*. Lusaka: NEDCOZ.

Sternberg, R., Conway, B., Ketron, J. and Bernstein, M. (1981). People's conceptions of intelligence. *Journal of Personality and Social Psychology* 4, 37–55.

Strauss, C. (1984). Beyond 'formal' versus 'informal' education: uses of psychological theory in anthropological research. *Ethos* 12, 195–222.

Street, B. (1984). *Literacy in theory and practice*. New York: Cambridge University Press.

Super, C.M. (1983). Cultural variation in the meaning and uses of children's intelligence. In J.B. Deregowski, S. Dziurawiec and R.C. Annis (eds.), *Expiscations in cross-cultural psychology*. Lisse: Swets and Zeitlinger, pp. 199–212.

Super, C.M. and Harkness, S. (1986). The development niche: a conceptualization at the interface of child and culture. *International Journal of Behavioural Development* 9, 545–69.

Taylor, C. (1971). Interpretation and the sciences of man. *Review of Metaphysics* 25, 3–51.

Tignor, R.L. (1976). *The colonial transformation of Kenya*. Princeton, NJ: Princeton University Press.

Todd, D.M. and Shaw, C.P. (1980). The informal sector and Zambia's employment crisis. *Journal of Modern African Studies* 18, 411–25.

Traoré, B. (1972). *Black African theatre and its social functions*. Ibadan, Nigeria: Ibadan University Press.

Trevarthen, C. (1980). The foundations of intersubjectivity: development of interpersonal and cooperative understanding in infants. In D. R. Olson (ed.), *The social foundations of language and thought: essays in honour of Jerome S. Bruner.* New York: Norton, pp. 316–42.

Tuchman, B. W. (1978). *A distant mirror: the calamitous fourteenth century.* New York: Knopf.

Turnbull, C. M. (1962). *The lonely African.* London: Chatto and Windus.

Turton, A. (1988). Reflections on 'cultural approaches' to development issues. Unpublished MS, University of London, SOAS.

van Rensburg, P. (1984). Looking forward from Serowe. A special supplement to the journal, *Education with Production.* Gaborone, Botswana: Foundation for Education with Production.

Vernon, P. E. (1967). Abilities and educational attainments in an East African environment. *Journal of Special Education* 1, 335–45.

(1969). *Intelligence and cultural environment.* London: Methuen.

von Eye, A. (1988). The General Linear Model as a framework for models in CFA. *Biometrical Journal* 30, 59–67.

von Eye, A. and Nesselroade, J. R. (1989). Types of change: application of configural frequency analysis in repeated measurement designs. Paper presented at the International Society for the Study for Behavioral Development, Jymskyla, Finland: July 1989.

Vygotsky, L. S. (1978). *Mind in society: the development of higher psychological processes.* Edited by M. Cole, V. John-Steiner, S. Scribner and E. Sonberman. Cambridge, MA: Harvard University Press.

Weisner, T. (1989). Cultural and universal aspects of social support for children: evidence from the Abaluyia of Kenya. In D. Belle (ed.), *Children's social networks and social supports.* New York: Wiley, pp. 70–90.

Wendland, E. R. (1979). Stylistic form and communicative function in the Nyanja radio narratives of Julius Chongo. University of Wisconsin: unpublished PhD dissertation.

Werner, D. and Bower, B. (1982). *Helping health workers learn.* Palo Alto, CA: Hesperian Foundation.

WHO/UNICEF (1978). Alma-Ata Declaration on Primary Health Care. Geneva: WHO.

Wilson, A. (1980). The infancy of the history of childhood: an appraisal of Philippe Ariès. *History and Theory* 19(2), 132–53.

Witkin, H. A. (1967). A cognitive style approach to cross-cultural reasearch. *International Journal of Psychology* 2, 233–50.

Wittgenstein, L. (1958). *Philosophical investigations* (trans. G. E. M. Anscombe). Oxford: Blackwell (2nd edition).

Wober, M. (1966). Sensotypes. *Journal of Social Psychology* 70, 181–9.

(1969). Distinguishing centri-cultural from cross-cultural tests and research. *Perceptual and Motor Skills* 28, 488.

(1974). Towards an understanding of the Kiganda concept of intelligence. In J. W. Berry and P. R. Dasen (eds.), *Culture and cognition: readings in cross-cultural psychology.* London: Methuen, pp. 261–80.

(1975). *Psychology in Africa.* London: International African Institute.

Wood, D. (1989). Social interaction as tutoring. In M. H. Bornsten and J. S. Bruner (eds.), *Interaction in human development*. Hillsdale, NJ: Erlbaum, pp. 59–80.

Wood, D. and Middleton, D. (1975). A study of assisted problem-solving. *British Journal of Psychology* 66, 181–91.

Wood, D., Bruner, J. S. and Ross, G. (1976). The role of tutoring in problem solving. *Journal of Child Psychology and Psychiatry* 17, 89–100.

World Bank (1988). *Education in sub-Saharan Africa: policies for adjustment, revitalization and expansion*. Washington, DC: ISRD.

Zec, P. (1980). Multi-cultural education: what kind of relativism is possible? *Journal of the Philosophy of Education* 14(1), 77–86.

Index of names

Subject Index